THE NEW MORMON HISTORY

REVISIONIST ESSAYS ON THE PAST

THE NEW MORMON HISTORY

REVISIONIST ESSAYS ON THE PAST

Edited by

D. Michael Quinn

Signature Books   Salt Lake City   1992

In memory of Juanita Brooks

COVER ILLUSTRATION: *RED SYMMETRY,* BY GARY COLLINS
COVER DESIGN: JULIE EASTON

© 1992 by Signature Books, Inc. All rights reserved.
Signature Books is a registered trademark of Signature Books, Inc.
Composed and printed in the United States of America.

96   95   94   6   5   4   3   2

Library of Congress Cataloging-in-Publication Data

The New Mormon history : revisionist essays on the past / edited by D.
    Michael Quinn
        p.   cm.
        Includes bibliographical references.
        ISBN 1-56085-011-6
        1. Mormon Church—History.   2. Church of Jesus Christ of Latter-
    day Saints—History   3. Mormon Church—Historiography.   4. Church
    of Jesus Christ of Latter-day Saints—Historiography.   5. Mormons—
    United States—Social life and customs.   I. Quinn, D. Michael.
    BX8611.N48   1992
    289.3'09—dc20
                                                    91-21224
                                                        CIP

CONTENTS

EDITOR'S INTRODUCTION

THE "NEW MORMON HISTORY," FOR WANT OF A BETTER TERM, BEGAN with the publication of Juanita Brooks's *The Mountain Meadows Massacre* in 1950 by Stanford University Press, but there were certainly antecedents. From the 1900s to the 1930s, assistant church historian Brigham Henry Roberts, despite his shortcomings as a historian, exemplified much of the philosophy later identified with the New Mormon History. The first generation of university-trained Latter-day Saint scholars also made important contributions from the 1930s to the 1950s.[1] Still the flowering of New Mormon History has occurred since the 1950s. In 1961 this outpouring caused *Brigham Young University Studies* to start publishing an annual "Mormon Bibliography."

One aspect of this trend is simply a reflection of a larger process of change in the writing of history generally. Since the 1950s American historians have adopted new techniques and emphases in reexamining familiar topics. This "new history" examines the experiences of "common people" and reverses the lack of emphasis on women, children, families, and ethnic minorities. The focus on large populations and common people has stressed the use of statistics and computer analysis. In addition, historians have gained new insights through cross-cultural comparisons and some of the methods and theories of the social sciences. At the same time, sociologists, political scientists, economists, anthropologists, and psychologists have used their skills for historical inquiry.[2] "New history" already applied to the 1960s historical profession when a Jewish historian coined the term "New Mormon History" in 1969.[3]

The New Mormon History includes all of the ingredients of "new history" in America at large but has one crucial addition: the effort to avoid using history as a religious battering ram. That is why I date the New Mormon History from the publication of Brooks's *Mountain Meadows Massacre*. No topic was more traditionally inviting for sensational exploitation, secular condescension, or smug defensiveness. Yet this devoted Mormon writer did the best a human being can do to be dispassionate in helping readers better understand the context and details of a horrifying act committed by her equally devoted co-religionists of an earlier era.[4]

In her landmark study Brooks avoided seven deadly sins of traditional Mormon history. She did not shrink from analyzing a controversial topic. She did not conceal sensitive or contradictory evidence.[5] She did not hesitate to follow the evidence to "revisionist" interpretations that ran counter to "traditional" assumptions.[6] She did not use her evidence to insult the religious beliefs of Mormons. She did not disappoint the scholarly expectations of academics. She did not cater to public relations preferences. Finally she did not use an "academic" work to proselytize for religious conversion or defection.[7] As a result, Brooks's approach produced seven virtues for writing about the Mormon past. Since 1950 both LDS and non-LDS historians have approached their task from the perspective of functional objectivity.[8] Brooks demonstrated that functional objectivity is attainable even in controversial religious history.[9]

By contrast ultimate "historical objectivity" is an impossible ideal because the observer historian brings his or her own limitations to the study of the past.[10] Only a person of infinite capacity can understand the past with "ultimate objectivity." This is why impassioned arguments against "historical objectivity" sound strange compared to the imprecise aspiration of writers to be "fair and objective."

Any history—new or old, devotional or secular—has fundamental limitations. No historical work is the last word in understanding the seamless past. History is the imprecise effort to give finite understanding to an infinity of separate events and pieces of evidence. No human can completely understand the past "as it was" or the present "as it is." The historian cannot discover all the circumstances surrounding even the simplest event. Therefore history is not the past. History is a quest to understand the past. The New Mormon

History is part of that quest.

The changing emphasis in Mormon history has influenced the work of traditional Mormon historians, even as "traditional" approaches continue.[11] This mirrors the situation in the history profession generally. Traditional history persists at the same time new history influences American universities and professional publications.[12]

Not everyone has applauded the functional objectivity toward which the New Mormon Historians strive.[13] One of the most recent critics, a Mormon political scientist, defined the New Mormon History as "a wholesale abandonment of categories of self–understanding internal to the community . . . retrograde debunking when faced with faithful accounts not based on the secular historian's objectivist assumptions." New Mormon Historians, he wrote, are "ill equipped to write meaningfully about those most fundamental aspects of the Mormon past" and instead produce "a wholesale revision . . . which denies a priori the claims of the Restoration."[14]

Readers of this volume must judge for themselves whether the above criticisms accurately describe the revisionist articles in this collection. Narrow definitions certainly ignore the diversity of publications the New Mormon History has produced—on demography, frontier teenagers, female auxiliary leaders, Mormon relations with native Americans, social origins of British converts, textual reconstruction of the King Follet sermon, and the biography of church president Spencer W. Kimball, for example. Instead critics use "New Mormon History" as a polemical term within narrow definitions rather than as a descriptive term for this massive and diverse new literature.[15]

In preparing this collection my first list included more than two hundred selections. This, of course, excluded an even larger body of unpublished papers, theses, and dissertations. Even so my list was conservative, since one historian found a thousand significant works since 1950.[16] Next I narrowed that list to seventy-seven articles or excerpts from books. That reduced list seemed so essential that I suggested this collection of essays be multi-volumed. Practical considerations dictated a far smaller compilation.

Surveying the authors of selections on my initial list confirmed that something "new" has indeed occurred in the writing of Mormon history in recent decades. They were women and men;

Mormon, RLDS, Catholic, Protestant, Jewish, Muslim, and Hindu; American, Belgian, British, Canadian, French, German, Indian, Israeli, Italian, New Zealander, and Palestinian; anthropologists, architects, archivists, artists, biblical scholars, biologists, business administrators, classicists, computer programmers, demographers, ecologists, economists, engineers, English teachers, film critics, folklorists, genealogists, geographers, healthcare specialists, historians, housewives, institute teachers, journalists, lawyers, librarians, linguists, mathematicians, museum curators, philosophers, physicians, physicists, political scientists, psychiatrists, psychologists, sociologists, statisticians, university administrators, as well as leaders of both the Church of Jesus Christ of Latter-day Saints and the Reorganized Church of Jesus Christ of Latter Day Saints. Such diversity is evidence of the interdisciplinary and cross-cultural character of the new history.

This collection features fifteen representative essays to demon-strate the impact of New Mormon History in recent decades. In some cases the selections here were the first major reassessments of particular topics and have since been revised by new revisionists. The very richness of the New Mormon History guarantees that any selective publication of "important" or "representative" works will be incomplete. Due to practical limits of size, scores of authors and crucial examples are absent. Therefore I can only apologize in advance for the omissions and acknowledge that others might choose differently.[17] It is an imperfect world, but I hope that these essays will provide a useful introduction to the New Mormon History.

Appreciation is extended to the following authors and publications for permission to reproduce, sometimes in a different format, the essays appearing here: to *Dialogue: A Journal of Mormon Thought* for essays by Thomas G. Alexander, James B. Allen, Leonard J. Arrington, Maurine Ursenbach Beecher, Mario S. De Pillis, and Klaus J. Hansen; to *Sunstone* magazine for essays by Kenneth L. Cannon II, Linda King Newell, and Ronald W. Walker; to the *Utah Historical Quarterly* for essays by Eugene E. Campbell and Bruce L. Campbell, and William G. Hartley; to the *Journal of Mormon History* for the essay by Jan Shipps; to the *Western Humanities Review* for the essay by Stanley S. Ivins; to the Charles Redd Center for Western Studies for the essay by Dean L. May; and to Coronado Press for the essay by Robert B. Flanders.

NOTES

1. Leonard J. Arrington, "Scholarly Studies of Mormonism in the Twentieth Century," *Dialogue: A Journal of Mormon Thought* 1 (Spring 1966): 15-28; David J. Whittaker, "Historians and the Mormon Experience: A Sesquicentennial Perspective," in *A Sesquicentennial Look at Church History* (Provo, UT: Religious Instruction, 1980), 293-327; Davis Bitton and Leonard J. Arrington, *Mormons and Their Historians* (Salt Lake City: University of Utah Press, 1988).

2. Allan J. Lichtman and Valerie French, *Historians and the Living Past: The Theory and Practice of Historical Study* (Arlington Heights, IL: AHM Publishing Co., 1978), 122-52, on "New History"; William O. Aydelotte, Allan G. Bogue, and Robert William Fogel, "Introduction" to their *The Dimensions of Quantitative Research in History* (Princeton, NJ: Princeton University Press, 1972); Theodore K. Rabb and Robert I. Rotberg, eds., *The New History, the 1980s and Beyond: Studies in Interdisciplinary History* (Princeton, NJ: Princeton University Press, 1982); Robert William Fogel, "'Scientific' History and Traditional History," in Fogel and G.R. Elton, *Which Road to the Past?: Two Views of History* (New Haven, CT: Yale University Press, 1983).

Examples of the New History's diversity are Phillipe Aries, *Centuries of Childhood: A Social History of Family Life* (New York: Knopf, 1962); Erik H. Erikson, *Young Man Luther: A Study in Psychoanalysis and History* (New York: Norton, 1962); Edward H. Spicer, *Cycles of Conquest: The Impact of Spain, Mexico, and the United States on the Indians of the Southwest, 1553-1960* (Tucson: University of Arizona Press, 1962); Lauro Martines, *The Social World of the Florentine Humanists, 1390-1460* (Princeton, NJ: Princeton University Press, 1963); Robert F. Berkhofer, *Salvation and the Savage: An Analysis of Protestant Missions and American Indian Response, 1787-1862* (Lexington: University of Kentucky Press, 1965); Peter Laslett, *The World We Have Lost* (London: Methuen, 1965); Robert R. Dykstra, *The Cattle Towns* (New York: Knopf, 1968); Kenelm Burridge, *New Heaven, New Earth: A Study of Millenarian Activities* (New York: Schocken Books, 1969); Paul Kleppner, *The Cross of Culture: A Social Analysis of Midwestern Politics, 1850-1900* (New York: Free Press, 1970); Carl N. Degler, *Neither Black Nor White: Slavery and Race Relations in Brazil and the United States* (New York: Macmillan, 1971); Tamara K. Hareven, ed., *Anonymous Americans: Explorations in Nineteenth-Century Social History* (Englewood Cliffs, NJ: Prentice-Hall, 1971); Stephan Thernstrom, *The Other Bostonians: Poverty and Progress in the American Metropolis, 1880-1970* (Cambridge, MA: Harvard University Press, 1973); Robert William Fogel and Stanley L. Engerman, *Time on the Cross: The Economics of American Negro Slavery* (Boston: Little, Brown, and Co., 1974); Robert V. Wells, *The Population of the British Colonies in America Before 1776: A Study of Census Data*

(Princeton, NJ: Princeton University Press, 1975); Lawrence Stone, *The Family, Sex and Marriage in England, 1500-1800* (New York: Harper & Row, 1977); Thomas Kessner, *The Golden Door: Italian and Jewish Immigrant Mobility in New York City, 1880-1915* (New York: Oxford University Press, 1977); Jean Louis Flandrin, *Families in Former Times: Kinship, Household, and Sexuality* (New York: Cambridge University Press, 1979); Carl N. Degler, *At Odds: Women and the Family in America from the Revolution to the Present* (New York: Oxford University Press, 1980); Howard R. Lamar and Leonard Thompson, eds., *The Frontier in History: North America and Southern Africa Compared* (New Haven: Yale University Press, 1981); Tamara K. Hareven and Kathleen J. Adams, *Aging and Life Course: An Interdisciplinary Perspective* (New York: Guilford Press, 1982); Robert V. Wells, *Revolutions in Americans' Lives: A Demographic Perspective on the History of Americans, Their Families, and Their Society* (Westport, CT: Greenwood Press, 1982); Arnoldo DeLeon, *The Tejano Community, 1836-1900* (Albuquerque: University of New Mexico Press, 1982); Susan Grigg, *The Dependent Poor of Newburyport: Studies in Social History, 1780-1830* (Ann Arbor: UMI Research Press, 1984); Christiane Klapisch-Zuber, *Women, Family, and Ritual in Renaissance Italy* (Chicago: University of Chicago Press, 1985); Jan Vansina, *Oral Tradition as History* (Madison: University of Wisconsin Press, 1985); John Demos, *Past, Present and Personal: The Family and the Life Course in American History* (New York: Oxford University Press, 1986); Kevin J. Christiano, *Religious Diversity and Social Change: American Cities, 1890-1906* (Cambridge, Eng.: Cambridge University Press, 1987); Steven Mintz, *Domestic Revolutions: A Social History of American Family Life* (New York: Free Press, 1988).

3. Moses Rischin, "The New Mormon History," *The American West* 6 (Mar. 1969): 49.

4. For tributes to the achievement of Juanita Brooks, see *Pacific Historical Review* 20 (May 1951): 180-81; *Journal of Religion* 31 (Oct. 1951): 285; *Pacific Northwest Quarterly* 42 (Oct. 1951): 248; *Journal of the West* 2 (Oct. 1963): 482-83; Charles S. Peterson, *"A Utah Moon": Perceptions of Southern Utah* (St. George, UT: Dixie College Department of Printing, 1984), 15-19; Levi S. Peterson, *Juanita Brooks: Mormon Woman Historian* (Salt Lake City: University of Utah Press, 1988), esp. 175-210, 218-20.

5. David B. Honey and Daniel C. Peterson, "Advocacy and Inquiry in Mormon Historiography," *Brigham Young University Studies* 31 (Spring 1991): 153, defend Mormon historians of faith-promoting motivation who "leave out less-than-desirable episodes, tell only one side of the story, or are incomplete in their treatment." In support of this, Honey and Peterson in n76 argue "that 'suppression of evidence' is in fact an essential step in the application of a 'viable tradition' of interpretation." They cite Peter Novick, *That Noble Dream: The "Objectivity Question" and the American Historical Profes-*

sion (New York: Cambridge University Press, 1988), 527, in support of this. Novick himself quotes without comment or evaluation an extended argument in favor of the suppression of evidence which contradicts an accepted scientific theory. In so doing, Novick misuses the concept of "suppression of evidence." "Withholding evidence" or "suppressing evidence" does not refer to omitting evidence that is unimportant or irrelevant to one's subject, as Honey and Peterson seem to indicate. Worse yet, Novick, Honey, and Peterson seem to actually endorse the view that one can withhold evidence from the reader that contradicts a writer's theory or contradicts evidence the writer does present. Since views of "withholding evidence" are indebted to legal concepts, it is well to remember that the legal process *requires* the "suppression" of irrelevant evidence. On the other hand, the legal process prohibits the suppression of "material evidence"—evidence which directly bears on the case at hand.

Contrary to Honey and Peterson, writers are certainly "dishonest or bad historians" if they fail to acknowledge the existence of even one piece of evidence they know challenges or contradicts the rest of their evidence. If this omission of relevant evidence is inadvertent, the author is careless. If the omission is an intentional effort to conceal or avoid presenting the reader with evidence that contradicts the preferred view of the writer, that is fraud whether by a scholar or non-scholar, historian or other specialist. If authors write in scholarly style, they are equally dishonest if they fail to acknowledge any significant work whose interpretations differ from their own.

Dishonest apologists insist on these standards for everyone but themselves and in every subject but their own. Honest apologists avoid suppressing material evidence, even as they seek to downplay the significance of controversial information. Traditional Mormon history has had (and continues to have) both honest apologists and dishonest apologists. Many "New Mormon Historians" are also honest apologists for what they see as the essential truths of Mormon theology and the basic goodness of the Mormon experience. These New Mormon Historian apologists often seek to downplay the significance, or "to put into context," any evidence they find which may discomfort believing Mormons. Traditional Mormon apologists discuss such "sensitive evidence" only when this evidence is so well known that ignoring it is impossible. Personally, I have always tried to write both as a New Mormon Historian and an honest apologist for the Mormon faith and experience.

6. Readers should avoid the mistaken assumption that "revisionist history" is a term invented by New Mormon Historians or that its application to Mormonism necessarily means the rejection of the supernatural, of the reality of angelic ministrations to humanity, or of prophetic calling. This is Louis Midgley's assertion in "Faith and History," *Student Review,* 4 Mar. 1987, 1; and in "Modernity and the Mormon Crisis of Faith: The Challenge of

Historical Consciousness," in John M. Lundquist and Stephen D. Ricks, eds., *By Study and Also By Faith: Essays in Honor of Hugh Nibley* . . ., 2 vols. (Salt Lake City: Deseret Book, 1990), 2:530-33. In briefest terms, "revisionist history" simply means the challenging of traditional approachs or interpretations toward any historical topic. The *Oxford English Dictionary* (2d ed.) quotes one historian that revisionist history occurs when there is a widely held interpretation "which, because of its unilateral emphasis or perspective, needs to be counter-balanced."

7. Some readers may question why I do not date the New Mormon History from the 1945 publication of Fawn M. Brodie's *No Man Knows My History: The Life of Joseph Smith the Mormon Prophet* (New York: Alfred Knopf). In my view, Brodie's erudite and literary biography has more in common with the sins of traditional Mormon history. She discussed fundamental issues of Joseph Smith's life without taking his religious claims seriously and filtered her evidence and analysis through the perspective that the Mormon prophet was at best a "parapath" and at worst a charlatan. It is silent evidence of the inadequacy of traditional Mormon history that for more than thirty years no scholary rival to Brodie appeared until the publication of Donna Hill's *Joseph Smith: The First Mormon* (Garden City, NY: Doubleday, 1977). For claims that Brodie's biography ushered in a "new era" of Mormon history, see Robert B. Flanders, "Some Reflections on the New Mormon History," *Dialogue: A Journal of Mormon Thought* 9 (Spring 1974): 35; and Gary Topping, "History of Historians," *Dialogue: A Journal of Mormon Thought* 22 (Spring 1989): 157.

8. For publications which give generally positive definitions and evaluations of the New Mormon History, see Leonard J. Arrington, "Preface," *Great Basin Kingdom: An Economic History of the Latter-day Saints, 1830-1900* (Cambridge, MA: Harvard University Press, 1958), esp. viii-ix; Marvin S. Hill, "The Historiography of Mormonism," *Church History* 28 (Dec. 1959): 418-26; Leonard J. Arrington, "Scholarly Studies of Mormonism in the Twentieth Century," *Dialogue: A Journal of Mormon Thought* 1 (Spring 1966): 15-32; Klaus J. Hansen, "Reflections on the Writing of Mormon History," *Dialogue: A Journal of Mormon Thought* 1 (Spring 1966): 156-57; Richard L. Bushman, "Taking Mormonism Seriously," *Dialogue: A Journal of Mormon Thought* 1 (Summer 1966): 81-84; Richard L. Bushman, "The Future of Mormon History," *Dialogue: A Journal of Mormon Thought* 1 (Autumn 1966): 23-26; Leonard J. Arrington, "The Search for Truth and Meaning in Mormon History," *Dialogue: A Journal of Mormon Thought* 3 (Summer 1968): 56-66; Richard L. Bushman, "Faithful History," *Dialogue: A Journal of Mormon Thought* 4 (Winter 1969): 11-25; Rischin, "The New Mormon History"; Robert A. Rees, "'Truth is the Daughter of Time': Notes Toward an Imaginative Mormon History," *Dialogue: A Journal of Mormon Thought* 6 (Autumn-Winter

1971): 15-22; Paul M. Edwards, "Why Am I Afraid to Tell You Who I Am?," *Courage: A Journal of History, Thought and Action* 1 (June 1971): 241-46; Marvin S. Hill, "Brodie Revisited: A Reappraisal," *Dialogue: A Journal of Mormon Thought* 7 (Winter 1972): 72-74; Richard P. Howard, "The Effect of Time and Changing Conditions on Our Knowledge of History," *Saints' Herald* 120 (June 1973): 54; William Mulder, "Fatherly Advice," *Dialogue: A Journal of Mormon Thought* 9 (Winter 1974): 77-80; Marvin S. Hill, "Secular or Sectarian History?: A Critique of *No Man Knows My History*," *Church History* 43 (Mar. 1974): 78-96; Robert B. Flanders, "Some Reflections on the New Mormon History," *Dialogue: A Journal of Mormon Thought* 9 (Spring 1974): 34-41; Richard P. Howard, "The Historical Method as the Key to Understanding Our Heritage," *Saints' Herald* 121 (Nov. 1974): 53; "History Is Then and Now: A Conversation with Leonard J. Arrington, Church Historian," *Ensign* 5 (July 1975): 8-13; William Mulder, "The Mormon Angle of Historical Vision: Some Maverick Reflections" and Marvin S. Hill, "The 'Prophet Puzzle' Assembled: or, How to Treat Our Historical Diplopia Toward Joseph Smith," *Journal of Mormon History* 3 (1976): 13-22, 101-05; Richard D. Poll, "Nauvoo and the New Mormon History: A Bibliographical Survey," *Journal of Mormon History* 5 (1978): 105-123; James B. Allen, "Line Upon Line," *Ensign* 9 (July 1979): 32-39; Charles S. Peterson, "Mormon History: Some Problems and Prospects," *Encyclia: Journal of the Utah Academy of Sciences, Arts and Letters* 56 (1979): 114-26; Mark P. Leone, "The Uses of History," in his *Roots of Modern Mormonism* (Cambridge, MA: Harvard University Press, 1979), pp. 194-209; "Mormon History: A Dialogue with Jan Shipps, Richard Bushman and Leonard Arrington," *Century* 2 [BYU] 4 (Spring-Summer 1980): 27-39; Richard Sherlock, "The Gospel Beyond Time: Thoughts on the Relation of Faith and Historical Knowledge," *Sunstone* 5 (July-Aug. 1980): 20-23; James L. Clayton, "History and Theology: The Mormon Connection: A Response," *Sunstone* 5 (Nov.-Dec. 1980): 51-53; Leonard J. Arrington, "The Writing of Latter-day Saint History: Problems, Accomplishments and Admonitions," *Dialogue: A Journal of Mormon Thought* 14 (Fall 1981): 119-29; Jan Shipps, "The Mormon Past: Revealed or Revisited?" *Sunstone* 6 (Nov.-Dec. 1981): 55-57; Davis Bitton, "Mormon Biography," *Biography: An Interdisciplinary Quarterly* 4 (Winter 1981): 1-16; F. Henry Edwards, "Engagement with Church History," *John Whitmer Historical Association Journal* 1 (1981): 30-33; Roger Elvin Borg, "'Theological Marionettes': Historicism in Mormon History," *Thetean: A Student Journal of History* (Provo, UT: Beta Iota Chapter of Phi Alpha Theta, Brigham Young University, 1981): 5-20; Mario DePillis, "Bearding Leone and Others in the Heartland of Mormon Historiography," *Journal of Mormon History* 8 (1981): 79-97; Lawrence Foster, "New Perspectives on the Mormon Past," *Sunstone* 7 (Jan.-Feb. 1982): 41-45; James L. Clayton, "Does History Undermine Faith?" *Sunstone* 7 (Mar.-Apr. 1982): 33-40; Ronald K. Esplin,

"How Then Should We Write History?" *Sunstone* 7 (Mar.-Apr. 1982): 41-45; Jay Fox, "Clio and Calliope: Writing Imaginative Histories of the Pacific," *Proceedings of the Mormon Pacific Historical Society, Third Annual Conference, April 10, 1982,* 12-19; Ronald W. Walker, "The Nature and Craft of Mormon Biography," *Brigham Young University Studies* 22 (Spring 1982): 179-92; Richard P. Howard, "Adjusting Theological Perspectives to Historical Reality," *Saints' Herald* 129 (Sept. 1982): 28; Davis Bitton, "Like the Tigers of Old Time," *Sunstone* 7 (Sept.-Oct. 1982): 44-48; C. Robert Mesle, "History, Faith, and Myth," *Sunstone* 7 (Nov.-Dec. 1982): 10-13; Martin E. Marty, "Two Integrities: An Address to the Crisis in Mormon Historiography," *Journal of Mormon History* 10 (1983): 3-19; Melvin T. Smith, "Faithful History/Secular Faith," *Dialogue: A Journal of Mormon Thought* 16 (Winter 1983): 65-71; Davis Bitton, "Ten Years in Camelot: A Personal Memoir," *Dialogue: A Journal of Mormon Thought* 16 (Autumn 1983): 9-20; Thomas G. Alexander, "Toward the New Mormon History: An Examination of the Literature on the Latter-day Saints in the Far West," in Michael P. Malone, ed., *Historians and the American West* (Lincoln: University of Nebraska Press, 1983), 344-68; Marion G. Romney, "Foreword" to D. Michael Quinn, *J. Reuben Clark: The Church Years* (Provo, UT: Brigham Young University Press, 1983), ix; Melvin T. Smith, "Faithful History/Secular Religion," *John Whitmer Historical Association Journal* 4 (1984): 51-58; Richard P. Howard, "The Problem of History and Revelation," *Saints' Herald* 131 (Oct. 1984): 24; Marvin S. Hill, "Richard L. Bushman: Scholar and Apologist," *Journal of Mormon History* 11 (1984): 125-33; Lavina Fielding Anderson, "The Assimilation of Mormon History: Modern Mormon Historical Novels," *Mormon Letters Annual, 1983* (Salt Lake City: Association for Mormon Letters, 1984), 1-9; Jan Shipps, "History as Text," in her *Mormonism: The Story of a New Religious Tradition* (Urbana: University of Illinois Press, 1985), 41-65; Paul M. Edwards, "Our Own Story," *Sunstone* 10 (Jan.-Feb. 1985): 40-41; Ronald W. Walker, "A Way Station," *Sunstone* 10 (Apr. 1985): 58-59; R. Laurence Moore, "Prophets in Their Own Country," *New York Times Book Review* (21 July 1985): 11; David Brion Davis, "Secrets of the Mormons," *New York Review of Books* (14 Aug. 1985): 15-18; Kent E. Robson, "Objectivity and History," *Dialogue: A Journal of Mormon Thought* 19 (Winter 1986): 87-97; Martin Ridge, "Joseph Smith, Brigham Young, and a Religious Tradition," *Reviews in American History* 14 (Mar. 1986): 25-33; Grant Underwood, "Re-visioning Mormon History," *Pacific Historical Review* 55 (Aug. 1986): 403-26; Paul M. Edwards, "The New Mormon History," *Saints' Herald* 133 (Nov. 1986): 12-14, 20; Thomas G. Alexander, "Historiography and the New Mormon History: A Historian's Perspective," *Dialogue: A Journal of Mormon Thought* 19 (Fall 1986): 25-49; W. Grant McMurray, "'As Historians and Not as Partisans': The Writing of Official History in the RLDS Church," and Roger D. Launius, "A New Historiographical Frontier: The Reorganization in the Twentieth Century," *John Whitmer Historical Association Journal* 6 (1986): 43-52, 53-63; Thomas G. Alexander, "No Way to Build Bridges," *Dialogue: A Journal of Mormon Thought* 22 (Spring 1988): 5; Marvin S. Hill, "The New Mormon History Reassessed in Light of Recent Books on Joseph Smith and Mormon Origins," *Dialogue: A Journal of Mormon Thought* 21 (Autumn 1988): 115-27; Richard D. Poll, *History and Faith: Reflections of a Mormon Historian* (Salt Lake City: Signature Books, 1989); Klaus J. Hansen, "Arrington's Historians," *Sunstone* 13 (Aug. 1989): 41-43; Henry Warner Bowden, "From the Age of Science to the Age of Uncertainty: History and Mormon Studies in the Twentieth Century," *Journal of Mormon History* 15 (1989): 105-20; "Coming to Terms with Mormon History: An Interview with Leonard Arrington," *Dialogue: A Journal of Mormon Thought* 22 (Winter 1989): 39-54; Paul M. Edwards, "A Time and a Season: History as History," *John Whitmer Historical Association Journal* 10 (1990): 85-90; Eric C. Olson, "The 'Perfect Pattern': The Book of Mormon as a Model for the Writing of Sacred History," and Honey and Peterson, "Advocacy and Inquiry in Mormon Historiography," 7-18, 154-62, 170-72; D. Michael Quinn, "On Being a Mormon Historian," in George D. Smith, ed., *Faithful History: Essays on Writing Mormon History* (Salt Lake City: Signature Books, 1992). For abstracts of most of the above articles, see Louis C. Midgley and David J. Whittaker, *Mapping Contemporary Mormon Historiography: An Annotated Bibliography* (forthcoming).

9. LDS apostle Dallin H. Oaks believes that official church publications are exempt from the responsibility to be balanced but that secular publications are not: "Balance is telling both sides. This is not the mission of official Church literature or avowedly anti-Mormon literature. Neither has any responsibility to present both sides. But when supposedly objective news media or periodicals run a feature or an article on the Church or its doctrines, it ought to be balanced. So should a book length history or biography. Readers of supposedly objective authors and publishers have a right to expect balance in writing about the Church or its doctrines" ("Reading Church History," an address delivered at the Church Educational System's Symposium on the Doctrine and Covenants, Brigham Young University, Provo, Utah, 18 Aug. 1985).

10. Novick, *That Noble Dream*.

11. This is reflected in previously ignored or denied historical evidence now being at least acknowledged by traditionalists. Examples are Truman G. Madsen (director of Brigham Young University's Religious Studies Center), *Defender of the Faith: The B. H. Roberts Story* (Salt Lake City: Bookcraft, 1980), 379; Francis M. Gibbons (secretary to the First Presidency of the LDS church), *Joseph F. Smith: Patriarch and Preacher, Prophet of God* (Salt Lake City: Deseret Book, 1984), 221; and Richard Lloyd Anderson (religion

professor at Brigham Young University), "The Mature Joseph Smith and Treasure Searching," *Brigham Young University Studies* 24 (Fall 1984): 489-560.

12. For the hostile backlash of a traditional historian against new historians, see Gertrude Himmelfarb, *The New History and the Old* (Cambridge, MA: Belknap Press, 1987).

13. For publications with generally negative evaluations of the New Mormon History, see Ezra Taft Benson, *The Gospel Teacher and His Message* (Salt Lake City: Church Education System, 1976); Ezra Taft Benson, "God's Hand in Our Nation's History," in *1976 Devotional Speeches of the Year, BYU Bicentennial Devotional and Fireside Addresses* (Provo, UT: Brigham Young University Press, 1977), 295-316; Joe J. Christensen, "The Value of Church History and Historians: Some Personal Impressions," *Proceedings of the Church Education System Church History Symposium* (Provo, UT: Brigham Young University Press, 1977), 12-17; Boyd K. Packer, "The Mantle is Far, Far Greater Than the Intellect," *Brigham Young University Studies* 21 (Summer 1981): 259-78; Neal W. Kramer, "Looking for God in History," *Sunstone* 8 (Jan.-Mar. 1983): 15-17; David Earl Bohn, "No Higher Ground: Objective History Is an Illusive Chimera," *Sunstone* 8 (May-June 1983): 26-32; Gordon B. Hinckley, "Stop Looking for Storms and Enjoy the Sunlight," *Deseret News* Church Section, 3 July 1983, 10-11; Gordon B. Hinckley, "Be Not Deceived," *Ensign 13* (Nov. 1983): 46; Scott C. Dunn, "So Dangerous It Couldn't Be Talked About," *Sunstone* 8 (Nov.-Dec. 1983): 47-48; Boyd K. Packer, "Dedication of Museum of Church History and Art," *Ensign* 14 (May 1984): 104; David Earl Bohn, "The Burden of Proof," *Sunstone* 10 (June 1985): 2-3; Gordon B. Hinckley, "Keep the Faith," *Ensign* 15 (Sept. 1985): 3-6; Gordon B. Hinckley's remarks at priesthood session in *October 1985 Conference Report*, 63-69; Louis Midgley, "Church Espouses Agency, Critics Accuse Authorities of Seeking Blind Obedience," *Brigham Young University Daily Universe*, 10 Dec. 1985, 18; Russell M. Nelson, "Truth—and More," *Ensign* 16 (Jan. 1986): 69-73; Robert L. Millett, "How Should Our Story Be Told?" and Louis Midgley, "Faith and History," in Robert Millet, ed., *"To Be Learned Is Good, If...": A Response by Mormon Educators to Controversial Religious Questions* (Salt Lake City: Bookcraft, 1987), 1-8, 219-26; Keith Perkins, "Why Are We Here in New England?: A Personal View of Church History," in Donald Q. Cannon, ed., *Regional Studies in Latter-day Saint Church History* (Provo, UT: Brigham Young University, 1978); M. Gerald Bradford, "The Case for the New Mormon History: Thomas G. Alexander and His Critics," *Dialogue: A Journal of Mormon Thought* 21 (Winter 1988): 143-150; Louis Midgley, "Which Middle Ground?" *Dialogue: A Journal of Mormon Thought* 22 (Summer 1989): 6-8; Arthur H. King and C. Terry Warner, "Talent and the Individual's Tradition: History as Art, and Art as Moral Response," and Louis Midgley, "Modernity and the Mormon Crisis of Faith: The Challenge of Historical Consciousness,"

in John M. Lundquist and Stephen D. Ricks, eds., *By Study and Also By Faith: Essays in Honor of Hugh Nibley on the Occasion of His Eightieth Birthday, 27 March 1990*, 2 vols. (Salt Lake City: Deseret Book Company, 1990), 2:484-501, 502-51; David Earl Bohn, "Our Own Agenda: A Critique of the Methodology of the New Mormon History," *Sunstone* 14 (June 1990): 45-49; Gary Novak, "Naturalistic Assumptions and the Book of Mormon," *Brigham Young University Studies* 30 (Summer 1990): 23-40; Louis C. Midgley, "The Myth of Objectivity: Some Lessons for Latter-day Saints," *Sunstone* 14 (Aug. 1990): 54-46. For abstracts of the above articles, see Midgley and Whittaker, *Mapping Contemporary Mormon Historiography*.

14. Bohn, "Our Own Agenda," 46, 47, 48.

15. Midgley acknowledges this in his "Modernity and the Mormon Crisis of Faith." Midgley and associates dismiss the rest of the New Mormon History as insignificant unless they find something in it worthy of critical attention.

16. James B. Allen, "Since 1950: Creators and Creations of Mormon History," in Davis Bitton and Maureen Ursenbach Beecher, eds., *New Views of Mormon History: A Collection of Essays in Honor of Leonard J. Arrington* (Salt Lake City: University of Utah Press, 1987), 432n7.

17. Earlier collections appeared in F. Mark McKiernan, Alma Blair, and Paul M. Edwards, eds., *The Restoration Movement: Essays in Mormon History* (Lawrence, KS: Coronado Press, 1973); Claudia L. Bushman, ed., *Mormon Sisters: Women in Early Utah* (Salt Lake City: Olympus Publishing Co., 1976); Richard H. Jackson, ed., *The Mormon Role in the Settlement of the West* (Provo, UT: Brigham Young University Press, 1978); Vicky Burgess-Olson, ed., *Sister Saints* (Provo, UT: Brigham Young University Press, 1978); Thomas G. Alexander, ed., *The Mormon People: Their Character and Traditions* (Provo, UT: Brigham Young University Press, 1980); Maurice L. Draper, et al., eds., *Restoration Studies: A Collection of Essays About the History, Beliefs, and Practices of the Reorganized Church of Jesus Christ of Latter Day Saints*, 4 vols. (Independence, MO: Temple School, 1980-88); Lyndon W. Cook and Donald Q. Cannon, eds., *A New Light Breaks Forth: Essays in Mormon History and The Exodus and Beyond: Essays in Mormon History*, 2 vols. (Salt Lake City: Hawkes Publishing, 1980); Thomas G. Alexander and Jessie L. Embry, eds., *After 150 Years: The Latter-day Saints in Sesquicentennial Perspective* (Provo, UT: Charles Redd Center for Western Studies, Brigham Young University, 1983); Lester Bush and Armand Mauss, eds., *Neither White Nor Black: Mormon Scholars Confront the Race Issue in a Universal Church* (Salt Lake City: Signature Books, 1984); Maureen Beecher and Lavina Anderson, eds., *Sisters in the Spirit* (Urbana: University of Illinois Press, 1987); Bitton and Beecher, *New Views of Mormon History*; Gary James Bergera, ed., *Line Upon Line: Essays on Mormon Doctrine* (Salt Lake City: Signature Books, 1989); Richard L. Jensen and

Malcolm R. Thorp, eds., *Mormonism in Early Victorian Britain* (Salt Lake City: University of Utah Press, 1989); and Dan Vogel, ed., *The Word of God: Essays on Mormon Scripture* (Salt Lake City: Signature Books, 1990).

1.
The Search for
Truth and Meaning in
Mormon History

Leonard J. Arrington

From its inception the Church of Jesus Christ of Latter-day Saints has sought to leave an accurate and complete record of its history. On 6 April 1830, the traditional date of the organization of the church, a revelation to Joseph Smith began, "Behold, there shall be a record kept among you . . ." (D&C 21:1). To accomplish this purpose the Second Elder of the church, Oliver Cowdery, was selected to serve as Church Recorder. When Cowdery was transferred to other work a year later, John Whitmer was appointed, by revelation, to "write and keep a regular history" (47:1). Whitmer served in this capacity until 1835 and wrote a manuscript narrative which is now in the possession of the Reorganized Church of Jesus Christ of Latter Day Saints in Independence, Missouri.[1]

Thus from the earliest years the church designated an official to record its story and preserve its records. Thirty-two men have been sustained from 1830 to 1991 as Church Historians and Recorders. In addition to the records kept by these men, each of the organizations of the church has kept minutes of its meetings and other documents, individuals have kept diaries and journals, and newspapers and magazines have published items of contemporary and earlier history. A surprisingly complete record of the church and its instrumentalities, from 1830 to the present, can be found in the church's library and archives in Salt Lake City. The records in church archives appear to be "honest," in the sense of presenting the facts as nearly as the designated historians could determine them, and there appears to be very little—if any—destruction of or tampering with the records or the evidence.

The second phase of official church historiography began in 1838 when Joseph Smith and his associates began preparing a documentary record entitled "History of Joseph Smith." This detailed chronology, written as an official diary of the prophet, appeared in serial form in the *Times and Seasons* (Nauvoo, Illinois), beginning in 1842. When that publication was discontinued in 1846, the remainder of the "History" was published in issues of the *Deseret News* (Salt Lake City) and the *Latter-day Saints' Millennial Star* (Liverpool), during the years 1853-63. A follow-up "History of Brigham Young" and of other church officials covered the years to 1844 and was published in the *Deseret News* and *Millennial Star,* 1863-65. In subsequent years Church Historians and Assistant Church Historians worked through these manuscripts, corrected errors, added corroborative material, and "improved" the narrative. The result was the seven-volume *History of the Church,* edited and annotated by B. H. Roberts (Salt Lake City, 1902-12), which is still the standard "documentary history" of the church.

A third stage in recording the history of the church was initiated by Andrew Jenson at the turn of the century, when he commenced three important projects: (1) preparing and accumulating biographies of the founders and subsequent officers of the church, many of which eventually found an outlet in the *L.D.S. Biographical Encyclopedia* (4 vols., Salt Lake City, 1901-36). Unfortunately, subsequent volumes have not been issued with information on church officials of the past fifty-five years. (2) Preparing an encyclopedia of church history, subsequently published as *Encyclopedic History of the Church* (Salt Lake City, 1941). (3) Preparing a massive multi-volume scrapbook record of the day-to-day activities of the church, with excerpts from available sources, both published and unpublished. This "Journal History of the Church" comprises more than 1,500 legal-size scrapbooks, from three to five inches thick. Happily there is an index to this mammoth collection so that one is able to trace references to individuals and organizations with considerable ease.

A fourth stage in the setting down of Mormon history was

the preparation of synthesis histories. Overlooking the fragmentary histories of Oliver Cowdery, John Whitmer, and John Corrill,[2] and the publication of various missionary tracts with historical sections, the first attempt of Mormon historians to set down a synthesis history was that of Edward Tullidge, who was granted access to materials in church archives for his *Life of Brigham Young; or Utah and Her Founders* (New York, 1876), *History of Salt Lake City* (Salt Lake City, 1886), and *History of Northern Utah and Southern Idaho* (Salt Lake City, 1889). Hubert Howe Bancroft also received extensive materials from the Historian's Office and had the personal help of Orson Pratt, Franklin D. Richards, John Taylor, and Wilford Woodruff for his *History of Utah* (San Francisco, 1889), which might be said to contain the first "professional" history of the Mormons. Bancroft's one-volume history was followed by Orson F. Whitney's four-volume *History of Utah* (Salt Lake City, 1898-1904), which was written almost exclusively from Mormon sources. The next history was B. H. Roberts's "History of the Mormon Church," which appeared in serialized form in *Americana* (New York), 1909-15. With some additions and changes it reappeared in *A Comprehensive History of the Church: Century I* (6 vols., Salt Lake City, 1930). A one-volume synthesis history, originally prepared as a manual for priesthood classes and since reissued many times with additional material, is Joseph Fielding Smith's *Essentials of Church History* (Salt Lake City, 1922).

With the exception of the Bancroft volume and some sections of Roberts's *Comprehensive History,* most of these and other Latter-day Saint histories and monographs represented what might be called "documentary histories." They attempted to give an account of the important events of the past without critical analysis or interpretation. They depended, essentially, on the statements of participants and observers, whose testimonies were excerpted and combined, with due regard for their trustworthiness, and "compiled" into a narrative. Some of the histories were written to prove a theological thesis, such as that the Lord looked after the Saints, punished them when disobedient, and frustrated their enemies. They dealt primarily with the externals of the events that transpired, and did not concern themselves with the internals—the underlying motives or thoughts of those who made the actions happen. Above all, our historians were perhaps unduly respectful of certain authorities, placing credence in accounts that should have been subjected to critical analysis.

This tradition of unquestioning "compiled external history" presented not only an authoritative narration of the succession of events, but also set the tone for a large proportion of the subsequent studies in Mormon history. These have dealt primarily with changes in the institutional structure of the church—with the development of its doctrine, program, and organization. Particularly popular objects of study have been histories of the missions, wards and stakes, auxiliaries, educational and cultural institutions and programs, and economic enterprises. One reason for the popularity of such studies is the survival and availability of the records of the organizations and programs. Personal records were hardly available to anyone outside of given families, and these were widely scattered. There was always a problem about family records because every family organization had at least *one* person who did not want anyone to know that grandpa once shared a bottle of wine with his Mormon Battalion buddies, or that Aunt Jane once served tea to an officer of the Relief Society. Thus, using organizational records rather than family records, scholars tended to describe the "outside" of the events.

There is, of course, another kind of history—the type which the British historian and philosopher, R. G. Collingwood, has called the history of the inside of the event. This history seeks to determine and expose the thoughts in the minds of the persons "by whose agency the events came about."[3] Historians do this by creatively re-thinking the thoughts of the participants in the context of their knowledge, analyzing them and forming judgments as to the validity of their explanations. They invest the narrative with meaning by consciously selecting from the sources what they think important, by interpolating in the reports of the participants and observers things which they do not explicitly say, and by rejecting or amending what they regard as due to misinformation or mendacity. Above all, they put their sources in the witness-box, and by cross-examination extort from them information which in their original statements they withheld, either because they did not wish to give it or because they did not realize they possessed it. In other words, Mormon historians, like other historians, must read contemporary accounts with a question in their mind and seek to find out, by inference and otherwise, what they want to find out from them. Every step in their research depends on asking a question—not so much whether the statement is true or

false, but what the statement means. Obviously, since their infor-
mants, by and large, are dead, historians must put the questions to
themselves.[4] These historians, as with scholars in other disciplines,
must engage in the continuous Socratic questioning that Plato described so well as "a dialogue of the soul with itself."

This kind of history, which we may call Socratic or interpretive history, must by its very nature be a private and not a church
venture. Although this history is intended to imbue the written
record with meaning and significance, the church cannot afford to
place its official stamp of approval on any "private" interpretation of
its past. Interpretations are influenced by styles and ideas of the
times, not to say the personalities and experiences of historians, and
the church itself ought not to be burdened with the responsibility of
weighing the worth of one interpretation against another. Contrari-
wise, historians ought to be free to suggest interpretations without
placing their faith and loyalty on the line.

Fortunately, the church's library and archives are arranged
to permit historians to get at the "inside" of the events in LDS history,
although some collections are closed.[5] Materials are filed in three
separate sections, each of which has its own card catalogues and
indexes: (1) Library Section. This includes a nearly-complete library
of books, pamphlets, tracts, and periodicals published by and about
the church, including "anti-Mormon" works. There are also newspapers and maps, films and filmstrips. (2) Manuscript Section. In
addition to the "Journal History of the Church," there are similar
journal or manuscript histories of each of the wards, stakes, and
missions; name files of several thousand church officials and members (and some non-members as well); and the diaries and journals
of several hundred persons. (3) Written Records Section. This section
features tens of thousands of minute books and other records of
wards, stakes, priesthood quorums, auxiliary organizations, and missions, as well as emigration records.

The alphabetically-arranged name files in the Manuscript
Section are of particular value in rewriting Mormon history. Typically, they include autobiographical sketches, newspaper clippings,
letters to and from the person, and other personal records and
documents. Thus, these files permit us to look at the record from the
standpoint of many individual participants. These records must be
examined with care, and because of the intimate family information

which they contain can sometimes be made available only to historians accustomed to handling confidential data.

After working through several hundred of these files, I do not see any major revisions of our history—that is, revisions of conclusions to which sophisticated historians have come in years past. Indeed, on some of the conclusions reached long ago by our historians but doubted by some recent historians, there is a wealth of material, heretofore unused, which corroborates the earlier point of view. The records contain numerous accounts and evidences of individual greatness, heroism, and sacrifice. My own impression is that an intensive study of church history, while it will dispel certain myths or half-myths sometimes perpetuated in Sunday school (and other) classes, builds faith rather than weakens it.

The more one works with the materials of Mormon history the more one becomes aware of certain built-in biases which have influenced our impressions of church history. Let me suggest five of these:

1. *The theological marionette bias.* One gets the impression from some of our literature and sermons that the prophets and their associates in the First Presidency and Quorum of the Twelve Apostles were pious personages who responded somewhat mechanically, as if by conditioned reflex, to explicit instructions from on high, and that God manipulated the leaders much as marionettes in a puppet show—that church leaders themselves were not significant as agents of history. While this may very well have been the case in some instances, all developments did not come about "naturally" or even "supernaturally," nor can we describe innovations naively as "expedients necessitated by the times." The introduction of theological and organizational changes is done by people—by learned scripturists, talented organizers, and energetic innovators. They may have operated individually or in groups; they may have been motivated by ambition, prestige, or the good of the church. In any event, they introduced new programs and organizational instrumentalities, and assumed the responsibility for the adjustment to external circumstances without which the programs would not work. To study the mentality, personality, and character of our leaders is to study the activators of history. Biographical and psychological studies are an indispensable but little-used vehicle for the study and comprehension of our history.

2. *The male bias.* This is the notion that men hold all the important policy-making positions, therefore they are the ones who determine the course of events. The priesthood holds the key leadership offices, we reason, so the priesthood is responsible for everything that happens. We are inclined toward a male interpretation of Mormon history. More than forty years ago, the Gospel Doctrine classes in Sunday school studied a manual prepared by Thomas C. Romney entitled *The Gospel In Action* (Salt Lake City, 1949). Each week we studied the life of one historic Latter-day Saint—and we discussed some truly interesting and inspiring lives. Forty-five biographies were given in the manual; and while half of the people attending Gospel Doctrine classes were presumably women, forty-two of the biographies were of men, and only three were of women. This pattern of assumed male dominance is characteristic of almost all our histories. Edward Tullidge gave biographies of thirty people in his *Life of Brigham Young*; all of the thirty were men. The fourth volume of Orson F. Whitney's monumental *History of Utah* contains the biographies of 351 people, only twenty-nine of which were women.

Anyone who spends a substantial amount of time going through the materials in church archives must gain a new appreciation of the important and indispensable role of women in the history of the LDS church—not to mention new insights into church history resulting from viewing it through the eyes of women.

3. *The solid achievement bias,* with emphasis on the word "solid." We have tended to remember the tangible, the material, the visible, simply because these have had greater survival value. We have tended to measure the accomplishments of the pioneers by such *durable* achievements as the construction of canals and dams, temples and meeting houses, houses and cooperative stores. We have forgotten that the pioneers also made contributions in thought, in human relations, in education. From the evidence of pioneer life still surviving, we are led to conclude that the Mormons were good farmers and engineers, but poor poets and philosophers. By thus giving emphasis to the achievements of the more active members of the community, we have overlooked the quiet and immeasurable achievements of the reflective and contemplative. An extended experience among the name files has convinced me that the role of the writer and the intellectual was greater than we have ever acknowledged. These contributions are more subtle—more difficult to discover and to

trace—but they are nevertheless there.

4. *The centrifugal bias*—the notion that the important influences and forces in Mormon history originated in the center and moved outward. This bias, which results partly from the greater survival value of materials collected and protected by the central church, has had a discernible effect on our attitudes. Some Latter-day Saints have seemed to think that their primary task is to sit down and wait for instructions from 47 East South Temple Street, Salt Lake City. This was clearly not the attitude of earlier generations, who were told by revelation that they were personally invested with the responsibility of contributing toward the building of the kingdom and did not wait on anybody to tell them when to start: "For behold, it is not meet that I should command in all things; for he that is compelled in all things, the same is a slothful and not a wise servant; wherefore he receiveth no reward. Verily I say, men should be anxiously engaged in a good cause, and do many things of their own free will, and bring to pass much righteousness; For the power is in them, wherein they are agents unto themselves" (D&C 58:26-29).

Clearly that revelation had an impact, for a large share of creativity in thought and practice in the church came from what might be called the "private sector"—the geographical and organizational periphery—and moved toward the center and universal adoption. To give some examples, the Relief Society originated as a voluntary women's aid society in Nauvoo and was quickly reconstituted as an official organization. The *Woman's Exponent,* first magazine for women west of the Mississippi River (with one fly-by-night exception), originated as a semi-private venture in which the leading part was played by a twenty-two-year-old female journalist from Smithfield, Utah. After many years of splendid service, it came to be recognized as the official organ of the Relief Societies. The *Contributor* and the *Young Woman's Journal,* the two periodicals which later formed *The Improvement Era,* were both initiated by young men and young women writers who wanted to make a literary contribution to the church. The United Order, established by the church in 1874, was modeled along the lines of cooperative general stores in Brigham City and Lehi. The Welfare Plan, as introduced in 1936, was built on experiences in St. George Stake, southern Utah, and in Liberty Stake, Salt Lake City. All missionaries know of "good ideas" that were tried in one mission and quickly spread to others. All of this is quite "natural" and, upon reflection, is what one would expect; an examination of the archives helps to demonstrate its validity. Brigham Young used to say that more testimonies were obtained on the feet than on the knees. What he obviously meant was that we must all be "about our Father's business."

5. *The unanimity bias.* This is the notion that Mormon society has, from the earliest years, been characterized by cooperation, concord, and consensus in thought and behavior. In this respect, Mormon historians have been so charmed with the unity of the Saints that they have not inquired into the process by which they made up their minds. As with other peoples, the Saints have had their controversies, conflicts, and questionings. The substantial disagreement on doctrine, practice, and collective policy becomes evident when one leaves the "official" sources to focus on the minds and careers of individuals. While the records of the church emphasize the triumphs of union and accord, individual diaries often dwell on the difficulties of resolving differences. When one studies certain controversies—doctrinal, economic, or political—one occasionally uncovers widely disparate positions, both among general authorities and among the "lay" members of the church. The Saints were not without opportunities for criticism and the free expression of opinion—in priesthood meetings, quorum meetings, and other encounters; and sometimes opinions were articulated with considerable vigor and determination. There was such debate over proper policy preceding the exodus from Nauvoo, before the coming of the railroad to Utah, and during the anti-polygamy "Raid" of the 1880s and the Depression of the 1930s.

It is with respect to the last bias, perhaps, that historians can make their greatest contribution to the church today. There is now, as in early epochs, a certain amount of dissent. Some of it has to do with the church's role in politics, some with the church's business operations, and some with the emphasis on certain doctrines and practices such as women and the priesthood. We cannot deny the uneasiness which these strains and conflicts produce. But anxiety seems so much easier to bear when we understand the magnitude of the tensions and challenges of earlier generations. Indeed, one might make a very good case for the fact that the LDS church has grown and prospered precisely *because* of the dissent and discord, the obstacles and difficulties. For our pioneer ancestors, worship was not a running away or withdrawal from the battles of the world; neither was it an ostrich-like refusal to look problems in the face. They could not, even if they had wished, gloss over their many obstacles, physical and human, external and internal.

In his autobiographical recollections and reflections, *Little Did I Know* (New York, 1963), the great Jewish novelist and Zionist Maurice Samuel asserts that the "authentic Jew" is "the one who understands and is faithful to his own personal and social identity. One who, in short, accepts his history."[6] May we not make an analogous definition of the Latter-day Saint? Are we authentic Latter-day Saints (i.e., real Mormons) unless we receive messages from our collective past? Our individual and collective authenticity as Latter-day Saints depends on the historians telling the truth, the whole truth, and nothing but the truth about our past. This includes the failures as well as the achievements, the weaknesses as well as the strengths, the individual derelictions as well as the heroism and self-sacrifice.

Since the late 1960s, the writing of Mormon history has flowered. Scholars have prepared several first-rate general histories of the church, many biographies of Latter-day Saint leaders and "ordinary" members, and many dozens of books, essays, and articles on specific incidents in our history, LDS institutions, organizational entities, the history of doctrine, and the history of communities where Latter-day Saints lived. Especially commendable have been the many book-length and article-length studies of the history of Latter-day Saint women.

History can give meaning and purpose to life; it can help to formulate attitudes and policies for the future. Hopefully, the images conveyed by our historians will help us to continue the restoration of the gospel and assist in building the Kingdom of God on earth.

NOTES

1. A similar history, overlapping the Whitmer account, is the "Far West Record," in archives, Historical Department, Church of Jesus Christ of Latter-day Saints, Salt Lake City, Utah; hereafter LDS archives. Parts of it were published in Joseph Smith, Jr., et al., *History of the Church*, ed. B. H. Roberts, 6 vols. (Salt Lake City: Church of Jesus Christ of Latter-day Saints, 1902-12). It was published in its entirety by Donald Q. Cannon and Lyndon W. Cook, eds., *Far West Record: Minutes of The Church of Jesus Christ of Latter-day Saints, 1830-1844* (Salt Lake City: Deseret Book, 1983).

2. A series of letters by Oliver Cowdery and W. W. Phelps in the *Latter-day Saints' Messenger and Advocate* (Kirtland, OH, 1834-37) contains much history. John Corrill published *A Brief History of the Church* (St. Louis, 1839).

3. R. G. Collingwood, *The Idea of History* (New York, 1956), 215.

4. Ibid., 235-37, 269, 273-75.

5. In addition to restrictions on the papers of all apostles and members of the First Presidency, certain materials are not in LDS archives at all. For example, minutes of meetings of the First Presidency, certain diaries of members of the First Presidency (such as those of George Q. Cannon and Francis M. Lyman), certain financial records, etc., are in the office vault of the First Presidency. Other records are also maintained in the office vault of the Quorum of Twelve Apostles.

6. In Daniel Stern, Review of Maurice Samuel, *Little Did I Know,* in *Saturday Review,* 25 Jan. 1964, 35.

2.
The Quest for Religious Authority and the Rise of Mormonism

Mario S. De Pillis

IF THERE IS TO BE HONEST DIALOGUE BETWEEN MEMBERS OF THE Church of Jesus Christ of Latter-day Saints (Mormons) and outsiders, the question of the historical origins of Mormonism is central. Nevertheless, no serious student of this issue can deny that the controversial "dialogue" of the past one hundred and sixty years has often been less than candid. It has long been true, however unfortunate some Mormons may find it, that historians who write our generally accepted social and intellectual history have rarely consulted such standard Mormon historians as B. H. Roberts, Orson F. Whitney, or Joseph Fielding Smith. This was true even before the writings of these historians became dated.

Until recently professional historians and serious writers outside of academia have been non-Mormons or implicitly anti-Mormon. This non-Mormon historiography, as "official" in its attitude as that of the approved LDS church historians, has been a failure in three basic ways. First, it has been dominated by interest in the later period of Mormon history: by Brigham Young and Utah, by the great "practical" leader and the first "successful" Mormon settlement. Second, and related to the first, the role of Joseph Smith the prophet has been problematic. Among Mormons he has never really lost ground to Young. But in accepted American history, he was an impractical visionary who belongs to the Jacksonian reform era.

13

Serious treatments of his career have emphasized the Book of Mormon and the revelations—an implicit concern with the decades-old question, important enough, of whether Mormon scriptures are authentic or not. Third, serious writings have rarely dealt with early Mormonism as a religion whose study was governed by the same canons of modern methodology as, say, Congregationalism. There is nothing in the official historiography of Mormonism to compare with the intense studies of Puritanism: in the editing of documents, the relationship with other groups, the personnel, the earliest environment and background, and above all in the religious ideas. Even Mormon historians have neglected to work on critical editions of such crucial documents as Joseph Smith's *History of the Church*.[1]

These failures are understandable. Among the many explanations of this regrettable state of affairs, the most plausible is the modern regional interpretation of the American West. Writers have emphasized the later period of Mormon history because they have worked under the influence of what may be called the myth of the Trans-Mississippi West, that is, the well-known image that associates Mormons with cowboys and Indians, gold miners, mountain men, and other heroic figures of the great, open, arid West. As residents of the trans-Mississippi region, most Mormons have tended in their historical public-ations to live up to the role expected of them: inflating the importance of Brigham Young in their history and diminishing the significance of Joseph Smith, Oliver Cowdery, Sidney Rigdon, Martin Harris, and other leading figures in the early church (1827-44). They celebrate Pioneer Day not Hill Cumorah Day.

The third failure in the academic study of the origins and theology of Mormonism may not seem apparent at first glance. Some will be quick to assert that Mormonism has not been neglected in thoroughness and breadth of research or in relationships to its environment; that, in fact, one may easily find many works that reasonably relate the new religion to a wide variety of historical elements: frontier conditions, reform movements, anti-Masonry, Jacksonian egalitar-ianism, theories concerning the Hebraic origin of the American Indians, the widespread evangelical rebellion against conservative Calvinist orthodoxy, and so on.

But while all trained historians may agree that these and other factors are necessary in any explanation of Mormonism, they have not formed any pattern of agreement or disagreement, as they have on Puritanism, the Reformation, or even Christian Science. Not even within the Mormon camp has there been any attempt to explain what made Mormonism unique in its appeal and in its surprising and even shocking heterodoxy.[2] One well-known historian even asserted that theology made no difference to the pragmatically-minded Americans of the nineteenth century. Mormons and similar believers were essentially incapable of distinguishing between the relatively simple teachings of the Methodists and the Presbyterians.[3]

This failure in approach is deficient chiefly in that it merely provides a traditional analysis of traditional factors without taking into account traditional elements of dogmatic theology. In other words non-Mormon historians have not taken Mormonism seriously *as a religion.* They have thought it sufficient to take a position on the golden plates and to relate the "movement" to the general history of the time. Mormonism ends up as a kind of religious Grahamism.

Mormon historians have, of course, taken the religious part of their history seriously. But motivated for the most part by apologetics, they are more likely to view their religious history through the new revelations rather than through the theological issues that gave birth to the new revelations. They have not related the doctrines of this new body of revelation to the historical and *theological* time and place of the Book of Mormon and the Doctrine and Covenants. They seem to reason that if these works are divine, true, and authentic, it is more important to expound and believe. Non-Mormons (and of course anti-Mormons) seem to reason that since the new revelations were human, false, and inauthentic, it is more important to *dis*believe such shocking hetero-doxies.

It is the aim of this essay to assess the rise and historical significance of Mormonism from the neglected point of view of historical theology and to show the crucial importance of the doctrine of authority.

If historians were to take Mormonism as seriously as, say, the Separatism of Plymouth, what could they discern as the chief religious appeal of the new revelation? For an answer they must look not merely to the Book of Mormon and the Doctrine and Covenants but also to the sincere concerns of the intensely religious people of western New York in the 1820s and 1830s. A good place to start is the explanation, never closely read by non-Mormons, of Joseph Smith himself.

The prophet's narrative of the events leading to his first vision is one of the most significant and revealing in early Mormon history. It occurs in essentially the same form in two different places: at the beginning of his own *History of the Church* (1838)[4] and in his letter to John Wentworth, editor of the *Chicago Democrat* (1842). In both places his explanation, following the bare facts of birth, family, and education, comes at the begnning at the very source of his whole life and career: "When about fourteen years of age, I began to reflect upon the importance of being prepared for a future state, and upon inquiring [about] the plan of salvation, I found that there was a great clash in religious sentiment; if I went to one society they referred me to one plan, and another to another; each one pointing to his own particular creed. . . . Considering that all could not be right, and that God could not be the author of so much confusion, I determined to investigate the subject more fully."

Retiring to a grove he began to call upon the Lord for wisdom and while so engaged was suddenly enwrapped in a heavenly vision, in which two persons appeared: "They told me that all religious denominations were believing in incorrect doctrines, and that none of them was acknowledged of God as His Church and kingdom: and I was expressly commanded 'to go not after them,' at the same time receiving a promise that the fullness of the Gospel should at some future time be made known unto me."[5]

There was no room for much detail in his letter to Wentworth, but in his more discursive *History* the prophet related his search to the particular religious conditions in the vicinity of Manchester: "[About 1820-21] there was in the place where we lived an unusual excitement on the subject of religion. It commenced with the Methodists, but soon became general among all the sects of that region. Indeed, the whole district of country seemed affected by it, and great multitudes united themselves to the different religious parties, which created no small stir and division amongst the people, some crying, 'Lo here!' and others, 'Lo there!' Some were contending for the Methodist faith, some for the Presbyterian, and some for the Baptist."

The prophet's family succumbed to Presbyterianism, which the early Mormons often equated with Congregationalism. Joseph, then fifteen years old, remained uneasy and undecided: "So great were the confusion and strife among the different denominations, that it was impossible for a person young as I was, and so unacquainted with men and things, to come to any certain conclusions who was right and who was wrong."[6]

Who was right and who was wrong—that was the issue at the root of Mormon beginnings. By what authority did the contending preachers lay claim to the one true road to salvation?

The issue of authority will not seem unusual to informed members of the Mormon church. But in the writing of history this criterion of salvation is rarely cited as an important explanation of the origins and immediate success of the early church. Non-Mormon historians and indeed most Mormons habitually attribute the rise and progress of the church to personalities: Joseph Smith, Sidney Rigdon, Oliver Cowdery, Brigham Young, or others; to the appeal of the Book of Mormon; to the "age of reform"; to the environment of the Burned-over District of Western New York with all its revivalism and religious emotionalism, its "far-out" reform movements; to the frontier environment.

These traditional explanations are relevant and necessary. But they do not make complete sense of the revivalism, the visions, the handful of Mormon baptisms that took place before the organization of the church in April 1830 nor of the Mormon insistence on the necessity of a High Priesthood (the Melchizedek Priesthood); of the new revelations (collected in the Doctrine and Covenants); of the social and economic instrument of restorationism represented by Mormon communitarianism (chiefly expressed in the United Order of Enoch); of the new historical framework (the Book of Mormon). All these may be explained by the thirst of Joseph Smith and his contemporaries for the religious authority of one true church, for divine authority.

When this thirst has been recognized by leading historians, most of whom have belonged to the liberal traditions, it has been dismissed as "authoritarian." The use of this pejorative denies to Mormonism any sincere concern with divine authority—and thus abjures any need to analyze Mormonism as seriously as one would analyze a more orthodox denomination. Thus a standard work in American intellectual history deals with Mormonism in this way: "The weakness of Protestantism in the Middle Period was its sectarianism. . . . Inevitably some anxious souls sought the reassurance of an authoritarian Church. Two such organizations played minor roles in the United States during the Middle Period. One, the Catholic Church, was old; the other, the Church of Jesus Christ of Latter-Day Saints, was new. The latter was indigenous."[7]

The "anxious souls" were many, not "some." They all refused to accept the three evangelical orthodoxies of Baptism, Methodism, and Presbyterianism. Some rebelled against any kind of formal doctrine of salvation and became Universalists, Unitarians, and "infidels." These sought authority and truth by relying in varying degrees on some concept of reason; others joined splinter groups like the Reformed Baptists, Reformed Methodists, Free Will Baptists, and others; some followed minor prophets like Joseph Sylks or Isaac Bullard; many joined various "Christian" groups and communitarian societies.

One "Christian" group, the Campbellites, and one communitarian movement, Shakerism, were strong advocates of religious authority as the foundation of salvation. And it is significant that these were the two groups whose history impinged most closely on Mormonism.

Alexander Campbell's quest for primitive Christianity and divine authority led him between 1808 and 1812 from Secession Presbyterianism to a kind of Baptist congregationalism. Authority was to be found in the ability of a congregation to find truth in scriptures. Campbell called the first such congregation assembled by him the "Christian Association." He found authority to ordain in the consent of his congregation—unlike the Mormons, who found this crucial exercise of authority in new revelations, especially the revelation on the High Priesthood.[8] For the Campbellites sectarianism was the chief evil[9]—one reason why they called themselves "The Church of Christ" and "The Disciples of Christ"; for the names implied non-sectarianism or "unity."

A second group that competed with the Mormons in the Western Reserve of Ohio and elsewhere was the United Society of Believers in Christ's Second Appearing, commonly called Shakers. The Shakers were also ardent anti-sectarians. Richard McNemar, who before his conversion to Shakerism had been one of the leading figures of the Kentucky Revival, wrote a poem in about 1807 ridiculing the sectarians and the age. One stanza runs: "Ten thousand Reformers like so many moles/ Have plowed all the Bible and cut it [in] holes/ And each has his church at the end of his trace/ Built up as he thinks of the subjects of grace."[10] Thirty years later he was preaching the same message. He made it clear that anti-sectarianism was a general feeling among the non-orthodox seekers of the early nineteenth century.[11] He and others like him sought one true church with the mark of divine approbation. It had become meaningless to pick one of the major contending denominations as an instrument of salvation.

Anti-sectarianism could of course lead to infidelity or to ration-alist simplifications of doctrine, but it usually meant, as it did with Joseph Smith, a fundamental rejection of the three dominant denominations of frontier and rural areas: Baptism, Methodism, and Presbyterianism. A seeker hardly wasted time with those denominations, and perhaps the spiritual history of the many anxious souls may be symbolized by the brief story of the religious experience of young Michael Hull Barton of western Massachusetts, an area that gave so much to the religious life of western New York.

After traveling extensively throughout New England seeking the one true church, Barton found himself torn between the Mormons and the Shakers. Finally in 1831 he started from western Massachusetts for Portsmouth, New Hampshire, to be baptized by a Mormon elder. On the way back to his home his "conscience seized him and his sins stared him in the face." Retiring to the woods to pray, he received the spiritual light which turned him toward the nearest Shaker community in the town of Harvard, Massachusetts.[12] If he had lived in western Pennsylvania, he might have joined the Campbellites.

To understand fully the importance of authority in early Mormonism, one must do more than take into account the religious milieu of the 1820s and the direct testimony of Joseph Smith. One must examine in detail, painful detail for the non-theologically inclined, the subsequent development of Mormon polity and doctrine. Does it prove the sincerity of Joseph's quest for authority? Did his followers also seek it? Does the elaboration of Mormon doctrine after 1830, and especially between 1839 and 1844, cast doubt upon his original quest?

Aside from the Book of Mormon (1830), the Mormon conception of authority rests chiefly on a special priesthood and on the revelations received by Joseph Smith. Most of the development of the priesthood and most of the revelations came after 1830.

For Mormons authority means the right of those holding the priesthood to act for God. This right and the priesthood that exercises it are given a historical rationale in the Book of Mormon (published in 1830) and acquired specific forms and goals through subsequent revelations and practices. Mormon religion was authoritative (a slightly different concept from that of authority) because God attested to its truth by direct revelation. To demonstrate that Mormonism was a continuing quest for authoritative religion, it is not necessary to enter into the question of whether these revelations were authentic or to show how the Mormons proved their doctrines to be true in contrast to those of all their competitors.

Both Mormon apologetics and anti-Mormon propaganda have always dwelt, and understandably for their purposes, on the historical authenticity of the golden plates and the divine authenticity of Joseph Smith's visions and revelations. This question of authenticity is basic for explaining the rise of the new religion but is not enough. What must be shown is how much stronger the Mormon quest for authority was than that of the Campbellites, Shakers, and others who preached against sectarianism, how much more elaborate and theologically central was the Mormon concern for authoritative religion than, for example, Campbell's reliance on the New Testament or the Shakers' faith in the post-millennial ministry of their foundress. Despite the intricate elaboration of their priesthood, Mormons never watered down its function: the right and power to act authoritatively for God. Only the restored priesthood could save a torn and divided Christianity.

The mitosis of churches, or what Kenneth Scott Latourette has called the "fissiparous genius of Protestantism,"[13] has been the classic problem of Protestantism, stemming from a belief in the individual interpretation of the scriptures, bibliolatry, and a rejection of sacerdotal authority.[14] And it antedates by at least two centuries the "Middle Period" of American history.

To simplify it may be said that there are three modes of establishing a theological claim to being the one true church: apostolic succession, miracles and "gifts" (as signs of divine approbation), and special revelations. With certain modifications Joseph Smith used all three methods. Since apostolic succession was Roman and alien,[15] he turned to a more familiar source of Protestant tradition, the Old Testament: he claimed a *prophetic* succession through a dual priesthood that allegedly existed among the Hebrews.[16] Miracles and gifts he used discreetly and sparingly; ambitious miracles, such as his attempt to raise a dead infant, were likely to fail.[17] As for special revelations,[18] they were central to the establishment of authority, and Joseph adopted them even before the church was organized; his mother, with her antinomian predilection for special inspiration, encouraged him to seek visions and revelations. Joseph believed that his additions to orthodox Christian-Jewish scripture—his revelations, the Book of Mormon, "lost books" like the Book of Enoch, and his revision of the King James Bible—constituted the "fulness of the gospel." In short while using some of its doctrines, Joseph rejected Protestantism as well as Calvinism: he claimed to bring an entirely "new dispensation." "Truth," he later said, "is Mormonism. God is the author of it."[19] This special status of Mormonism as a fourth major religion is generally accepted in American society.[20]

The idea of a religious authority established by means of prophetic succession and direct revelation originated not in the Book of Mormon but in the mind of Joseph Smith. The historical foundation or authority supplied by that book was of little practical use to the prophet in defining the polity and doctrine of the new religion. For the non-Mormon it is almost as though he had simply composed a Hebrew-and-Indian novel with no thought of making it the Bible of a new religion. Even the uneducated agrarians who had read it with relish seemed to sense this, for they usually felt compelled to visit the prophet and hear what was concretely required of them for salvation. At first the prophet had little to offer them beyond baptism and his own impressive personality. Many heard him preach, but by January 1831 less than eighty persons in western New York had embraced the gospel—eleven years after Smith's first vision and six months after the publication of the Book of Mormon.[21]

Converts soon discovered that Mormon polity and doctrine would consist of what God revealed through Joseph Smith, month by month, in direct revelations. It was Smith's revulsion against the sectarianism of the Burned-over District and his consequent quest for a new source of authority that made direct revelation necessary. And it was in the newer wests of Ohio, Missouri, and Illinois that most of the doctrine and much of the polity took form.

In spite of these facts, students of Mormonism have usually

assumed that the religion sprang full-blown from the brain of Joseph Smith in the form of the Book of Mormon. This myth may be traced back to a single sentence in a book published in 1832, a sentence quoted in almost every work touching upon early Mormonism. In that year the Rev. Alexander Campbell, founder of the Campbellites, or "Reformed Baptists," published *Delusions,* the first serious, critical analysis of the Book of Mormon. Campbell wrote that the Mormon bible had provided final answers to every theological problem of the day: "infant baptism, ordination, the trinity, regeneration, repentance, justification, the fall of man, the atonement, transubstantiation, fasting, penance, church government, religious experience, the call to the ministry, the general resurrection, eternal punishment, who may baptize, and even the question of freemasonary [sic], republican government and the rights of man."[22]

This was the bitter attack of a man who had lost his best preacher, Sidney Rigdon, to Joseph Smith's new religion and who resented being identified as a friend to Mormonism. Hardly any of these "answers" was much more than hinted at in the Book of Mormon and certainly not in any way that was unique to what is now termed Mormonism. The prophet gave his answers, answers which diverged from the Book of Mormon, in the form of nearly one hundred revelations issued after 1830 in accordance with what Fawn M. Brodie calls his extraordinary "responsiveness to the provincial opinions of his time."[23] So great seemed his doctrinal departures from the Book of Mormon that one heretical offshoot of the church called the Whitmerites made opposition to such changes their chief point of doctrine.[24] In fact, the justice of the Whitmerite position is well attested by the evolution of the main elements of Mormonism between 1830 and 1844: church government, the nature of God, and the nature (the Fall) of humankind. A brief discussion of each of these elements shows that Mormonism was mainly a product of these later years.

Mormon church government was based on two priesthoods, the priesthood of Aaron and the priesthood of Melchizedek. This dual priesthood provided a sacerdotal authority for the latter-day gospel, and between 1830 and 1844 the prophet organized and elaborated a whole hierarchy of offices founded on this dual priesthood. The dual priesthood not only developed outside of and after the Book of Mormon, it also came in answer to specific needs.

The first need arose even before the Book of Mormon was finished—from the skepticism of Oliver Cowdery, one of the prophet's scribes in the translating of the golden plates. Cowdery pointed out that the Book of Mormon did not provide the "keys" or authority for performing baptism.

Cowdery's skepticism[25] was immediately overcome by a vision in which John the Baptist in the form of an angel conferred upon the two chosen ones the lower priesthood of Aaron with authority to baptize the first converts to the new faith. Thereupon in the spring of 1829 Smith and Cowdery baptized one another in the chilly Susquehanna River and became the first members of the church. A year later the Book of Mormon was published and almost simultaneously, on 6 April 1830, the little church of less than thirty people—most of them closely related—was formally organized.[26]

This solution, the restoration of the Aaronic priesthood, did not lay the question of authority to rest. The Book of Mormon had implied that all elders could ordain priests and teachers. But the relations among the Melchizedek priesthood, the Aaronic priesthood, and church government were not crystal clear, and subsequent, clarifying revelations were needed to supplement the Book of Mormon. Accordingly, in April 1830 the prophet issued a revelation on church government which outlined the duties of elders, priests, teachers, and deacons and the manner of baptism. Over the next year and a half he issued two revelations teaching that the second or higher priesthood of Melchizedek would be necessary for ordaining and being ordained to teacher, deacon, the new office of bishop, and "all the lesser offices."[27]

By June of 1831 the rapid growth of his church in Ohio persuaded the prophet to announce at an important conference in Kirtland that the Lord had restored the special office of high priest.[28] The prophet may have been encouraged to make this announcement by an influential new Ohio convert named Sidney Rigdon.

The office of high priest has often been confused with the Melchizedek priesthood, even by Mormons. And well it might be, for it was not until after the death of Joseph Smith that the complex, vague, and shifting relationship between the High Priesthood and the Melchizedek priesthood could be stabilized.[29] The distinctions were blurred in Smith's time, for between 1830 and 1844 he issued many revelations which expanded the two priesthoods of Aaron and

Melchizedek, not to speak of the high priesthood. In 1832 he provided them with a genealogy or "succession" going back to Adam and
Aaron respectively.[30] That same year he made the dual priesthood
indispensable for personal salvation and for the salvation of the
world. In March 1835 the prophet elaborated the biblical background
of the higher priesthood and its manifold relations to all other offices.
By 1841 the priesthood of Melchizedek was the most important
institution of church government. And toward the end of his life, the
prophet seemed to be clothing it with the power of binding and
loosing of sins.

The entire government of the church came to rest on the
dual priesthood. The primitive officialdom of the Palmyra years—
priests, teachers, deacons—was incorporated into the lesser or Aaronic priesthood. The high offices of the high council, the Quorum of
the Twelve Apostles, the Patriarch, the Seventies, and the First
Presidency all arose after 1830-31.

It is apparent that the dual priesthood had a genesis and
history of its own. Its theological *raison d'etre* was the principle of
teaching authority, a central principle of Mormonism to this day. This
principle was a response to the "social sources" of rural Jacksonian
society in western New York, a society which burned with religious
fervor but was torn by sectarianism. At the time and place there were
many other responses to religious yearnings and sectarianism, but
Smith clearly saw the need for authority, and this might have made
Mormonism a relatively unique solution even if his new, heterodox
scriptures had not been published.

Of course the Book of Mormon did provide the basic historical rationale for prophetic succession (restored in the nineteenth
century), and consequently the "Mormon Bible" is strongly emphasized among Latter-day Saints as the main historical source of teaching authority of the church. Non-Mormon historians, on the other
hand, have tended to ignore the theological claims described above.
They have looked to "the frontier," to the New England mind, and
to Jacksonian reform for explanations of Mormonism. These three
non-theological explanations will always remain relevant; and so too
will the Book of Mormon as the historical foundation for the basic
doctrine that Mormonism is a new or "restored" historical religion.
But the only non-theological element that seems to explain the
unique content and appeal of Mormon religion is the one that most

clearly shows it to have been a quest for religious authority: the element is the fluid, sectarian, torn society of rural (or "frontier") New York and northern Ohio.

It was here and in the subsequent, socially fluid, western environments of Missouri and Illinois that the principle of authority was spun out in the revelations of Smith and in Mormon institutions, the most important of which was the dual priesthood. (As a set of Mormon institutions, the communitarian United Order of Enoch, begun in Ohio, was possibly even more important in early Mormonism than the dual priesthood, but it was an answer to social as well as theological problems.) The dual priesthood and a peculiarly Mormon obsession with authority arose outside of and in large part after the Book of Mormon. And it arose in a special social environment as a result of specific needs confronting the young prophet. In logical order skepticism over the Book of Mormon had to be overcome, converts made and baptized, and leaders ordained—all tasks requiring authority. Particular ordinances connected with the dual priesthood, chiefly baptism and ordination, were widely enlarged as the church moved west, grew in numbers, and encountered everywhere people and printed matter which cannot be identified solely with the New England mind, the Book of Mormon, the Turnerian "frontier," or Jacksonian reformism. In sum Mormonism and its characteristic doctrine of authority was a growth made possible by the social conditions of Smith's time and place: the rural, northern society emerging between the 1820s and the martyrdom of the prophet in 1844.

Alexander Campbell was right in an important sense: Smith supplied people in this fluid society with answers to every perplexing theological question and even some social questions of the day (a day when social questions were still approached theologically). But Campbell wrote too early: in 1831-32, just after the appearance of the Book of Mormon. To the outsider writing well over a hundred years later, the Book of Mormon seems much less decisive in the rise of a full-blown Mormonism than the astonishing developments in revelation and practice between 1831 and 1844.

These conclusions can be confirmed by comparing one partly non-theological explanation of the rise of Mormonism—New England religions and culture—with the prophet's authoritative doctrinal solutions for the contentions of his day. Two revealing Mormon teachings are those outlining the nature of God and humanity. His teaching on property relations (Campbell's "communism") is even more instructive. His complex property arrangements under a set of communitarian institutions known as the United Order of Enoch supplied the social fabric for the millennial kingdom of God on earth. The order is not within the scope of this essay. Nevertheless the revolutionary changes in the rural fringes of New England's society are almost equally well reflected in Smith's definition of God and in his conception of the behavior required of those who want to be saved.

When non-Mormon historians consider the rise of Mormonism as a religion, they tend to overlook its setting in western New York and northern Ohio. Their instinct is to see it in relation to the religious aspect of New England culture or even as a throwback to the polygamous, millennial Anabaptists of the Reformation era.[31] This generalized view loses sight of historical time and place and thus of the principle of authority which Smith preached to the settlers of New York and Ohio.

New England no doubt endowed the prophet with his willful, ordering, moral, religious, theorizing, institutional cast of mind. But it was from the alchemy of his personal life, his reading, his daily experiences, from the reception accorded the Book of Mormon, and from the social opportunities of his time and place that he extracted a new socio-theological system that repudiated the age-old system of his forefathers. The New England culture he had inherited was shaped by Puritanism, now modified to a kind of combined Congregationalism-Presbyterianism (early Mormon missionaries used the two names interchangeably). And early Mormon teachings on the nature of God and humanity lucidly illustrate how profoundly Smith rejected this heritage.

The God of Mormonism was not Calvinistically and unpredictably stern. God was, as Joseph's mother had taught him, friendly, immediately present,[32] easily consulted, and to one who reads the revelations, knowledgeable and down-to-earth. To the older New England, the ways and "providences" of God were inscrutable. To a rebellious son of New England living in an age of secret societies with strange signs and special ceremonies, God was quite scrutable, but only to those who were initiated. Some Mormons knew more than others and the one who knew most was the prophet, who acted as the medium of God's revelations.[33] These revelations are only the most obvious kind of evidence for the knowableness of the Mormon God. The stalwart apostle Parley P. Pratt demonstrated in his *Autobiography* how the minutest occurrence could clearly and indubitably reveal the scrutable will of God and how those closest to the prophet enjoyed the most complete understanding of the Divine Will.

God was not only knowable; he was material and plural. There are three persons in the godhead. A revelation given in 1843 stated that of these three the Father and the Son have bodies "of flesh and bones as tangible as man's."[34] The Holy Ghost is less important than the Father and the Son; he is a spirit but still matter—more finely divided. A few days later another revelation put it bluntly: "There is no such thing as immaterial matter."[35] But these are not the only gods, said the prophet in a sermon. There are others above them,[36] and man below them can attain equality with the gods[37] and rule kingdoms. God himself was a man in the beginning. He had risen to a high position in heaven, as indeed every American of that egalitarian period hoped to do on earth.

Mormonism as it evolved between Kirtland, Ohio, and Nauvoo, Illinois, also rejected the pre-eminence of faith over works, a doctrine which has always had direct implications for the behavior of men and women. The *Evening and the Morning Star* comes, said the editor of this first Mormon newspaper, "to declare that goodness consists in doing good, not merely in preaching it . . . all men's religion is vain without charity."[38] The allusion, of course, is to what Luther called the "straw epistle" (James 1-2). But charity did not drive the Mormon into a philosophy of supererogation. He wholeheartedly accepted the worldly "creature" (earthly pleasure) that had plagued the old Calvinist conscience. The best-known work on early Mormonism stresses this acceptance:

"Mormon theology was never burdened with otherworldliness. There was a fine robustness about it that smelled of the frontier and that rejected an asceticism that was never endemic to America. The poverty, sacrifice, and suffering that dogged the Saints resulted largely from clashes with their neighbors over social and economic issues. Though they may have gloried in their adversity, they certainly did not invite it. Wealth and power they considered basic among the blessings both of earth and of heaven, and if they were to be denied them in this life, then they must assuredly enjoy them in the next."[39]

While some may cavil at the psychological interpretation of the "frontier" here, it is far more dubious to see, as anti-frontier historians often do, a kind of anti-liberal "puritanism" that "shaped" Mormonism in the East and to state that Mormonism "was nearly extinguished on the frontier."[40] Mormonism was, if anything, a moderate liberal revolt. Like Transcendentalism on its higher plane,[41] Mormonism avoided the extremes of Unitarianism and Calvinism. The frontier produced neither Turnerian frontier liberalism nor conservatism. A fluid frontier society was simply a stimulus to change in any direction.

Mormonism flourished in the fluid, socially confused, newer settlements—and sometimes in the decayed, confused areas of older settlements. This is what makes it a "frontier religion." Much of what is peculiar to Mormon doctrine developed west of, or better, after Palmyra and Manchester. The Book of Mormon of Palmyra days was anti-Masonic; in Far West, Missouri, and Nauvoo, Illinois, Joseph became more Masonic than the Masons.[42] The earlier Book of Mormon doctrine of baptism for the remission of sins, little different from that of neighboring Free Will Baptists, was metamorphosed in Nauvoo by the teaching that baptism could be accepted after death. Indeed it was not until the Far West and Nauvoo period of Mormon history (1838-44) that Mormon theology came to its "full flowering."[43] One of the greatest of official Mormon church historians, Brigham H. Roberts, once wrote that no one could understand the wondrousness of his faith without a knowledge of this "essentially . . . formative" period: "It was in Nauvoo that Joseph Smith reached the summit of his remarkable career. It was in Nauvoo he grew bolder in the proclamation of those doctrines, which stamp Mormonism as the great religion of the age."[44] It was in Nauvoo that Joseph taught the "higher and more complex doctrines of Mormonism"—baptism for the dead, the functions of the priesthood, the correct methods of spiritual exegesis, the kingdom of God, the time of the coming of the Son of God, the resurrection of the dead, the being and nature of God (his "materiality," the "plurality of Gods"), the immortality of matter, the spirit prison, and many others.[45]

Theologically Joseph Smith's moral and physical departure from New England may be summed up in the second and tenth "articles of faith," which were not formulated until 1841.[46] Article Two explicitly rejected the old Puritan maxim that in "Adam's fall we sinned all." Not only had God become predictable, but the Calvinistic man who was a sin-laden worm was replaced by an individualistic Arminian who "will be punished for his own sins and not for Adam's transgression" (Article Two). Article Ten insured the fact that these optimistic Americans, by "gathering" in the "lands of their inheritance," were to move west.

One should conclude from this essay that Alexander Campbell's description of Mormonism on the basis of the Book of Mormon, a description avidly accepted by anti-frontier historians over a century later,[47] was wrong in that it considered the Book of Mormon alone to be the essence of Mormonism. But he was unwittingly right in noting that Smith sought authoritative answers for every perplexing theological problem of the day.

Joseph Smith hoped to establish the authority of what early Mormons called "the one true church" over against the theological potpourri of competing sects that surrounded him as a young man in the Burned-over District. Later elaborations of doctrine never obscured this goal. New revelations merely reinforced the uniqueness of the one true church.

A great deal of additional evidence for this central concern of Mormonism could be cited. Even after he had been excommunicated, Sidney Rigdon, for example, preached the Mormon doctrine of authority. In 1845 he defended the truth of Mormonism against criticisms of the Roman Catholic bishop of Pittsburgh.[48] But nowhere is the concern more apparent than in the Book of Mormon itself. That work expresses only contempt for sectarianism.[49] The danger of "going astray" from doctrinal truth and the need for establishing the one true fold are major and recurrent themes of the Book of Mormon.[50] These themes are, it seems to me, the only real theological themes of the book.

The prophet hated the contentions and contradictions of sectarianism and hoped in a sense to establish a sect to end all sects. Indeed the origin and whole doctrinal development of Mormonism under the prophet may be characterized as a pragmatically successful quest for religious authority, a quest that he shared with many other anxious rural Americans of his time, class, and place. Historians who do not take this quest seriously enough to examine it do not take Mormonism seriously enough for rigorous historical inquiry.

NOTES

1. Except for this sentence and one or two others in the notes I have not altered the text of the original article; and I still stand by both the text and the interpretation. But fairness and clarity require that I point out that, largely as a result of the New Mormon History, the historiographical landscape has changed. Leonard J. Arrington's work, cited below, still appeared execptional in the 1950s. Since then, other historians have produced scores of books and articles on early Mormon history which, like the work of Arrington, command the respect of both Mormons and non-Mormons. The new works range as widely as the quasi-philosophical work of Jan Shipps to the detailed local history of Richard L. Bushman. See Shipps, *Mormonism: The Story of a New Religious Tradition* (Urbana: University of Illinois Press, 1985), and Bushman, *Joseph Smith and the Beginnings of Mormonism* (Urbana: University of Illinois Press, 1984).

Standard Mormon historians like Roberts, Whitney, and Joseph Fielding Smith have, of course, done much writing on the early period, but they are not consulted by people who write American history.

Except to Mormons, Fawn Brodie's *No Man Knows My History* (New York: Alfred A. Knopf, 1945) is not clearly polemical. Intellectual honesty requires this opinion to be stated at the outset at the risk of offending some Mormon readers. Though hardly pro-Mormon, Brodie's book does not clearly fit either of my two categories of Mormon and non-Mormon. Leaders of Mormon thought have yet to come to grips with the influence of her book.

The sole Mormon authority is B. H. Roberts, but his six-volume *Comprehensive History of the Church of Jesus Christ of Latter-Day Saints* (Salt Lake City: Deseret News Press, 1930) is too sprawling and undigested to be of much use, and though it is listed by the *Guide,* one very rarely finds it cited by non-Mormon historians.

In alluding to recent changes in the acceptability of works by loyal Mormons, I have in mind such works as Leonard J. Arrington's excellent and definitive *Great Basin Kingdom* (Cambridge: Harvard University Press, 1958). Significantly, perhaps, this does not deal with early Mormonism or its theological milieu.

2. Milton Backman's *American Religions and the Rise of Mormonism* (Salt Lake City: Deseret Book, 1965) never gained an acceptance outside the church comparable with Arrington's *Great Basin Kingdom.* For the haphazard nature of non-Mormon interpretations, see note 31.

3. Henry Steele Commager, *The American Mind: An Interpretation of American Thought and Character Since the 1880's* (New Haven: Yale University Press, 1950), 9.

4. See Brigham H. Roberts, ed., *History of the Church of Jesus Christ*

of Latter-day Saints. Period I. History of Joseph Smith, the Prophet by Himself, 7 vols. (Salt Lake City: Deseret News Press); hereafter cited as HC. Knowledgeable Mormons will point out that this work, though it goes back to as early as 1838, cannot be so precisely dated. But in so doing they underline the fact that Brigham H. Roberts, the editor, was not following the rules of modern critical editing, rules which were in full flower when he published the work.

5. Ibid. 1:3-4.

6. Reprinted in ibid. 4:536.

7. Ralph Henry Gabriel, The Course of American Democratic Thought, 2d ed. (New York: The Ronald Press Co., 1956), 57. Another leading historian in this tradition hardly admits the existence of sectarianism, noting erroneously that the word sect was only "occasionally used" in nineteenth-century America. Kenneth Scott Latourette, The Great Century, A.D. 1800-A.D. 1914, vol. 4, A History of the Expansion of Christianity (New York: Harper and Brothers, 1941), 429.

8. Robert Richardson, Memoirs of Alexander Campbell, 2 vols. (Philadelphia: J. B. Lippincott, 1868-70), 1:387-91. Campbell's doctrine of adult baptism for the remission of sins has often and erroneously been stated to be the model for the similar Mormon doctrine. But the doctrine was a kind of afterthought for Campbell (391-400). For both Campbell and Smith (and many others) it was simply the way of the apostolic church, to which almost all sectarians appealed for the authority of their doctrine.

9. See Campbell's prospectus for his projected newspaper (The Millennial Harbinger) in the Western Reserve Chronicle, 3 Dec. 1829; also the earlier Campbellite announcements of 28 Feb. and 18 Mar. 1828.

10. "The Mole's little pathways" (1807?), MS copy, Shaker Papers, Library of Congress.

11. Richard McNemar, A Friendly letter to Alexander Mitchell (Union Village, OH, 1837), reprinted by the Shakers from the Western Review.

12. Letter from the Ministry of Harvard to the Ministry of New Lebanon, Harvard, MA, 9 Nov. 1831, MS, Western Reserve Historical Society.

13. The Great Century, A.D. 1800-A.D. 1914, vol. 4 History of the Expansion of Christianity, 261.

14. For an excellent short statement of the problem of authority, see Robert McAfee Brown, "A Protestant Viewpoint: Protestantism and Authority," Commonweal 81 (9 Oct. 1964): 69-71.

15. Mormons became sensitive to the accusation that they had glossed over apostolic succession. See Henry Caswall, City of the Mormons; or, Three Days at Nauvoo, in 1842, 2nd ed., rev. (London: J. G. F. & J. Rivington, 1843), 17, 39, 42.

16. The Prophet, 4 Jan. 1845; HC 1:40-41. A priesthood did, of course,

exist among the Hebrews; and some orthodox Christian denominations believe in a continuation in some manner of this priesthood. Such Christians point, as do Mormons, to the appropriate verses in the seventh chapter of Hebrews, where the familiar phrase occurs: "Thou art a priest for ever after the order of Melchisedec." But the dual priesthood and the special elaboration of the Mormon priesthood of Melchizedek (spelled Melchisedec in the King James version) is peculiarly Mormon.

Mormon readers will also be aware that Joseph Smith claimed apostolic succession through Peter or more accurately through Peter, James, and John. But this is far less important to the definition of Mormonism than the belief that the apostles were "prophets and revelators" in a prophetic succession from Moses on down through Solomon, John the Baptist, and Christ to Joseph Smith. See James E. Talmage, *Articles of Faith* (Salt Lake City: Deseret News Press, 1901), 300-301.

17. Brodie, *No Man Knows My History,* 104, 112.

18. For revelation in general as a source of authority, see Parley P. Pratt, *A Voice of Warning* (New York: W. Sandford, 1837), 119.

19. HC 3:297.

20. This separate, "fourth" position of Mormonism achieved a kind of quasi-official recognition in a film used in the Democratic party convention of 1956 and shown on nationwide television networks. In 1985 Jan Shipps made this notion of Mormonism as a new, fourth religious tradition the central thesis of her *Mormonism: The Story of a New Religious Tradition.*

21. I mean here the conversions in the area of western New York under the direct influence of the prophet. It is true that in the fall of 1830 about one hundred persons had been converted in the vicinity of Kirtland, Ohio, mainly from a group of former Campbellites there known as Rigdonites. In January 1831 there were not more than a hundred converts in the area, most of whom had been baptized a few weeks before. The Ohio conversions differed from those in western New York, where the leadership, presence, and revelations of the prophet were of primary importance. See HC 1:77n, 120, 124, 146.

22. Alexander Campbell, *Delusions. An Analysis of the Book of Mormon . . . and a Refutation of Its Pretenses to Divine Authority* (Boston: Benjamin H. Greene, 1832), 13. The title is an allusion to 2 Thes. 2:11.

23. Brodie, *No Man Knows My History,* 69, 86. This is also emphasized strongly by Stow Persons in his *American Minds: A History of Ideas* (New York: Holt, 1958), 183.

24. David Whitmer, *An Address to All Believers in Christ. By a Witness to the Divine Authenticity of the Book of Mormon* (Richmond, MO: David Whitmer, 1887), 4, 50.

25. Smith also wondered about the need for authority to baptize,

but he was not weak in faith as was Cowdery throughout his life.

26. HC 1:64-79, 84.

27. D&C 20. This extremely important revelation was received in April 1830, and Smith may already have revised it while preparing it for its first printing in the Book of Commandments (Independence, MO, 1833). In August another revelation stated that the higher priesthood of Melchizedek, then held by Smith and Cowdery, bore "the keys of ministry." See D&C 27:12. The predominance of the Melchizedek priesthood in general and of its first presidency in particular was first strongly asserted in November 1831 in D&C 78:15-22. When the Book of Commandments (1833) was revised and re-printed with additional revelations as the Doctrine and Covenants (1835), Smith added verses 65, 66, and 67 to D&C 20. In these verses he defined more precisely the right of ordaining and being ordained, a right that was the key to the complex hierarchy of offices from apostle down to deacons and church members. In short the Melchizedek priesthood and the powers associated with it were elaborated even before the first printing of the revelation on church government in D&C 20. Elaboration continued at least up to 1841 in subsequent revelations.

28. HC 1:176.

29. Some time after 1844 the relationship between the two institutions was reduced to the seemingly simple notion that the high priesthood is a category to which the eldership and high priesthood belong as offices. A high priest also always holds the Melchizedek priesthood or is "within" it. But actually there is extensive overlapping of offices and categories even today.

30. Brodie has suggested that the concept of the dual priesthood came directly from two books published by one Rev. James Gray in Philadelphia and Baltimore in 1810 and 1821. See *No Man Knows My History,* 111.

31. See D. B. Davis, "The New England Origins of Mormonism," *New England Quarterly* 26 (June 1953): 148-49 for the comparison of Joseph Smith with the Anabaptist, John of Leiden. None of the standard works on American intellectual history treats Mormonism in the same way; nor are there patterns or schools of disagreement. Ralph H. Gabriel stresses its authoritarianism, as pointed out in the text. See *The Course of American Democratic Thought,* 57. He also considers it a "product of the New England frontier" (35). Stow Persons emphasizes its eschatological elements (also mentioned by Gabriel, 35). See Persons, *American Minds,* 182. But he is also the only non-Mormon writer who clearly asserts that Smith's neighbors were "yearning for an authoritative dispensation of the truth [and] Smith came to such people with an unqualified claim of authority" (1840). Merle Curti makes it one of the many new utopian experiments of the age of reform. Curti, *The Growth of American Thought,* 3d ed. (New York, 1964), 304. Henry Steele Commager describes it, together with Christian Science, as a "native

American religion." *The American Mind,* 186. Since the early 1980s patterns of interpretation have been emerging, even among faithful members of the church.

32. Brodie, *No Man Knows My History,* 6-7.

33. Ibid., 141n2. Brodie makes much of this. It is doubtful that the prophet veiled his actions in the particular incident which she cites here, but some Saints thought so. The well-known fact that the prophet permitted only a select group of Saints to know the spiritual wife doctrine (polygamy) may also be recalled.

34. D&C 130:22.

35. D&C 132:7

36. George F. Partridge, ed., "Death of a Mormon Dictator; Letters of Massachusetts Mormons, 1843-1848," *New England Quarterly* 9 (Dec. 1936): 594. The doctrine caused many to apostatize.

37. "King Follett Discourse," a funeral sermon given in 1844 and printed in [Joseph Smith,] *The Voice of Truth* (Nauvoo, IL: John Taylor, 1844). See 60-62 and also D&C 132:20, 37 (1843). Smith had hinted at the plurality of Gods as early as 1832 (D&C 76:58).

38. *Evening and Morning Star* 1 (June 1832): 7.

39. Brodie, *No Man Knows My History,* 187-88. To non-Mormons the most famous of the heavenly pleasures was the retention of one's earthly spiritual wives.

40. Davis, "The New England Origins of Mormonism," 153-54, 162. Davis is trying to refute "frontier historians [who] say that Mormon theology is mostly absurd and meaningless, but can be explained as a Western revolt against Calvinism" (153). In this anti-frontier interpretation of Mormonism, Davis follows the widely accepted but shaky interpretation of Whitney R. Cross in *The Burned-Over District: the Social and Intellectual History of Enthusiastic Religion in Western New York, 1800-1850* (Ithaca: Cornell University Press, 1950). For a fairly successful attempt to refute Cross's interpretation of Mormonism, see Alexander Evanoff, "The Turner Thesis and Mormon Beginnings in New York and Utah," *Utah Historical Quarterly* 30 (Spring 1965): 157-73.

41. Frederic Ives Carpenter, *Emerson Handbook* (New York: Hendricks House, 1953; rep. 1967), 129-31.

42. Brodie, *No Man Knows My History,* 64-66, 367, 380-82.

43. Ibid., 277.

44. Brigham H. Roberts, *The Rise and Fall of Nauvoo* (Salt Lake City: Deseret News Press, 1900), 17. Daryl Chase, another professing Mormon, echoes this in *Joseph the Prophet* (Salt Lake City: Deseret Book Co., 1944), 74-75. See also HC 3:379-81, 386ff.

45. Roberts, *Rise and Fall of Nauvoo,* 165-215.

46. See Talmage, *Articles of Faith*. This in its various editions is the official church statement of the articles.

47. Davis, "The New England Origins of Mormonism," 153, 155; Cross, *Burned-Over District,* 145. The most thorough historian of early Mormonism also quotes the Campbell litany but does not state that the doctrines listed were Mormon doctrines. They merely reflect, like the anti-Masonic elements, the fiery issues of the Burned-Over District in the 1820s; Brodie, *No Man Knows My History,* 69.

48. *Latter-Day Saints Messenger and Advocate* (Pittsburgh), 1 June 1845.

49. 1 Ne. 22:23-25; 2 Ne. 3:12.

50. See the dream of Lehi, 1 Ne. 8. Also Al. 41:1; 2 Ne. 12:5 (where, astonishingly, "astray" is added to Isaiah); 2 Ne. 26:21; and 2 Ne. 28:3-6.

3.
The Significance of Joseph Smith's "First Vision" in Mormon Thought

James B. Allen

IN THE YEAR 1838 JOSEPH SMITH BEGAN DICTATING HIS *HISTORY OF THE Church.* The history commenced with the now famous account of what has been termed the "first vision," in which he told of the appearance to him in 1820 of two heavenly personages. The vision, according to the Mormon prophet, came as a result of his prayerful inquiry concerning which church to join, and in it he was forbidden to join any of them, for all were wrong. Although not specifically named in the story, the two personages have been identified by Latter-day Saints as God the Father and Jesus Christ; Joseph Smith indicated that the one said of the other, "This is My Beloved Son, Hear Him!"

This singular story has achieved a position of unique importance in the traditions and official doctrines of the Mormon church. Belief in the vision is one of the fundamentals to which faithful members give assent. Its importance is second only to belief in the divinity of Jesus of Nazareth. The story is an essential part of the lessons given by Mormon missionaries to prospective converts, and its acceptance is necessary before baptism. The nature and importance of the vision is the subject of frequent sermons by church members in all meetings and by authorities of the church in semi-annual conferences.

Not only is belief in the first vision of primary importance to

Mormonism, but the story of the vision has what might be termed a
number of secondary, although highly important, utilitarian functions. Joseph Smith's original purpose in writing the story was to
clarify facts that had been distorted in the public mind. In our time,
however, it is used by church leaders and teachers to demonstrate
for believers other aspects of the Mormon faith: the idea that God
actually hears and answers prayers; the concept that there is a
personal devil who tries to stop the progress of truth; and perhaps
most fundamental of all, the Mormon doctrine that the divine
Godhead are actually separate, distinct, physical personages, as opposed to the Trinitarian concept of traditional Christianity.

     The person who would understand the history of any insti-
tution must be concerned not only with chronology but also with an
understanding of what the people in that institution were thinking,
what they were being taught, and how these ideas compare with
present-day thought. In connection with the story of the vision then,
it is important to ask certain questions: When was it first told? When
was it first published? Did it have the significant place in early
Mormon thought that it has today? If not, when did it begin to take
on its present significance in the writings and teachings of the
church? Some thoughts on these questions might open the door to
a better understanding of Mormon history and also demonstrate by
example the gradually changing pattern of thought which one would
expect to find in any church.

     According to Joseph Smith, he told the story of the vision
immediately after it happened in the early spring of 1820. As a result,
he said, he received immediate criticism in the community. There is
little if any evidence, however, that by the early 1830s Joseph Smith
was telling the story in public. At least if he was telling it, no one
seemed to consider it important enough to have recorded it *at the
time,* and no one was criticizing him for it. Not even in his own history
did Joseph Smith mention being criticized in this period for telling
the story of the first vision. The interest, rather, was in the Book of
Mormon and the various angelic visitations connected with its origin.

     The fact that none of the available contemporary writings
about Joseph Smith in the 1830s, none of the publications of the
church in that decade, and no contemporary journal or correspondence yet discovered mentions the story of the first vision is convincing evidence that at best it received only limited circulation in those

early days. In February 1830, for example, a farmer who lived about fifty miles from Palmyra, New York, wrote a letter describing the religious fervor in western New York and particularly the coming forth of the Book of Mormon. No mention was made, however, of the idea that Joseph Smith had beheld Deity.[1] The earliest anti-Mormon literature attacked the Book of Mormon and the character of Joseph Smith but never mentioned the first vision. Alexander Campbell, who had some reason to be bitter against the Mormons because of the conversion of his colleague Sidney Rigdon in 1830, published one of the first denunciations of Joseph Smith in 1832. It was entitled *Delusions: An Analysis of the Book of Mormon* and contained no mention of the first vision. In 1834 E. D. Howe published *Mormonism Unvailed,* which contained considerable damaging material against Joseph Smith but again no mention of the first vision. In 1839 John Corrill, a former Mormon, published a history of the Mormons, but he made no reference at all to Joseph Smith's claim to having conversed with the members of the Godhead. In 1842 J. B. Turner published *Mormonism in All Ages,* which included one of the most bitter denunciations of the Mormon prophet yet printed, but even at this late date no mention was made of the first vision.[2]

Not until 1843, when the *New York Spectator* printed a reporter's account of an interview with Joseph Smith, did a *non-Mormon* source publish any reference to the story of the first vision.[3] In 1844 I. Daniel Rupp published *An Original History of the Religious Denominations at Present Existing in the United States,* which contained an account of the vision provided by Joseph Smith himself. After this time non-Mormon sources began to refer to the story. It seems probable, however, that as far as non-Mormons were concerned there was little if any awareness of it in the 1830s. The popular image of Mormon belief centered around such things as the Book of Mormon, the missionary zeal, and the concept of Zion in Missouri.

As far as Mormon literature is concerned, there was no specific reference to Joseph Smith's first vision in any published material in the 1830s. Joseph Smith's history, which was begun in 1838, was not published until it ran serially in the *Times and Seasons* in 1842. The famous "Wentworth Letter," which contained a much less detailed account of the vision, appeared 1 March 1842 in the same periodical. Introductory material to the Book of Mormon as well as publicity about it told of Joseph Smith's obtaining the gold plates and of angelic visitations, but nothing was printed that suggested earlier visitations. In 1833 the church published the Book of Commandments, forerunner to the present Doctrine and Covenants, and again no reference was made to Joseph's first vision, although several references were made to the Book of Mormon and the circumstances of its origin. The first regular periodical to be published by the church was *The Evening and the Morning Star,* but its pages reveal no effort to tell the story of the first vision to its readers. Nor do the pages of the *Latter-day Saints Messenger and Advocate,* printed in Kirtland, Ohio, from October 1834 to September 1836. In this newspaper Oliver Cowdery, who was second only to Joseph Smith in the early organization of the church, published a series of letters dealing with the origin of the church. These letters were written with the approval of Joseph Smith, but they contained no mention of any vision prior to those connected with the Book of Mormon. In 1835 the Doctrine and Covenants was printed at Kirtland, Ohio, and its preface declared that it contained "the leading items of religion which we have professed to believe." Included in the book were the "Lectures on Faith," a series of seven lectures which had been prepared for the School of the Prophets in Kirtland in 1834-35. It is interesting to note that in demonstrating the doctrine that the Godhead consists of two separate personages, no mention was made of Joseph Smith having seen them, nor was any reference made to the first vision in any part of the publication.[4] The *Times and Seasons* began publication in 1839, but as indicated above, the story of the vision was not told in its pages until 1842. From all this it would appear that the general church membership did not receive information about the first vision until the 1840s and that the story certainly did not hold the prominent place in Mormon thought that it does today.

The story of the first vision had little if any importance in missionary work in the 1830s. The best missionary tool in that day was the Book of Mormon, and most early converts came into the church as a result either of reading the book or of hearing the "testimony" of others who declared their personal knowledge of its authenticity. Such important early converts as Parley P. Pratt, Sidney Rigdon, Brigham Young, and Heber C. Kimball all joined because of their conversion through the Book of Mormon, and none of their early writings indicates that any understanding or knowledge of the first vision was in any way part of their conversion. John Corrill tells of his first contact with Mormons through Parley P. Pratt, Oliver Cowdery, Peter Whitmer, and Ziba Peterson. These were the famous missionaries to the "Lamanites" of 1830. Their message concerned the Book of Mormon, but Corrill reported nothing of a prior vision.[5] When Parley P. Pratt converted John Taylor in 1836, the story he told him was of angelic visitations connected with the Book of Mormon, of priesthood restoration, and of the organization of the church. There is no evidence that anything was said of the first vision. Rather, Taylor was converted on the basis of the Book of Mormon and the fact that Mormonism taught certain principles which he had already concluded were essential and which he had been waiting to hear someone preach.[6]

The first important missionary pamphlet of the church, the *Voice of Warning*, published in 1837 by Parley P. Pratt, contains long sections on items important to missionaries of the 1830s, such as fulfillment of prophecy, the Book of Mormon, external evidence of the book's authenticity, the Resurrection, and the nature of revelation, but nothing on the first vision. It seems evident that at least in the 1830s, it was not considered necessary for prospective converts to Mormonism to know the story. It is assumed, of course, that if they believed in the authenticity of the Book of Mormon as well as the other claims of Joseph Smith to divine authority and revelation, the story of the first vision would not have been difficult for them to believe once they heard it.

To summarize, it is apparent that the story of Joseph Smith's first vision was not given general circulation in the 1830s. Neither Mormon nor non-Mormon publications made reference to it, and it is evident that the general membership of the church knew little if anything about it. Belief in the story certainly was not a prerequisite for conversion, and it is obvious that the story was not being used to illustrate other points of doctrine. In this respect at least, Mormon thought of the 1830s was different from Mormon thought of later years.

A possible explanation for the fact that the story of the vision was not generally known in the 1830s can be found in Joseph Smith's conviction that experiences such as these should be kept from the general public because of their sacred nature. It is noted by some that in 1838 he declared that his basic reason for telling it even then, years after it happened, was in response to "reports which have been put in circulation by evil-disposed and designing persons" who had distorted the facts.[7] Furthermore, the young prophet said that he had been severely rebuffed the first time he told the story in 1820; and since it represented one of his most profound spiritual experiences, he could well have decided to circulate it only privately until he could feel certain that in relating it he would not receive again the general ridicule of friends.

Perhaps the closest one may come to seeing a contemporary diarist's account of the story is in the journal of Alexander Neibaur, which is located in LDS church archives. It must be observed, however, that Neibaur did not become associated with Joseph Smith until the 1840s and that he did not hear the story until well after other accounts of the vision, including Joseph Smith's, had been written and published.

In spite of the foregoing discussion, there is some evidence to suggest that the story of Joseph Smith's first vision was known, probably on a limited basis, during the formative decade of church history. One of the most significant documents of that period yet discovered was brought to light in 1965 by Paul R. Cheesman, then a graduate student at Brigham Young University. This is a handwritten manuscript composed about 1832, dictated and written in part by Joseph Smith. It contains an account of the early experiences of the Mormon prophet and includes a version of the story of the first vision. While the story varies in some details from the version presently accepted, enough is there to indicate that at least as early as 1832 Joseph Smith contemplated writing and perhaps publishing it. The manuscript had been in the Church Historian's office for many years, and yet few if any who saw it realized its significance. The existence of the manuscript, of course, does not prove or disprove the authenticity of the story, but it demonstrates the fact that in the early 1830s the story of the vision was beginning to find place in the formulation of Mormon thought.[8] Fawn Brodie suggested that the story of Joseph Smith's first vision was something he invented after 1834.[9] This argument must be revised.

Another document of almost equal importance was brought to light by a member of the staff at the Church Historian's office in the mid-1960s.[10] It is located in the back of Book A-1 of the handwritten manuscript of the *History of the Church* (commonly referred to as the "Manuscript History"). The writing of the "Manuscript History" was supervised by Joseph Smith beginning in 1838. Under the date of 9 November 1835, the story is told of a visit to Joseph Smith by a man calling himself Joshua, the Jewish Minister. The conversation naturally turned to religion, and it is recorded that the Mormon prophet told his guest "the circumstances connected with the coming forth of the Book of Mormon, as recorded in the former part of this history."[11] From reading the "Manuscript History," therefore, as well as the printed *History of the Church,* one would get the impression that at this time Joseph Smith related only the Book of Mormon story. In the back of the book, however, is a revealing document that almost certainly comprises the original notes from which the "Manuscript History" was later compiled and is actually a daily account of Joseph Smith's activities in 1835 as recorded by a scribe. The importance of the manuscript here lies in the fact that the scribe wrote down what Joseph Smith said to his visitor, and he began not by telling the story of the discovery of the Book of Mormon but with an account of the first vision. Again, the details of the story vary somewhat from the accepted version, but the manuscript at least demonstrates that by 1835 the story had been told to someone.

The only additional evidence that Joseph Smith's story was being circulated in the 1830s is found in reminiscences of a few people who were close to him in that decade. While reminiscences are obviously open to question, for it is easy for anyone after many years to read back into his own history things which he accepts at the time of the telling, some of them at least sound convincing enough to suggest that the story might have been circulating on a limited basis. In 1893 Edward Stevenson published his reminiscences. He first saw the Mormon prophet in 1834, and according to Stevenson: "In that same year, 1834, in the midst of many large congregations the Prophet testified with great power concerning the visit of the Father and the Son, and the conversation he had with them. Never before did I feel such power as was manifested on these occasions. . . . We were proud, indeed, to entertain one who had conversed with the Father and the Son, and been under the tuition of an angel from heaven."[12]

Lorenzo Snow heard Joseph Smith for the first time when he was seventeen years old. Years later he recalled the experience in these words: "As I looked upon him and listened, I thought to myself that a man bearing such a wonderful testimony as he did, and having

such a countenance as he possessed, could hardly be a false prophet.
. . . for when he testified that he had had a conversation with Jesus
the Son of God, and talked with Him personally, as Moses talked with
God upon Mount Sinai, and that he also heard the voice of the Father,
he was telling something that he either knew to be false or to be
positively true."[13]

If this statement is accurate, it means that Joseph Smith was
telling the important story in 1831. When reading the statement in
context, however, it will be noted that Snow did not say that he heard
Joseph tell the actual story—only that he heard him testify that he had
conversed with the Son and heard the voice of the Father. Other
reminiscences may be found which would indicate that the story was
being told in the 1830s, but the weight of evidence suggests that it
was not a matter of common knowledge, even among church members, in the earliest years of Mormon history?

The question for historical consideration, then, is when and
how did the story of Joseph Smith assume its present importance not
only as a test of faith for the Mormons but also as a tool for illustrating
and supporting other church doctrines.

It seems apparent that after Joseph Smith decided to write
the story in 1838 the way was clear for its use as a missionary tool. It
is not known how generally the membership of the church knew of
the story by the end of the decade, but in 1840 Orson Pratt published
in England a missionary tract entitled *Interesting Account of Several
Remarkable Visions and of the Late Discovery of Ancient American Records.*
This early pamphlet contained a detailed account of the first vision
which elaborated upon several details that Joseph Smith touched on
only briefly. Smith's own account was published in 1842. In the same
year Orson Hyde published in Germany a pamphlet entitled *A Cry
From the Wilderness, a Voice from the Dust of the Earth.* This also
contained an elaborate account of the vision. It is evident then that
in the early 1840s the story of Joseph Smith's first vision took its place
alongside the story of the Book of Mormon as a missionary message,
and it is possible that Joseph Smith's decision to write it in 1838 was
a sort of "go ahead" for this action.

By the 1850s the story of the vision had become an important
part of church literature. In 1851 it appeared in the first edition of
the Pearl of Great Price, published in England by Franklin D. Richards. This volume was accepted as one of the "standard works" of the

Mormon church in 1880.[14] By this time the story had become well known both to members and non-members alike and was being used as a basic missionary tool.

A more difficult question to answer concerns the various utilitarian functions of the story. As far as any recorded material reveals, Joseph Smith never used the story of his vision to illustrate specific doctrinal teachings.

When did church members begin to make such use of the story? Apparently the early teachers of the church relied on scriptural evidence alone to demonstrate the Mormon doctrine of God, and not until well into the Utah period did they begin to use Joseph Smith's story to illustrate it. One of the earliest recorded sermons to make this use of the story was given by George Q. Cannon of the First Presidency on 7 October 1883. Said Cannon:

"Joseph Smith, inspired of God, came forth and declared that God lived. Ages had passed and no one had beheld Him. The fact that he existed was like a dim tradition in the minds of the people. The fact that Jesus lived was only supposed to be the case because eighteen hundred years before men had seen him. . . . The character of God—whether He was a personal being, whether His center was nowhere, and His circumference everywhere, were matters of speculation. No one had seen him. No one had seen any one who had seen an angel. . . . Is it a wonder that men were confused? that there was such a variety of opinion respecting the character and being of God? . . . Brother Joseph, as I said, startled the world. It stood aghast at the statement which he made, and the testimony which he bore. He declared that he had seen God. He declared that he had seen Jesus Christ. . . .

"After that revelation faith began to grow up in men's minds and hearts. Speculation concerning the being of God ceased among those who received the testimony of Joseph Smith. He testified that God was a being of body, that He had a body, that man was in his likeness, that Jesus was the exact counterpart of the Father, and that the Father and Jesus were two distinct personages, as distinct as an earthly father and an earthly son."[15]

Probably there were earlier sermons or writings that used the story of the first vision to demonstrate the Mormon doctrine of God. Evidence indicates, however, that they were rare and that only gradually did this use of the story find place in the traditions of the church. Suffice it to say that by the turn of the century the device was regularly used. James E. Talmage, for example, in his *Articles of Faith* used the story to illustrate the godhead doctrine, and Elder Joseph Fielding Smith in *Essentials in Church History* makes a major point of this doctrinal contribution. In 1961 the church required all missionaries to use the story in their first lesson as part of the dialogue designed to prove that the Father and the Son are distinct personages and that they have tangible bodies.

As the story of Joseph Smith's vision was told and retold, both by himself and others, there were naturally some variations in detail. The account written about 1832 told of his youthful anxiety over the "welfare of my immortal soul" and over his sins as well as the sins of the world. Therefore, he declared, "I cried unto the Lord for mercy for there was none else to whom I could go and to obtain mercy and the Lord heard my cry in the wilderness and while in the attitude of calling upon the Lord in the 16th year of my age a piller of light above the brightness of the sun at noon day came down from above and rested upon me and I was filled with the Spirit of God and the Lord opened the heavens upon me and I saw the Lord and he spake unto me saying Joseph my son Thy Sins are forgiven thee, go thy way walk in my Statutes and keep my commandments behold I am the Lord of glory I was crycifyed for the world."[16]

In this story only one personage was mentioned, the Son, for he spoke of having been crucified. If Edward Stevenson's account is correct, however, he heard Joseph Smith say in 1834 that he had seen both the Father and the Son.

In 1835, when Joseph Smith's scribe heard him tell the story to a visitor, the Mormon leader's words were "nearly as follows":

"Being wrought up in my mind respecting the subject of Religion, and looking at the different systems taught the children of men, I knew not who was right or who was wrong but considered it of the first importance to me that I should be right in matters of so much moment, matter involving eternal consequences. Being thus perplexed in mind I retired to the silent grove and there bowed down before the Lord, under a realising sense (if the Bible be true) ask and you shall receive knock and it shall be opened, seek and you shall find, and again, if any man lack wisdom, let of God [sic], who giveth to all men liberally & upbraideth not. Information was what I most desired, at this time and with a fixed determination to obtain it. I called on the Lord for the first time in the place above stated, or in other words, I made a fruitless attempt to pray My tongue seemed to be swollen in my mouth, so that I could not utter, I heard a noise behind me like some one walking towards me, I strove again to pray, but could not; the noise of walking seemed to draw nearer; I sprang upon my feet and looked around. but I saw no person, or thing that was calculated to produce the noise of walking. I kneeled again, my mouth was opened and my tongue loosed; I called on the Lord in mighty prayer. A pillar of fire appeared above my head; which presently rested down upon me, and filled me with unspeakable joy. A personage appeared in the midst of this pillar of flame, which was spread all around and yet nothing consumed. Another personage soon appeared like unto the first: he said unto me thy sins are forgiven thee. He testified also unto me that Jesus Christ is the son of God. I saw many angels in this vision."[17]

In this account Joseph emphasized the difficulty he had in uttering his first prayer, and the "noise of walking" seems to suggest the evil opposition which became an essential element in the official version of the story. Furthermore, he told of having seen two persons, although one preceded the other. The two persons looked alike, and the second assured him that his sins had been forgiven. The most unusual statement, however, is Joseph's declaration that he saw many angels in this vision.

When Smith finally dictated the "Manuscript History" in 1838, he told of his great uneasiness in the midst of the religious confusion of 1820 and his quest to determine which of the churches was right. After reading James 1:5 he retired to the woods and began to pray. In this account he told of a force of darkness which tried to stop him from proceeding, then the appearance in a pillar of light of two personages. When the light appeared, the force of darkness left. One of the personages said to Joseph, "This is my beloved Son, hear him." The crux of the message from the Son was that he should join none of the churches, for all of them were wrong. "When I came to myself," he said, "I found myself lying on my back looking up into Heaven."[18] The story as told in Joseph Smith's published history of 1842 and in the Pearl of Great Price does not differ appreciably from his manuscript history.

The account published by Orson Pratt in 1840 contains a great deal of amplification upon the story as told by Joseph Smith.[19]

He describes in more detail, for example, the problems running through young Joseph's mind when he was "somewhere about fourteen or fifteen years old." The appearance of the light is described in more vivid detail, and the whole account takes on a more dramatic air than any recorded story told by Joseph himself. Describing the light, for example, Pratt wrote: "as it drew nearer, it increased in brightness, and magnitude, so that, by the time that it reached the tops of the trees, the whole wilderness, for some distance around, was illuminated in a most glorious and brilliant manner. He expected to have seen the leaves and boughs of the trees consumed, as soon as the light came in contact with them; but, perceiving that it did not produce that effect, he was encouraged with the hopes of being able to endure its presence. It continued descending, slowly, until it rested upon the earth, and he was enveloped in the midst of it. When it first came upon him, it produced a peculiar sensation throughout his whole system; and, immediately, his mind was caught away, from the natural objects with which he was surrounded; and he was enwrapped in a heavenly vision, and saw two glorious personages."[20] According to this account the young man was informed that his sins were forgiven and that the "fullness of the gospel" would be made known to him in the future. Neither of these statements is contained in the Pearl of Great Price account, but the first one is included in both the 1832 and 1835 manuscripts.

The Wentworth Letter published in 1842 and Rupp's history published in 1844 contain identical but very short accounts of the vision. The force of opposition was not mentioned, and the description of the visitation was shorter than in Joseph's earlier account. He told, however, of seeing two personages while he was "enwrapped in a heavenly vision" and said that "they" told him that all religious denominations were believing incorrect doctrines. The idea that the "fullness of the gospel" should be given to him in the future was recorded here in agreement with Orson Pratt's account.

Orson Hyde's account published in 1842 is similar to the stories told by Joseph Smith and Orson Pratt. The two personages were not defined or quoted directly, but they were said to exactly resemble each other, and the promise to reveal the fullness of the gospel was mentioned.

The variations in these and other accounts suggest that in relating his story to various individuals at various times, Joseph Smith emphasized different aspects of it and that his listeners were each impressed with different details. This, of course, is to be expected, for the same thing happens in retelling any story. The only way to keep it from changing is to write it only once and then insist that it be read exactly that way each time it is to be repeated. Such an effort would obviously be unrealistic. Joseph Smith told his story several times before he released it for publication. People who heard it may have embellished it a little with their own literary devices as they retold or recorded it.

In this connection four accounts are especially interesting, for each suggests that although two personages appeared in the vision, one preceded the other. The 1835 story is the earliest that makes this distinction. In 1843 Joseph Smith told the story to a non-Mormon editor, who later quoted him in an article in the *New York Spectator*. As quoted by the editor, Joseph said: "While thinking of this matter, I opened the New Testament promiscuously on these words, in James, 'Ask of the Lord who giveth to all men liberally and upbraideth not.' I just determined I'd ask Him. I immediately went out into the woods where my father had a clearing, and I kneeled down, and prayed, saying, 'O Lord, what church shall I join?' Directly I saw a light, and then a glorious personage in the light, and then another personage, and the first person said to the second, 'Behold my Beloved Son, hear Him.' I then addressed this second person, saying, 'O Lord, what church shall I join?' He replied, 'Do not join any of them, they are all corrupt.' The vision then vanished."[21]

The third contemporary account to repeat the idea that one personage preceded the other is the diary of Alexander Neibaur. Writing on 24 May 1844, Neibaur said that Joseph Smith had told him that day of his early quest for religion. In Neibaur's words Joseph Smith "went into the woods to pray, kneels himself down . . . saw a fire toward heaven come nearer and nearer; saw a personage in the fire; light complexion, blue eyes, a piece of white cloth drawn over his shoulders, his right arm bear [sic]; after a while another person came to the side of the first."[22] A fourth reference to this idea is in the diary of Charles L. Walker on the date of 2 February 1893. Walker wrote of hearing John Alger declare in "Fast meeting" that he had heard Joseph Smith relate the story of the vision, saying "that God touched his eyes with his finger and said, 'Joseph this is my beloved Son, hear him.' As soon as the Lord had touched his eyes with his finger he immediately saw the Saviour."[23] The latter, of course, is only reminiscence, but together with the earlier narratives it demonstrates at least that a few people had this concept of the vision as it gradually took its place among the fundamental teachings of the church.

Additional accounts by people close to the Mormon prophet would undoubtedly reveal similar variations and amplifications. Through it all, however, there seems to be no deviation from Joseph Smith's apparent intent in telling the story in the first place: to demonstrate that he had had a visitation from deity and that he was told that the religions of his day were wrong. The account published in the Pearl of Great Price in 1851 has become the standard account and is accepted by Mormons as scripture.

In conclusion, this essay demonstrates the need for new approaches to Mormon history by sympathetic historians. Can we fully understand our heritage without understanding the gradual development of ideas and the use of those ideas in our history? An understanding of the story of Joseph Smith's vision dawned only gradually upon the membership of the church during his lifetime and new and important uses were made of the story after his death. In what other respects has the Mormon mind been modified since the 1830s? What forces and events have led church leaders to place special emphasis on special ideas in given periods of time? What new ideas have become part of the Mormon tradition since the exodus from Nauvoo or even in the twentieth century; what old ideas have been submerged if not forgotten; and what ideas have remained constant through the years? As in the case of other institutions and movements, there is still room in Mormonism for fresh historical scholarship—not necessarily for the apologist, although he or she will always be necessary and will always make an important contribution, and certainly not for the debunker. What is needed is the sympathetic historian who can approach his or her tradition with scholarship as well as faith and who will make fresh appraisal of the developments of the Mormon mind.

NOTES

1. The letter is reproduced in William Mulder and A. Russell Mortensen, eds., *Among the Mormons* (New York: Alfred A. Knopf, 1958), 28.
2. It is probable that Turner had not seen Joseph Smith's written

account of the vision when he was preparing his book, for both were published the same year. Turner shows familiarity with the earlier publications of church history and would certainly have included the history published in the *Times and Seasons* if he had seen it. Orson Pratt's account published in 1840 may also have escaped him as he prepared his manuscript, for Pratt's work was published in England for circulation there.

3. A quotation from the article appears later in this study.

4. See N. B. Lundall, comp., *A Compilation Containing the Lectures on Faith* (Salt Lake City, n.d.). It is interesting to observe in connection with the general question of how certain precise teachings of the church in the 1830s differed from those of today that in *The Lectures on Faith* the Father is defined as a "personage of glory and power," the Son is defined as a "personage of tabernacle," and the Holy Spirit is defined as the mind of the Father and the Son (see Lecture 5). As far as the vision is concerned, the only possible allusion to it is in Section I of the Doctrine and Covenants, which reads, "Wherefore I the Lord, knowing the calamity which should come upon the inhabitants of the earth, called upon my servant Joseph Smith, Jr. and spake unto him from heaven, and gave him commandments; and also gave commandments to others, that they should proclaim these things unto the world." The same statement is in the 1833 Book of Commandments, but most would agree that it hardly constitutes a direct reference to the first vision.

5. John Corrill, *Brief History of the Church of Jesus Christ of Latter-day Saints* (St. Louis: by the Author, 1839), 1.

6. Parley P. Pratt, *Autobiography of Parley P. Pratt* (Salt Lake City: Deseret Book, 1961), 136-51.

7. B. H. Roberts, ed., *History of the Church of Jesus Christ of Latter-day Saints* (Salt Lake City: Deseret Book, 1946), 1:1, hereafter cited as HC.

8. See Paul R. Cheesman, "An Analysis of the Accounts Relating Joseph Smith's Early Visions," M.A. thesis, Brigham Young University, 1965.

9. Fawn M. Brodie, *No Man Knows My History* (New York: Alfred A. Knopf, 1946), 25.

10. The document was brought to my attention in June 1966. Since it is bound with the "Manuscript History," it is unusual that someone had not found it earlier and recognized its significance. It seems apparent, however, that as in the case of Cheesman's document, few if any people have been aware of it. The fact that the use of the "Manuscript History" was restricted and that any research done in it was done through a microfilm copy could help account for the fact that researchers generally had not discovered what was in the back of the book.

11. Compare HC 2:304.

12. Edward Stevenson, *Reminiscences of Joseph, the Prophet* (Salt Lake City: by the Author, 1893), 4-5.

13. Quoted in LeRoi C. Snow, "How Lorenzo Snow Found God," *Improvement Era,* Feb. 1937, 83.

14. T. Edgar Lyon, *Introduction to the Doctrine and Covenants and the Pearl of Great Price* (Salt Lake City: Latter-day Saints' Department of Education, 1955), 109; James R. Clark, *The Story of the Pearl of Great Price* (Salt Lake City: Bookcraft, 1955), 186-221.

15. *Journal of Discourses,* 24:340-41.

16. As transcribed in Cheesman, 129. This account records the first vision as having occurred when Smith was sixteen years old. In Smith's 1838 account, he said it happened in the 15th year of his age. Orson Pratt and Orson Hyde both said that it happened when Joseph was "somewhere about fourteen or fifteen years old." The Wentworth letter said "when about fourteen years of age." Joseph's brother, William Smith, wrote that the Smith family's concern with the prevailing religions of the day came when Joseph was about seventeen. See William Smith, *William Smith on Mormonism* (Lamoni, IA: Printed at Herald Steam Book and Job Office, 1883). William, however, did not record the story of the first vision. He related the religious revival which he described to the discovery of the Book of Mormon. The only contemporary account to date the vision in a definite manner as occurring in the spring of 1820 is that written by Joseph Smith in 1838.

17. "Documentary History of the Church" (MS), in archives, Historical Department, Church of Jesus Christ of Latter-day Saints, Salt Lake City, Utah. From a separate section in the back of Book A-1, 120-21.

18. For a transcribed copy of the handwritten manuscript, see Cheesman, Appendix A.

19. For a copy of the Pratt story, see Cheesman, Appendix C.

20. O. Pratt, *An Interesting Account of Several Remarkable Visions, and of the Late Discovery of Ancient American Records* (Edinburgh: Printed by Ballantyne and Hughes, 1840), 5.

21. *New York Spectator,* 23 Sept. 1843, in Preston Nibley, *Joseph Smith the Prophet* (Salt Lake City: Deseret News Press, 1946), 31.

22. As quoted in Cheesman, 29.

23. Diary of Charles L. Walker, in Cheesman, 30.

4.
The Prophet Puzzle: Suggestions Leading toward a More Comprehensive Interpretation of Joseph Smith

Jan Shipps

JOSEPH SMITH WAS ONE OF A PROLIFERATION OF PREACHERS AND prophets who found God along the stony ridges and narrow lakes of western New York in the first half of the nineteenth century. It was a place and a time of intense interest in religion: pathways to paradise ran in all directions. Prospective pilgrims had a choice, and many a wanderer journeyed a little way down first one path and then another, testing alternate routes to heaven. The story of the strange systems and unusual faiths that resulted is essentially a record of unsuccessful experiments with religion. Some survived for a season, but most disappeared at the death of their leaders—if they lasted that long. Of all the unorthodox theological systems introduced in the New York hinterland between 1800 and 1850, the only one that has become an important American religion is the Church of Jesus Christ of Latter-day Saints.

The Mormon church found scant support in New York state, however. Within a year after the formal organization of the church, the Mormons started their celebrated westward hegira by moving to Ohio. Because the phenomenal growth of the organization began

53

after this initial move from New York state, the successful development of the church has generally been predicated on evidence found
in the subsequent history of Mormonism. Although tendentious
histories—whether pro or con—almost invariably begin with the
events that preceded the founding of the church in 1830, for a long
time the *objective* (i.e., critical as opposed to traditional) historiography of Mormonism was largely made up of studies which explained
how Mormons built the Kingdom of the Saints following the removal
of that realm from western New York.

    In the mid-1960s the "Case of the Missing Information about
Mormon Origins," as Truman G. Madsen, of Brigham Young University's religion department, once styled the problem posed by the
paucity of information on the New England-New York background,
was reopened. BYU history professor James B. Allen's article on "The
Significance of Joseph Smith's 'First Vision' in Mormon Thought"
was published in 1966, and the following year an intensive reexamination of Mormon beginnings was spurred headlong by the challenge
to the integrity of Joseph Smith represented in the outcome of the
Reverend Wesley P. Walters's investigation of the religious situation
in and around Palmyra, New York, in the 1820s.[1] So much research
has been carried out since then that a steady stream of articles, essays,
and books on the early period in Mormon history is pouring forth.[2]

    While some of these new works are little more than argu-
ments about the validity of Philastus Hurlbut's interviewing techniques when gathering material for *Mormonism Unvailed* (sic), much
of it is interesting—and significant. Richard L. Bushman's description
of what one can learn from a close reading of the rhetoric of the Book
of Mormon, for example, was not only intrinsically useful but meth-
odologically important. Mario S. De Pillis also made a methodological
contribution with his analysis of dream accounts while adding to our
understanding of the initial appeal of Mormonism.[3] At a less theoretical level, Dean Jessee's work with holograph writings has provided
precise information about who wrote what when and, at the same
time, demonstrated the procedures employed in the original production of such basic works as the Book of Mormon and Joseph Smith's
history.[4]

    Nevertheless, complacency is not in order. It is true that
many major points have been clarified and many minor issues settled,
but there are still loose ends not neatly tied up between the covers

of various professional and general interest magazines and journals; inconsistencies still exist that must be resolved before the case can be considered closed. In the meantime all that can be said is that while a great deal is known about the methods used in building up this extraordinary religious society, its creation is still surrounded by mystery.

Throughout the nineteenth century, when the Mormon church was regarded as a threat to the social and political fabric of the nation, those who wrote about it were less concerned with the mysterious nature of Mormon origins than with their perceptions of present dangers. For a long time the mystery connected with Mormonism appeared to be corporate—and criminal—and its solution, therefore, was seen less as a matter of understanding Mormon origins and theological beliefs than discovering the secrets of the temple and penetrating the plottings of the "sinister" hierarchy.[5] When polygamy and the political kingdom were shorn away, the mystery for a time seemed to dissipate. Emphasis on the radical and revolutionary elements in Mormonism diminished, and the Saints seemed destined to fade unobtrusively into the American religious landscape. From the outside it even looked as if, in their search for acceptance and respectability, they might find a place if not in the fold then certainly along the fringes of American Protestantism.

In an essay Klaus J. Hansen speculated that something of this sort has in fact happened. After reviewing the reasons that explain Mormonism's failure to fit into the pluralistic, voluntaristic pattern of nineteenth-century American religion, he pointed out that in the twentieth century these reasons no longer function as boundaries marking Mormon peculiarity and that, as a result, Mormonism as a "distinct cultural unit" has more or less ceased to exist.[6] Hansen's argument is persuasive. Here, however, agreement must be made contingent on a clear understanding of the difference between a "cultural entity" and a religio-theological unit. While the homogeneous character of Mormondom is plainly giving way, the Saints are still set apart—certainly in their own self-consciousness—as a "community of the faithful." Despite a value structure and belief in Jesus Christ which Mormons share with middle-class American Protestants, the Saints have not been absorbed into Protestantism. A chosen people living in the new dispensation of the fulness of times cannot be a party to the denominational contract; they retain an identity as separate and distinct from American Protestantism as either Roman Catholicism or Judaism.[7] For that reason the "mysteries" of Mormonism, particularly the early years, remain matters of concern not only for Latter-day Saints who wish a deeper understanding of their faith but also for historians who would fully comprehend American religion.

Now that the nineteenth-century bias toward Brigham Young as the "real" genius of Mormonism is clearing away, it is obvious that the logical place to begin is with the study of Joseph Smith's life. That is not an easy task, however. As is so often the case with controversial figures, the prophet's adherents and detractors built up public images which they have been at pains to protect, leaving apparently irreconcilable interpretations of the Mormon leader's life. As a result the historian must cope with the contradictory accounts found on the one hand in memoirs penned by apostates and in affidavits collected from Smith's neighbors and on the other in the official *History of the Church,* a reconstruction of events compiled by diverse people including the prophet himself, which was commenced in 1838 with the express purpose of countering the reports that were circulated by "evil-disposed" persons clearly designed to militate against the character of the church and its prophet. The situation is further complicated by the need to establish the extent to which the contents of the Book of Mormon, the Pearl of Great Price, and the revelations of the prophet can be utilized as primary source material.

All these difficulties notwithstanding, a continuing effort must be made to solve the mystery of Mormonism by coming to understand the enigma at its core. The image that now exists is fragmented and incomplete. The perspective must be lengthened through a consideration of the prophet in the context of the social, political, economic, and theological milieu from which he came; the range of resources must be expanded to utilize the information and the insight that can be found in the Mormon canon; and the entire project must be approached with an open mind, a generous spirit, and a determination to follow the evidence that appeals to reason from whatever source it comes, wherever it leads. Only then will the outcome be a picture of the prophet and an account of the foundations of the Mormon faith which will be convincing to both *tough* minds, which demand empirical facts, and *tender* minds, comfortable in the presence of leaps of faith. What follows here are some suggestions leading in that direction.

In the first quarter of the nineteenth century, western New York was in effect the New England frontier. As they crossed the Adirondacks, emigrants from New England left behind the Half-way Covenant that had allowed church membership to be handed down from generation to generation. On the frontier the social satisfactions that had accompanied full standing in the Congregational churches of the older regions all but disappeared. Even long after the frontier character of this area had passed away, religion ministered primarily to the emotional rather than social needs of the populace. The unfolding economic opportunity that attended the building of the Erie Canal seemed to make everyone an heir to fortune; status came with success, and society no longer gave church members special social or religious privilege.

This fluid economic and social environment made an anachronism of the theological doctrine of divine election, and yet the Protestant community was still too close to the Reformation to alter the balance between faith and works in favor of the latter. As a result, the way of conventional Christianity throughout the district was the way marked out by George Whitefield and Gilbert Tennent during the Great Awakening in New England in the 1740s. Beyond the mountains, doctrinal distinctions denoting denominationalism were blurred by a stylized evangelism that forced the wide thoroughfare of Protestant Christianity into the confines of the sawdust trail. Whether the ecclesiastical connection of the minister made the service a Baptist gathering or a Methodist meeting, the sermon followed the predicted pattern of its "New Light" Presbyterian prototype.

With jeremiads that were painstaking catalogues of sins that would lead to destruction—and they were legion—Charles Finney and his fellows cautioned the unregenerate to beware the day of judgment. While penitents approached the sinner's benches, these lamentations were extended into compelling crescendos of exhortation designed to disturb the indifferent and terrify the wicked with speculation about the fate of unrepentant sinners abandoned to the wrath of an angry God. As fear and guilt pulled heartstrings taut, the preacher watched with practiced eye for signs that the limits of emotional stress were near. Sounds of weeping and audible appeals for mercy were the prelude to skillful modulation from admonition to invitation and promise. When a contrite soul accepted the pledges of forgiveness and love and yielded absolute trust in God, release and rejoicing—sometimes verging on ecstacy—followed. Another Christian had been born again.

As unquestionably effective as such techniques were, their often transitory results reflected the limitations of a theology that attempted a compromise between the uncertainty inherent in the doctrines of predestination and divine election and the ineffable assurance of the interior religious experience. Using conversion as a catalyst, the Puritan theologian Jonathan Edwards had sought to merge mystic rapture and Calvinistic logic into a stable compound, but the subtleties of the speculations of this great philosophic intellect were lost when lesser minds proved unable to keep conversion at the center of Christian life where it had been placed by the Northampton divine. One result was the development of an emotional evangelism that made conversion the capstone of religious experience.

Edwards had kindled such a fire as has never yet been put out, but seldom has the flame blazed so brightly or for so long as it did beside the banks of the Erie Canal during the youth of Joseph Smith. Revivalistic fervor swept through western New York state with such regularity that Orthodoxy back across the Adirondacks looked on the region as the "Burned-over District." The religious holocaust predicted by use of this derogatory designation failed to occur, however, and in 1825 it was clear that the fire that raged over the area was like the fire in the midst of the bush that burned and was not consumed. As if increase of appetite had grown by what it fed on, the spiritual longings of the people had created one of those spheres of genuine religious exploration that have served from time to time throughout human history as the seedbed for new theological systems.

Within a span of twenty-five years after the frontier gave way to the settled community life that paralleled the building of De Witt Clinton's canal, this "burnt" district sheltered a multitude of small bands and large congregations that had turned aside from traditional faiths to travel toward eternity along unmarked trails. As guides, contemporaries might follow Andrew Jackson Davis, the "Poughkeepsie Seer," and the amazing Fox Sisters into Spiritualism, or William Miller into Millennialism; they could make a more total commitment and move to Oneida to search for Perfection with John Humphrey Noyes; they could join the Shakers at New Lebanon or the Community of the Publik Universal Friend at Jerusalem in Yates County—or any of a host of lesser known groups that sought God with creeds embracing vegetarianism, sexual abstinence, communism, complex marriage, or some other equally esoteric doctrine.

But men and women have a way of packing the past among their personal possessions when they move from place to place, and most of those who settled in the area had come with Protestant traditions so firmly fixed that no alternative was acceptable. The overwhelming majority of western New Yorkers looked for religious assurance in the old familiar places, and Presbyterians (and Congregationalists under the Plan of Union), Baptists, and Methodists all hastened to provide ministers to preach the gospel to the community beyond the Catskills. Unfortunately, these virtually simultaneous home missionary efforts of the several Protestant denominations sometimes brought religious chaos not spiritual comfort, for when conversion rather than spiritual guidance and pastoral care was made the primary purpose of the Protestant ministry, success became a matter of numbers. And since this quantitative criterion was not limited by the sum of uncommitted souls, the successful evangelist often had to build his church by tearing others down. There was a buyer's market in salvation, and in the confusion of contested credentials and conflicting claims, it was not at all unusual for a single soul to have been saved several times.

Although the Mormon prophet emerged from this volatile psychic ground, no evidence exists to indicate that religious tensions there caused him to move—as many other incipient religious leaders did—through a succession of affiliations with different religious groups, searching for satisfactory answers to spiritual questions. Like his father, Joseph Smith stood aside and refused to join any of the churches in the Palmyra region.

According to a biographical sketch written by his mother, Joseph Smith's father, Joseph Sr., did not become a member of any of the churches that were already established because he interpreted a dream (or vision) which he had had in 1811—the elder Smith like the father of Nephi in the Book of Mormon regarded dream and vision as synonymous—as a warning that these churches were the outposts of Babylon.[8] Joseph Jr. came to the same conclusion in a not

altogether different fashion. When he dictated the explanatory pro-
logue to the official *History* in 1838, the prophet described the way
that the bewildering religious landscape had confused him. He said
that in 1820 he had made prayerful inquiry about which church he
should join and that the prayer had been answered in a vision wherein
he saw two "personages" and was told that he should join none of the
established churches as they were all wrong.[9]

Since the account of the first vision published in the *History
of Joseph Smith, the Prophet* (the official history) seems to tie it chronologically to a revival that was going on in 1824 and 1825, since the
prophet apparently mentioned this vision rarely if at all before 1830,
and since no description of it seems to have been written down until
almost a dozen years after it is said to have happened, Fawn Brodie,
Jerald and Sandra Tanner, Wesley P. Walters, and others take the
position that the first vision never occurred—that the prophet invented it in order to defend himself when his credibility was under
attack.[10]

Certainly Walters's reconstruction of the events surrounding
the 1824 revival, his argument that this was the "war of words and
the tumult of opinions" the prophet spoke of, is more convincing
than the counter-argument that Smith was referring to an awakening
that took place not in the immediate Palmyra-Manchester area but
nearby around 1820.[11] But using the confused chronology presented
in the official *History* as the basis for assuming that an early vision—
one which led Joseph Smith to stay away from organized religion—
never occurred is less persuasive.

In addition to William Smith's earliest known recollection of
his brother Joseph's conversion, which does not connect the first
vision to the 1824 revival, and in addition to the general tenor of the
prophet's personal diaries, from which an attitude of piety and
devoutness can be read back,[12] the evidence which has not been
adequately brought to bear on this question is the Book of Mormon
itself. Although this work has been considered—often at length—in
general histories of Mormonism, it has by and large been neglected
as a source which might facilitate a better understanding of Joseph
Smith's early career.

The reasons for this center on the answers that have usually
been given to questions about who wrote the Book of Mormon and
what its intrinsic merit is. Most Mormons have taken the position that

Joseph Smith was the translator of the book, not its author, which means of course that since they believe the prophet did not write the book, they could not regard it as a potential source of insight into his early life. Throughout the nineteenth and much of the twentieth century, many non-Mormons were led to a similar conclusion, not because they thought the substance of the Book of Mormon had been taken from the plates of Nephi *et al.* but because the work was widely believed to have been plagiarized.[13] Even if this notion was wrong and Joseph Smith had written the book, taking the work into account in explaining his career seemed foolish; after all, what could an amateurish historical novel masquerading as scripture reveal about a man's spiritual history?

In his 1957 sociological study of Latter-day Saints, Thomas F. O'Dea made it clear that scholars would be mistaken to accept Mark Twain's assessment of the Book of Mormon as "chloroform in print" and in taking at face value Judge Cradlebaugh's description of the book as "a conglomeration of illy cemented creeds from other religions."[14] As a result historians have reconsidered the Book of Mormon. And it is becoming increasingly obvious that whatever its source—whether it was translated from engravings on metal plates or dictated directly from Joseph Smith's extraordinary mind—this book functions as a powerful and provocative synthesis of biblical experience and the American dream, and it occupies a position of importance in both the religious and intellectual history of the United States.

It is likewise evident that beneath its crude exterior, the Book of Mormon reflects knowledge of the Bible, familiarity with theological currents, perception of the problems posed by Protestant denominationalism, and experience with extra-rational religious phenomena that simply are not consistent with the theory that its religious framework was an afterthought.[15] Such a position requires a greater leap of faith than accepting a naturalistic explanation which holds (1) that Joseph grew up in a family fascinated with religion; (2) that, as he said, he thoroughly searched the scriptures and came to know them well; (3) that around 1820 he probably did have a vision or go through some other non-rational experience, which at least left him convinced that his father's dream about the organized churches all being in error was true; (4) that in the throes of revivalistic excitement he could well have come to doubt his earlier conclusion about the Protestant churches, leading him to inquire about the matter a second time, thereby stimulating a second vision around 1824; (5) that (as will be discussed below) in connection with his money-digging activities, he actually found some Indian artifacts, or hoped to do so, which inspired the writing of the Book of Mormon. Leaving aside the question of whether the book has captured eternal truths, it plainly reflects the religious experiences and concerns that had been an important part of Joseph Smith's life until that time.

If the foregoing conceptualization of the events of Joseph Smith's youth is not completely congruent with what really happened, it does nevertheless assist us in understanding his complex personality. Reports of visions not unlike those described by this strange young man were by no means unknown in western New York in the 1820s, but these experiences were sufficiently singular to convince Joseph Smith that he was set apart from his peers. His recognition of separateness may well account for the apparently compulsive need for acceptance that led him into "vices and follies" after he had been rejected "by those who ought," he said, "to have been my friends and to have treated me kindly." He wanted to belong but could not; he did not fit the pattern of men whose worlds were limited by scant schooling, mortgaged homesteads, and revivalist religion. He was different; he knew it, and the knowledge made him abnormally sensitive to the opinions of others. Although it was camouflaged in later years by his self-confident, almost cocksure, personality, this sensitivity persisted throughout his life. It caused him to place an unwarranted value on flattery and praise, and it made him react to criticism with an intensity that at times approached paranoia in his transformation of slight censure into "bitter persecution."

It was not his propensity to prophetic vision that first made Joseph Smith's difference distinct and introduced him to condemnation, however, for he was also gifted with what his contemporaries called "second sight." Using a "peepstone" (a luminous semi-precious gemstone which served as a screen for mental images) as a kind of psychic Geiger counter, Smith attempted to supplement the meager farm income of his family by assisting in the location of lost articles and buried "treasure." Because ventures of this nature which proved unsuccessful left the "peeper" vulnerable to charges of dishonesty and fraud, Smith was brought to trial in 1826 after he had failed to locate a silver mine he had promised to find, and he was charged with being a disorderly person and a fraud.

A year or so following the conclusion of that trial, Smith reported that he had in his possession a book, "written upon gold plates, [containing] an account of the former inhabitants of this continent and the sources from which they sprang." The existence of the plates, Smith said, had been revealed by an angel; they were instruments of divine revelation, which would, after translation, be the occasion of the ushering in of the new dispensation of the fullness of times. When the translation of the plates was completed and published to the world, the juxtaposition of these two apparently antithetical activities—digging for money and translating holy scripture—was used to bring the prophet's integrity into question and to cast doubt on the validity of his claims.

Testimony was collected in 1833 from almost a hundred people who had lived in the same general area where the prophet grew up, and their affidavits almost uniformly maligned the reputation of the Smith family and featured reports of the prophet's youthful search for buried treasure. Mormon apologists have sought to discredit these affidavits by charging muckraking and demonstrating how the information the witnesses supplied was contaminated by the attitude of the investigators. But attempts to discredit the information gathered by Philastus Hurlbut and Eber D. Howe can never prove that the attitudes reflected in the affidavits were not current or that the information in them is necessarily wrong, because newspaper articles and first-hand accounts written by Obadiah Dogberry, the Reverend Diedrich Willers, and James Gordon Bennett published in 1831—a full two years before the preparation of *Mormonism Unvailed*—contain precisely the same information.

The fact that so many of Smith's neighbors and acquaintances used the reputation of the Smith family and the "money-digging" to demonstrate the incongruity between the man they knew and a man of God is not surprising if the extraordinary difference between their perception of jovial Joseph and their Old Testament notions of appropriate prophets is kept in mind.

The situation can perhaps be compared to one occasionally encountered in today's world. A "model" devout church-going teen-aged boy suddenly kills his father, and neighbors and acquaintances—finding it difficult to immediately alter their perception of the boy—explain over and over again that the young man had been a perfect child. Just as these explanations are crucial in developing a psychic profile which will facilitate an understanding of the patricidal act, so the Dogberry, Bennett, and Hurlbut and Howe reports of the way the people of Palmyra perceived the prophet are crucial to the development of a complete religious profile of Joseph Smith.[16]

Although Marvin Hill is right in his assertion that magic and religious faith were not incompatible in nineteenth-century America,[17] it is nevertheless clear that the prophet and those who participated with him in the compilation of the official *History of the Church* were anxious not to emphasize the prophet's early connection with the divining art. It seems reasonable to conclude that the motive for playing down this part of the prophet's background was the knowledge that it could be used as the basis for charges that might endanger his reputation. But by glossing over that part of his life in the preparation of his history, Smith left himself vulnerable to the charges that have been used from that day forward to prove at best his insincerity, at worst outright fraud.

If the prophet's preference for leaving the money-digging part of his career out of the picture is ignored, and the events of that part of his life are placed alongside the clearly defined spiritual events of his early years, a pattern emerges which leaves little room for doubting that Smith's use of the seerstone was an important indication of his early and continued interest in extra-rational phenomena and that it played an important role in his spiritual development.

ca. 1820	Smith had his first vision.
1822	He discovered a peepstone in a well.
1823-24	He said that an angel revealed gold plates to him.
1824-26	He participated in money-digging activities.
1826	He was tried as a "glass looker."
1827	He reported possessing the gold plates.
1828-29	He "translated" the engravings on the plates by means of "Urim and Thummim," an instrument which operated on the same principle as his peepstone.

Integrated in this fashion the early events of Smith's life add up to a coherent whole that makes more sense than the charlatan-true prophet dichotomy which has plagued Mormon history from the beginning.

Historians who deal with Joseph Smith's post-1830 career are also faced with disparate interpretive models, but since the fruits of the prophet's labors after the church was established are more amenable to assessment, these models do not represent the same sort of polar opposites that have been developed to explain the Book of Mormon. The building up of Kirtland, Far West, and Nauvoo, the formation of an efficient and effective organizational structure for the church, and the overall development and remarkable growth of Mormonism were substantial achievements which can hardly be credited to a ne'er-do-well, practiced in the magic arts and proficient at deception and trickery or for that matter to a prophet intoxicated with divinity.

Some students of the Mormon past have denied Smith's crucial role as the leader of the church—suggesting that he was a dreamer, a visionary, or a madman, who was fortunate enough to have Brigham Young around to handle practical things, and who managed to be martyred, as Bernard DeVoto said, "at precisely the right time" to allow his blood to become "the seed of the church." But this view, like the notion that someone other than Smith wrote the Book of Mormon, has not survived in the wake of Fawn Brodie's *No Man Knows My History*. Historians are now generally agreed that the prophet's influence was the decisive factor in almost every phase of the construction of the Mormon kingdom, though they do not agree on the reasons why this is so. Devotional interpretations explain almost everything in terms of the "Will of the Lord," but historical interpretations of Smith's later career are variations on two themes: Joseph Smith as charismatic personality and Joseph Smith as pragmatic prophet.

These two themes are not diametrically opposed; as categories they are not mutually exclusive; each depends on the other. Biographical treatments of that part of Smith's life which follows the founding of the church, therefore, betray less anti-Mormon/pro-Mormon bias than the portrayals of his youth. The images remain distressingly different even so. Difficult questions are not adequately answered either with the explanation that the prophet was an effective leader because he was ultimately taken in by his own deception or with the reminder that the prophet was a prophet only when he was acting as such.

Perhaps the situation will be clarified if the problem is approached from another direction. Joseph Smith was a dynamic personality, it is true; and there was undoubtedly a charismatic quality to his leadership. If his charisma is seen not as a function of his personality but as an integral part of his role as prophet, seer, and revelator, the reasons for the reactions to his leadership of both Mormons and non-Mormons will be more intelligible. While the distinction being made here was not important for the large portion of the Saints who perceived his personality and his prophet's role as one, it is important in fathoming the behavior of those Saints who made Smith's ability to carry everything before him contingent on their ideas about the authenticity of his prophetic position. When his pronouncements and actions led certain Saints to conclude that Smith was a fallen prophet, his charisma, for them, evaporated.

The prophet, seer, and revelator *role* then is central to an understanding of the prophet's life. Because this role grew out of and was defined by the Book of Mormon and the circumstances surrounding its "translation," it is there that we must look to get a glimpse of how the prophet's role was perceived by Smith and by his followers. There too we must turn if we would begin to analyze the importance of the *role* of the prophet as a factor in early Mormonism's appeal.

The Book of Mormon claimed to be the history of the western hemisphere between 600 B.C. and 400 A.D., but its account of that millennium was interspersed with such an astonishing variety of philosophical notions and theological speculations that it was immediately apparent that this was no ordinary history. The work recounted stories of voyages and battles and tales of intrigue and treason. Yet the most striking passages in the Book of Mormon are those which are essentially explications of ideas that had also been a part of the visions of Joseph Smith's youth. Allusions to the ideas which, according to Smith's own account, were conceived in the course of his extraordinary experiences, were particularly clear in the second section of the book. This section, 2 Nephi, included a series of chapters which detailed the state of society existing when the plates of gold would be opened to the man chosen of God. These prophetic predictions returned again and again to the themes of the visions; that churches already current were corrupt and that a book containing a "revelation from God from the beginning of the world to the ending thereof" would be delivered into the hands of a "seer" whom the Lord would bless, whose name like that of his father would be Joseph, who would bring the people who loved the Lord to salvation.[18]

Since a far greater portion of the book was concerned with a fanciful history of the western hemisphere, it stands to reason that its initial appeal was not entirely religious. This was a time when the people of the United States were busily engaged in the manufacture of instant heritage, substituting inspiration for antiquity with regard to the Constitution and producing a veritable hagiography of popular biography designed to turn America's political leaders into national heroes in the shortest possible time. Joseph Smith's visionary account of the American past was therefore not entirely out of place.[19] The passages which referred to the United States as the "land of promise" and as "a land which is choice above all other lands" appealed to (and reflected) the nationalistic sentiment of the age in overt fashion. And in addition Smith's golden book was a fascinating expression of the prevalent American desire to declare cultural independence from Europe. In a pseudo-Elizabethan prose style that recalled the King James version of the Bible, the Book of Mormon maintained that the American Indians were remnants of the twelve tribes of Israel and that Jesus Christ had appeared on this continent in 34 A.D. Thus the book provided a link between the history of the United States and the Judeo-Christian tradition that by-passed the European culture filter altogether.

Nevertheless, this unconventional pre-Columbian history of the western hemisphere must in large measure be regarded as suits and trappings for the prophetic device that reiterated the errors of established churches and promised that the seer who read the record found on the golden plates would be the agency through which the ancient church in all its purity should be restored:

"And it shall come to pass that my people . . . shall be gathered home unto the lands of their possessions. . . .

"If they will repent and hearken unto my words, and not harden their hearts, I will establish my church among them, and they shall come into the covenant and be numbered among his remnant of Jacob, unto whom I have given this land for their inheritance . . . that they may build a city which shall be called the New Jerusalem.

"And blessed are they who shall seek to bring forth Zion."[20]

Joseph Smith said that the "miracle" of translation was accomplished by means of a "curious instrument which the ancients called 'Urim and Thummim,' . . . two transparent stones set in the rim of a bow fastened to a breastplate," that somehow allowed him to read the "reformed Egyptian" engravings as if they were English.[21] As news of his unusual project spread across the countryside, a small band of followers including Martin Harris, Oliver Cowdery, Joseph Knight, several members of the family of Peter Whitmer, and most of Smith's own immediate family gathered round. They watched the progress of the work as Smith dictated it from behind a makeshift curtain to be written out on foolscap paper by Cowdery or Harris or his new bride Emma, and they were convinced that Joseph Smith had a divine calling.

Martin Harris's wife Lucy was convinced otherwise, and so after a portion of the manuscript had been completed, Harris persuaded the translator to let him take those pages home in order to prove to Lucy that the work was inspired of God. But Lucy Harris was not impressed. She had never liked Smith, and she heartily disapproved of her husband's association with him. She feared, not without reason, that Harris intended to use his modest fortune to make publication of Smith's golden Bible possible; and consequently when she got her hands on the manuscript, she destroyed it.

The crisis that resulted profoundly affected the new religion. Joseph Smith prayed for guidance and received two revelations directing that the lost section should not be retranslated. Lest the devil arrange publication of the missing section, God would provide another set of plates which would summarize the account contained in the missing chapters.[22] Thus did Joseph Smith don the prophet's mantle.

O'Dea has suggested that the exigency of the situation with which Smith was faced simply proved to be the necessary occasion for the introduction of contemporary revelation; he says that a belief in continuing revelation was vital to the secure establishment of the new religion and that it should probably have come in any case.[23] Brodie failed to credit the translator with so much foresight; she concluded that the revelations were a ruse—perhaps an unconscious one—to conceal the fact that the story of the golden plates was false and that Smith merely capitalized on their effect among his followers.[24] Yet Brodie and O'Dea agree that this event was decisive in

Mormon history, and most students of Mormonism concur, so that accounts of the origins of the Church of Jesus Christ of Latter-day Saints usually trace the doctrine of continuing revelation to this juncture in Joseph Smith's career.

Notwithstanding the importance of the doctrine of continuing revelation in the development of the faith, few serious attempts have been made to delineate the difference between these revelations and Smith's earlier esoteric activities. Church doctrine makes no distinction between the divine character of the Book of Mormon and the prophet's revelations. From the outside all the reports of visions and revelations and the writing of golden Bibles and the pursuit of treasure with a peepstone tend to become so confusing that it is entirely understandable that historians often dismiss the problem by saying that it is all a matter of faith. And indeed it is. But just as Vernon Louis Parrington and Perry Miller were obliged to go to theological polemics to fully comprehend the social and economic and political developments in Puritan New England, so the student of Mormon history must seek the explanation of many of the significant events in Joseph Smith's life in the subtle distinction between vision and revelation.

In the eyes of the Latter-day Saints, Joseph Smith's early visions and his later revelations are both dialogues between God and humanity. The difference turns on who initiated the conversation. Whether it is regarded as a metaphysical event or a psychic phenomenon, a religiously-oriented vision is an intensely realistic subjective experience which leaves the individual who has experienced it with a definite sense of having been in direct communion with God. Like other spiritual mani-festations, the hearing of transcendental voices, infused meditation, illumination, and so on, visions are spontaneous occurrences apparently independent of the conscious human mind.

Although it is true that many of the prophet's revelations— particularly the ones having to do with theology or the organization of the restored church—were accompanied by visions, voices, or some other metaphysical phenomena, much of the revelation in Mormonism proceeds from a more prosaic but more dependable method of communicating with God. As it worked out in Mormon history, this process of revelation involves asking for divine instructions and receiving an "impression" of the will of the Lord in return. In theological terms God initiates the vision and humanity responds;

men and women ask for revelation and God responds.[25]

The difference was clear even to the prophet. The visions left him with no doubts about the reality of what he had seen and heard. When William James said that persons who have undergone traumatic religious experiences "remain quite unmoved by criticism from whatever quarter it may come, [because] they have had their vision and they *know,*" he could have been referring directly to Joseph Smith who wrote, "Why does the world think to make me deny what I have actually seen? For I had seen a vision; I knew it and I knew God knew it, and I could not deny it."[26]

This same confidence did not always extend to the revelations, however. David Whitmer wrote that Smith himself said "some revelations are of the devil."[27] Historians who deal with the prophet's life and the history of the church must take note of the implications of that statement and weigh the possibility of considering the revelations according to some classification scheme. This does not mean—*must not mean*—that a dash through the Doctrine and Covenants identifying revelations of a first, second, and third order is necessary. It means rather coming to realize and consciously accept what Robert Flanders's *Nauvoo: Kingdom on the Mississippi* and Leonard Arrington's *Great Basin Kingdom* demonstrate implicitly: a recognition of the fact that a continuum on which the revelations can be placed *exists.* At its highest terminal point are the revelations which came during those moments when a higher reality erupted into the prophet's everyday world; at its opposite are the revelations which can perhaps best be marked not, as Smith said, "of the devil" but as wishful thinking.

Taxonomical exercises in history are always dangerous, frightfully so when the subject is the history of religion. But in view of Mormon history's double interpretative strand of Joseph Smith as man of God and Joseph Smith as fraud who exploited his followers for his own purposes—lately summed up as a religious versus a rational being—it is possible that drawing distinctions between the character of the different parts of the Mormon canon will allow us to see the prophet's mature life as more coherent than is now possible. I am not an expert on Joseph Smith. But I do know that the mystery of Mormonism cannot be solved until we solve the mystery of Joseph Smith.

In a biography I once heard described as the best biography

ever written of an American historical figure, Carl Van Doren described Benjamin Franklin as a "harmonious human multitude." We do not have a comparable biography of the prophet. Joseph Smith was also a "human multitude," an extraordinarily talented individual, but our picture of him is anything but harmonious. What we have in Mormon historiography are variations on two Josephs: the one who started out digging for money and when he was unsuccessful, turned to propheteering; and the one who had visions and dreamed dreams, restored the church, and revealed the will of the Lord to a sinful world. While the shading was varied, the portraits have pretty much remained constant; the differences are differences of degree, not kind.

The approach I am suggesting at least has the virtue of providing a different perspective from which to view the prophet's life. The result cannot be harmony, because Joseph himself had difficulty integrating the many facets of his complex career. But it might allow us to reconcile enough of the inconsistency to reveal not a split personality but a gifted, pressured, sometimes opportunistic, often troubled, larger-than-life *whole* man.

NOTES

1. James B. Allen, "The Significance of Joseph Smith's 'First Vision' in Mormon Thought," *Dialogue: A Journal of Mormon Thought* 1 (Autumn 1966): 29-45, and reprinted in this compilation. Madsen's remarks were made at the 1968 Edwardsville Conference on the Mormons in Illinois. Walters's article, "New Light on Mormon Origins from the Palmyra Revival," was first published in 1967 as an Evangelical Theological Society tract and was reprinted in *Dialogue: A Journal of Mormon Thought* 4 (Spring 1969): 60-81.

2. Concentrated research in the available records relevant to Mormon history in New York was carried out under the direction of a committee of Mormon historians and scholars headed by Madsen. The first fruits of this project were presented in the Spring 1969 issue of *Brigham Young University Studies*. The 1970 spring issue of the same journal was also devoted to the New York period. In addition, see Marvin S. Hill, "Joseph Smith and the 1826 Trial: New Evidence and New Difficulties," *Brigham Young University Studies* 12 (Winter 1972): 223-33; and "Brodie Revisited: A Reappraisal," *Dialogue: A Journal of Mormon Thought* 7 (Winter 1972): 72-85; Milton V. Backman, Jr., *Joseph Smith's First Vision* (Salt Lake City: Bookcraft, 1971); and Richard L. Bushman, "The First Vision Story Revived," *Dialogue: A Journal of Mormon*

Thought 4 (Spring 1969): 82-93; and Reverend Walters's reply to same, 94-100.

3. Bushman and De Pillis read papers reporting the results of their research at a session on "Early Mormonism in Its American Setting" at the annual meeting of the Western Historical Association in New Haven, Connecticut, 13 Oct. 1972.

4. See also Dean C. Jessee, "The Writing of Joseph Smith's History," *Brigham Young University Studies* 11 (Summer 1971): 439-73.

5. In analyzing a chronologically stratified representative sample of articles on Mormons and Mormonism published between 1860 and 1895, I found that 74 percent contained references to Mormonism as a threat to the American political system, 66 percent contained pejorative references to the internal control church leaders exercised over the LDS community, but only 57 percent contained references which were coded as "unflattering descriptions of Joseph Smith, of the origins of Mormonism, or of the religion itself." Jan Shipps, "From Satyr to Saint: American Attitudes Toward the Mormons," a paper presented to the annual meeting of the Organization of American Historians, Chicago, Mar. 1973.

6. "Mormonism and American Culture: Some Tentative Hypotheses," in *The Restoration Movement: Essays in Mormon History,* eds. F. Mark McKiernan, Alma R. Blair, and Paul M. Edwards (Lawrence, KS: Coronado Press, 1973), 1-25.

7. This conclusion agrees with the characterization of Mormonism as the fourth major religion generally accepted in American society found in Mario S. De Pillis, "The Quest for Religious Authority and the Rise of Mormonism," *Dialogue: A Journal of Mormon Thought* 1 (Spring 1966): 78, and reprinted in this compilation. The full effect of the abandonment of the policy of the "literal gathering" is more apparent today than it was in 1966. While cultural distinctiveness is disappearing—an inevitable consequence, in any case, of the international outreach of both major branches of Mormonism—it is possible that the dispersal of LDS "communities of the faithful" throughout the nation and the world has resulted in a heightened consciousness of Mormon peculiarity, both from within and from without.

8. Lucy Mack Smith, *History of the Prophet Joseph* (Salt Lake City: Improvement Era, 1902), 54. The 1908 edition of this work has been reprinted by Arno Press, New York.

9. Joseph Smith, Jr., *History of the Church of Jesus Christ of Latter-day Saints: Period I, History of Joseph Smith the Prophet,* ed. B. H. Roberts, 6 vols., 2nd ed. rev. (Salt Lake City: Church of Jesus Christ of Latter-day Saints, 1955), 1:4-6; hereafter cited as HC.

10. See Fawn M[cKay] Brodie, *No Man Knows My History: The Life of Joseph Smith, the Mormon Prophet* (New York: Alfred A. Knopf, 1945), 25; Jerald and Sandra Tanner, *Joseph Smith's Strange Account of the First Vision* (Salt Lake

City: Modern Microfilm, n.d.), 3; Walters, "New Light on Mormon Origins," 71-73.

11. See Bushman, "The First Vision Story Revived"; Larry C. Porter, "Reverend George Lane—God 'Gifts,' Much 'Grace,' and Marked 'Usefulness'," *Brigham Young University Studies* 9 (Spring 1969); Porter, "The Church in New York and Pennsylvania, 1816-1831," chap. 1 in McKiernan et al., *Restoration Movement*; and Backman, *Joseph Smith's First Vision*.

12. Hill, "Brodie Revisited," 76, 78-81.

13. Brodie categorized the Mormon Bible as merely one of several ostensibly inspired sacred books made up of "an obscure compound of folklore, moral platitude, mysticism, and millennialism" (67). Readers of *No Man Knows My History* come away convinced, however, that the "compound" is Joseph Smith's own.

14. See chap. 2 of O'Dea's *The Mormons* (Chicago: University of Chicago Press, 1957). Mark Twain's sally is in the appendix to *Roughing It*. Judge Cradlebaugh's description was given in his testimony before Congress in 1863. It is reprinted in Andrew J. Hanson, "Utah and the Mormon Problem," *Methodist Quarterly Review* 64 (Apr. 1882): 213. The description is of course not unique: it is a variation of Alexander Campbell's 1832 charge that the book contained answers to every conceivable theological question. Nineteenth- and early twentieth-century anti-Mormon literature, especially that portion of it publish-ed in religious periodicals, is shot through with similar charges that the Book of Mormon is made up of wholesale borrowings from other religions. It is likely that Sterling McMurrin's *Theological Foundations of the Mormon Religion* (Salt Lake City: University of Utah Press, 1965) was also a factor in the reappraisal of the Book of Mormon.

15. Walters summarizes this position in the concluding section of "New Light on Mormon Origins." With reference to this same point, Brodie states: "What had been originally conceived as a mere money-making history of the Indians had been transformed at some point early in the writing, or possibly even before the book was begun, into a religious saga" (83).

16. The Dogberry editorials and selections from affidavits collected by Hurlbut and Howe are reprinted in the appendix to *No Man Knows My History*. Bennett's articles are reprinted in Leonard J. Arrington, "James Gordon Bennett's 1831 Report on the 'Mormonites,'" *Brigham Young University Studies* 10 (Spring 1970): 353-64. See also Rodger I. Anderson, *Joseph Smith's New York Reputation Reexamined* (Salt Lake City: Signature Books, 1990).

17. Hill, "Brodie Revisited," 78.

18. Specific references to the errors of already established churches are found in 2 Ne. 26:20-21; 28:3-20. The content of the records engraved on the plates of gold are described in 2 Ne. 27:6-11; 28:2. The prophecy about

the seer to be called Joseph is in 2 Ne. 3:1-19.

19. The German historian Peter Meinhold has commented at length on the way in which the Book of Mormon provided America with a usable past. See "Die Anfaenge des Amerikanischen Geschichtsbewusstseins," *Saeculum* 5 (1954): 65-86. This work is discussed in Klaus J. Hansen's chapter on "Mormonism and the American Dream," *Quest for Empire* (East Lansing: Michigan State University Press, 1970).

20. 2 Ne. 19:14; 3 Ne. 21:22-23; 1 Ne. 13:37.

21. In his 1974 Mormon History Association Presidential Address, "'Is There No Help for the Widow's Son': Mormonism and Masonry," Reed C. Durham alluded to a Masonic legend which utilized many of the same elements—metal plates, stones called Urim and Thummim, and Egyptian hieroglyphics—found in Smith's account of the origin of the Book of Mormon. The quotation is from the Wentworth letter, HC 4:537.

22. HC 1:22-28.

23. O'Dea, *The Mormons,* 19-20.

24. Brodie, *No Man Knows My History,* 55-57.

25. The two categories, vision and revelation, which are being put forth here are not intended to be mutually exclusive; they are rather semantic symbols intended to encompass *process* (the means by which communications between God and the Mormon prophet were initiated) as well as the extra-rational phenomena themselves.

26. HC 1:7-8. While this quotation is taken from the official history, which account has been called into question, the reality of the prophet's perception of his having been made responsible for translating the plates is substantiated in chaps. 2, 4, and 9 of the Book of Commandments (1833; reprt., Independence, MO: Herald House, 1972), 8-13, 22-27.

27. David Whitmer, "An Address to All Believers. . . .," reprinted in Keith Huntress, *Murder of an American Prophet: Events and Prejudice Surrounding the Killings of Joseph and Hyrum Smith; Carthage, Illinois, June 27, 1844* (San Francisco: Chandler Publishing Co., 1960), 23. This point must not be confused with Smith's clear distinction between his actions as a prophet and his actions as a "mere man."

5.
Dream and Nightmare: Nauvoo Revisited

Robert Bruce Flanders

HAD JOSEPH SMITH OFFERED A PRIZE TO THE SAINTS FOR THE BEST NAME of their new city in Illinois (instead of naming it himself), "City of Joseph" surely would have been the popular entry. It was a day when many government seats were named for American heroes, dead or alive, and Joseph Smith—despite the homely name—was a very special American hero to his followers (even to his enemies, in reverse, for whom he was a special villain).

"City of Joseph" would have been a fitting name for a new Mormon capital, for Smith fulfilled in his person and his life many facets of the Great American Dream. He was a self-made man, rising from poverty to power, from semi-literacy to knowledge of both worldly and heavenly mysteries, from anonymity to fame, from being nobody to being somebody. He was a shaper of both present and future, a man who seemed to make history rather than merely reacting to it—qualities much prized in early America. Personally he exemplified other ideals: he was big, strong, blond, handsome, virile, young, ambitious, hearty, humorous, at once earthy and godlike, articulate but not pedantic, possessed of a vanity and pomposity more admired than ridiculed and enormously attractive to both men and women. That is enough to make any American some kind of hero, to name at least one town after.

But more important Smith was star-crossed—an American prophet by more than one definition. To generations of faithful followers he was and is a demi-god. Smith's vision of God's New Israel

75

in America created a religious movement that intended to sanctify American history—past, present, and future—by fulfilling the promises of the Promised Land. "The latter-day glory is probably to begin in America," said the great New England divine Jonathan Edwards a hundred years earlier. In fulfillment of the prophecy of his spiritual forebear, Smith gave the world the Book of Mormon for an American scripture ("by the gift and power of God," as he described it) and the true church restored from heaven to earth in America. He founded the Kingdom of God in the Mississippi Valley (which Americans were wont to consider the Garden of the World), and he was fountainhead of a newly sanctified, divinely commissioned ruling group—the Mormon priesthood ("the government of God," Apostle Parley Pratt called it).[1]

From among a nation of immigrants, Smith made a special call to the Old World from the New: Come claim your inheritances in Zion; come build up the waste places of God; come fulfill human destiny at the close of time. Tens of thousands believed and came. And he would convert governments too. Kings and rulers must come up to Zion and learn her ways, said Smith, and he projected a great hotel, the Nauvoo House, on the banks of the Father of Waters to lodge them. Ultimately the word of ancient prophecy would be fulfilled, and the kingdom, become a mighty American empire of righteousness, would roll forth and fill the whole earth like the "stone cut out of the mountain without hands."

Modern Latter-day Saints who are distressed that Joseph Smith sought the American presidency do not understand that it was a day when Ralph Waldo Emerson could propose Jesus Christ for the same office and have many Americans concur that it was the only reasonable nomination. America was to be truly "God's New Israel." Early converts to Mormonism usually were not difficult to convince of all this. A broad stratum of people in America and Europe believed it in principle before the Mormon elders arrived to announce that it was coming to pass. Thus the phenomenon of ministers and their congregations being baptized *en masse* (Sidney Rigdon, Isaac Morley, Lyman Wight, and others in Kirtland, Ohio, for example) and the remarkable fact that men were often baptized, ordained, and sent to preach the restoration message on the same day. The "mission miracle" of the early church was a kind of rapidly expanding, organized grapevine that got the word around.

The essential heart—the *sine qua non*—of the whole thing was the prophet Joseph Smith, the living oracle. He became an institution before his death—one might say a set of institutions. There was even an unstudied, folksy titling of the great man: "the Prophet Joseph" or just "Joseph," never "Joe," except by "enemies." He sealed it all (unwillingly to be sure) with martyr's blood and then became a myth. It was an American success story to make Horatio Alger's fictional heroes mean, crass, and pitiable by comparison.

On the other hand, Smith and his people were sorely vexed with troubles of which his own bullet-riddled body sprawled on the well curb at Carthage jail is only a sample. Nauvoo, Illinois, began as a wretched refugee camp peopled with five thousand Mormons who survived the holocaust in northwest Missouri in 1838-39. They were broken in spirit, sick, maimed, dying, possessed only of the goods they had carried with them. Joseph was in Liberty jail and probably would be lynched or executed, "Missouri justice" either way.

But Smith survived the ordeal, was allowed to escape (an act of Missourians not to be interpreted as a grant of amnesty), and appeared on the Illinois scene in April 1839. It was a decisive moment. There was considerable sentiment among refugees to "scatter off" and avoid another attempt at corporate, communal enterprise, after the awful persecutions in Missouri. There was also some crisis of confidence in the leadership of Smith, Sidney Rigdon, and others in the hierarchy of power. Things had not been handled judiciously at Far West, Missouri. The fanatical extremism of the Danites had gone unchecked, provoking Saints and gentiles alike. Many able Mormons left or were driven from the movement, never to return. There must be some kind of new deal; the past did not bear repeating. Smith now reasserted his charismatic power of leadership. Though he was not a man to forget, neither was he given to looking backward; and now he directed attention to the future, to the destiny of the Saints in the Last Days. They would gather not scatter, they would draw thousands and tens of thousands to the cause, and they would, as Smith put it, build up a city in the land of their exile, the State of Illinois.

In retrospect Smith had little choice but to found Nauvoo if he were to survive as the leader of Mormonism—indeed if Mormonism itself were to survive, at least in the form that he had outlined. He was locked into a series of decisions and a course of events that were productive of new difficulties. The site of the new city was apparently accidental. Isaac Galland, a real estate speculator, had lands to sell near the Mississippi River in Illinois and Iowa at the northeast corner of Missouri, and he attracted the attention of the Saints. It was the only location considered, it seems, "no better place having presented itself," as Smith put it. He was willing to view the lack of alternative possibilities as providential: God would provide; it was the Lord's work. The purchase of 15,000 acres in Lee County, Iowa, for some $40,000 (on credit) brought trouble and turmoil, ill feeling in the church and out, and ultimate failure, stemming from the fact that Galland did not own the lands he sold to the Mormons. Smith regarded Galland at the outset as "one of our benefactors." "When we were strangers," said Smith, "he took us in." How indeed they had been taken in by Galland, Smith was to learn subsequently with pain and embarrassment.

By another accident, however, Smith avoided compounding the Iowa land fiasco by locating himself and the main body of Saints on the Illinois side, just across the river. The main acreage purchased here was from a group of speculators headed by one Horace Hotchkiss of Connecticut. This area, about five hundred acres, constituted much of what was to be the city of Nauvoo, and was subsequently known as the Hotchkiss Purchase. Hotchkiss was shrewd enough to see a city coming on his property, and the price he exacted was enormous—$50,000 principle and $64,500 interest to be paid over twenty years. Considering the fact that the time was one of deep economic depression and that much of the land was malarial swamp unfit for human habitation, the amount would suggest that Smith was duped again. But perhaps both seller and buyer were considering the odds. Land speculation then was a gamble at best, and Hotchkiss like Smith had to hope that the future would bring the payoff. The deal was a land contract with the purchaser having the rights of occupation but not the deed until full payment was made. In the end Hotchkiss received only a fraction of the total due him from the church and had the taxes on a growing city to pay as well, inasmuch as he was still the legal owner. So it is a question as to who took advantage of whom. In any event in order to attempt to meet payments, Joseph Smith was forced into the real estate business in a big way; it was a business filled with care and anxiety, enormously taxing of time and energy. The problem of obtaining a deed to lots and lands which the church sold to the gathering Saints was one that could not be solved.[2]

In an 1841 letter to Hotchkiss Smith fumed, "I presume you are no stranger to the part of the city plot we bought of you being a sickly hole [and] although we have been keeping up appearances, and holding out inducements to encourage immigration . . . we scarcely think it justifiable in consequence of the mortality that almost invariably awaits those who come." This was one of the rare occasions when Smith did not "keep up appearances" as all real estate promoters must do and alluded to one of Nauvoo's great problems. Endemic malaria was the worst natural scourge of the Mississippi Basin, and Smith had located his town on a wet river bottomland that swarmed in summer with infected mosquitoes. The plague was an annual event of the hot season, and hundreds died, victims of the "unhealthy air." Draining the area helped, but new settlers in particular remained susceptible to infection by mosquitoes breeding in nearby islands and sloughs.

Other consequences of Nauvoo having been a refugee camp were less tangible than land purchase or health problems but perhaps more lasting. Injury, deprivation, anxiety, bereavement, disappointment, frustration, when unrelieved and unrequited, have a cumulative effect on the character of individuals and groups. Despite "keeping up appearances," the brief Illinois sojourn brought neither security nor requital of past hurts. Indeed trouble was repeated and compounded, and for those who "stayed with the Church" the next flight to the valley of Great Salt Lake was to be an epic journey both in space and of the spirit. The character of the Mormon people was in process of formation, a character grounded in the experiences of the Saints in Ohio and Missouri in the 1830s, which came to a sort of early maturity in Nauvoo. Utah began in Nauvoo, as did the "dissenting" sects of Mormonism, such as the Reorganized Church of Jesus Christ of Latter Day Saints, if in a different way.

To attempt descriptions of group character is risky at best, but in Nauvoo certain Mormon characteristics began to become permanent and settled. One was a quality of deep, mystical faith. By "believing in" the Book of Mormon and the prophet, Mormon converts had at once taken a step beyond the run of evangelical Protestants to a new para-meter of faith commitment. By continuing to follow Smith and participate in his ventures, of which Nauvoo and the missions begun there were the most extensive, their investment deepened. Mormons were committing their lives, fortunes, and "sacred honor" to a kind of new, sacred American revolution, from which it was difficult to turn back. A mystical faith in both the sacred and secular leadership of the prophet and the priesthood was "essential to salvation," not only in the life to come but to psychic and physical survival in this life as well. As the historian Jan Shipps put it: "Always the prophet drew his followers into a circle distinctly Mormon, setting them apart from those who refused to recognize the claims of the 'restored gospel' and therefore remained gentiles outside the covenant of Jacob. Secure within the circle, all Israel listened as plans for a New Jerusalem, and for a self-sufficient social and economic community which should flower there, were revealed in great profusion and minute detail. With faith in their prophet and in the restored priesthood which he headed—and with precious little else to sustain them—the Saints began to build their latter-day Zion at Nauvoo on the banks of the Mississippi in frontier Illinois."[3] For those who turned away—and there were many—the costs could be great: economic loss, shattering of dreams, spiritual agony, guilt, consignment by the faithful to the special oblivion reserved for "apostates," and perhaps persecution by *both* Mormons and gentiles.

Another trait of Mormon character originating partly in circumstance but partly in Smith himself was a kind of paranoid style. In a way such a statement is both a truism and an exaggeration, like saying that the burned child who dreads the fire is consequently paranoid. Of course Mormons were haunted by the specter of lynchings, burnings, and drivings. Naturally the prophet feared kidnapping and lynching. But there was in addition an aggressive, truculent temper in Smith and many whom he attracted and promoted to leadership—Sidney Rigdon and Brigham Young are different examples of the phenomenon—that seemed to promote war rather than peace. The Mormons were not easy peacemakers, either with critics within or critics without. One of the many examples in the Nauvoo period was the case of Dr. John Cooke Bennett. Smith felt compelled to make Bennett a great man overnight and then was unable to avoid making a dedicated and powerful enemy of him. Bennett's loose morals and Smith's nascent spiritual wife system did not quite mesh gears and the consequent mutual hatred of the two became personal. But it was a clash that Smith in his position could ill afford. The details of the affair between the two are uncertain, but it would appear that before he left Nauvoo, Bennett genuinely feared for his life, as many of Smith's enemies claimed to do. And he subsequently published newspaper articles and a book that aroused national antagonism toward the Mormons. Smith claimed among other things that Bennett was author of a plot to kill him, which may have been true but probably was not. Smith suffered for at least the final two years a chronic anxiety that there were plots against his life. Significantly he feared those inside the movement as much or more than those outside.

After the Bennett affair certain police-state characteristics begun in Far West were augmented in Nauvoo and persisted in Mormonism: informers, secret police, bodyguards, and gangs of enforcers. The Nauvoo Legion, a private army organized by Bennett in which Smith played general, created anxiety in Illinois and terrified Hancock County people. A case can be made that all this was a legitimate response to real dangers and insecurities. But upon reflection it seems that a paranoid temper developed in Joseph Smith that carried over into the style and *modus operandi* of the movement itself. Currying the enmity rather than the favor of both political parties in Illinois, the Bennett affair, losing control of the secret celestial marriage doctrine, the constant war on critics within the church, all cost the Saints dearly. It is necessary in this context to examine the celebrated Boggs shooting.

Lilburn Boggs, ex-governor of Missouri, was shot in the back of the head in Independence in 1842 by a person unknown. Miraculously he lived, and the assassin was not apprehended. But public opinion in Missouri and Illinois could scarcely have been more aroused had Boggs died with the alleged Mormon assailant caught standing over his body. The crime was laid to Orrin Porter Rockwell, a simple, illiterate, utterly faithful and loyal Mormon who was from childhood a close friend of Smith and devoted to him as courier, bodyguard, enforcer, and general factotum. He was a tough, rugged man, a skilled horseman and gunman. Rockwell was in Independence *incognito* at the time of the shooting for an apparently legitimate reason—he wanted to be near his pregnant wife, who was staying with her parents. He fled Missouri immediately afterward and returned to Nauvoo. Rockwell was always a man of reliable veracity, according to his biographer, and the fact that he never denied having done the deed is significant. He only denied that Smith ordered him to do it. Furthermore, it is not difficult to imagine that Rockwell was guilty; rather it is difficult under the circumstances to imagine him innocent. He was there, had abundant motive, and—important in retrospect— subsequently killed so many "enemies" of the church that the Boggs shooting is in character. Joseph Smith's affection for Rockwell seemed to increase after the affair—perhaps only because Rockwell was to suffer exile and prison as a result, in Smith's eyes unjustly, but perhaps because he knew that Rockwell was the assassin and he condoned the act. Perhaps Smith's prophecy of a violent end for Boggs (he also prophesied that Illinois governor Thomas Carlin would wind up dead in a ditch, which caused Carlin some anxiety) and Rockwell's being in Independence were among those extraordinary coincidences of history that occur from time to time. But perhaps not. Whatever the truth, Smith and Rockwell sought to dissociate themselves from the affair legally but not morally. If they were otherwise innocent—Rockwell of the act and Smith of the notion—they were willing to take the credit.[4]

Incredible as it may seem to Latter-day Saints today, the possibility that Smith and Rockwell were culpable in the Boggs shooting should be considered along with the consequences accruing to the Saints. But it should be considered in historical perspective. Boggs was a special miscreant, a vindictive, vengeful man whom the political process of Missouri elevated to the governorship. Boggs had in 1838 ordered the state militia to "expel or exterminate" the Mormons. The uprooting and slaughter of whole groups are the ultimate acts of violence which can be visited upon men and women, and the carrying out of the Boggs directive left an ineradicable mark upon the souls of those who survived it. Mormon hatred of Missouri in general and Boggs in particular knew no bounds. And in nineteenth-century America, the killing of individuals to "settle accounts" was common, especially on the frontiers. Executions, lynchings, duels, bushwhackings, premeditated and unpremeditated, brought violent ends to hundreds of people believed deserving of punishment for whatever reason. Theft, injury, insult, lack of patriotism, threats real or imagined to public or private safety, all were sufficient to bring mortal retribution. The lines between legal and extra-legal actions were blurred in young and underdeveloped frontier societies, and for people to "take the law into their own hands" was to be both democratic and faithful to the traditions of the American revolution. For Lilburn Boggs to suffer a nearly fatal assault was sensational but not on a different level of "punishment" than that of his own extermination order. If Smith was in any way responsible for the Boggs shooting, it is in retrospect both understandable and inexcusable, like all the violence between Mormons and gentiles. The Boggs incident caused an escalation of anti-Mormon feeling in Missouri and Illinois that the Saints could not afford but which Smith neither anticipated nor seemed to regret.

Smith's hatreds and vendettas were not more exaggerated than those of many prominent men; and, as in the case of Andrew Jackson, helped make him the public figure he was. But for Smith and the Mormons a paranoid style was counterproductive in the short run; and in the long run festered in the Mormon spirit to spawn qualities of illiberality and alienation that continue in Mormon culture.

Another Mormon trait that can be discerned developing in Nauvoo was a strong, distinctive sense of group loyalty, of common purpose and destiny. Described negatively, it was the feeling that those not for us are against us. In an obvious sense group loyalty under conditions of danger and suffering is a natural human response. But beyond this Mormons forsook the celebrated American individualism for "groupthink"; forsook a society egalitarian for one authoritarian and hierarchical. Though Americans were neither as free nor as equal as they believed, to become a loyal Mormon was to give up much of both. Perhaps the "strain of freedom," as one historian put it, was too great for some of them to bear. Unquestionably Americans in the 1830s and 1840s were under great stress due to a variety of circumstances. The response of Mormons, as of masses of Americans, to the Old Hero Andrew Jackson illustrates their ambivalence about the substance of democracy. While Mormons scorned Martin Van Buren, a real democrat and consequently weak—a compromiser and deal-maker—they admired the old tyrant Jackson who destroyed his enemies with power and righteous indignation, like some Old Testament prophet, and who implied that the only "real" Americans were his supporters.[5] Though insecure in the things of this world and beset by worldly powers, Mormons were secure in the knowledge of The Truth, their own identifiable, explicit calling and destiny to build the Kingdom of God. They scorned the tentative,

uncertain religious values of gentiles. Nauvoo, though short-lived and
in many ways chaotic, was the one place where Joseph Smith came
close to "getting it all together." There Mormons began to become a
people—even a nation. After Nauvoo and the trek West, to call them
merely a church was to understate the case.[6]

Between 15,000 and 20,000 Mormons finally settled in Hancock County, Illinois, with a maximum of perhaps 12,000 in and
around Nauvoo. They were not only welcomed into Illinois at the
outset, they were enthusiastically received. Governor Thomas Ford
said that when the Mormons arrived, the citizens were "justly distinguished for feelings and principles of the most liberal and enlight-
ened toleration in the matters of religion. The Mormons were
received as sufferers in the cause of their religion. Several counties
and neighborhoods vied with each other in offers of hospitality and
in endeavors to get the Mormons to settle among them."

The Prairie State, only twenty-one years in the union in 1839,
was vast, sparsely populated, under-developed, and floundering in a
sea of troubles. The state had undertaken a canal and railroad
building scheme in the late 1830s that seemed to promise quick
development and wealth for the state and its citizens. But the time
was wrong, the plan too big, the money borrowed, and worst of all,
the government had no idea what it was doing or how to do it. Then
depression struck the nation—the worst in twenty years. The result
was that the state was near financial and moral collapse when the
Mormons arrived. The influx of so many skilled and industrious
citizens, though poor, was a needed shot in the arm for Illinois.
Viewed apart from all the strife that quickly ensued, Nauvoo had the
potential to be a great urban center built on the industries of
transportation, manufacturing, commerce, religion, and education.
The river provided a power potential to turn mills, and Nauvoo lay
on a line between Chicago and Kansas City for the railroad when it
came. By 1846 Joseph's city was larger than any other in Illinois. And
while it could not have been another Chicago, it could conceivably
have become such a complex as Davenport-Moline-Rock Island-Mus-
catine or even Minneapolis-St. Paul (which also began with mills at a
minor falls of the Mississippi).

Illinois, though an accidental choice for Mormon settlement
in 1839, had advantages compared with many other western states
for the development of a culturally different, highly particular society

such as the Mormons were becoming. The problem of slavery was absent; and for Yankees and English immigrants with abolitionist leanings a free state was essential. Missouri was, for example, no fit place for a Zion—especially one with such a New England odor about it. Yankees were by contrast welcome in Illinois and were pouring into the northern half of the state. Cultural diversity was already a fact of life, albeit an uneasy one, with Yankee and Southerner, free people of color, French-Canadian, Irish Catholic, Jews, and many new British immigrants already there. Though Illinois was in trouble in 1840, the state was rich and was soon to "take off" on a boom of development that made it the economic and political hub of western America by 1860 when the chief presidential candidates, Lincoln and Douglas, were both Illinois men who had grown up facing each other as leaders of the state's Whig and Democratic parties.

The stumbling blocks in the way of opportunity for Mormons were considerable. In addition to Nauvoo's bad climate and general economic unease, Illinois politics was a cockpit of fierce partisanship. The ferocity of political struggles in the Jacksonian period tends to amaze modern observers. In Illinois partisan feelings were particularly embittered. Both Whigs and Democrats wanted the new Mormon vote, were subsequently angered by what they considered Mormon duplicity and unpredictability, and finally held the Mormons in fear and contempt, as politicians are wont to hold any privately controlled swing-voting bloc. The situation offered the Mormons opportunity, but one which had to be handled delicately. Unfortunately, in political management Joseph Smith was at his worst. Inexperienced in politics, he was swayed by vanity, delusions of power, and an unwarranted certainty that he could master the situation. Particularly in the elections of 1842 and 1843, his political behavior was gross. And in 1844 he was running for the U.S. presidency, hardly a course designed to calm troubled waters, although he was killed before much came of it. The truth is that Smith did not understand or accept many of the fundamental premises of American politics. He was by 1840 basically in opposition to a democratic, two-party, brokered political system. He favored rather rule by a *partie unique*, a theocracy as represented by the Mormon priestly hierarchy and described as "unity of the faith" and "obedience to counsel." His experience—with a New York court in his youth and later with Ohio bank law, with executive and judicial politics in Missouri, and with a government in Washington that failed to indemnify the Saints for their losses in Missouri or "impeach" that state for failing to have a constitutional form of government—tended to settle Smith into a critical apprehension of worldly governments.

In the 1843 congressional election, Smith promised the Mormon vote to the Whig candidate and then delivered it to the Democrat. Though not entirely cynical, it was careless, a provocative act of staggering proportions. It lends credence to the notion that from the Bennett scandal and the Boggs shooting in 1842 to the *Nauvoo Expositor* incident and Smith's own death in 1844, Smith was losing control of many affairs and perhaps of himself. "From this time forth [the election of 1843]," wrote Governor Thomas Ford, "the Whigs generally, and a part of the Democrats, determined upon driving the Mormons out of the state; and everything connected with the Mormons became political." For his part, Smith had said on the eve of the fateful election, "I am above the kingdoms of this world, for I have no laws." It was an apocalyptic not a political position. By 1844 he believed the "government of God" must inevitably replace all the governments of this world, including that of the United States and the various states. The only courses the Mormons could have pursued successfully in Illinois would have been to remain scrupulously apolitical or to cultivate a skillful bi-partisanship. Smith seems at the outset to have considered both possibilities but quickly gave way to various pressures and the temptations of his paranoid style.[7]

Another problem the Mormons had to face was that of inevitable enmities in their home county of Hancock. Hancock County had been organized for only ten years when the Mormons came, was on the frontiers of Illinois settlement, seemed at the time to be out-of-the-way, and stagnant. Hancock had at most a population of 5,000 on the eve of Mormon settlement. There was no newspaper, and the largest town, Warsaw, a little river community fifteen miles below Nauvoo, had fewer than 300 inhabitants. Most of the population was in the townships around the edges of the county, leaving Carthage, the county seat, a little village in a kind of central no-man's-land. The population was apparently Southern in origin and Whiggish in political proclivity. The Mormons swept in on this quiet frontier backwater like a tidal wave. Had the resident population been 500 or 50,000, things might have been easier. As it was Hancock was populous enough to resist Mormon influence but not populous enough to do so decisively. Civil war in Hancock might have been avoided by a willingness on both sides to co-exist and by the skillful and imaginative application of cultural pluralism and political and economic federalism. Unfortunately neither side was much prepared or disposed for such a course of action.[8]

Mormons believed at the beginning of Nauvoo that they had a great future in Illinois. Illinoisans tended to agree and to offer the Saints many inducements and opportunities, including the remarkably liberal Nauvoo charter and an early tendency to side with the Saints against Missouri vindictiveness. So the Saints might have prospered in the Prairie state, all other things being equal. But that is not what happened. Joseph Smith must bear the burden of responsibility for the failure. He mismanaged many crucial things. Especially disastrous was his failure to cultivate successfully the good will that the Mormons inherited when they first arrived and to keep his political fences mended. He was naive and inexperienced and attracted to bad advice and bad advisors. His proclivity to control the church absolutely and to destroy what he could not control produced a crop of bitter ex-Mormons who spread scandal over the state. And his program to protect honest and innocent men (including himself) from the long, unjust arm of the law by erecting an independent judicial fiefdom in Nauvoo naturally attracted the dishonest and the guilty who coveted the same protection. Smith failed to preserve a healthy public image, and in an important measure he failed to preserve a healthy private substance. The plural wife system though officially secret was known in various exaggerated forms everywhere and added fuel to the fire. After the Boggs affair, Smith was branded a conspiratorial murderer, and the Mormons stood convicted in the court of public opinion as moral bankrupts and political firebrands.

Smith and the Mormons were of course not solely to blame. Illinois was alive with opportunists, public inflamers who worked for enmity rather than comity with the Mormons. Newspapers built their circulation on anti-Mormon yellow journalism, from Thomas Sharp's scurrilous *Warsaw Signal* to the august Springfield *Sangamo Journal*. No less a figure than Stephen A. Douglas skillfully played both ends against the middle. Bigots and sharpers of all kinds made fair game of the Mormons, especially when they began to bleed. Thomas Ford stands out among the jackals for a degree of integrity. He never pretended to like the Mormons and was honest enough to say that he despised them. But he was equally convinced of their civil rights and tried in his weak way against overwhelming odds to protect them.

If the Mormons failed in Illinois, if they were obsessed with dreams of a kingdom of righteousness beyond their grasp, it was a magnificent obsession. The inexperience, the lack of maturity, the human fallibility of the young prophet were thrown into bold relief by the enormous responsibilities he assumed, which were thrust upon him by events and by an adoring, demanding people. But he did speak prophetically to his generation about the sanctification of American history, the revolutionizing of American life. He proposed to change it from a confused, secularized, anarchic chaos where freedom had deteriorated to mere license, into a Christian kingdom, an empire of communities ruled by God's restored priesthood. The Mormon church was not to be just another church but was to be the new holy catholic religion that was to refresh the earth in preparation for the end of time and the Second Coming. Of course every new sect is the sect to end all sects, and Mormonism was not in its pretensions entirely unique. But Smith offered a religious "plan" to organize and legitimate one of America's most powerful historic impulses—the movement of millions of settlers to new lands, to open new farms, form new towns, found new businesses, new govern-ments, new societies.

The secular manifestation of the American imperative to multiply and have dominion was the formation of the new western states—Ohio, Illinois, Missouri. The Latter-day Saints wanted to sacralize the process, to form instead the kingdom of God. To give a sacred meaning, a divine sanction, to the creating of America repre-sented by the constant, endless begetting—westering, settling, build-ing, speculating, risking, hoping, dying, of the millions engaged in the process—was the unique contribution of Mormonism. Those Americans who had a strong Protestant evangelical tradition worried that religion was increasingly separated from the daily meaning of life. Being saved, going to church, evidencing a pious, respectable lifestyle were well and good but were more and more subordinated to secular concerns. The land was new, raw, open; life was hard but opportunity beckoned.

Mormonism by contrast brought religion and life together in an inextricable mix. The land belonged to God as did the people, the settlements, the businesses, the governments. Human work could be achieved by human aspiration, ingenuity, and sweat. But it was God's good pleasure that his Saints should inherit the earth, in preparation for the end. To readers acquainted with the religious ethic of the seventeenth-century Puritan settlements in New England, this will sound familiar, because Mormonism was in many ways a new efflorescence of the same ethic. But now it was American not English, and the vision was much broader, more encompassing in scope. By 1844 Smith saw Zion as spreading over the entire western hemisphere. When John C. Bennett wrote that the Mormons had a vast, deep-laid plot afoot to conquer the states of middle America and erect upon their ruin a priestly tyranny, he was being both absurd and profound (though he intended to be neither), like one who might have said that the Puritans in Massachusetts Bay plotted to conquer the wilderness, overthrow Satan's kingdom, and establish the rule of righteousness.

The Mormon idea of a literal kingdom of God—towns, organizations, governments—represented a new way for Christians to approach the end of time and the Second Coming. Smith and the Mormons were convinced millennarians, expecting the second advent in a few years. It was indeed a part of the faith of multitudes of Christians in Europe and America. Most millennarians, however, had concerned themselves with the *time* of the parousia; to predict the date when Jesus would come, either from divining scripture or through prophecy, was the common style of millennarian leaders. Smith was different. Instead of appointing a time, he appointed a place. To westering Americans and European immigrants who were on the move to somewhere—perhaps anywhere—in the vast land, Smith issued the call: Come to Zion, come home. Receive your inheritances, build the temple, receive your blessings and endowments, go out with the good news of the kingdom. The story of Mormonism is "gathering"—a peculiarly Mormon thing, moving in, settling, building, developing, being nurtured in the community of faith—and going out on mission. Mormon lay missionaries seemed to be a class of men who were scarcely ever at home, yet among the few Americans who knew for sure where home was. It was for them in Zion.

Nauvoo was the first full-scale model of the Mormon kingdom. This was its essential significance, although other occurrences during the period were important—for example, the development of a distinctive Mormon eschatology and political style. Despite the fact that Nauvoo lasted only seven years, a very short time for a major town to rise and fall, it articulated the Mormon faith in a tangible way for Saint and gentile alike; it was an early proving ground for Mormonism. And it was, so to speak, the last will and testament of Joseph Smith, a fact which sanctified the memory of Nauvoo for succeeding generations of Mormons. It set permanently in Mormonism the communitarian vision and mode and fastened a "glorious lost cause" image upon the Mormon imagination. For the gentile world, Nauvoo had a different fascination, ranging from curiosity to horror. And for those Saints who dissented from the "church" during the period but did not deny the "faith" (many made such a distinction), Nauvoo meant something different. It was neither easy to accept entirely nor to reject. Members of the Reorganized church, for example, have always had difficulty interpreting the Nauvoo experience, because its meaning is ambivalent to them. Joseph Smith's commitment to the kingdom and his sacrifice, along with the investment of a heroic founding generation of Saints, Reorganized Saints have made a part of their own faith tradition. But many of the details such as celestial marriage, the politicizing of the church, Smith's temporal roles in Nauvoo, Mormonism as a vehicle for the immediate revolutionizing of society, and the real meaning of the Nauvoo temple have been generally rejected or denied.

Life was hard in Nauvoo, but there was alluring economic opportunity for individuals, for private groups of business partners, and for the church corporation. There was "political opportunity" too, although the term is not exactly appropriate to the process by which men (and a few women) could rise in influence by moving closer to the center of power where the prophet stood. Examples of the more successful were John C. Bennett and Brigham Young, men so different yet so much alike. The warm, fraternal society of Saints was a satisfying and successful feature of life in Nauvoo and its satellite settlements, and it filled deep psychic needs of frontier people. The Nauvoo community, though brief, was on balance the most mature, homogenous, and settled—the most "Mormon"—of all the Latter-day Saint colonies up to that time.

Religious life in Nauvoo was centrally important of course but is difficult to characterize in any concise manner. In a city whose purpose was so explicitly pious, whose heritage was Puritan, and whose leaders were mostly devout Yankees, the absence of even one meeting house for the observance of divine worship must have seemed an extraordinary omission to visitors. Nor was there one clergyman whose sole vocation it was to minister. On the other hand, every dwelling was a meeting house for the Saints, though the meeting would be necessarily small. And virtually every male Mormon was a lay priest. Smith himself was of course *the* minister (among other things). In the Mormon definition, he and the priestly structure he headed were the only legitimate ministry in existence. The wards of the town took on a combination civil-ecclesiastic significance that persisted and became a permanent feature of Mormon life. The ward was both an articulated neighborhood—a civil community—and a religious congregation. To imply a dichotomy between sacred and secular for the purposes of description is to skew the truth, for in fact there was no separation of concept, function, or leadership. Church and state were combined, from the ward "priesthood" at the grassroots to the prophet-president-mayor-general-trustee-in-trust at the top.

The only way to understand religious life in Nauvoo is to understand that religion *was* life, that such a mode was fundamental to the Mormon way, and that it was deeply satisfying to its adherents. "Administering to the sick," for example, meant not only nursing and caring for those who were down but also anointing with consecrated oil in a rite of prayer. "Going to meeting" meant (in good weather) generally repairing *en masse* to a grove of trees near the temple site, where a speaker's platform stood. The addresses by the "priesthood" might be one or many, with any mixture of exegesis, admonition, or exhortation of subjects religious, political, social, economic, or personal (for personalities were often of public concern in Nauvoo). So "service" was usually a mix of Protestant-style worship-revival and New England town meeting (the latter aspect being more theocratic than democratic).

Beneath these ordinaries (or extraordinaries) of life in the New Jerusalem lay other characteristics perhaps less apparent but vital. There was a sense of mystery, of excitement, of great events, great beginnings only dimly perceived which were omens of far greater things to come as yet unimagined: "For thus said the Lord, . . . to them [the Saints] will I reveal all mysteries . . . yea, even those which eye hath not seen, nor ear heard, nor yet entered into the heart of man." The Mormon faith was not burdened with guilt and con-demnation but was afire with hope, promise, exultation. "We thank thee, O God, for a prophet, to guide us in these latter days," sang the Saints; and in another favorite hymn: "The Spirit of God like a fire is burning; the latter-day glory begins to come forth. . . . We'll sing and we'll shout with the armies of heaven, hosanna, hosanna, to God and the Lamb . . . henceforth and forever, amen and amen." Nauvoo Saints sensed themselves caught up in the ending of an era and the beginning of another. Nothing symbolized this part of the life mode better than the great temple rising slowly on the hill and the creation of the Council of Fifty, the "living constitution" of the kingdom.

Few public buildings were erected in Nauvoo, churches included, because of the enormous investment being made in the temple. It was to be *the* meeting house, *the* public building, of a great city yet to rise. But it was to be much more, just as the temple at Jerusalem was more to ancient Jews than a big synagogue. The Nauvoo temple was a shrine and a monument for Mormonism. But more than this, the temple was a building to link heaven and earth in some mystical-literal manner that was peculiarly Mormon (al-though the influence of Freemasonry on Smith's conception cannot be doubted). Here, Smith's prophetic promises of enlightenment and blessing were to be fulfilled. To miss this meaning of the temple is to miss much of the meaning of Mormonism and Nauvoo. Nauvoo was to be the "temple city" of Mormonism. The meaningful historic analogy was Jerusalem—an analogy well understood by the Saints. Smith did not live to preside in that vast, unusual structure, but the ordinances of the new Mormon eschatology celebrated there and in subsequent Mormon temples originated in his vision. "Temple Work"—rites for the dead, "sealings" of family relationships "for time and eternity," "endowments" (all significant Mormon expressions)—seemed less than the sum of their parts to "gentiles" but the opposite to devout Mormons.

American culture was poor in symbols, dramas, imaginative images. Americans hungered for them. One observer compared nineteenth-century political campaigns in America to traditional religious festivals of Europe. In the Mormon temple time and space were fused symbolically in an awesome, mysterious way. Past, pres-ent, and future—heaven and earth—time and eternity—the hidden things of humanity and God—were to be made known. The extent to which the expectations of devotees were satisfied there obviously varied, but of the expectations themselves, there can be no doubt. Mormonism was a religion of great expectations, of drama, of high mystery, and of restrained ecstasy, mostly contained within the priesthood structure. Perhaps subsequent Mormon temples were in part a memory of Joseph's City Beautiful and its dream of the kingdom. The early abandonment and subsequent melodramatic destruction of the sacred edifice, like the death of the young prophet at the apparent full flower of his powers, left impressions upon the romantic nineteenth-century Mormon imagination that can scarcely be exaggerated. But the impact was felt by dissenters as well, who interpreted these twin symbols of the fall of Nauvoo to be retribution more than tragedy—divine wrath falling upon the church in consequence of the new, unholy doctrines and politics.

Joseph Smith's vision of the kingdom sought to sanctify not only the American quest for a new society but the American dream of empire as well. The founding generation of Mormons and their contemporaries grew up as the young republic was enhanced by the Florida Cession and the Louisiana Purchase. In their maturity they were to witness the extension of the nation into a vast continental empire—Texas, the Mexican Cession, including Alta California and the Oregon country. Western Americans in particular tended to doubt that the empire was complete even so. Nauvoo occurred just at the time when excitement over Texas, Oregon, and California approached a climax—when Manifest Destiny was a household idea if not a household word in much of the country. Smith shared the excitement, and just before his death in 1844, the focus of his planning for the future expansion of the kingdom became continental, even hemispheric. He began to conceive mission-colony-states as part of a great system of kingdom societies that might stretch from Oregon and California to Texas, Mexico, Central America, and the Caribbean.

It was in this context that Smith organized the Council of Fifty to launch his imperial plans. Actually fifty-three men including the church hierarchy, leading men of practical affairs, and at least one non-Mormon, the group was secret, like much of import that went on within the structure of power. Its operations as projected by Smith were shadowy and foreshortened by his own early demise. But it is clear that they were a central planning and administrative circle charged with both conception and execution of the new imperial concepts. The group initiated proposals to detach Nauvoo from the state of Illinois and create a self-governing, powerfully-garrisoned, virtually independent state under the guise of a federal territory; to create a Mormon state in west-central Texas; to launch specific para-military colonizing ventures into the trans-Missouri west; and to elect Joseph Smith president of the United States.[9]

The Mormon quests for power and political sovereignty were real. The founding of Utah and its subsequent expansion were neither simply the unique, divinely revealed courses of action supposed by generations of the Mormon faithful nor the accidental and fortuitous consequences of the Nauvoo debacle assumed by secular historians. Utah was in the beginning a fragment of larger schemes salvaged and built upon by Brigham Young. The heroic but pitiful struggles in Texas and Minnesota of Lyman Wight and Alpheus Cutler—members of the Council of Fifty who broke with Young to discharge what they believed to be Joseph Smith's commission to them—are shadowy historic reminders of many secret plans made in Nauvoo in the spring of 1844 when anything seemed possible. It should become more clear to members of the Reorganized church and other dissenting sects of Mormonism that their "founding fathers" broke with Brigham Young about other issues in addition to authority and polygamy: they dissented in many instances from the political and imperial kingdom conceived by Smith and continued by Young.

No matter how the historian approaches Nauvoo—whether with a focus on the socio-economy, the church, doctrine, religious experience, politics, or some combination—he or she should consider the ultimate concern of Nauvooans themselves: the matter of life and death. Joseph Smith had miraculously survived in Ohio and Missouri, but he did not survive in Illinois. And for the corporate Mormon people, the end in Illinois was in effect a repeat of the Missouri experience: expulsion or extermination. The Mormons again got caught up in a civil war that they could neither win nor survive. Although Mormon-gentile conflict is long past now, its effects on Mormonism are not, nor probably its effects on gentiles. War and violence change the survivors and their culture, no matter who is victor or vanquished. Mormons were the repeated victims of violence but were not themselves pacifist; Mormons publicly and privately accepted the idea of force, threatened to use it, and did so occasionally. To condemn the Mormons for their use of violence is not any more just or reasonable than to argue that Indian and slave uprisings justified the awesome brutality visited upon them. But the Mormons were provocative and even dangerous locally, and in particular situations aroused the same kind of general, massive retaliation triggered by slave or Indian threats. One should probably not carry the analogy between oppression of Mormons and blacks or Indians much farther. The Mormon and the gentile thinking about the use of force was much the same: each side was reared in the vigilante tradition. Here, perhaps, is a new way to think about Mormon-gentile conflict in Illinois and elsewhere.

Vigilantism in America, born during the Revolutionary era, was popularized and legitimated by the War for Independence. The philosophy passed into the pantheon of the new United States: Americans must be vigilant, or freedom, so hard bought, might be threatened. A vigilante posse was usually representative of the local population or some portion of it and was more or less respected (if for nothing more than derring-do bravado). Sometimes they were led by "the leading men of the community." They ranged from mobs to para-military organizations, and their purpose was the extra-legal protection, by whatever means they deemed necessary, of the locale from the British, the Indians, the horse thieves, the blacks, the sheep men, the nesters, other vigilance groups, or whoever else threatened at the moment.

In the nineteenth century, the vigilance ethic fed on emotionalism, romanticism, evangelical salvationism, and popular democracy. It was a powerful idea, and it gripped the imagination of Americans: the continuing right of revolution and the right to self preservation and the protection of property. In the economic circumstances of a newly developing region, a human life could be judged less valuable than a horse or a barn. They might trail, run down, and whip or lynch in one operation. Legal niceties and questions of degrees of innocence were uninteresting. Vigilantes responded frequently to the fear in sparsely populated regions that undesirable elements—usually organized bands of desperadoes—would take over, if allowed. Such fears were frequently well founded. By the early 1830s some regions of the states in the lower Mississippi Valley were under the virtual control of such outlaw bands until driven out—many north, up the Mississippi—by massive vigilante action. This may be one reason why Illinois was in the 1830s and early 1840s so plagued with organized rural crime. Thomas Ford described much of the population of Hancock County as of "low character" and thought perhaps the Mormons were drawn there by some natural affinity with such people. Illinois had its own vigilante response. One of the most spectacular occurred in the Rock River Valley in 1841 where outlaws controlled or terrified county governments, including sheriffs and courts. After a great vigilante uprising and the civil war that ensued, offenders were exterminated or expelled.

Vigilantes were apparently like a refiner's fire, and the innocent were consumed with the guilty. When a county seat newspaper published an editorial mildly chiding the vigilantes for their tactics, the newspaper office was burned to the ground the same night. "Law and order" were apparently restored. The Rock River vigilance served the subsequent anti-Mormon vigilance as a powerful model. The locals in particular and many Illinoisans in general feared the Mormons—that they would "take over." Governor Ford tried during the *Nauvoo Expositor* crisis of 1844 to exercise control through the agency of the militia system and the state executive, but he failed. He tried again in the fall of 1845 with partial success, allowing the Mormons a truce to prepare their exodus. It was at least some improvement over their expulsion from Missouri.

But Mormons had their own vigilance. They believed in local, even regional and state, political control; in the expulsion of undesirable elements; in short, in Mormon popular sovereignty. The Mormon ethic as a force to revolutionize American life fitted neatly with the belief that the vigilante tradition preserved that continuing revolution. The Danites may perhaps best be understood as a kind of special, romantic vigilante organization, in some ways not unlike the Ku Klux Klan, the Knights of the Golden Circle, or other secret groups pledged to defend the truth. The Nauvoo Legion was different of course but was not perceived as less dangerous by the gentiles. As a matter of fact, Mormonism attracted a sort of nineteenth-century "freedom fighter" type, as all beleaguered causes and all civil wars have done throughout history—men whose motives are mixed, complex, and often confused.[10]

The most fateful act of Mormon vigilantism in Illinois was Joseph Smith's destruction of the *Nauvoo Expositor* press in June 1844.

It set in motion a swift train of events that ended with his own murder on June 27. Only the first issue of the newspaper was published before Smith's order that it all be destroyed, but a few copies survived, and reproductions are now widely available in libraries. Reading the *Expositor* today gives one pause. It is moderate enough—compared with most "opposition" newspapers of the day. Joseph Smith was criticized and condemned for many of his actions to be sure, but the editors were still in "the faith" of Mormonism, although they had broken with "the church." Any good Whig editor who had cursed the name of Andrew Jackson in print would have disdained it as no expose at all. Polygamy, centralization and "usurpation" of power by Smith and the hierarchy, attempted control of the economy, charges of "covering up" the true state of affairs, duping the people, etc., all are there. But such is the standard fare of any independent newspaper that criticizes the prevailing power structure. Apparently Smith's real problem was that the paper was independent and that it threatened his monopoly over public expression and the formation of public opinion. Furthermore the paper was part of a continuing conflict of community elites. Smith and the church dominated the "lower town" in Nauvoo, but a group of gentile and dissident Mormon businessmen dominated a rival commercial district on the "hill." The rivalry had become acrimonious by 1844. Smith had already suffered just about all the inflammatory newspapers he could stand around the state, given his personal sensitivity to public criticism. The *Nauvoo Expositor,* in his own town and run by traitorous former brethren, was the last straw.

The destruction of newspapers was in the vigilante tradition. In frontier America, given the widespread illiteracy and the paucity of printed material, a newspaper constituted a sort of monopoly on the flow of printed information and propaganda to the literate, opinion-forming segment of the population. Hence the regular destruction of "unpopular" presses. The Mormons had had their own *Evening and Morning Star* press destroyed in Independence, Missouri, in 1833. The most celebrated destruction of a newspaper by mob vigilance was the abolitionist press of Elijah Lovejoy in Alton, Illinois, in 1837, where Lovejoy was killed. Smith's action certainly had precedent, and he apparently gave it little thought. But the aggrieved *Expositor* editors saw Smith unexpectedly playing into their hands and used the incident to destroy the prophet—though there is no evidence that they were involved in the plot to kill him that resulted.

What Nauvoo was may become more clear in our generation. Joseph Smith was not only the founder of the faith but proved to be the unique Mormon prophet as well. For him there was never a replacement. His death brought a succession crisis that changed Mormonism through schism and metamorphosis. Nauvoo was the occasion for the "final" Mormon expulsion, this time from the United States, and was followed by flight into the wilderness. Nauvoo was the end of the beginning. It was also the fork in the road for Mormons; those who accepted Nauvoo and what it meant tended to go west with Brigham Young and the Mormon corporation. Those who had serious doubts, including many who had not actually lived in Nauvoo, chose the road of dissent that led to the churches of the dispersion or out of organized Mormonism altogether. For all, Nauvoo tended to be a guide, a model of what to do or what not to do. What might have been, had Nauvoo survived, we can only surmise.

Nauvoo was a volatile mixture of elements—American patri- otism, immigrant dreams of the promised land, displaced-person desperation, religious mysticism and fanaticism, free experimenta- tion with new social, ethical, and politico-economic modes, optimism, opportunism, energy—and escalating violence, within and without. But no matter that Smith, his religious corporation, and his people were in the end not entirely innocent victims—they were victims nevertheless. The threat they supposedly posed to their neighbors was not sufficient to warrant the response. In the end the result was another typical case of overkill. Americans could not yet conceive of themselves living together in the Promised Land with others of fundamentally different values and goals, of possibly resolving their conflicts peaceably. Coexistence is a new idea even in the following century, and one with which many Americans are still uneasy. Of course Mormons themselves denied the notion of cultural federal- ism—of the right of others to be "wrong"—and were themselves oppressed when that right was denied them.

In 1838 Abraham Lincoln said in a speech in the Illinois legislature that internal violence was the supreme threat to American political institutions. He spoke of "the increasing disregard of law which pervades the country; the growing disposition to substitute the wild and furious passions in lieu of the sober judgment of courts. . . ."

Americans need not fear foreign conquest, he continued. "If destruction be our lot, we ourselves must be its author and finisher. As a nation of freemen, we [will] live through all time, or die by suicide."[11]

NOTES

1. Conrad Cherry, ed., *God's New Israel: Religious Interpretations of American Destiny* (Englewood Cliffs, NJ: Prentice-Hall, 1972), is a collection of essays that offers insight into the vision of an American kingdom of God such as Smith explicated.

2. The land purchases and real estate business in Nauvoo are described in Flanders, *Nauvoo: Kingdom on the Mississippi* (Urbana: University of Illinois Press, 1965), esp. chaps. 2 and 5.

3. Jan Shipps, "The Mormons in Politics: The First Hundred Years," Ph.D. diss., University of Colorado, 1965, 41.

4. Harold Schindler, *Orrin Porter Rockwell: Man of God, Son of Thunder* (Salt Lake City: University of Utah Press, 1966), is a provocative biography. Schindler obviously suspects that Rockwell was the Boggs assailant as does Fawn Brodie in her biography of Smith, *No Man Knows My History* (New York: Alfred A. Knopf, 1945), which offers a balanced account of the affair. Neither Schindler nor Brodie believed Smith to have been involved directly.

5. For an examination of the politico-cultural setting for early Mormonism in the Jacksonian period, see Marvin Meyers, *The Jacksonian Persuasion: Politics and Belief* (Palo Alto, CA: Stanford University Press, 1957).

6. Perhaps the first writer to explicate this idea was Thomas O'Dea in his *The Mormons* (Chicago: University of Chicago Press, 1957), 50.

7. For detailed treatments of the Mormons and Illinois politics, see Flanders, *Nauvoo*, chap. 8, and "The Kingdom of God in Illinois: Politics in Utopia," *Dialogue: A Journal of Mormon Thought* 5 (Spring 1970).

8. For an unusual and thoughtful discussion of the problems of immigrant groups of heterodox culture, see Louis Hartz, "A Comparative Study of Fragment Cultures," in Hugh David Graham and Ted Robert Gurr, eds., *The History of Violence in America: Historical and Comparative Perspectives* (New York: F. A. Praeger, 1969).

9. For extended discussions of these matters, see Klaus J. Hansen, *Quest for Empire: The Kingdom of God and the Council of Fifty in Mormon History* (Wayne State University Press, 1967), and Flanders, *Nauvoo*, chap. 10.

10. This discussion of vigilantism follows Richard Maxwell Brown, "The Vigilante Tradition in American History," in Graham and Gurr, *Violence in America*. See also Thomas Rose, ed., *Violence in America* (Boston: Houghton Mifflin, 1967); Robert Lee and Martin Marty, eds., *Religion and Social Conflict*

(New York: Oxford University Press, 1964); and Horace M. Kallen, *Cultural Pluralism and the American Idea* (Philadelphia: University of Pennsylvania Press, 1956).

   11. Quoted in Arthur M. Schlesinger, Jr., *Crisis of Confidence: Ideas, Power, and Violence in America* (Boston: Houghton Mifflin, 1969), 13, 14.

6.
A Gift Given, A Gift Taken: Washing, Anointing, and Blessing the Sick among Mormon Women

Linda King Newell

FOR MEMBERS OF THE MODERN LDS CHURCH, THE TERM "WASHING and anointing" is synonymous with the initiatory ordinances of the temple endowment. Joseph Smith first introduced the practice to male members of the church in the Kirtland Temple; he included women when he gave the endowment and sealing ordinances to his select "Quorum of the Anointed" in Nauvoo.[1] By the time Mormons had established a refuge in the Great Basin, washing and anointing had also been combined with healing. Although it grew out of the temple ordinances in Nauvoo, the practice by women was carried on outside the temple. Even after the establishment of the Endowment House in Salt Lake in 1855, the ordinance took place both within the confines of sacred structures and in the privacy of individual homes. The wording took different forms as the occasion demanded. One of the most common uses of the washing and anointing blessing came as women administered to each other prior to childbirth.

That women could and did participate in blessing and healing the sick was a clearly established and officially sanctioned fact by the time the Saints established a refuge in the Great Basin. Women such as Sarah Leavitt and Edna Roberts left records of their experiences with healings in Kirtland, Ohio.[2] In Nauvoo the prophet Joseph

Smith not only formed the Relief Society as an essential part of the church, but he also introduced the ceremony of the temple endowment, including washings and anointings. With the coming of the Relief Society, women had an organization through which they manifested the gifts of the spirit. Of this period Susa Young Gates, a daughter of Brigham Young, wrote: "The privileges and powers outlined by the Prophet in those first meetings [of the Relief Society] have never been granted to women in full even yet." Then she asked, "Did those women, do you and I, live so well as to be worthy of them all?"[3]

There is considerable evidence in the minutes of the Nauvoo Relief Society meetings to suggest that Joseph Smith envisioned the Relief Society as an independent organization for women parallel to the priesthood organization for men.[4] Yet both seemed to come under the aegis of the priesthood as a power from God, not as an administrative entity.

Women themselves saw their organization as more than a charitable society. Spiritual gifts such as speaking in tongues and healing the sick were not only discussed but openly practiced by the sisters. With Smith's approval, his wife Emma and her counselors laid hands on the sick and blessed them to be healed. The fifth time the Relief Society convened, Sarah Cleveland invited the sisters to speak freely, and women stood one at a time in this testimony meeting. Sister Durfee was among those who spoke. She "bore testimony to the great blessing she received when administered to after the last meeting by Emma Smith and [her] Counselors [Sarah] Cleveland and [Elizabeth] Whitney, she said she never realized more benefit through an administration." She added that she had been healed and "thought the sisters had more faith than the brethren." Following the meeting Sarah Cleveland and Elizabeth Whitney administered to another Relief Society sister, Mrs. Abigail Leonard, "for the restoration of health."[5]

In the intervening week someone apparently reported to Joseph Smith that women were laying their hands on the sick and blessing them. His reply to the question of the propriety of such acts was simple. He told the women in the next meeting "there could be no evil in it, if God gave his sanction by healing. . . . there could be no more sin in any female laying hands on the sick than in wetting the face with water." He also indicated that there were sisters who were ordained to heal the sick and that it was their privilege to do so. "If the sisters should have faith to heal," he said, "let all hold their tongues."[6]

In 1857 Mary Ellen Kimball recorded her visit to a sick woman in company with Presindia, her sister-wife. They washed and anointed Susannah, cooked her dinner, and watched her "eat pork and potatoes" with a gratifying appetite. "I felt to rejoice with her for I shall never forget the time when I was healed by the power of God through faith in him which power has again been restored *with* the priesthood" (a phrase which indicates a distinction in Mary Ellen's mind): "But after I returned home I thought of the instructions I had received from time to time that the priesthood was not bestowed upon woman. I accordingly asked Mr. [Heber C.] Kimball if women had a right to wash and anoint the sick for the recovery of their health or is it mockery in them to do so. He replied inasmuch as they are obedient to their husbands, they have a right to administer in that way in the name of the Lord Jesus Christ but not by authority of the priesthood invested in them for that authority is not given to woman." Mary Ellen then noted an argument that would calm apprehensions for the next four decades: "He also said they might administer by the authority given to their husbands in as much as they were one with their husband."[7]

At the same time strong official encouragement for women to develop and use their spiritual powers is evident. Brigham Young, speaking on 14 November 1869, scolded both men and women for not improving themselves. The example he cited was of a sick child. "Why do you not live so as to rebuke disease?" he demanded. "It is your privilege to do so without sending for the Elders." He laid down some practical advice; if the child was ill of a fever or of an upset stomach, treat those symptoms by all means, beware of too much medicine, and remember that prevention is better than cure. He ended by addressing himself specifically to mothers: "It is the privilege of a mother to have faith and to administer to her child; this she can do herself, as well as sending for the Elders to have benefit of their faith."[8] Having enough faith to heal was clearly, for Young, "practical religion" like having enough food on hand.

The year before in Cache Valley, Elder Ezra T. Benson had called on all the women who had been ordained to wash and anoint to exercise their power to rebuke an unspecified disease which so destructively coursed its way through the valley.[9] This record neither identifies the ordained women nor who ordained them. It only said they were "ordained to wash and anoint." Zina Huntington Young's journal mentions several healings. On Joseph Smith's birthday in 1881, she washed and anointed one woman "for her health" and administered to another "for her hearing." She remembered the prophet's birthday and reminisced about the days in Nauvoo when she was one of his plural wives: "I have practiced much with My Sister Presendia Kimball while in Nauvoo & ever since before Joseph Smiths death. He blest Sisters to bless the sick." Three months later in March 1890: "I went to see Chariton [her son] & administered to him, felt so sad to see him suffer." The next year she notes with satisfaction hearing an address by Bishop Whitney wherein he "blest the Sisters in having faith to administer to there own families in humble faith not saying by the Authority of the Holy priesthood but in the name of Jesus Christ."[10]

Still, healing by women caused some confusion. This quiet, routine practice on the local level occasionally raised questions which, when answered publicly by church leaders or the Relief Society, seemed to start a ripple of uneasiness which sooner or later set off another inquiry. Church leaders began to issue general cautions about women blessing the sick. Angus Cannon, president of the Salt Lake Stake, included the following in his answer to a question about women holding the priesthood: "Women could only hold the priesthood in connection with their husbands; man held the priesthood independent of woman. The sisters have a right to anoint the sick, and pray the Father to heal them, and to exercise that faith that will prevail with God; but women must be careful how they use the authority of the priesthood in administering to the sick."[11] Two years later on 8 August 1880, John Taylor's address on "The Order and Duties of the Priesthood" reaffirmed that women "hold the Priesthood, only in connection with their husbands, they being one with their husbands."[12]

A circular letter sent from Salt Lake that October "to all the authorities of the Priesthood and Latter-day Saints" described the organization of the Relief Society, its composition, its purposes, the qualifications for its officers, and their duties. The letter includes a section called "The Sick and Afflicted": "It is the privilege of all faithful women and lay members of the Church, who believe in

Christ, to administer to all the sick or afflicted in their respective families, either by the laying on of hands, or by the anointing with oil in the name of the Lord: but they should administer in these sacred ordinances, not by virtue and authority of the priesthood, but by virtue of their faith in Christ, and the promises made to believers: and thus they should do in all their ministrations."[13] It seems clear that the First Presidency was answering one question: anointing and blessing the sick is not an official function of the Relief Society since any faithful member may perform this action. However, by specifying women's right to administer to the sick "in their respective families," church leaders raised another question: what about administering to those outside the family? They gave no answer, although the practice of calling for the elders or calling for the sisters had certainly been established.

Another question also bears on the topic: "Is it necessary for sisters to be set apart to officiate in the sacred ordinances of washing, anointing, and laying on of hands in administering to the sick?" Eliza R. Snow used the columns of the *Woman's Exponent* in 1884 to answer: "It certainly is not. Any and all sisters who honor their holy endowments, not only have the right, but should feel it a duty whenever called upon to administer to our sisters in these ordinances, which God has graciously committed to His daughters as well as to His sons; and we testify that when administered and received in faith and humility they are accompanied with all mighty power. Inasmuch as God our Father has revealed these sacred ordinances and committed them to His Saints, it is not only our privilege but our imperative duty to apply them for the relief of human suffering." Eliza Snow in 1884 then echoed the language of Joseph Smith in his 28 April 1842 instructions to the Relief Society: "thousands can testify that God has sanctioned the administration of these ordinances [of healing the sick] by our sisters with the manifestation of His healing influence."[14]

In answering the question of who should "officiate in the sacred ordinances" Eliza Snow's language is instructive. By limiting its performance to those who have been endowed, she definitely placed the source of their authority under the shelter of those ordinances in the temple. In other words she saw washing and anointing the sick as an *ordinance* that could and did take place outside the confines of the temple. Women through their endowment had both the authority and obligation to perform them.

Two differing points of view were not in print. Eliza Snow and the First Presidency agreed that the Relief Society had no monopoly on the ordinance of administration by and for women. The First Presidency, however, implied that the ordinance should be limited to the woman's family without specifying any requirement but faithfulness. Eliza Snow, on the other hand, said nothing of limiting administrations to the family—indeed the implication is clear that anyone in need of a blessing should receive it—but said that only women who have been endowed may officiate.

As washings and anointings continued, women attending a Relief Society conference in 1886 heard a Sister Tenn Young urge them: "I wish to speak of the great privilege given to us to wash and to anoint the sick and suffering of our sex. I would counsel every one who expects to become a Mother to have these ordinances administered by some good faithful sister." She later gave instructions how it should be done. Her counsel was endorsed by Mary Ann Freeze who "said she attended to this and the curse to bring forth in sorrow was almost taken away."[15]

But doubts kept surfacing among women whose desire for approval from their presiding brethren inevitably led to questions of propriety. Answers varied, however, depending on who provided them.

In 1888 Emmeline B. Wells, editor of the *Exponent* and soon to be president of the Relief Society, sent church president Wilford Woodruff a list of questions on the topic of washing and anointings. Her questions, and his response, follow:

"First: Are sisters justified in administering the ordinance of washing and anointing previous to confinements to those who have received their endowments and have married men outside of the Church?

"Second: Can anyone who has not had their endowments thus be administered to by the sisters if she is a faithful Saint in good standing and has not yet had the opportunity of going to the temple for the ordinances?"

"To begin with," wrote Woodruff, "I desire to say that the *ordinance* of washing and anointing is one that should only be administered in Temples or other holy places which are dedicated for the purpose of giving endowments to the Saints. That *ordinance* might not be administered to any one whether she has received or has not received her endowments, in any other place or under any other circumstances.

"But I imagine from your questions that you refer to a practice that has grown up among the sisters of washing and anointing sisters who are approaching their confinement. If so, this is not, strictly speaking, an ordinance, unless it be done under the direction of the priesthood and in connection with the ordinance of laying on of hands for the restoration of the sick.

"There is no impropriety in sisters washing and anointing their sisters in this way, under the circumstances you describe; but it should be understood that they do this, not as members of the priesthood, but as members of the Church, exercising faith for, and asking the blessings of the Lord upon, their sisters, just as they and every member of the church might do in behalf of the members of their families."[16]

Woodruff's distinctions between the *temple ordinance* of washing and anointing, the church *member's practice* of washing and anointing, and the *priesthood ordinance* of anointing in connection with a blessing did not directly address the position Eliza R. Snow had taken earlier that only endowed women should administer to others. But the issue became more confused. When the same act was performed and very nearly the same words used among women in the temple, among women outside the temple, and among men administering to women, the disinction—in the average mind—was shadowy indeed.

In 1889 Zina D. H. Young, addressing a general conference of the Relief Society, gave the sisters advice on a variety of topics. Between wheat storage and silk culture came this paragraph: "It is the privilege of the sisters, who are faithful in the discharge of their duties, and have received their endowments and blessings in the house of the Lord, to administer to their sisters, and to the little ones, in time of sickness, in meekness and humility, ever being careful to ask in the name of Jesus, and to give God the glory."[17] Although she does not specify whether the "privilege" refers to washing and anointing or both, she reaffirms—without saying so—that it is not a priesthood ordinance. She also reiterates Eliza's position that it was a privilege of the endowed.

As the last decade of the nineteenth century closed, refinements were being added, both officially and in the wards and stakes.

In 1893 the *Young Women's Journal* advised girls to get enough faith
to be healed since it is "much easier, . . . much less troublesome and
expensive" than medical treatment. The writer then offered a program for increasing faith: "Do not wait until you are sick nigh unto
death before making a trial of your faith and the power of God. The
next time you have a headache take some oil and ask God to heal you.
If you have a touch of sore throat, try the oil and a little prayer before
you try a single thing besides. Go to bed and see if you are not better
in the morning. If you are, then go on adding experience to experience until you have accumulated a store of faith that will all be needed
when your body is weak, and you are sick unto death . . . and if you
still feel sick ask your mother or your father to administer to you. Try
that; then if that fails, and they wish to call in Elders, let them do so,
and thus exhaust the ordinances of the priesthood before you take
the other step [of calling a doctor]."[18] This brisk matter-of-factness
echoes Brigham Young's practical heartiness—there is nothing mysterious or mystical here about faith and spiritual gifts. But perhaps
most revealing is the attitude of spiritual self-sufficiency and the
interchangeability of the mother and father as administrators. If this
article reflects practice among the membership at large, administrations were far from being confined to men holding the priesthood.

Another revealing example occurred in 1895 when Brother
Torkel Torkelson, widely in demand in his community to bless the
sick, records that two sisters "came to my house to wash and anoint
my wife before her confinement. Since it happened that I was at
home, the sisters called upon me to bless her. After I had blessed her
and then sealed the holy ordinance which the sisters had performed,
. . . I could see the power of God come upon" her, and she prophesied
in tongues upon him, his household, and the unborn child.[19] It is
interesting that Torkelson blessed his wife because "it happened that
I was at home" and that he terms the sisters' service a "holy ordinance." The distinction drawn at the high levels was not so restricting
at the lower.

In the twentieth century, controversy continued over the
traditions and policies touching on women's administrations to the
sick in general and washing and anointing specifically. On 16 September 1901 a general board meeting of the Relief Society discussed
"whether the sisters should seal the annointing after washings and
annointings. Pres. [Elmina S.] Taylor said that she thought it was all

right. She had received just as great benefit from the sealing of the sisters as from the brethren, but thought it wise to ask the Priesthood to seal the annointing when it was get-at-able." Her own testimony that she had been as greatly benefited from the sisters as from the brothers suggests that she did not believe that a man with priesthood ordination might be more efficacious, only that she thought there was wisdom in including the priesthood holders as much as possible. This interpretation is borne out by her next statement: "And if the brethren decided that women could not seal the annointing then we should do as they say," but she could not see any reason why women could not: "Aunt Zina did."

Over five years earlier, Ruth Fox recorded a discussion with the same gently-redoubtable Zina Young. "When asked if women held the priesthood in connection with their husbands, [she said] that we should be thankful for the many blessings we enjoyed and say nothing about it. If you plant a grain of wheat and keep poking and looking at it to see if it was growing you would spoil the root. The answer was very satisfying to me."[20]

But always someone was eager to poke, and each time the spiritual roots of the women were imperiled. Some, such as Louisa Lulu Greene Richards, former editor of the *Woman's Exponent*, responded indignantly. On 9 April 1901 she wrote a terse letter to church president Lorenzo Snow concerning an article she read in the *Deseret News* the previous day which stated: "Priest, Teacher or Deacon may administer to the sick, and so may a member, male or female, but neither of them can seal the anointing and blessing, because the authority to do that is vested in the Priesthood after the order of Melchisedek." The question of sealing was thus added to the long list of ambiguities. Lulu said, "If the information given in the answer is absolutely correct, then myself and thousands of other members of the Church have been misinstructed and are laboring under a very serious mistake, which certainly should be authoritatively corrected." She gives a hint of the kind of authority that would be necessary by stating firmly, "Sister Eliza R. Snow Smith, who received the instructions from the Prophet Joseph Smith, her husband [the man to whom she is writing is Eliza's brother], taught the sisters in her day, that a very important part of the sacred ordinance of administration to the sick was the sealing of the anointing and blessings, and should never be omitted. And we follow the pattern she gave us continually. We do not seal in the authority of the Priesthood, but in the name of our Lord and Saviour, Jesus Christ."[21]

Over the next few years, however, an emerging definition of priesthood authority and an increased emphasis on its importance would remove more and more spiritual responsibilities from women and cluster them to the priesthood. The very statements authorizing the continuance of women's blessings only signaled their dependence on that permission. One month later the general presidency of the Relief Society sent President Snow a copy of President Woodruff's letter of 1888 to Emmeline B. Wells. This letter, discussed earlier, distinguished between washings and blessings as an ordinance (and hence confined to the temple under priesthood authority) and as a sisterly act.[22] As president of the church, Snow reaffirmed this position with the exception that blessings should be "confirmed" rather than "sealed."[23]

Sometime during the first decade of the new century, the Relief Society circulated a letter on Relief Society letterhead called simply "Answers to Questions." Undated, it ended with the notation: "Approved by the First Presidency of the Church." This two-page letter was the most complete document on the subject thus far.

Depending on the extent to which this letter was circulated, it may have been a response to an unsigned 1903 *Young Woman's Journal* lesson that asserted: "Only the higher or Melchisedek Priesthood has the right to lay on hands for the healing of the sick, or to direct the administration . . . though to pray for the sick is the right that necessarily belongs to every member of the Church."[24] This may be the earliest published claim that only the Melchizedek priesthood had authority to heal. But the Relief Society's approved letter directly countered that position.

This letter clarified some issues that had previously been ambiguous or contradictory. Administrations by women to the sick did not necessarily fall as a Relief Society function, but it clearly indicated that women did not need priesthood permission or participation to perform these duties. Quoting Eliza R. Snow's position gave any endowed woman authority to perform such services. Confining the blessings to one's own family was not necessary. The letter also cautioned women to avoid resemblances in language to temple ceremonies, and although the blessings should be sealed, the sisters did not need a priesthood holder to do it.[25]

Nephi Pratt, LDS mission president in Portland, Oregon, wrote church president Joseph F. Smith in 1908 to inquire if in setting Relief Society sisters apart he should give them authority to wash and anoint sisters for their confinement and also whether there were any forms they should follow. President Smith answered that the washings and anointings in question was a practice that "Some of our Relief Society Sisters appear to have confounded . . . with one of the temple ordinances. . . . We desire you therefore to impress upon the sisters of your Relief Society that this practice is in no sense whatever an ordinance, and must not be regarded as such, unless it be attended to under the direction of proper authority in connection with the ordinance of laying on of hands for the healing of the sick."

He emphasized, however, that even women who had not received their endowments could participate in these washings and anointings "as there is no impropriety whatever in their doing so, inasmuch as they do it in a proper way, that is, in the spirit of faith and prayer, and without assumption of special authority, no more in fact than members of the church generally need to be barred from receiving a blessing at the hands of faithful women. . . . As to the particular form of words to be used, there is none, not any more than there is for an elder to use in administering to the sick."[26]

On 17 December 1909 the First Presidency, still headed by Joseph F. Smith, again endorsed President Woodruff's 1888 letter to Emmeline B. Wells, making one correction: "namely in the clause pertaining to women administering to children, President [Anthon H.] Lund had said those sisters need not necessarily be only those who had received their endowments, for it was not always possible for women to have that privilege and women of faith might do so [give blessings]."[27]

Apparently for the first time, directly and decisively, a president of the church enunciated a policy about who could give and receive such blessings, separating such actions from temple ceremonies and making them rites accessible to any member of the church, male or female. But the matter was not yet laid to rest. The quiet practice of washing and anointing among women went on, but it was accompanied by greater uneasiness, by more questions, and by greater uncertainty about the propriety of such actions.

The Oakley (Idaho) Second Ward Relief Society minute book contains in a rare undated entry, the written-out blessing to be pronounced in washing, anointing, and sealing that anointing for pregnant women prior to giving birth. Even though Joseph F. Smith had said there were no special forms for such occasions, it seems that the sisters were more comfortable with one written out. To what extent they followed the pattern or deviated from it is not known, but the very existence of such a document bespeaks an insistence that it be done, that it be done in a certain way, and that it be linked to the Relief Society. They did follow earlier counsel to avoid the wording used in the temple.

The first two blessings follow each other very closely with only minor changes in the wording. They were specific and comprehensive: "We anoint your spinal column that you might be strong and healthy no disease fasten upon it no accident belaff [befall] you, your kidneys that they might be active and healthy and preform their proper functions, your bladder that it might be strong and protected from accident, your Hips that your system might relax and give way for the birth of your child, your sides that your liver, your lungs, and spleen that they might be strong and preform their proper functions, . . . your breasts that your milk may come freely and you need not be afflicted with sore nipples as many are, your heart that it might be comforted." They continued by requesting blessings from the Lord on the unborn child's health and expressed the hope that it might not come before its "full time" and "the child shall present right for birth and that the afterbirth shall come at its proper time . . . and you need not flow to excess. . . . We anoint . . . your thighs that they might be healthy and strong that you might be exempt from cramps and from the bursting of veins. . . . That you might stand upon the earth [and] go in and out of the Temples of God."[28]

The document combines practical considerations, more common to women's talk over the back fence, with the reassuring solace and compassion of being anointed with the balm of sisterhood.[29] The women sealed the blessing: "Sister _____ we unitedly lay our hands upon you to seal this washing and anointing wherewith you have been washed and anointed for your safe delivery, for the salvation of you and your child and we ask God to let his special blessings to rest upon you, that you might sleep sweet at night that your dreams might be pleasant and that the good spirit might guard and protect you from every evil influence spirit and power that you may go your full time and the every blessing that we have asked God to confer upon you and your offspring may be litterly fulfiled that all fear and dread may be taken from you and that you might trust in God. All these blessings we unitedly seal upon you in the name of Jesus Christ Amen."[30] The tender attention to both the woman's psychological and physical state is an example of loving service and gentleness.

That this widespread practice continued in similar form for several more decades is illustrated in an account written by a Canadian sister: "In the years from the early 1930s on, in the Calgary Ward R. S. under presidents—Bergeson, Maude Hayes, Lucile Ursenbach, the sisters often asked for a washing and blessing before going into the hospital for an operation or childbirth. In this ordinance two sisters washed the parts of the body, pronouncing appropriate words of prayer and blessing, being advised to avoid similarity to expressions used in a temple ordinance, and at the conclusion put their hands on the head of the recipient and, in the name of the Lord pronounced a further blessing."[31]

In Cache Valley a 1910 Relief Society meeting was given over to testimonies of healing. President Lucy S. Cardon "read some instructions to the sisters on the washing and anointing [of] the sick and how it should be done properly." One sister then "asked a question of the subj." of washing and anointing, and Martha Meedham, with a brisk earthiness that comes off the page, answered that "she had done as much washing and anointing as anyone in this Stake. Related an experience of a blessing which she had given while she was in Salt Lake. Said she wanted to spend the rest of her life in doing good to others and blessing and confirming them. Related of experiences where all had blessed and anointed people. Said she had written Pres. J. F. Smith on the sub. and he told her to keep on and bless & comfort as she had done in the past. It was a gift that was only given to a few, but all sisters who desired and are requested can perform this."

Along with a number of other women the local Relief Society president, Margaret Ballard, "spoke of her exp[erience] in washing and anointing and said they had carried out these instructions given." The next sentence speaks volumes not only for the independence of the Relief Society but perhaps also of mingled pride and trepidation: "The sisters felt that the Bishop should be acqua[i]nted with the work we do."[32] Ballard continued, telling the sisters "how she had been impressed to bless and administer to her father who was sick and suffering and he had been healed. Had also been impressed to bless her husband and he was healed." The meeting closed appropriately with singing "Count Your Many Blessings."

Two years later, in October 1914, President Joseph F. Smith and his counselors sent a letter to bishops and stake presidents, establishing official policy on "Relief Society Sisters Regarding Anointing the Sick." For the first time such a document did not come through the Relief Society itself.[33] Little of the information was new. It formalized policy that had taken shape over the years: Lorenzo Snow's stipulation that the blessing be confirmed rather than sealed, Wilford Woodruff's that it was not a Relief Society function and neither was it an ordinance. The only new policy seems to be that such work comes under "the direction of" the bishop.

At the 13 April 1921 general conference, Elder Charles W. Penrose reported women asking "if they did not have the right to administer to the sick" and he, quoting Jesus' promise to his apostles of the signs that will follow believers, conceded that there might be "Occasions when perhaps it would be wise for a woman to lay her hands upon a child, or upon one another sometimes, and there have been appointments made for our sisters, some good women, to anoint and bless others of their sex who expect to go through times of great personal trial, travail and 'labor;' so that is all right, so far as it goes. But when women go around and declare that they have been set apart to administer to the sick and take the place that is given to the elders of the Church by revelation as declared through James of old, and through the Prophet Joseph in modern times, that is an assumption of authority and contrary to scripture, which is that when people are sick they shall call for the elders of the Church and they shall pray over them and officially lay hands on them."[34] Even though he cited the authority of Joseph Smith, Penrose contradicted the extension of healing privileges to women by Smith. In fact Smith had cited that same scripture in the 12 April 1842 Relief Society meeting but ironically had made a far different commentary: "These signs . . . should follow all that believe whether male or female."[35]

Throughout the 1920s church leaders drew bolder lines between spiritual gifts and priesthood powers. With the clarification of the priesthood role in healing came further restrictions of a woman's sphere. Church leaders made it clear that women did not have right to priesthood power. Continuing redefinition of priesthood held that healing, anointing with oil, and so on were exclusive functions of elders.

By 1928 President Heber J. Grant defended the priesthood against "complaint . . . about the domination of the people by those who preside over them." He quoted the description of the ideal way in which priesthood authority is to function, found in Doctrine and Covenants 121, and then asked rhetorically, "Is it a terrible thing to exercise the priesthood of the living God in the way that the Lord prescribes: 'By kindness and gentleness'"?[37] The pattern had now been established, clarified, and validated.

The strength of that pattern can be seen through a letter from Martha A. Hickman who wrote to the Relief Society general president, Louise Yates Robison, asking:

"Is it orthodox and sanctioned by the Church today to perform 'washing' and 'anointings' for the sick (sisters) especially in preparation for confinement in childbirth?

"Some have advocated that the proper procedure would be to have a special administration by some member bearing the Priesthood for those desiring a special blessing at this time.

"Some years ago when our temples did away with this ordinance for the sick and expectant mothers, in many of our wards in this stake, as well as adjoining stakes, committees of sisters, generally two or three in each committee, were called and set apart for this work of 'washing' and 'anointing,'" in their respective wards, wherever this ordinance was desired.

"I happen to be the head of this committee in the First Ward of Logan Stake. We have officiated in this capacity some ten years, have enjoyed our calling, and have been appreciated. However, since above questions have arisen we do not feel quite at ease. We would like to be in harmony, as well as being able to inform correctly those seeking information. Our Stake Relief Society President, nor our Stake President seem to have nothing definite on this matter."[38]

Robison sent Hickman's letter back to her local stake Relief Society president with an attached letter explaining:

"In reference to the question raised, may we say that this beautiful ordinance has always been with the Relief Society, and it is our earnest hope that we may continue to have that privilege, and up to the present time the Presidents of the Church have always allowed

it to us. There are some places, however, where a definite stand
against it has been taken by the Priesthood Authorities, and where
such is the case we cannot do anything but accept their will in the
matter. However, where the sisters are permitted to do this for
expectant mothers we wish it done very quietly, and without any
infringement upon the Temple service. It is in reality a mother's
blessing, and we do not advocate the appointment of any committees
to have this in charge, but any worthy good sister is eligible to perform
this service if she has faith, and is in good standing in the Church. It
is something that should be treated very carefully, and as we have
suggested, with no show or discussion made of it.

"We have written to Sister Hickman and told her to consult
you in this matter, as it is always our custom to discuss matters of this
kind with our Stake [Relief Society] Presidents, and have them advise
the sisters in their Wards."[39]

There is an air of almost wistful timidity about Robison's
letter that bespeaks near resignation toward the change that was
happening, not necessarily because the policy against blessings had
change *per se* but because policy about the priesthood in general had
changed the environment in which the blessings by women occurred.
Non-priesthood blessings were now suspect. One of the last docu-
ments on the subject is a little notebook containing a record of
"Washing[s] and Annointing[s] done by sisters in 31st Ward" in Salt
Lake City. It begins in 1921: "Sister Dallie Watson for confinement,
Dec. 1, 1921—by Emma Goodard and Mary E. Creer. 1033 Lake
Street." Every few weeks there is another entry, usually for childbirth
or illness. The last entry is a 2 July 1945 washing and anointing for
Jane Coulam Moore by three sisters, one of whom is the same Emma
Goddard who had officiated twenty-four years earlier at the first
anointing.[40]

The next year brought the official death knell of this particular spiritual gift. On 29 July 1946 Elder Joseph Fielding Smith of the
Quorum of the Twelve Apostles wrote to Belle S. Spafford, the Relief
Society general president, and her counselors, Marianne C. Sharp
and Gertrude R. Garff: "While the authorities of the Church have
ruled that it is permissible, under certain conditions and with the
approval of the priesthood, for sisters to wash and anoint other
sisters, yet they feel that it is far better for us to follow the plan the
Lord has given us and send for the Elders of the Church to come and

administer to the sick and afflicted."[41] It would certainly be difficult for a sister to say that she did *not* wish to follow "the plan the Lord has given us" by asking for administration from her sisters rather than from the elders. One Relief Society worker in Canada recalled: "This ordinance was a comfort and strength to many. But it was discontinued and the sisters were asked to call for administration by the Priesthood instead when necessary and desirable."[42] Elder Smith's pronouncement ended the practice where it had not already stopped. We have no further evidence of washing and anointing blessings being given by women. However, since the original publication of this essay in 1981, over a dozen women have told the author of their experiences with blessings and healing. One woman gathered her sister's frail, cancer-ridden body in her arms and blessed her with one pain-free day. Two other women, in separate instances, each blessed and healed a child in her care. Neither of these women had ever discussed the blessing with anyone before for fear it would be considered "inappropriate." Several women together blessed a close friend just prior to her having a hysterectomy. Others asked that their experience not be mentioned—again fearing that what had been personal and sacred to them would be misunderstood and and viewed as inappropriate by others. Of course, the same kinds of blessings, when performed by priesthood holders, are commonly told in church meetings as faith-promoting experiences and are accepted by members of the church in that spirit.[43]

A 1981 article in the church's *New Era* magazine, entitled "President Kimball Speaks out on Administration to the Sick," bears on the topic at hand. Although it does not deal with the practice of washing and anointing the sick, it does state what appears to be current church policy in regard to blessing the sick: "The administration proper is an ordinance of two parts, the anointing and the sealing. An elder pours a small quantity of oil on the head of the one to be blessed, near the crown of the head if convenient, *never on the other parts of the body* [italics added], and in the name of the Lord and by authority of the priesthood, he anoints the person for the restoration of health. The sealing is performed by two or more elders, one of whom, as mouth, seals the anointing and gives an appropriate blessing, also in the name of Jesus Christ and by authority of the priesthood." Allowances can be made for unusual circumstances, for example, when only one Melchizedek Priesthood holder is present.

In this case, the article states, a "substitute program is followed." One elder, presumably acting alone may "give a blessing, likewise in the name of the Lord and by authority of the Melchizedek Priesthood. . . . Only by the priesthood are results manifested."

Nowhere in the article does it mention an instance where a mother, wife, or other female could assist the priesthood holder. It does, however, state: "Then there is the prayer that is unlike the administration; it makes request to the Lord to heal and may be offered by any soul who has a desire to do so and is not an ordinance in the same sense. The prayer is a request for the Lord to act, whereas the blessing or the administration is given by the brethren in the name of Christ."[43]

Perhaps Mormon women today can gain some measure of comfort from Elder James E. Talmage, who wrote: "When the frailties and imperfections of mortality are left behind, in the glorified state of the blessed hereafter, husband and wife will administer in their respective stations, seeing and understanding alike, cooperating to the full in the government of their family kingdom. Then shall women be recompensed in rich measure for all the injustice womanhood has endured in mortality. . . . Mortal eye cannot see nor mind comprehend the beauty, glory, and majesty of a righteous woman made perfect in the celestial kingdom of God."[44] But President Joseph Fielding Smith spoke more to the point when he said: "There is nothing in the . . . gospel which declares that men are superior to women. . . . Women do not hold the priesthood, but if they are faithful and true, they will become priestesses and queens in the kingdom of God, and that implies that they will be given authority."[45]

Susa Young Gates's statement still rings clear, "The privileges and powers outlined by the Prophet [Joseph Smith] . . . have never been granted to women in full even yet." When the lives of Latter-day Saint women—their faith, spirituality, devotion, and sacrifice—are seen across the history of the church, we find a record as venerable as that of men. We must respond to Susa's question, "Did those women . . . live so well as to be worthy of them all?" in the affirmative.

NOTES

1. For the most comprehensive studies to date of the history of the temple ordinance, see D. Michael Quinn, "Latter-day Saint Prayer Circles,"

Brigham Young University Studies 19 (Fall 1978), David John Buerger, "The Development of the Mormon Temple Endowment Ceremony," *Dialogue: A Journal of Mormon Thought* 20 (Winter 1987), and Andrew F. Ehat, unpublished paper in author's possession.

    2. For examples of women participating in healing in Kirtland, see Linda King Newell and Valeen Tippetts Avery, "Sweet Counsel and Seas of Tribulation: The Religious Life of the Women in Kirtland," *Brigham Young University Studies* 20 (Winter 1980). For additional accounts, see Carol Lynn Pearson, *Daughters of Light* (Salt Lake City: Bookcraft, 1973).

    3. Susa Young Gates, "The Open Door for Woman," *Young Women's Journal* 16 (1905): 117.

    4. See Newell, "Gifts of the Spirit: Women's Share," *Sisters in Spirit: Mormon Women in Historical and Cultural Perspective* (Urbana: University of Illinois Press, 1987), 114-16, for a more detailed discussion of this issue.

    5. "A Record of the Organization, and Proceedings of The Female Relief Society of Nauvoo," 19 Apr. 1842, microfilm of original, Joseph Smith collection, archives, Historical Department, Church of Jesus Christ of Latter-day Saints; hereafter cited as LDS archives; also microfilm and typescript, Library and Archives, Reorganized Church of Jesus Christ of Latter Day Saints, Independence, Missouri.

    6. Ibid., 28 Apr. 1842.

    7. Mary Ellen Kimball Journal, 2 March 1856, LDS archives (italics added).

    8. *Journal of Discourses* (Liverpool and London, 1856), 13: 155; hereafter cited as JD.

    9. Cache Valley Stake Relief Society Minute Book A, 1869-81, 18 June 1868, LDS archives.

    10. Zina Diantha Huntington Smith Young Diary, Vol. 13, Aug.-Dec. 1881, LDS archives.

    11. *Woman's Exponent* 7 (1 Nov. 1878): 86.

    12. JD 21:367-68.

    13. Circular Letter, Salt Lake City, Utah, 6 Oct. 1880, LDS archives.

    14. *Woman's Exponent* 13 (15 Sept. 1884): 61.

    15. Cache Valley Stake Relief Society Minute Book B, 46-48, 11 Sept. 1886, LDS archives.

    16. Wilford Woodruff to Emmeline B. Wells, editor, *Woman's Exponent*, 27 Apr. 1881, Correspondence of the First Presidency, LDS archives.

    17. *Woman's Exponent* 17 (15 Aug. 1889): 172.

    18. *Young Woman's Journal* 4 (4 Jan. 1893): 176-77.

    19. Diary of Torkel Torkelson, 7 Nov. 1895, LDS archives; translated by Richard Jensen.

20. Diary of Ruth May Fox, 8 Mar. 1896.

21. Louisa L. G. Richards to President Lorenzo Snow, 9 Apr. 1901, LDS archives.

22. Relief Society Minutes, 1901, LDS archives.

23. Relief Society Minutes, special meeting of officers of the general board, 2 May 1901, 1:352, LDS archives.

24. *Young Woman's Journal* 14 (8 Aug. 1903): 384.

25. James R. Clark, ed., *Messages of the First Presidency*, 6 vols. (Salt Lake City: Bookcraft, 1965-75), 4:314-15.

26. Joseph F. Smith to Nephi Pratt, 18-21 Dec. 1908, Correspondence of the First Presidency, LDS archives.

27. Relief Society Minutes, 17 Dec. 1909, 136.

28. Oakley [Idaho] 2nd Ward Relief Society Minutes, LDS archives.

29. Maureen Ursenbach Beecher, Comments, n.d., 1-2, in author's possession.

30. Oakley [Idaho] 2nd Ward Relief Society Minutes, LDS archives.

31. Lucile H. Ursenbach statement, 14 Aug. 1980, in possession of Maureen Ursenbach Beecher.

32. For this and other testimonies born that day, see Cache Valley Stake Relief Society Minute Book B, 1881-1914, 5 Mar. 1910, 2:438-40, LDS archives.

33. *Messages of the First Presidency*, 4:314-15.

34. *Conference Reports*, 3 Apr. 1921, 190-91.

35. Relief Society Minutes of Nauvoo, 12 Apr. 1842.

36. For a more detailed discussion, see Newel, "Gifts of the Spirit," 36.

37. *Conference Reports*, 5 Oct. 1928, 8-9.

38. Martha A. Hickman to Pres. Louise Y. Robison, 28 Nov. 1935, LDS archives.

39. Louise Y. Robison, 5 Dec. 1935, copy in author's possession.

40. Photocopy of holograph, courtesy Charlott Boden Erickson, LDS archives.

41. Quoted in *Messages of the First Presidency*, 4:314.

42. Ursenbach, statement.

43. Newell, "Gifts of the Spirit: Women's Share," 149 n115.

44. "President Kimball Speaks out on Administration to the Sick," *New Era*, Oct. 1981, 46, 50.

45. James E. Talmage, "The Eternity of Sex," *Young Women's Journal*, 25 (Oct. 1914): 602-603.

46. *Doctrines of Salvation*, 3:178 as quoted in *Choose You This Day*, Melchizedek Priesthood Personal Study Guide, 1980-81 (Salt Lake City: Church of Jesus Christ of Latter-day Saints, Salt Lake City, 1979), 200.

7.
A Demographic Portrait
of the Mormons, 1830-1980

Dean May

THERE ARE FEW BENCHMARKS IN EARLY MORMON HISTORY THAT provide a clear fix on how many Saints there were at any given time. Indeed the first systematic series of data on the number of Mormons worldwide begins in 1879. Before that time most reports on Mormon population were sporadic, partial censuses, or unreliable impressionistic estimates. Moreover Mormons had a vexing habit of avoiding federal censuses; the timing of the Ohio, Missouri, and Illinois migrations made the federal census of little use in reconstructing Mormon population. Add to this the complexities of trying to account for changing birth and death rates, as well as rates of apostasy and conversion, and the task becomes enormously complicated and in the end more speculative than we would wish. Nonetheless, by keeping estimates within limits set by the sporadic censuses which were taken, together with the known demographic behavior of comparable populations, it is possible to come to conclusions that hopefully will be better than intuitive estimates commonly encountered.

By the end of 1830 Mormon congregations in New York and Ohio numbered perhaps 200-500 souls. Joseph Smith reported 70 Mormons in New York,[1] and Parley P. Pratt reported baptizing 127 in Kirtland, Ohio, on his way west in 1830. This number, Pratt wrote, "soon increased to one thousand."[2] Marvin S. Hill, C. Keith Rooker, and Larry T. Wimmer have estimated the overall Kirtland population—Mormon and non-Mormon—between the years 1830 and 1840 from the number of personal property owners taxed each year. They

show the total population growing rapidly from just over 1,000 in
1830 to a peak of 2,500 in 1837, then declining sharply in 1838 and
1839 to a low of 1,704. Milton V. Bachman has reworked the Kirtland
data and found the estimates of Hill, Rooker, and Wimmer to be low
by 700.[3]

As about a third of the Kirtland population was non-Mormon, we can safely conclude that there were at the peak of the Saints'
stay in the area no more than 2,500 Mormons, perhaps fewer. The
decline noted by Hill, Rooker, and Wimmer of 796 persons in
1838-39 can be attributed to Mormons moving to Missouri, but
non-Mormon towns in the area suffered noticeable declines as well,
apparently in response to the economic crisis precipitated by the
panic of 1837. By their data 796 would be the maximum number of
Mormons moving from Ohio to Missouri. Backman, however, reports
the whole population declining by 1,630 persons between 1838-39,
with 1,900 Mormons leaving and 270 non-Mormons moving in. Only
515 left Kirtland as part of the Kirtland Camp en route to Missouri
in July 1838, the rest either leaving the church or making their way
eventually on their own to join the main body of Saints.[4]

By the time they left, the Mormon population in Caldwell
County, Missouri, is reported to have been about 4,900.[5] This figure
indicates a larger population than that suggested by the first formal
church count of Mormons, called "the Lesser Priesthood Enumeration," taken in Nauvoo, Illinois, in 1842. This census lists only 3,000 in
Nauvoo and perhaps 1,000 in the environs—and this after 500-1,000
Saints from Ohio and Canada had joined the Missouri Saints in
Illinois and after the first English migrations to Nauvoo had begun.[6]
Apparently the lesser priesthood brethren took the census with less
than perfect efficiency. Hamlin Cannon listed 2,989 leaving Britain in
1840-42, which, if they all made it to Nauvoo, would by themselves
account for three-quarters of the whole census population.[7]

Perhaps some sense can be made of the matter if we work
backwards from the 1845 census reported in the *Times and Seasons*
(15 November) showing 11,057 in Nauvoo proper and "without the
[city] limits it is supposed there is a third more." Let us assume that
the elastic phrase "it is supposed" is accurate, giving a total Nauvoo-
area Mormon population of 14,742. I have tried to simulate the order
of growth required to reach that population in six years (1840-45,
inclusive), assuming that 90 percent of the annual British migration

reached Nauvoo, a birth rate of 50 per 1,000 and high death rate of 20 per 1,000. If the base population of 1840 was 5,000 and there was a non-British in-migration of 600 each year, the population six years later would be 14,676, or very close to that estimated in the 1845 census. Thus 11,816 persons—5,000 leaving Missouri, 3,600 entering from other states, and 4,216 arriving from England—could have produced the census population of 14,742 in the time shown with an average birthrate and a fairly high death rate.[8]

One could adjust these estimates upward or downward somewhat—but not greatly—without straining credulity. If the 1842 priesthood census was accurate, it would have taken an average non-British in-migration of 1,500 persons each year from 1842-45 to approximate the 1845 census figures. I thus am inclined to consider the 1842 priesthood census incomplete and to have more confidence in an initial population of 5,000 Mormons gathered to Nauvoo from Missouri and Ohio, which provided the base upon which the Mormon population grew by the end of 1845 to 14,000 or 15,000.

Estimating the number of Mormons elsewhere presents equally difficult problems. Wilford Woodruff recorded that in April 1841 there were 5,814 Saints in England.[9] The precision of this figure possibly makes it an actual count of members. Using the same crude rate of natural increase, adding Hamlin Cannon's data on conversions and deducting his recorded out-migration figures and 20 percent decrease for disaffiliation, British membership would have grown to 9,882 by the end of 1846. If we were to allow another 1,000 for Saints elsewhere in Europe and 5,000 for Saints elsewhere in North America, total church membership by 1846 would have been 30,882. I am comfortable with a working estimate of 30,000 for the whole church population, half of which resided in the Nauvoo area, at the time wagons began to pull out into the mire of the Iowa countryside in 1846 on the Saints' way west.

It is also difficult to determine how many of these Saints left Nauvoo and came west. The next figures that can be extrapolated from actual counts come from the 1850 federal censuses for Pottawattamie County, Iowa, and for Utah territory.[10] However, there are problems with using these enumerations. Lowell C. Bennion and Marilyn Wagner in separate studies have found evidence of redundancy in the 1850 census, with some persons being counted twice as residents of settled areas and of new colonies. Moreover it is impossible to know precisely how many non-Mormons were in Utah and in Pottawattamie County at the time. Assuming a 3.5 percent crude rate of natural increase, 2 percent out-migration, 20 percent under-registration of the census, and apply reasonable allowances for the non-Mormon population, I estimate a total western U.S. population of Mormons in 1850 of 17,072, with 41 percent, nearly half, still living in western Iowa.[11]

How many of these 17,072 were recent arrivals from England? We have already accounted for English immigrants up to 1846. By that time they and their children numbered about 4,708 or 32 percent of the population of Nauvoo. From 1846 to 1852, some 6,597 more Mormons boarded emigrant ships in England. If we again assume that about 10 percent stopped along the way in New Orleans, St. Louis, or other river towns and allow a 3 percent rate of natural increase, the new arrivals account for 4,272 persons by 1850. Substracting them from the 17,072 total in the west leaves about 12,800 who could have come west from Nauvoo, but we must consider that a good many of these were born between 1846 and 1850.

A base population of 11,150 leaving Nauvoo could have grown to 12,800 (our calculated figure) by the end of 1850, even if we cut the rate of natural increase to 2 percent for 1846 to allow for high mortality along the Missouri River. But some of the American Saints along the Missouri and in Far West in 1850 had never been part of the Nauvoo population. Those sailing from the east coast and traveling overland from the south numbered at least 338, and it is likely that many other, less well documented, raised the total of the non-Nauvoo American emigration considerably, perhaps to as much as 1,000. Thus about 10,150 (69 percent) of our estimated 14,742 Nauvoo 1846 population had followed Brigham Young and the apostles to the west by 1850. If the proportion of British Saints following Brigham Young west was the same as their proportion of the whole Nauvoo population (probably it was higher) they, together with the British who came after 1845, made up over half (8,980 or 53 percent) of the 17,072 Mormons in the west by 1850. These calculations suggest that the proportion of Mormons migrating west from Nauvoo may have been somewhat less than has been thought (69 percent) and that a very high proportion (53 percent) of western Mormons were British.

After the 1850s we have no clear readings on the population

of the Mormons until 1879, when the first reasonably complete series of official annual LDS statistical reports appeared.[12] Even then the data are difficult to use and to compare with other sources, as they report all church membership only for 1880 and thereafter do not include mission statistical reports, at least not as part of the same listing. I have calculated the Utah church population to 1860, using migration data as 20 percent under-registered, a 3.5 percent rate of natural increase, and a 2 percent out-migration rate, and find the estimated population including 1860 in-migrants to be 41,303. Given the general under-registration of federal censuses after 1850, I find this estimate not unlikely. It is 5,743 short of Wayne Wahlquist's 47,046 estimate of total Utah population—Mormon and non-Mormon—for the same year and some 1,030 greater than the 40,273 federal census count. If Wahlquist's territorial estimate is correct, Mormons accounted for 88 percent of the total territorial population.

These data give us some insight into another interesting question concerning the Mormon population, or at least the Utah Mormon population: how prophetic Colonel Patrick Connor was in suggesting that the influx of non-Mormons following the opening of the precious metal mining industry would diminish if not overcome Mormon control of the territory. Comparing church membership data for Utah with the federal census, we find that eighteen years after the railroad made large-scale mining feasible Mormons had dropped from our 1860 estimate of 88 percent of the population to 79 percent. This figure declined to 66 percent by 1890.[13] Mormons accounted for 67 percent in 1900, 61 percent in 1910, and reached a low point of 55 percent in 1920. Thereafter the proportion of Mormons rose steadily a few percentage points a year, reaching a twentieth-century high of 71.5 percent in 1970, according to data compiled independently by Joseph L. Lyon and Lowell C. Bennion. County percentages for 1970 ranged from 21.9 percent Mormon in Grand County to 93.5 percent in Wayne County. Colonel Connor's hope was realized, though more slowly and not to the degree he had planned. And finally it was the mining of industrial metals and coal—not precious metals—that brought Mormons to near-minority status in 1920. Since 1970 random polls have since consistently found that 75-78 percent of adults in Utah report their religious preference as LDS. In addition, Mormons have had until the mid-1980s almost twice the birthrate of non-Mormons in Utah.[14]

How then can we summarize this profile of Mormon growth over the last 160 years? If my procedures are sound, the numbers are considerably less than is often thought, at least for the Illinois and early Utah periods. The 5,000 leaving Missouri to settle Nauvoo is not far from contemporary estimates. The peak population of 14,000 to 15,000 for Nauvoo is also close to what has been thought, but the estimation of 10,150 leaving Nauvoo to go west is somewhat lower than many have assumed. The 30,000 worldwide population in 1846 is substantially less than contemporary accounts (see *Times and Seasons* 6:1052), which suggest 57,000 to 200,000. Furthermore, it is clear that the 1850 Mormon population was over enumerated in the federal census. I am surprised at my small out-migration estimates to California and elsewhere. I frankly began these calculations expecting to find the territory a wide-open sieve on the California side, an expectation that clearly was not realized. Finally I am impressed with how large a component the English and their children were of the whole western church population by 1850—apparently making up 53 percent of church membership.

Now let me proceed to point out one or two important aspects of Mormon growth. Of all distinctive aspects of Mormon demography, high fertility has been most often noticed. This much is known of Mormon fertility. Mormons had fertility rates approaching natural rates until the 1870s, when evidence of fertility control becomes apparent. Since that time Mormon fertility has tended to follow national trends, though at higher levels. The influence of peer groups, which probably brought a decline in fertility rates in the 1870s, is evident today. Mormons living among non-Mormons have higher fertility rates than their non-Mormon neighbors but smaller fertility rates than Mormons living in predominantly LDS areas.[15] Mormon fertility rates remained high and actually increased during the late 1970s, but declined in the 1980s. The Mormon crude birth rate has tended to be about twice the national average. It is interesting that this maintenance of higher birthrates has continued in spite of increasing affluence and educational status. While the fertility rates of other traditionally high fertility groups have dropped as socioeconomic status has risen, rates among Mormons persist.[16]

The interesting question is: Why do Mormon fertility rates maintain themselves at such high levels? Numerous studies have noted high fertility rates among American frontier populations, but there are also significant declines after the first generation to levels close to the national average.[17] Mormon fertility remains high, one suspects, not because of the frontier heritage *per se* but because of the doctrines and ceremonies established during the frontier period.

One argument for this point of view stems from the attitude of Mormons toward children. In 1960 Phillip Aries pointed out that attitudes toward children have changed dramatically from the Middle Ages, when children mingled freely in adult society and were seen as miniature adults, to the nineteenth century, when children were viewed as occupying a special position and place in society. Nineteenth-century Americans treated children as one does a spaniel— pampering and petting them but not permitting them in adult society or taking them seriously as individuals until they reached an appropriate level of maturity.[18] Some have seen the Mormon fondness for children as a direct heritage of this nineteenth-century predilection, and I would suggest that in part it is—but only in part.[19]

Beginning with the visit of William Chandless in 1855 and continuing through 1975, non-Mormon visitors have kept up a running commentary on the behavior of Mormon children.[20] These observers maintain that Mormon children are doted upon, are present and accepted in adult society, and are not taught to know their place. They are assertive, bold, even brassy, and do not respect adults. I have not researched the subject sufficiently to offer conclusions with confidence, but I wonder if we do not see in Mormondom a combination of the indulgence characteristic of the nineteenth century and the acceptance of children as adults common to an earlier time. Mormon children are doted upon, but equally important they are invited into adult society, as almost every non-Mormon attending Mormon church services has noted. They are accepted in adult society and recognized as individuals from an early age on—given more liberties and accorded more trust than is generally the case in contemporary American society.

All this can be tied, I suspect, both to historical experience and doctrinal roots. Mormon stress on the spiritual maturity and eternal importance of the individual, including the youngest of children, has helped perpetuate among them attitudes toward children that once were widespread but subsequently almost disappeared in nineteenth-century America. It is a persuasive argument for how important the persistence of older traditions can be when they are locked into a provincial culture at a critical time. I will comment on this later, but I see in a similar manner contemporary Mormon fertility rates as an artifact of Mormons' having been a frontier people and then being prevented by provincial self-consciousness from dropping frontier values and habits, especially in those areas where doctrine and belief reinforce the frontier condition.

I have deliberately avoided discussing polygamy as it relates to fertility, but one observation might be appropriate here. Those studies that find an inverse relationship between fertility rates per woman and the practice of polygamy—that women in polygamy bear less children per woman than women in monogamy—an effect noted by several researchers, tend to have been derived from low fertility elite segments of the population and have not considered the effects of polygamy on fertility rates in the aggregate.[21] My guess is that as more sophisticated studies take these factors into consideration we will find that polygamy enhanced rather than depressed aggregate fertility rates.[22]

Another common observation on Mormon fertility is the suggestion that the absence of husbands on missions lowered fertility rates. Obviously in individual instances it did, but since the 1840s the proportion of Mormon men on missions has never reached even half of 1 percent of the whole church membership. Thus the percentage of Mormon men on missions was never enough to be significant.[23]

One other point pertaining to the components of Mormon growth deserves mention. From the church's inception until about 1880, the major portion of new members each year came from convert baptisms. The only nineteenth-century listing that I can find of child baptisms and convert baptisms churchwide was for 1880. It indicates that 3,042 children and 3,606 adults were baptized during the year, with the great portion of adult converts (2,286) coming from Europe.[24] It would seem likely that the church in the 1880s was about to enter an era of some eighty years when the bulk of its growth would be internal. When such data appeared again in 1925, the ratio of child baptisms to convert baptisms had changed significantly—from roughly equal to more than double (225 to 100). The same ratio persisted into 1930 but then dropped sharply in 1935 (189 to 100). During World War II the ratio leapt dramatically (325 to 100), obviously because of the curtailment of European mission activity. Except for the war years, the trend until 1955 was toward a balance between the two. Converts began to outnumber child baptisms at some point between 1955 and 1960. From that time on the ratios drop consistently to a low of 41.4 to 100 in 1979, reversing the 1925 ratio.[25] Mormon fertility remains high but can no longer compete with missionary work in increasing the overall numbers of church members.

Mormon death rates are as notable for being low as Mormon birthrates are for being high. It is unfortunate that we have no data with which to test the hypothesis that Mormon mortality was low in crossing the plains compared with that of other overland migrants. The first death statistics I have been able to find come from a church census of 1852. The federal census for 1850 listed a notoriously high death rate of 21 per 1,000 for Utah territory that year, a statistic which was corrected in the 1860 census, either by better health or by sharper statisticians.

According to these data, church death rates are consistently lower than the national average. It is difficult to explain why except to observe that Utah's urban centers did not have the high concentrations of populations found elsewhere in the United States that served to increase the national average.[26]

Nineteenth-century Mormons were not noted for their careful observance of the Word of Wisdom, especially its proscriptions regarding alcohol and tobacco. However, such observance of the church's dietary laws is apparently the main reason for the present low death rates among their descendants. Joseph L. Lyon and others have studied this phenomenon carefully. Their report, showing incidence of cancer standardized for age and other factors among LDS and non-LDS persons in Utah, indicates that in most types of cancer, including those that should not be affected by tobacco or alcohol, Mormons have substantially lower incidences of cancer than non-Mormons living in Utah.[27] These and other data on Mormon health add up to an expectation of life at birth for Mormon men five years longer than for non-Mormon men and three years longer for Mormon women than for non-Mormon women. These studies do not, however, consider the likely positive effects of Mormon health practices on pregnancy, childbirth, and birth defects.

I have previously noted the high proportion of English Saints in the Mormon church by 1850. I would like to draw upon work done by Charles M. Hatch pertaining to Cache Valley in northern Utah in the nineteenth century to make a point about the cultural importance of the high proportion of foreign-born Mormons in Utah. In a day of general xenophobia, a common charge of nineteenth-century anti-Mormons was that the Saints harbored a high proportion of foreign born who in coming to Utah from their native lands had never been exposed to American values and thus were susceptible to Mormon culture. In 1860 the Cache Valley population was about two-thirds American-born. Ten years later 62 percent were American born, just under two-thirds, and about the same proportion prevailed in 1880. The data indicate a fairly consistent pattern of large American-born majorities who presumably set the social, religious, and cultural tone of Cache Valley towns in the nineteenth century.

A closer look, however, reveals a more complicated picture. Examining the structure of a population uncovers nuances the aggregate figures conceal. A high birth rate or high crime rate, for example, may be a product of how young or how old the population as a whole is rather than of the social habits peculiar to the group. Looking at the age structure of the general population for Cache County in 1860, 1870, and 1880 reveals the broad base characteristic of high fertility populations: a sizable group of young and early middle-aged adults and a sharp drop in the forty-years-old and older categories. In general these were young people, as was common in American frontier areas.

Considering how the foreign-born population fit into the age structure reveals differences more specific to the Mormon frontier. Most of the children, except for those of very recent immigrants, were born in America. The foreign-born population was concentrated in the older age categories, and from age twenty on the proportion of foreign-born exceeded that of the U.S.-born substantially. This phenomenon, clearly evident in 1860, becomes more pronounced in the 1870 population and persists strongly in 1880. Thus if a time machine would permit us to look in on a typical Cache Valley street any time between 1860 and 1880, almost every adult we would greet would be foreign-born, either British or Scandinavian.

Where then would be the two-thirds American majority suggested by the aggregate data? They are virtually all children under the age of fifteen. As we look at the older age groups, the number of American-born is a diminishing part of the total, the great bulk of the population being recent European immigrants to the Mormon Zion.[28]

At first glance one might conclude from this that the tone of society in Utah *was* set by foreigners—persons alien to American traditions. Undoubtedly the contributions of the European population to the cultural heritage of Cache Valley have been greater than is often supposed. But nonetheless most immigrants came to Zion eager to abandon Babylon and to learn from those having authority and status within the Mormon kingdom. Social, cultural, and religious norms were set by this American elite—those who taught the Mormon gospel in Europe, arranged the voyage to America, directed the overland journey, and welcomed the incoming Saints.

If life in nineteenth-century Mormon towns seemed un-American to visitors from the East, the fault (if fault it was) lay with the old Mormons and not the new. They were the most influential shapers of Utah society. This observation may make a point worth noting for Mormons in the late twentieth century. Changes brought about by conversion and full participation in Mormonism are profound. Moreover, in the past the old Mormons, if you will, have at times been a minority in the church yet their value system has for the most part been successfully imparted to those who enter the faith. Growth brings its challenges, but one suspects that the Rocky Mountain Mormon is not likely in the near future to become extinct. Rocky Mountain Mormons still command a numerical majority in the church, but more importantly they dominate culturally.[29]

I remember once asking the teenage daughter of an English regional church leader to name the presidents of the Latter-day Saint church. She did so without hesitation. I then asked her to name the monarchs of Britain. She could not get further than Elizabeth II. This incident argues for the great power of Mormonism to "traditionalize" (to use Brigham Young's term) converts into identifying with the Saints, and adopting values and points of view taught by the significant few sent out from church headquarters—whether missionaries, mission presidents, or general authorities.

This becomes more interesting when we note that some of the cultural traits of Rocky Mountain Mormons are probably as much heirlooms of nineteenth-century historical experience as of official church doctrine and principle. Perry Miller, who thought much about provincial societies and their relationship to the parent society, offered a profound insight in his *The New England Mind from Colony to Province*: "Recurrently the mind of America falls into isolation:

axioms brought to this country—Puritanism, the social contract, Romanticism—and here successfully tried out, have, by the time the American experiment is completed, ceased to be meaningful in Europe; America is repeatedly left, so to speak, with an institution on its hands."[30]

A similar dynamic operated on Mormons in the nineteenth century; axioms of many kinds, such as attitudes toward children or government influence in local affairs, found fertile root among Latter-day Saints and then became institutions that now go out from the Rocky Mountains to all parts of the world as part and parcel of what it means to be Mormon. I do not presume to say whether this is good or bad. But my observations indicate that the historical experience of Mormons has helped greatly to shape Mormon society, including fertility, mortality, and migration patterns. Attitudes formed in the past are now being imparted to hundreds of thousands of converts from all parts of the world by messengers sent out from the heartland of Mormonism. The cultural effects of this process in the twentieth as in the nineteenth century are powerful and enduring.

NOTES

1. Joseph Smith, *History of the Church of Jesus Christ of Latter-day Saints,* ed. B. H. Roberts, 6 vols. (Salt Lake City: Deseret Book Co., 1946-50), 1:133.

2. Parley P. Pratt, *The Autobiography of Parley P. Pratt, ed. Parley P. Pratt, Jr.* (Salt Lake City: Deseret Book Co., 1964), 48.

3. Marvin S. Hill, C. Keith Rooker, and Larry T. Wimmer, "The Kirtland Economy Revisited: A Market Critique of Sectarian Economics," *Brigham Young University Studies* 17 (Summer 1977): 389-482; Milton V. Backman, *The Heavens Resound: A History of the Latter-day Saints in Ohio, 1830-1838* (Salt Lake City: Deseret Book, 1983), 140. Backman's data indicate a maximum of 3,230 in Kirtland in 1838, 2,000 of whom were Mormons.

4. Backman, 140, 335.

5. From *History of Caldwell County* (St. Louis: National Historical Co., 1896), 113, as quoted in B. H. Roberts, *A Comprehensive History of the Church of Jesus Christ of Latter-day Saints,* 6 vols. (Salt Lake City: Deseret News Press, 1930), 1:425.

6. Information from the "Lesser Priesthood Enumeration" was supplied by James L. Kimball. The original of this document is in archives, Historical Department, Church of Jesus Christ of Latter-day Saints, Salt Lake City, Utah; hereafter LDS archives.

7. M. Hamlin Cannon, "Migration of English Mormons to America," *American Historical Review* 57 (Apr. 1947): 436-55.

8. The English figure is Cannon's estimate of numbers of British Saints emigrating less 10 percent to allow for those who, in the United States, did not migrate to Nauvoo.

9. Roberts, *Comprehensive History*, 2:85.

10. There was also an 1853 LDS bishops' census in Utah, representing the population of the territory after the great 1852 migration had reached Utah.

11. U.S. manuscript 1850 census returns for Pottawattamie County, Iowa, and for the Territory of Utah. See also Wayne A. Wahlquist, "Population Growth in the Mormon Core Area: 1847-70," in Richard H. Jackson, ed., *The Mormon Role in the Settlement of the West,* Charles Redd Monographs in Western History, no. 9 (Provo, UT: Brigham Young University Press, 1978), 107-33. For a more detailed discussion of how these numbers were arrived at, see the original version of my article in Thomas G. Alexander and Jessie L. Embry, eds., *After 150 Years: The Latter-day Saints in Sesquicentennial Perspective,* Charles Redd Monographs in Western History, no. 13 (Provo, UT: Charles Redd Center for Western Studies, 1983), 37-69. Tables I-III included various possibilities and calculations of the 1850-53 Mormon population.

Some numbers in the present version of this study are different from the original published version because of more refined calculations and because of an egregious error in the earlier version, pointed out to me by Richard L. Jensen of the Joseph Fielding Smith Institute for Church History at Brigham Young University. In the original essay I underestimated the number of Mormons leaving Nauvoo to come west and also the proportion of English born in that migration. Some demographic data on the Missouri settlement is in Richard E. Bennett, *Mormons at the Missouri* (Norman: University of Oklahoma Press, 1987).

12. Presiding Bishop's Office Statistical Reports for the years indicated in the text and charts, LDS archives.

13. The Utah Mormon population figure is from the Presiding Bishop's Office Reports cited above; the territorial population is from the published U.S. census reports. These figures are:

Year	Territorial Population	Mormon Population	% Mormon
1880	143,963	113,828	79
1890	210,779	138,059	65
1900	276,749	186,341	67
1910	373,351	226,355	61

14. The 1920 and subsequent estimates are from unpublished calculations done independently by Joseph L. Lyon and Lowell C. Bennion using LDS church population records and federal census returns. The telephone polls were conducted by University of Utah scholars in a random survey for medical research.

15. See M. Skolnick et al., "Mormon Demographic History: Nuptiality and Fertility of Once-Married Couples," *Population Studies* 32 (1978): 5-19; Donald W. Hastings, Charles H. Reynolds, and Ray R. Canning, "Mormonism and Birth Planning: The Discrepancy Between Church Authorities' Teachings and Lay Attitudes," *Population Studies* 26 (1972): 19-28; Brian Pitcher, Phillip R. Kunz, and Evan T. Peterson, "Residency Differentials in Mormon Fertility," *Population Studies* 28 (1974): 143-51; James E. Smith and Phillip R. Kunz, "Polygyny and Fertility in Nineteenth-Century America," *Population Studies* 30 (1976): 465-80; and Judith C. Spicer and Susan O. Gustavus, "Mormon Fertility Through Half a Century: Another Test of the Americanization Hypothesis," *Social Biology* 21 (1974): 70-76.

16. The Mormon rate is from the Presiding Bishop's Office Statistical Reports before 1910 and from published *LDS General Reports* thereafter (normally April Conference). The 30.7 figure is from the April 1979 *LDS Conference Report*. The national rates through 1970 are from U.S., Department of Commerce, Bureau of the Census, *Historical Statistics of the United States: Colonial Times to 1970*, Bicentennial Edition, Part I (Washington, D.C.: Government Printing Office, 1975), 49. Thereafter in *Statistical Abstracts*, esp. 1979, 60. (The original published version of this article included Graph I, which charted the crude birth rate from 1840 to 1980 of Mormons versus the United States population in general.)

17. Merle Curti, *The Making of an American Community: A Case Study of Democracy in a Frontier County* (Stanford, CA: Stanford University Press, 1959); John Modell, "Family and Fertility on the Indiana Frontier 1820," *American Quarterly* 23 (1971): 615-34; and Richard A. Easterlin, George Alter, and Gretchen Condran, "Farms and Farm Families in Old and New Areas: The Northern States in 1860," in Tamara K. Hareven and Maris A. Vinovskis, eds., *Family and Population in Nineteenth-Century America* (Princeton, NJ: Princeton University Press, 1978), 22-85.

18. Phillip Aries, *Centuries of Childhood: A Social History of Family Life*, trans. Robert Boldick (New York: Vintage Books, 1962). See also Bernard Wishy, *The Child and the Republic: The Dawn of Modern America Child Nurture* (Philadelphia: University of Pennsylvania Press, 1968).

19. Davis Bitton is among scholars who have given special attention to these concerns. See his "Zion's Rowdies: Growing up on the Mormon Frontier," *Utah Historical Quarterly* 50 (Spring 1982): 182-95. For an excellent recent study of Mormon demographic behavior, based on genealogical

records, see Lee L. Bean, Geraldine P. Minear, and Douglas Anderton, *Fertility Change on the Mormon Frontier* (Berkeley: University of California Press, 1990).

20. See, for example, William Chandless, *A Visit to Salt Lake and . . . Mormon Settlement in Utah* (London: Smith, Elder & Co., 1857), 192; Elizabeth Wood Kane, *Twelve Mormon Homes. . .* (Philadelphia, 1874), 25-26, 43, 49, 58, 77; and "Letters to the Editor," *Utah Holiday* (10 Nov. 1975): 58.

21. Among such studies are Kimball Young, *Isn't One Wife Enough?* (New York: Henry Holt & Co., 1954); and James E. Smith and Phillip R. Kunz, "Polygyny and Fertility in Nineteenth-Century America," *Population Studies* 30 (1976): 465-80.

22. Larry Logue has found, since this essay was originally written, that polygamy did not suppress the fertility of women in St. George in the 1880s. See Larry M. Logue, *A Sermon in the Desert: Belief and Behavior in Early St. George, Utah* (Urbana: University of Illinois Press, 1988).

23. Computed from data in *Church Almanac* (Salt Lake City: Deseret News, 1977), 170-71.

24. Presiding Bishop's Office, Statistical Reports, 1880, LDS archives.

25. *LDS General Conference Reports,* April 1925 to present.

26. Presiding Bishop's Office, Statistical Reports, LDS archives; U.S. Census Bureau, *Seventh Census of the United States, 1850* (Washington: Robert Armstrong, 1853), appendix, xii.

27. Joseph L. Lyon and Steven Nelson, "Mormon Health," *Dialogue: A Journal of Mormon Thought* 12 (Autumn 1979): 61-69.

28. Charles M. Hatch, Dean L. May, and Ron R. Brown, "The People of Cache Valley's Jensen Farm Area in the 19th Century" (a report prepared for The Ronald V. Jensen Historical Farm and Man and His Bread Museum, Utah State University, 1979), 15-21. (Again, the original published version of this essay included Graphs III-V charting the age structure [foreign- and native-born] in Cache County for the years 1860 and 1880.)

29. Dean R. Louder and Lowell Bennion, "Mapping Mormons Across the Modern West," in Jackson, 135-67.

30. Perry Miller, *The New England Mind: From Colony to Province* (Boston: Beacon Press, 1961), 119.

8.
Mormons, Crickets, and Gulls: A New Look at an Old Story

William G. Hartley

WITHIN PICTURESQUE TEMPLE SQUARE IN SALT LAKE CITY STANDS the graceful bronze and stone Sea Gull Monument commemorating a highly dramatic experience in Mormon pioneer history. Soon after Mormons reached the shores of Great Salt Lake, so the story goes, their desperately needed first crops were invaded by vociferous black crickets. When the battle to save fields and gardens seemed doomed, the pioneers prayed earnestly for deliverance. Thereupon, miraculously, thousands of sea gulls suddenly appeared. In short order these divinely sent birds ate and disgorged huge quantities of crickets until the insects were eliminated, and the threatened Mormon crops were saved.

The cricket war of 1848, popularly known as the "Miracle of the Gulls," has assumed legendary characteristics in the folk history of the Rocky Mountain West.[1] And like many frontier legends, this one invites scholarly probes into the past in order to determine how well the traditional story is supported by historical evidence.

In assessing current accounts of the 1848 event, a number of questions must be considered. Were gulls and crickets inhabiting the Great Salt Lake area prior to the Mormon arrival in 1847? Did the gulls actually prevent major destruction of the Mormon crops? Was the event considered miraculous by contemporary observers? How unique was the encounter when compared with the natural history

137

of the Utah area? Current historical research has produced some unexpected answers to these questions while revealing some new problems with the traditional story.

The cricket war of 1848 occurred during the Mormons' first year in the Great Salt Lake Valley. A vanguard company of pioneers entered the area on 22 July 1847 followed by Brigham Young two days later. Other Mormon companies arrived soon thereafter, with the largest immigration coming in September. Young soon returned to Iowa, leaving a high council presidency in charge of the new settlements during the winter of 1847-48 and through the cricket attacks the subsequent spring.

These pioneers were new to the area but gulls and crickets were not. Their pre-Mormon presence is established by trapper and explorer records kept during the preceding decades. As early as 1825 British fur trapper Peter Skene Ogden noticed sea gulls near the present Utah-Idaho border, according to his 5 May diary entry: "Our course This day was west over a fine Plain Covered with Buffaloes & thousands of Small Gulls the latter was a Strange Sight to us I presume some large body of water near at hand at present unknown to us all."[2]

Years later the energetic American explorer, John C. Fremont, reported the presence of gulls near the Great Salt Lake in his journal entry for 12 September 1843: "We had to-night a supper of seal gulls, which [Kit] Carson killed near the lake."[3] These two notations show that sea gulls were not strangers to that region when the Mormons came.

Crickets were but slightly mentioned in early diaries. Again Ogden's journal specifically notes their presence not far from the Great Salt Lake on 2 May 1825: "As for insects we have no Cause to complain, Fleas Wood lice Spiders & crickets by millions."[4] There is no record, however, of gulls attacking crickets anywhere in the Rocky Mountain West prior to 1848, although a novelized account reported the rescue of the Comondu Mission in California when threatened by crickets and saved by gulls.[5]

The first Mormons to enter the Salt Lake Valley in 1847 were impressed by the quantity of large crickets they encountered. "The ground seems literally alive with very large black crickets crawling around up grass and bushes," commented William Clayton.[6] Orson Pratt described crickets the size of a man's thumb.[7] Brigham Young received a message from the vanguard party similarly descriptive: "In many places the grasses, rushes, etc. are 10 feet high, but no mire. Mammoth crickets abound in the borders of the Valley."[8] Crickets were still busy in the valley as late in the summer as 29 August, when John Steele wrote that his daily labors included "planting buckwheat, irrigating crops, killing crickets, etc."[9] It is notable, however, that these pioneer diarists did not mention the presence of gulls before the birds' impressive appearance in the spring of 1848.

Throughout the winter of 1847-48 nearly 1,700 Mormons prepared the dry valley soil for cultivation. Many lived at the Old Fort, a walled-in series of cabins forming the nucleus of the community later designated as Salt Lake City. Other pioneers had settled at the present sites of Kaysville and Bountiful and along the Weber River. Fences enclosed more than 5,000 acres, about one-fifth of which was sown with grain. A mild winter allowed for an early planting.[10]

Harvest prospects were bright by the next spring. On 16 April 1848 John Steele rejoiced that "green stuff is coming very fast" and that his "wheat, corn, beans and peas are all up and looking grand and grass is 6 inches high."[11] In a 9 June letter valley leaders advised Brigham Young that prior to the arrival of the crickets a large amount of spring crops had been planted and had been doing well.[12]

By late May, however, tragedy struck. Completely unexpected by the Mormon farmers, the nights turned cold, producing killer frosts, while sunlight activated armies of crickets. John Taylor noted crickets in some fields as early as 22 May.[13] Mrs. Lorenzo Dow Young despaired over their destructive appearance as part of her 27 May entry in her husband's diary: "We have grappled with the frost ... but today to our utter astonishment, the crickets came by millions, sweeping everything before them. They first attacked a patch of beans for us and in twenty minutes there was not a vestige of them to be seen. They next swept over peas, then came into our garden; took everything clean. We went out with brush and undertook to drive them, but they were too strong for us."[14]

The psychological damage caused by the dual enemies—frost and crickets—became apparent the next day to Eliza R. Snow: "This morning's frost in unison with the ravages of the crickets for a few days past produces many sighs, and occasionally some long faces."[15] That same day, 28 May, Isaac Haight matter-of-factly described his losses: "Frost again this morning. Things killed in the garden such as beans, cucumbers, mellons, pumpkins, and squash. Corn hurt some and some wheat killed and the crickets are injuring the crops."[16] Mrs. Lorenzo Young's description that day is similar: "[May] 28th: Last night we had a severe frost. Today the crickets have commenced on our corn and small grain. They have eaten off 12 acres for Brother Rosacrants, 7 for Charles and are now taking Edmunds."[17]

The horror of crickets engulfing fields, barns, houses, clothes, and cupboards continued day after day. Mrs. Lorenzo Young began to fear for the future outcome: "Today [29 May] they have destroyed 3/4 of an acre of squashes, our flax, two acres of millet and our rye, and are now to work in our wheat. What will be the result we know not."[18] Another diarist, Patty Sessions, wrote on 30 May of her son's efforts: "Mr. Sessions has gone to the farm to keep the crickets off the crops; they are taking all before them that they come to. The frost killed a good deal."[19]

That the quantity of crickets destroying the vegetation was overwhelming is shown in John Steele's "catch-up" journal entry which summarized at least a week of destruction: "Sunday, June 4th, there is a great excitement in camp. There has come a frost which took beans, corn and wheat and nearly everything, and to help make the disaster complete, the crickets came by the thousands of tons."[20] Although Isaac Haight did not admit disaster, his mood that same Sabbath was similarly gloomy: "Quite cold and very dry. Crops begin to suffer for want of rain. The crickets destroyed some crops and are eating the heads off the grain as soon as it heads out. The prospects for grain are discouraging."[21]

This anxiety caused some Mormon leaders and members to doubt Brigham Young's inspiration in selecting such a place for settlement. Haight perceived that "Many of the Saints begin to think of leaving the valley for fear of starvation."[22] Steele recorded that "the cry is now raised, 'we cannot live here, away to California,' and the faith of many were shaken."[23] Other farmers stated their intentions of leaving for the eastern states or Oregon. Even John Young, a counselor in the governing high council presidency, urged that an express be sent to warn Brigham Young not to bring more Mormons to the valley for fear of starvation.[24]

Subsequent entomological research regarding the characteristics of the Mormon cricket justifies the fear felt by these pioneers. The black insects, technically identified as *Anabrus simplex,* measure 1.25 inches in length and are wingless. They generally inhabit the

mountain country but occasionally become plentiful enough to de-
scend into the valleys in outbreaks which last from two to six years.
Traveling in bands the size of a city block to a square mile or more,
these sluggish insects move from one-eighth to almost two miles per
day. Relishing garden crops, small fruits, and grains, they also are
cannibalistic and have been seen consuming leather harnesses and
large rattlesnakes, evergreen trees, and sagebrush.[25]

Every conceivable defensive tactic was tried by the farmers
to fight this "army of famine and despair."[26] In an account written
nine years later, Jesse N. Smith said that initially water was turned
into ditches surrounding the fields. This method, however, proved
ineffective because "it seemed impossible to drown them, as they
would recover after being a long time under water." Then, he added,
the pioneers took advantage of the crickets' cannibalism. Since they
"showed some preference for the dead or disabled of their own
number," crickets were killed at the borders of the fields to keep other
crickets fed.[27]

Sticks, clubs, brooms, brushes, and willows were used to
knock the black creatures off the plants. Fires were built into which
the crickets were driven. Some Mormons discovered that the insects
disliked certain noises, so women and children went into the fields
with bells and sticks and tin pans to scare the black villains.[28] A
five-year-old girl was given a wooden mallet with which to smash
crickets.[29] Possibly the oddest technique was tried by John Young
who, with his brother, pulled a rope back and forth across the tops
of the grain to knock off the climbing crickets before they could reach
the heads of the wheat.[30] Initially ignorant of cricket habits, the
pragmatic pioneers soon claimed to be gaining a "fund of knowledge"
about the enemy.[31]

The harassed farmers "prayed and fought and fought and
prayed" for almost two weeks against the crickets—which some Mormons jokingly described as a cross between a spider and a buffalo.[32]
It is difficult to pinpoint exactly when the California gulls first arrived
to assist, but on 9 June valley leaders described the dramatic event in
a letter to Brigham Young: "The sea gulls have come in large flocks
from the lake and sweep the crickets as they go; it seems the hand of
the Lord is in our favor."[33] Daily gulls flew to the Mormon fields to
consume crickets. Twelve days later another letter to Brigham Young
noted the continuing activity of the crickets despite the gulls: "Crick-

ets are still quite numerous and busy eating but between the gulls and our own efforts and the growth of our crops we shall raise much grain in spite of them."[34] John Smith remembered that the gulls "came every morning for about three weeks, when their mission was apparently ended, and they ceased coming."[35] It appears that the 1848 cricket invasion lasted for at least a month and probably longer. In that time crickets had swept through some grain fields two or three times.

The spectacle of innumerable screaming sea gulls, filling the sky and shading earth from sun, seemed at first to portend a third plague for the Mormon crops. John Smith left this description: "The first I knew of the gulls, I heard their sharp cry. Upon looking up I beheld what appeared like a vast flock of pigeons coming from the Northwest. It was about three o'clock in the afternoon. . . . There must have been thousands of them. Their coming was like a great cloud; and when they passed between us and the sun, a shadow covered the field. I could see gulls settling for more than a mile around us."[36] Initially the gulls were feared because their presence in the valley was strange to many of the new settlers. Summarizing the history of the Mormon church up to 1850, Thomas L. Kane told the Pennsylvania Historical Society that gulls "were before strangers to the valley," an opinion he must have gained from a valley resident.[37] Likewise a letter published in the Little Rock, Arkansas, *Democrat* in 1849 claimed that "mountain men" familiar with the Great Salt Lake area said that gulls had never been seen there prior to 1848.[38] Needless to say such a belief would enhance the drama of the gulls' appearance.

The California gulls, now regular inhabitants of the Great Salt Lake region during spring and summer months,[39] amazed the beleaguered pioneers not only by the amount of crickets they killed but also by the unusual manner of consumption. The gulls would feed on crickets until full, drink some water, and then regurgitate prior to consuming more crickets. Therefore it appeared that their main objective was to kill crickets rather than to feed on them. George Q. Cannon, for example, received such an impression after walking along water ditches where he saw "lumps of these crickets vomited up by those gulls."[40] To ornithologists, however, such vomiting by gulls is not unusual. Responding to Cannon's description, gull expert F. E. L. Beale judged that "these 'lumps of crickets' were undoubtedly 'pellets' of indigestible parts habitually disgorged by the birds."[41]

Mormon pioneers, alone in the Great Basin wilderness, devout in their faith, and convinced that they were God's chosen people, attributed much of their experience as a religious body to the divine will. Thus in 1848 some, but not all, who witnessed the cricket war felt that God had performed a miracle in their behalf by sending the gulls. As noted earlier, the 9 June letter to Brigham Young expressed belief that "the hand of the Lord" guided the gulls.[42]

That such a belief became popular in a short time is shown in a most descriptive diary entry penned later in 1848. Henry Bigler, a member of the Mormon Battalion returning from Mexican War duty in California, was impressed by the story of the cricket war he heard immediately upon arriving in Salt Lake City: "[Sept. 28] The whole face of the earth I am told was literally covered with large black crickets that seemed to the farmers that they [the crickets] would eat up and completely destroy their entire crops had it not been for the gulls that came in large flocks and devoured the crickets. I am told that the gulls would feast themselves on the crickets to the full and straight way disgorge them and begin again and thus they did destroy the crickets and save the crops and . . . all looked upon the gulls as a God send, indeed, all acknowledged the hand of the Lord was in it, that He had sent the white gulls by scores of thousands to save their crops."[43]

Various pioneers familiar with the 1848 episode likewise affirmed years later that the gulls had been divinely sent. Typical is this 1853 tribute by Thomas S. Terry: "God who was ever ready to bless his Faithfull Children, Sent the Gulls, who was timely Saviours in our behalf, and Saved our Crops from total ruin."[44]

Immediate reverence for the gulls was expressed in laws adopted to protect them. A number of documents indicate that it was forbidden to shoot, kill, or annoy gulls with firearms.[45] Bigler wrote that this protection was afforded because "all" the pioneers looked upon the gulls as a "God send."[46]

The "Miracle of the Gulls" has been a popular faith-promoting story in Mormon circles for a half-dozen generations. The first mention of the "miracle" in a Mormon general conference was made by Apostle Orson Hyde on 24 September 1853 when he asserted that the gulls had been agents prepared by the hand of providence.[47] Two years later the *Deseret News* offered this encouragement for Mormon farmers then suffering a devastating grasshopper plague: "We do not feel . . . the least apprehension for the final result of the present destruction. . . . As for the Saints we are perfectly aware that through faith and obedience they can prevail in the grasshopper war, at least as well as they did in the cricket war of 1848."[48]

Similarly versions found in such Mormon periodicals as the *Improvement Era* and the *Instructor* and in the standard church histories by B. H. Roberts and Joseph Fielding Smith positively assert the miraculous nature of the event.[49]

Surprisingly a number of the contemporary sources which should have contained accounts of the "Miracle of the Gulls" make no mention of it. Various memoirs and autobiographies, for example, retrospectively tell of the cricket invasion in 1848 but say nothing of the gulls. Also all of the diarists quoted earlier for the day-by-day account of the cricket advances—Haight, Snow, Steele, Sessions, and Mrs. Young—ceased making diary entries during the first week of June, when the crickets were at their worst, and then said nothing about the gulls when their diaries were later reactivated. For example, Eliza R. Snow's next diary reports were dated 10 June and 15 June; they bemoan the general agricultural situation but ignore the newly arrived sea gulls.[50] Similarly unusual is the non-mention of gulls by the outspoken apostle, Parley P. Pratt. Neither his 1848 letters to his brother Orson in England nor his later autobiography mention gull attacks on crickets, even though Parley witnessed—and lamented in these sources—the 1848 difficulties.[51]

Likewise unusual is the lack of mention of the event in the official Mormon newspaper in England, the *Latter-day Saints' Millennial Star*. Not only Parley Pratt's letters but all valley reports reaching the *Star* painted an unduly optimistic picture of 1848 valley agricultural conditions. Very slight reference to cricket damage plus a passing remark printed in 1849 about the gulls is all that English Mormons were told about the cricket war of 1848.

Some understanding of this silence comes when the actual significance of the gulls for the ensuing 1848 harvest is evaluated. Was it a successful harvest? If so how much did the gulls contribute to that success?

On the one hand are glowing production reports like those sent to England by Parley Pratt. In September, for example, he wrote that a successful harvest had been produced: "Wheat harvest commenced early in July, and continued till August. Winter and spring wheat have both done well, some ten thousand bushels have been raised." He added that a surplus of ten to twenty thousand bushels was expected.[52]

A more moderate estimate comes from Henry Bigler: "Their crops were prity much harvested. . . . Buck wheat was good, potatoes fine, but the corn crop was light and fodder short."[53] On the other hand are more pessimistic reports. Isaac Haight, optimistic in July, wrote that his final wheat harvest was poor.[54] John Steele's harvest consisted of a mess pan full of corn ears.[55] A. J. Allen only produced five bushels of wheat from two acres.[56] Chapman Duncan wrote five years later that the 1848 harvest had been light due to lack of irrigation.[57]

Official Mormon church reports, more than any other source, indicate that the 1848 harvest was far from successful. They objectively discuss the factors which, in addition to the crickets, were to blame. The high council presidency, in evaluating the valley's agricultural situation for Brigham Young on 21 July 1848, rated the gulls as helpers but certainly not as rescuers: "The brethren have been busy for some time watering their wheat and as far as it is done the wheat looks well and the heads are long and large. The crickets are still quite numerous and busy eating, but between the gulls and our own efforts and the growth of our crops we shall raise much grain in spite of them. Our vines, beans and peas are mostly destroyed by frost and the crickets; but many of us have more seed and are now busy replanting. . . . Some of our corn has been destroyed, but many large fields look very well and corn is growing very fast."[58]

This letter identifies four factors which are important for any assessment of the role played by the gulls. Individual pioneer actions, in addition to gull efforts, are credited for controlling crickets. Also frost initially was every bit as damaging as the crickets. In addition specific crops such as corn and beans were hurt more than others by crickets. Undoubtedly individual farmers responded to the gulls according to the amount of cricket damage their fields did or did not receive and to the final amount produced by their own fields. Another factor noted in other sources was insufficient irrigation.

The gulls were completely slighted in a more significant letter written the next year. The first valley epistle officially sent by the First Presidency of the Mormon church to scattered non-Utah Mormons included a thorough evaluation of the 1848 harvests. Negative factors received the greatest emphasis: "The brethren had succeeded in sowing and planting an extensive variety of seeds at all seasons, from January to July, on a farm about twelve miles in length, and from one to six in width, including the city plot. Most of their early crops were destroyed, in the month of May, by crickets and frost, which continued occasionally until June. . . . The brethren were not sufficiently numerous to fight the crickets, irrigate the crops, and fence the farms of their extensive planting, consequently they suffered heavy losses."[59]

It must not be overlooked that this official summary of valley experiences from the first arrival of the pioneers until 1849 nowhere mentions the gulls, despite prominent notice paid to the cricket plague. According to this evaluation, crop losses were severe. Therefore the actual physical benefit brought by the gulls was not as extensive as is popularly believed.

The cricket war of 1848 is sometimes confused in pioneer writings with similar occurrences during the subsequent two years, when the gulls were more responsible for halting the crickets. Both gulls and crickets arrived earlier in 1849. Plover, a specie of shore bird native to the Great Salt Lake area, arrived before the gulls, according to a general church epistle dated 9 April 1849: "The month of March and April, to the 4th, was very mild and pleasant, and many small crickets have made their appearance, but large flocks of plover have already come among them, and are making heavy inroads in their ranks."[60] By 6 June California gulls were also attacking the crickets.[61] Two days later Brigham Young and others were reported to be "busy killing crickets, building fences, etc."[62] According to Thomas L. Kane the early arrival of the gulls "saved the wheat crop from all harm whatever" in 1849.[63]

Crickets invaded the valley again in 1850.[64] They were allied with grasshopper hordes in 1855, a year in which gulls again were on the attack.[65]

The "Journal History" compiled by the historian's office of the Mormon church contains a number of newspaper articles describing gull and cricket activities in Utah and the western United States. Millions of crickets, for example, invaded Rush Valley, Utah, in 1904.[66] Mandan, North Dakota, reported thousands of sea gulls in the grain fields in 1921 attacking grasshoppers.[67] A Montana report in 1924 said that gull flocks numbering from 4,000 to 5,000 birds preyed upon grasshoppers for more than six weeks.[68] Colorado reported thousands of gulls attacking grasshoppers in 1926.[69] An estimated one million gulls were feeding on Saskatchewan grasshoppers in 1933.[70] Four years later gulls feasted on Mormon crickets in Oregon.[71] An estimated 5,000 to 8,000 gulls raided crickets southeast of Tooele City, Utah, in 1937 during a cricket invasion which lasted until the next year.[72] More recently gulls battled crickets in Oregon in 1947[73] and in Utah in 1952.[74]

In 1848 Mormon farmers felt that their experience was unique. But these numerous examples suggest that encounters between gulls and crickets are common to the natural history of the western United States.

Current research alters the traditional sea gull/cricket story in many respects while substantiating its basic facts. As a result, the following information should be taken into account in credible versions of the dramatic struggle:

(1) The gulls were not strangers to the valley. Records before and since show that various types of gulls, including the California gull in 1848, regularly inhabit the Great Salt Lake area. These birds are natural enemies of various insects, including crickets.

(2) Gulls habitually regurgitate the indigestible parts of insects they have swallowed.

(3) Gulls did not arrive until after severe cricket damage had already occurred. Even after the gulls had been "feasting" on crickets for two weeks, the insects still were "quite numerous and busy eating."

(4) In 1848 Mormon crops were seriously damaged by three enemies—frost, crickets, and drought—and the gulls dealt with only one of these.

(5) The "miraculousness" of the event was not clearly recognized by contemporaries. The Mormon church's First Presidency was notably silent concerning any "Miracle of the Gulls" in its letters. Likewise the *Millennial Star* never told the English Saints about such a miracle. Diarists who detailed the cricket advance did not mention the gulls.

(6) Since 1848 gulls frequently have been on the wing to feast on crickets and other insects, making the 1848 encounter hardly unique.

Like other popular accounts of important and unusual his-

torical events, the details of the cricket war of 1848 over the years
have been oversimplified, improved upon, and given somewhat
legendary characteristics.

Yet the fact remains that the 1848 Mormon pioneers would
have suffered more had not the gulls come to their aid. Physically the
gulls helped avert a complete agricultural disaster; the amount of
crickets which thousands of gulls could consume in two or three
weeks would be a staggering figure. And the birds did relieve hard-
pressed farmers from arduous toil against the crickets. More importantly, the gulls provided mental and emotional rejuvenation.
Undoubtedly threats of leaving for California were diminished by the
sudden appearance of the gull flocks. At a nadir of discouragement
the farmers must have felt their burden lightened and their hopes at
least temporarily raised by their unexpected ally.

The "Miracle of the Gulls" story remains appropriate as an
expression of the faith held by Mormon pioneers and their descendants. To them God can and does intervene in the everyday affairs
of men and women when faith is exercised. Whether or not the gulls
performed some type of "miracle" under God's direction in 1848 is
not as important as is the confidence Mormons feel that God could
so act if he willed. In the final analysis it is this belief as well as the
benefit gulls have periodically provided Utahans that is honored by
the impressive Sea Gull Monument.[75]

NOTES

1. Austin E. Fife, "Popular Legends of the Mormons," *California Folklore Quarterly* 1 (Apr. 1942): 114.

2. David E. Miller, ed., "Peter Skene Ogden's Journal of His Expedition to Utah, 1825," *Utah Historical Quarterly* 20 (Apr. 1952): 171-72.

3. Quoted in Vasco M. Tanner, "A Chapter on the Natural History of the Great Basin, 1800 to 1855," *The Great Basin Naturalist* 1 (July 1939): 46.

4. Miller, "Peter Skene Ogden's Journal," 170.

5. See Antonio de Fierro Blanco, *Journey of the Flame*, trans. Walter de Steiguer (New York: Literary Guild, 1933), 170-76.

6. William Clayton, *William Clayton's Journal: A Daily Record of the Journey of the Original Company of "Mormon" Pioneers* . . . (Salt Lake City: Clayton Family Association, 1921), 311.

7. Orson Pratt, "Extracts from the Journal of Orson Pratt," *The Utah*

Genealogical and Historical Magazine 17 (Jan. 1926): 211.

8. Claire Noall, *Intimate Disciple: A Portrait of Willard Richards* (Salt Lake City: University of Utah Press, 1957), 538.

9. John Steele, "Extracts from the Journal of John Steele," *Utah Historical Quarterly* 6 (Jan. 1933): 18-19.

10. Orson F. Whitney, *History of Utah* (Salt Lake City: George Q. Cannon and Sons, 1892), 1:375-77.

11. Steele, "Journal of John Steele, 21-22.

12. Quoted in Pauline Udall Smith, *Captain Jefferson Hunt of the Mormon Battalion* (Salt Lake City: Nicholas G. Morgan, Sr., Foundation, 1958), 308.

13. Dale L. Morgan, *The Great Salt Lake* (Indianapolis: Bobbs Merrill and Co., 1947), 213-14.

14. J. Cecil Alter and Robert J. Dwyer, eds., "Journal and Biography of Lorenzo Dow Young," *Utah Historical Quarterly* 14 (1946): 166.

15. Eliza R. Snow, *Eliza R. Snow, An Immortal: Selected Writings* (Salt Lake City: Nicholas G. Morgan, Sr., Foundation, 1947), 364-65.

16. Isaac C. Haight, "Biographical Sketch and Diary of Isaac Chauncey Haight, 1813-1862," 49, Special Collections, Harold B. Lee Library, Brigham Young University, Provo, Utah.

17. Alter and Dwyer, "Lorenzo Dow Young," 166.

18. Ibid.

19. Quoted from a diary kept by Mrs. Sessions in "Gull Monument," *Improvement Era* 17 (Nov. 1913): 70.

20. Steele, "Journal of John Steele," 22.

21. Haight, "Biographical Sketch and Diary of Isaac Chauncey Haight," 49.

22. Ibid.

23. Steele, "Journal of John Steele," 22.

24. Journal History, 9 June 1848, archives, Historical Department, Church of Jesus Christ of Latter-day Saints, Salt Lake City, Utah.

25. Frank T. Cowan, *Life Habits, History and Control of the Mormon Cricket,* U.S. Department of Agriculture Technical Bulletin No. 161 (Washington, D.C., 1929), 26-27.

26. Whitney, *History of Utah,* 1:377.

27. Jesse N. Smith, *Journal of Jesse N. Smith: The Life Story of a Mormon Pioneer, 1834-1906* (Salt Lake City: Deseret News Publishing Co., [1953]), 13.

28. Sarah P. Rich, "Journal of Sarah De Armon Pea Rich," 2, Special Collections, Harold B. Lee Library.

29. Manomas Andrus, "Biography of Manomas Lavina Gibson Andrus: 1842-1922," 2, Special Collections, Harold B. Lee Library.

30. John R. Young, *Memoirs of John R. Young, Utah Pioneer, 1847* (Salt

Lake City: Deseret News Press, 1920), 148.

31. Journal History, 21 June 1848.

32. Sir Richard F. Burton, *The City of the Saints, and Across the Rocky Mountains to California,* ed. Fawn M. Brodie (New York: Alfred A. Knopf, 1963), 314.

33. Smith, *Captain Jefferson Hunt,* 136-37.

34. Journal History, 21 June 1848.

35. Ibid., 9 June 1848.

36. Ibid.

37. Thomas L. Kane, "The Mormons," *Utah Genealogical and Historical Magazine* 2 (July 1911): 122.

38. Reprinted by *Deseret News,* 15 June 1850.

39. Arthur C. Bent, *Life Histories of North American Gulls and Terns* (Washington, D.C., 1921), 124.

40. Whitney, *History of Utah,* 1:377.

41. W. L. McAtee and F. E. L. Beale, *Some Common Game, Aquatic, and Rapacious Birds in Relation to Man,* U.S. Department of Agriculture Bulletin No. 497 (Washington, D.C., 1912), 22.

42. Smith, *Captain Jefferson Hunt,* 136-37.

43. "Diary of Henry W. Bigler, 1846-1850," 1:106, Special Collections, Harold B. Lee Library.

44. "Diary of Thomas Sirls Terry, 1825-1877," 11, Special Collections, Harold B. Lee Library.

45. "Journal of Sarah Rich," 82; Kane, "The Mormons," 2:123.

46. "Diary of Henry W. Bigler," 107.

47. *Journal of Discourses,* 26 vols. (Liverpool, England, 1854-1886), 2:114.

48. "The Crops and the Grasshoppers," *Deseret News,* 23 May 1855.

49. B. H. Roberts, *A Comprehensive History of the Church of Jesus Christ of Latter-day Saints,* 6 vols. (Salt Lake City: Church of Jesus Christ of Latter-day Saints, 1930), 3:331-33; Joseph Fielding Smith, *Essentials in Church History* (Salt Lake City: Deseret News Press, 1960), 467-68; "Early Life in the Valley," *Juvenile Instructor* 9 (17 Jan. 1874): 22; "Saved By Gulls," *Improvement Era* 4 (July 1901): 671-73; J. L. Townsend, "The Sea Gulls and the Crickets," *Improvement Era* 8 (July 1905): 565-68; James E. Talmage, "Were They Crickets or Locusts and When Did They Come?" *Improvement Era* 13 (Dec. 1909): 97-108; Peter Madsen, "The Grasshopper Farmer—The Mullet and the Trout," *Improvement Era* 13 (Apr. 1910): 516; Elsie Hoffman Buchanan, "Our Historical Insect Foe," *Improvement Era* 37 (July 1934): 418-20, 448.

50. Snow, *Eliza R. Snow,* 365.

51. Parley P. Pratt, *Autobiography of Parley P. Pratt* (Salt Lake City: Deseret Book Co., 1938).

52. *Latter-day Saints' Millennial Star* 11 (1849): 21.

53. "Diary of Henry W. Bigler," 106.

54. "Diary of Isaac Chauncey Haight," 49.

55. "Journal of John Steele," 28.

56. "Diary of A. J. Allen," 9, Special Collections, Harold B. Lee Library.

57. Chapman Duncan, "Biography of Chapman Duncan, 1812-1900," 1849 comments, Special Collections, Harold B. Lee Library.

58. Journal History, 21 June 1848.

59. *Latter-day Saints' Millennial Star* 11 (1849): 227.

60. Journal History, 9 Apr. 1849.

61. Ibid., 6 June 1849.

62. Ibid., 8 June 1849.

63. Kane, "The Mormons," 123.

64. Talmage, "Crickets or Locusts."

65. *Deseret News,* 23 May 1855.

66. "Feasting on Crickets," *Improvement Era* 3 (Sept. 1904): 890.

67. *Salt Lake Tribune,* 25 Aug. 1921.

68. *Gazette* (Billings, MT), 26 Aug. 1924.

69. *Salt Lake Tribune,* 17 Aug. 1926.

70. Journal History, 9 Feb. 1935.

71. *Salt Lake Tribune,* 21 June 1937.

72. C. J. Sorenson and H. F. Thornley, "Mormon Crickets and Their Control in Utah Since 1923," *Proceedings of the Utah Academy of Sciences, Arts and Letters* 15 (1938): 63-70.

73. *Deseret News,* 23 May 1947.

74. Ibid., 9 June 1952.

75. The Sea Gull Monument, erected on Temple Square on 13 September 1913, is the work of Mahonri M. Young, a grandson to Brigham Young.

9.
The "Leading Sisters": A Female Hierarchy in Nineteenth-Century Mormon Society

Maureen Ursenbach Beecher

MORMON APOSTATE WRITER JOHN HYDE WAS ACCURATE IN HIS OBSER-vation of an elite group in early Mormon Utah. He wrote in 1857: "Miss Eliza R. Snow, the Mormon poetess, a very talented woman, but outrageously bigoted, and one or two kindred souls, are the nuclei for all the female intellect at Salt Lake. Let any recant from their creed, or oppose it, she and her band of second Amazons crush the intrepid one down."[1]

While Hyde may have exaggerated the vengeance of these ladies against nonconformists, he has suggested that a female elite existed among the early society of the Latter-day Saints and has illustrated some of its characteristics. It centered in one strong woman, charismatic, widely visible, powerful, and around that hub was a select group of "kindred" women; it demanded of its members unstinting adherence to a "creed," a spoken or otherwise understood set of tenets and behaviors. What Hyde missed was that this elite group not only led in matters intellectual but ruled informally the whole society of Mormon women. Because of the nature of Mormon-ism—the all-pervasive reach of the radical theology—there was not an aspect of living which the religion did not touch, and the chief disseminator of the religion to the women was Eliza Roxcy Snow,

153

termed by one historian "the female voice of the male hierarchy."[2]

Historians of Mormon culture have long noted Snow's importance to the religious and secular life of the Great Basin Saints. What they have largely neglected is the group of women who performed for the female Saints functions parallel to those carried out for the whole membership by the general authorities assembled around Brigham Young. It is the purpose of this essay to examine that female elite and determine how they arose and where they fit in the Mormon social order.

In their study of organizational patterns in the Mormon church, Jill and Brooklyn Derr point out differences between formal and informal power sources. Authority is conveyed, they assert, through formal organizations such as wards, stakes, priesthood quorums, and, after the 1870s, Mutual Improvement Associations, Primaries, and Relief Societies. In all those formal bodies, the male priesthood administration carries the decision-making power. Since in Mormon practice women hold no generally acknowledged priesthood authority, the formal structure shows them totally under the direction of their male leaders. On the other hand, as the Derrs stress, informal structures also function in organizations, stimulating, facilitating, or interrupting the formal system when it proves inadequate to the needs or counter to the best interests of the people it serves. It is in their use of informal methods, the Derrs demonstrate, that women have been most effective.[3] The very founding of the Nauvoo Relief Society from a chance conversation in a young woman's parlor illustrates the informal undercurrent moving with the mainstream as women bring about their own kind of changes in the system.

Titles and ranks make it easy to identify the key men in Joseph Smith's or Brigham Young's administrations. In the absence of such organization, it is less simple to name the women who were their equivalents in early church administration. For some periods there were Relief Society presidencies, but often there was no Relief Society, and equally often it was women other than the officially appointed ones who seem to have been directing women's activities. Close reading of minutes of women's meetings during Utah's later settlement days reveals several "leading sisters" whose words seem to have the force of law to their sisters in the outer settlements. Unofficial in the sense of having no titles or conference-approved general boards, these women carried messages from headquarters, gave assignments, encouraged specific projects, and generally preserved the continuity and sense of community of the women.

A list of "leading sisters" drawn from minute books in the 1870s squares almost without exception with the key women listed by Augusta Joyce Crocheron in an 1884 publication entitled *Representative Women of Deseret*.[4] The book, a compilation of brief biographies, was published to accompany a large composite photograph of twenty women. Crocheron's list is more representative of the elite than the mainstream. Though she includes leaders of women's organizations, she also selected some women not in the formal presidencies and left off some who were. Her list includes the following, grouped in five sections: (1) Eliza R. Snow [Smith], whom Crocheron titles "President of the Latter-day Saints' Women's Organizations"; Zina D. H. Young, first counselor; Mary Isabella Horne, treasurer (Crocheron neglects to title her with her more active callings—president of the Salt Lake Stake Relief Societies and president of the Cooperative Retrenchment Society, of which more will be said later); and Sarah M. Kimball, secretary (also president of the Fifteenth Ward Relief Society).

These four women also comprised the presidency of the Relief Society Central Board, counselor Elizabeth Ann Whitney, deceased since 1883, not having been replaced. The Relief Society board and the presidency of Women's Organizations were composed of the same people, which suggests that the Relief Society was mother organization to the female-directed "auxiliaries": the Young Ladies' Mutual Improvement Association and the children's Primary.

Next treated in the book are four women who, not holding specific callings, still had to be included, according to Crocheron's sense of who was really important: Phoebe Woodruff, Bathsheba W. Smith, Prescendia [sic] Kimball, and Elizabeth Howard. These two groups then were the core women, the *leading* leading sisters. The third group formed a second echelon: Elmina S. Taylor, general president of the YLMIA; Mary A. Freeze, her Salt Lake Stake counterpart; Louie B. Felt, Primary president; and her stake counterpart, Ellen C. Clawson.

The fourth group was made up of the artists Emily Hill Woodmansee, Hannah T. King, and Helen Mar Whitney (these latter two were noted for far more than their verse and prose); and the author, Augusta Joyce Crocheron. The fifth and last group was comprised of Emmeline B. Wells, editor of the *Woman's Exponent,* and Romania B. Pratt, physician at the woman-sponsored Deseret Hospital (both of whom were a generation younger than the central group); and Zina Young Williams, age thirty-four, and Louie Wells, twenty-two, who were included, Crocheron wrote, to suggest the "rising generation" of leaders. Zina did rise to leadership; Louie died at age twenty-five.

Minute books, personal accounts, newspapers, and magazines indicate that it was these "leading sisters" who interpreted the doctrines and set the behavioral standards for their sisters; who discovered worthy causes and organized effective social programs; and who made alliances and identified enemies. The corporate and often private lives of all Mormon women, remote from the central Salt Lake Stake, were affected by the doings and sayings of these few.

But how did such a group arise? How was its membership determined? What had these leading women in common? D. Michael Quinn has found as the single most significant characteristic of the priesthood hierarchy their shared familial relationships.[5] The female leaders, not surprisingly, derived much of their status from the men to whom they were connected. Of the central eight, six were wives of apostles or, in two instances, of the president of the church. Of the second echelon in Crocheron's configuration, another six were either wives or daughters (adopted in one case) of general church authorities.

Yet factors other than kinship helped determine membership in the female leadership group. The Mormon society which established itself in Utah took its form from those that developed or were established in Nauvoo, Illinois. There the most significant event affecting women was the founding in 1842 of the Relief Society, an organization whose repeated demises and resurrections demand reinterpretation. It is often overlooked that, though the "official" founding of the organization took place on 17 March in the Masonic Lodge room, the first Relief Society was actually a grass roots movement which earlier had brought together in Sarah M. Kimball's parlor a group of neighbors with the purpose of providing aid to men working full time building the temple. In her own account Kimball, a young but relatively wealthy matron, tells of her conversation with her seamstress and of the meeting they called in the Kimballs' small house. After that first meeting Kimball requested of Eliza R. Snow, a spinster known to be gifted in writing, a set of by-laws for the newly founded group.[6] Snow then took her effort to Joseph Smith for his approval, expecting to present it to the group which was scheduled to meet the following Thursday.

Joseph Smith took the fledgling organization under his wing and created for it a place in the general priesthood organization of the church. Under his direction twenty women were invited to an official founding meeting two weeks after the first unofficial gathering. The twenty whose names appear in the minutes, and their circumstances, provide some insight into the pattern which would emerge of female networks among Mormons.[7]

Analysis of the members of the charter Relief Society meeting suggests two social-geographical bases for their having been invited: those who were Sarah Kimball's friends from the first meeting and those later invited for the 17 March meeting. In the absence of a contemporary list of women who participated in the initial gathering in the Kimballs' parlor, we can only surmise that they would be Sarah's neighbors, women who lived within a short walk's distance of her home in northwest Nauvoo.

The later additions, presumably Joseph Smith's choice, were women who lived within four blocks of the Smith household, which itself was only a block from the red brick store where the meeting took place. Many factors intrude here—Joseph Smith's acknowledged bent for housing his leading men and their families near his own house; the tendency of a leader to know and trust kinsmen of his co-workers; the probability that the wives of church leaders, having suffered the privations which proved their husbands, were likewise proven faithful. These factors most likely had some bearing on the women chosen for the first meeting, as well. About half the second group, however, were women with no familial attachment to leaders, either present or past, or to boarders or servants in the Smith household or to dwellers on the Smith property. As the Relief Society was being organized eleven people shared the Homestead property with Joseph and Emma Smith and their family, and three of these were at the meeting.[8]

Those groups then with some overlap make up the first meeting, the inner core around which 1,400 Nauvoo women would rally in the next two years. But just as the women gathered from different backgrounds, so they assumed divergent agendas for the organization. Sarah Kimball's group had begun with the almost exclusive purpose of providing benevolent services; that purpose became the society's most lasting characteristic. But a close reading of the minutes reveals other purposes and achievements. To the stated objectives of "administering to [the] wants" of the poor were added other responsibilities: "correcting the morals and strengthening the virtues of the female community" (*female* has been stricken out in the original); admitting no woman to the society without a recommend as to her worthiness; expounding doctrine, which charter had been given Emma Smith in her Doctrine and Covenants revelation; and exercising spiritual gifts. That so much of the impact of the society should be in areas other than temporal welfare suggests that in the mind of Joseph Smith at least, as perceived in his sermons, there was an agenda more essential than the care of the poor.

The timing of the organization of the Relief Society is significant.[9] The day before the 17 March meeting, Joseph Smith had organized in the same room the Nauvoo lodge of the Masonic order. Three weeks later he would induct a chosen group of his male associates into the Holy Order, the name by which the priesthood temple endowment was identified. In succeeding weeks the two rituals, Masonic and priesthood, would be conducted in the same room in which the Relief Society met, the Masonic orders in the evenings and the endowments in the afternoons.

Considering the significance of women to the endowment, and reading carefully Joseph Smith's sermons to the Relief Society, it becomes apparent he was preparing the women of the church for the eventuality when they too would participate in the priesthood endowment. That the prophet anticipated that this "society of the virtuous and those who will walk circumspectly" remain small and "select" is revealed in his comments to the third meeting that society members "were going too fast"—the original twenty members had already grown to eighty-eight.[10] His agenda altered with the interest of so many women in joining, however, and by 28 April, when he preached his most powerful sermon, he was willing to agree that "if you do right, [there is] no danger of going too fast." Even so at that meeting he required that women whose worthiness had not been proved be excused, that only those accepted as faithful hear his message. Priesthood, spiritual gifts, keys of authority, and proper church organization being stayed "until the Temple is completed" were dealt with in his address. Its overtones of coming blessings for women is underscored a month later when Bishop Newel K. Whitney, himself recently endowed, "rejoiced at the formation of the Society that we might improve upon our talents and to prepare for those blessings which God is soon to bestow upon us." That four of the women present at the first meeting were among those endowed during Joseph Smith's lifetime does not prove a hidden intent but adds to other indications of a dual purpose in organizing the women in 1842.[11]

Lists compiled by Dean Jessee and Jeffery Johnson might bear on the women invited to the 17 March meeting. Closely connected to the endowment in the minds of church leaders was the principle of celestial or plural marriage. Of the twenty women at the meeting, one was first wife to Joseph Smith, one gave him her daughter as a plural wife, two were offered the chance to become his wives but declined, and five more, thus invited, accepted. Most of these negotiations took place within weeks before or after the 17 March meeting. Besides those involved with Joseph Smith in plural marriage, three women of the group were married to other men who took plural wives.

The spiritual component of the Relief Society in Nauvoo is undeniable: after the 14 April meeting the Relief Society presidency administered to Sister Durfee for her health; during the next meeting, her testimony of the healing was followed by manifestations of other spiritual gifts. Eliza R. Snow blessed Presendia Buel, prophesying over her; Abigail Leonard and others testified to the truth of the prophesies; Sarah Cleveland spoke in tongues and Mrs. Sessions (presumably Patty Sessions) interpreted. At the next meeting, Joseph Smith, taking his text from 1 Corinthians 12 and 13, approved the limited use of these charismatic expressions. Thus were institutionalized the ritual observances which would mark the practice of Mormon women for the next half century, rituals fostered by and most characteristic of the "leading sisters."

The benevolent, or "relief," aspect of the society was, however, the more pervasive, even in Nauvoo. During the second season of its existence (the society met only during the summer months, mainly because of the lack of space large enough to house the meetings), all but two of the charter members faded from the records, and the activities of the second group of leaders were almost exclusively welfare oriented.

The third season began auspiciously in the spring of 1844 with Emma Smith again taking the lead. Knowing the limits of space, she conducted the same meeting four times, at ten o'clock and one o'clock on March 9 and 16. There she delivered a double-talk indictment of plural marriage, a coded but unmistakable opposition to the practice which her husband was ever more widely promulgating. After those four sessions, as John Taylor later explained, "the meetings were discontinued" because "Emma Smith the Pres[ident] taught the sisters that the principle of plural marriage . . . was not of God."[12] Eliza R. Snow left the situation ambiguous by acknowledging to a Relief Society in 1868 that "Emma Smith . . . the Presidentess . . . gave it [Relief Society] up so as not to lead the society in Erro[r]."[13]

Out of the Nauvoo Relief Society then came women who would add other shared experiences: temple endowments, sealings, participation in plural marriage, and the trials of continued loyalty and unflagging obedience to church leaders. Of the charter members four women would be counted among the female elite in Utah forty years later: Sarah M. Kimball, Elizabeth Ann Whitney, Eliza R. Snow, and Bathsheba W. Smith. Four others, Zina D. H. Jacobs [later Young], her sister Presendia L. Buel [later Kimball], Mary Isabella Horne, and Phoebe Woodruff, all joined the Nauvoo Relief Society within its first months, and though their association was not demonstrably close, the shared knowledge gained there became a later binding force for them.

The practices and relationships begun at Nauvoo solidified in Winter Quarters, that shanty-town on the Missouri River where the first groups of Saints waited almost a year before finishing their trek from Illinois to the Great Basin. The significance of the events of that place that first winter have not been fully assessed, especially as far as women's affairs are concerned. It was there that the associations and ordinances of Nauvoo tightened into the bonds of families real and adopted, which formed a basis of selection into the leadership positions of the male hierarchy. Similarly among the women bonds not only of kinship in newly acknowledged plural families but of sisterhood born of proximity and necessity were formed whose ties would continue in many cases into the next century.

Readers of Eliza R. Snow's Winter Quarters diary and that of Patty Sessions have noted the proliferation of "blessing meetings" which filled the afternoons and evenings from midwinter until the time of departure of the various companies. Kenneth Godfrey in a description of Winter Quarters through the eyes mainly of Mary Haskins Parker Richards observed that those meeting were restricted mainly to the ecclesiastical elite.[14] If he is right, then the thesis is even more accurate than supposed: in Winter Quarters women who subsequently lead out in women's affairs in Utah identified themselves, set their standards, re-established certain rituals, and thus cemented the ties which held their group.

A significant occasion took place on Christmas 1846, when a group of the women gathered for a visit. Eliza R. Snow wrote of the event in her diary: "This mor[ning] take leave of the female family and visit sis. [Patty] Sessions with Loisa [Beaman] and Zina [D. H. Jacobs] very pleasantly. Last eve we had a very interesting time to close my five-day visit with the girls, for whom my love seem'd to increase with every day's acquaintance. To describe the scene alluded to would be beyond my pow'r. Suffice it to say, the spirit of the Lord was pour'd out and we receive'd a blessing thro' our beloved mother Chase and sis Clarissa by the gift of tongues."[15]

Two significant notes grow from this account: first, the women were perpetuating the spiritual activity which bound them together in commitment to the faith. Such meetings would escalate in Winter Quarters the following spring, continue as feasible across the plains, carry on for the first few years in the valley, and be relived for a time in Cardston, Alberta, and Snowflake, Arizona. The emotional bonding of women under such circumstances has been described in Carroll Smith Rosenberg's 1975 study of "The Female World of Love and Ritual" as characteristic of the homo-social patterns of the nineteenth century.[16] The ritual blessing of each other could not but strengthen whatever individual friendships might be forming under the adverse and isolated conditions of the winter's camp.

The second significant note deals with the individual women named in that and adjacent entries. It is apparent that in Winter Quarters, for the first time above whispers, plural wives were identifying themselves to each other. In the case cited, Brigham Young was a husband to all but one of the "female family," Mother Chase, and she was mother of Clarissa Ross, Young's plural wife since 1844. Loisa Beaman and Zina Jacobs who accompany Eliza, and Eliza herself, were all Young's wives; and Patty Sessions, whom the three women afterward visit had also been a plural wife of Joseph Smith.

Among the participants in subsequent Winter Quarters blessing meetings were most of the wives of Brigham Young and of Heber C. Kimball, Young's next in command. Eliza R. Snow, whose reputation in Nauvoo had been based mainly on her intellectual and poetic gifts, here emerges as a spiritual leader, an honor she shares with Patty Sessions who plays a lieutenant's role to Eliza's general. Legitimized by her marriage since October 1844 to Brigham Young, Eliza could also speak of her earlier preference by Joseph Smith, a fact she continued to emphasize in later years.

Two sisters prominent in the Winter Quarters accounts are Zina Huntington Jacobs and Presendia Huntington Buel (or Buell), both of whom had chosen Joseph Smith over their living husbands and since had been relocated—Zina in Brigham Young's family and Presendia in Heber Kimball's. Winter Quarters brought them together as wives of the two leading elders. Bolstered by each other and by their friendship with Eliza Snow and Patty Sessions, they rose to some heights in the blessing meetings, as indicated by the frequency with which the diaries mention their names. Vilate Kimball and Mary Ann Young, the first surviving wives of their husbands, figured in the meetings but as attenders more than as active participants. Not herself of the Young-Kimball group but certainly linked by affection and by the marriages of her son and daughter to Kimball's families was Elizabeth Ann Whitney, who had taken an active role in the Nauvoo Relief Society. In Winter Quarters her gifts of tongues and prophecy gained her the respect of her sisters, and her title of "Mother Whitney" became even more widespread.

That the women varied widely in age seemed no deterrent to their mutual affection and concern. The test of faith which plural marriage was becoming had cut across age barriers, as women in their late forties found themselves sister wives to women half their ages. The meetings in Winter Quarters joined more than divided the women in their common cause: older wives mentored younger ones, delivered their babies, coached them in their exercise of "the gifts," while younger ones performed tasks for their older sister wives, visited with them, honored them with the title "Mother." The accounts of the meetings show a second echelon of younger women learning their roles: such names as Helen Mar Kimball, Mary Isabella Horne, and Emmeline Harris Whitney [later Wells], occasionally mentioned in Winter Quarters, would appear increasingly during the thirty years following their arrival in Utah.

For the first few years in Great Salt Lake City, the informal meetings continued as they had in Winter Quarters.[17] They were then succeeded by a rash of various associations for very disparate purposes, none of which seem to have brought together the same groups of women. In 1854 the Polysophical Society in Apostle Lorenzo Snow's hall collected an intellectual elite of both sexes, Lorenzo's sister Eliza being central to the enterprise. The Council of Health and its female counterpart interested the more practical Patty Sessions and other midwives and lay practitioners. Elocution societies, the Universal Scientific Society, the Horticultural Society, the Deseret Philharmonic Society, and the Deseret Agricultural and Manufacturing Society attracted their separate followings. One such thrust was especially significant: with the blessing of Brigham Young, Relief Societies sprang up in at least twenty-two wards, this time with the express purpose of providing clothing for Indian women and children. But there was no central organization, and though some of the women who composed the ecclesiastical and social elite of the community were involved, they were not together in one group. Only in their individual callings as workers in the Endowment House might the leading women have served together.

The 1850s Relief Societies, disrupted in most wards by the Utah War, continued in others almost exclusively as a welfare service, looking to the needs of the poor of the ward. The winter of 1866-67, however, brought some innovations which suggest a widening official view of women and their roles. Brigham Young reestablished the School of the Prophets among the men of the church and announced on at least one occasion his intention to so organize the women. The cooperative movement with its drive to monopolize purchasing to local outlets drew attention to the need to involve women, both as consumers and as workers in the operation. The General Sunday School Union called attention to the rearing of children. And above all, on the highest spiritual plane, Brigham Young as holder of the keys began administering the sacred second anointing, an ordinance which men cannot receive without their wives.[18]

That the Relief Society should experience its third birth at that time seems consistent and that it should have a spiritual focus was inevitable. Eliza R. Snow, who had been officiating as matron in the Endowment House and whose reputation as prophetess and priestess had spread far, was called to head the women's work. She had been secretary for the Nauvoo society and promulgated the example of that organization by carrying with her its minutes, reading from Joseph Smith's sermons as she instructed local leaders. Although her 1867 call to organize the Relief Society carried no official title, she made of it the supreme office among Mormon women: "Presidentess of the female portion of the human race" was the honor accorded her by one over-eager ward secretary as she traveled about organizing local units.

But in her calling she served alone at first. Not until 1869 did she have a coterie of aides to assist in the work. It was in the organization of the Retrenchment Association that the "leading sisters" came together and became the force behind the local Relief Societies.

The Senior and Junior Cooperative Retrenchment Association began when Mary Isabella Horne, one of the younger stalwarts from Nauvoo and Winter Quarter days, was visiting her son, the bishop in the central Utah community of Gunnison, when Brigham Young and his entourage arrived en route to the Dixie colonies. Young was disturbed that the women in the various towns seemed to be such Marthas about the fine meals they prepared that they were losing the Mary-like values of his visits. He assigned to Mary Isabella the task of teaching her sisters a simpler way, encouraging them to "retrench" from their elaborate preparations. Arriving back in Salt Lake City, Sister Horne called on Sister Eliza Snow and Sister Margaret Smoot, and the three approached President Young for clarification.[19] That one meeting seems to have been his total official involvement in the setting up of a group which would meet thereafter for at least two decades with agendas expanded far beyond the initial goals of the retrenchment movement. The women elected their own president, Sister Horne, and six counselors and established a pattern of meeting on alternate Thursdays. Called finally the "ladies semi-monthly meeting," it was the only continuous gathering of women which crossed ward and stake lines, was not accountable to local authority, and brought together the "leading sisters" in a network which was capable of unhindered activity.

A reading of the three years of minutes of that group reveals the working of the network.[20] It was there that the women not only shared personal witness and affirmed sisterhood but learned of activities they would later more formally support: the retrenchment program itself, various Relief Society programs, cooperatives, home manufacture, civic duties, the MIA for young men (which would grow out of their young women's example), Primary Associations, and the United Order. In each case the group assembled in the Fourteenth Ward building felt it entirely appropriate to take unilateral action towards the goals it espoused, often with no more suggestion than a casual comment of Brigham Young. After he had spoken to Emmeline B. Wells about the necessity for storing grain, for example, she stewed for a while, wrote an editorial for the *Exponent,* and then the women in their regular meeting, directed by Eliza Snow, elected a central board to oversee the project. What began as an assignment to Wells became the responsibility of the whole group.[21] Following similar steps, the women of the semi-monthly meeting, especially those who traveled as companions to Eliza Snow on her frequent tours to various settlements, directed affairs of their sisters throughout Mormondom, independent of hierarchical authority chains.

A group as powerful as this, it can safely be assumed, would of necessity have as its core those women who individually held the reins of leadership among their sisters—an elite not only ecclesiastically but socially and politically. A tally of the women named in the minutes, noting the frequency with which they are mentioned, confirmed the thesis with which this essay began: (1) there was an elite among the Mormon women in Utah, (2) that elite had power in its sphere, (3) the women who made up the power base were those who had come earliest into the valley, having undergone the early formative experiences in Nauvoo and Winter Quarters. The names which recur most frequently in the minutes are familiar: Eliza R. Snow, Zina D. H. Young, Presendia L. Kimball, Elizabeth Ann Whitney, Sarah M. Kimball, Bathsheba W. Smith, Mary Isabella Horne, and Phoebe Woodruff. These were the leaders. They had in common more than just those characteristics of primacy and longevity. They lived in the central wards of Salt Lake City. (Margaret Smoot, who often traveled with Eliza Snow, pled distance as excusing her from the meetings; she lived in the 20th Ward, six blocks from downtown.) Six of the eight here named were married to general authorities of the church. All were plural wives; all had belonged to the Nauvoo Relief Society and all but one had participated in the Winter Quarters experience.

Next to this inner elite was a second echelon of "leading sisters," identified in most cases by their association with the inner core. These women, such as Emmeline Wells, Hannah T. King, Willmirth East, Elizabeth Howard, Zina Y. Williams, and Helen Mar Whitney, shared some but not all the characteristics of the leading group. Emmeline Wells had been at Winter Quarters but had not participated then or in the early years in Salt Lake City in blessing meetings; Hannah King was married to a non-Mormon (though she was later sealed to Brigham Young), and Elizabeth Howard had not entered into polygamy; Willmirth East moved to Arizona; Zina Young Williams, who later moved to Canada, was a daughter and Helen Mar Kimball Whitney a daughter-in-law of the older leading sisters.

These and other second echelon women, well schooled in the advantages of a united corps of strong women, carried on much the same pattern of unhindered leadership in women's projects as they functioned remote from the central group. Jane S. Richards, living in Ogden, too far for intimate involvement with the inner group, nevertheless kept in close touch with them by mail and visits each way. Willmirth East, writing from Arizona, acknowledged the primacy of Eliza Snow's advice over that of her local priesthood authority in the affairs of the women. And Zina Young Williams, emigrating to southern Alberta in 1887 with her new husband Charles Ora Card, maintained strong ties with her mother's inner circle in Salt Lake City, thus reinforcing the position of leadership which she held by virtue of her role as wife of the president of the colony, not as Relief Society president. In these as in other colonies, the women continued those rituals which bound them together in their female groups—the blessing meetings, the washings and anointings, the administrations, as well as the institutionalized Relief Society—in much the same patterns as had been established in the original settlement of Salt Lake City a generation earlier.

Meanwhile, after 1877 when stake organizations regionalized some of the responsibility and created a new level of administration, and when the women's organizations, Relief Society, MIA, and Primary, were given each its own head, the power of the Salt Lake City central group gradually diminished. The "old girls" died, albeit slowly—Bathsheba Smith remained president of the Relief Society until 1910—and the younger women had less in common. But for that half century there was a powerful elite running as an effective undercurrent in the tides of Mormonism. Rulers in women's sphere, "free to create their own forms of personal, social and political relationships,"[22] they participated parallel to their brothers in building God's kingdom. Brigham Young knew the power of the women. He said, "I may preach to the female portion of this community until I am as old as Methusaleh; but when they, the sisters, themselves, take hold to reform they will wield an influence that will be successful, and will save many thousands of dollars yearly to the community. It is utterly vain for me to try to exert such an influence."[23]

The statement, flippant though it sounds, reflects an organizational reality. Women were their own acknowledged and unquestioned leaders. With operational power thus vested in a cohesive group of faithful, conscientious women, it is not surprising that they and their sisters contributed so remarkably to the political, educational, economic, and social well-being of the Mormon community of the Intermountain West. As Leonard Arrington concluded, with atypical restraint, their "contributions to Mormon economic and territorial growth have not been negligible."[24]

NOTES

1. John Hyde, Jr., *Mormonism: Its Leaders and Designs* (New York: W. P. Fetridge & Company, 1857), 127-28.

2. Beverly Beeton in conversation with the author, spring 1975.

3. Jill Mulvay Derr and C. Brooklyn Derr, "Outside the Mormon Hierarchy: Alternative Aspects of Institutional Power," MS in my file.

4. Augusta Joyce Crocheron, *Representative Women of Deseret* (Salt Lake City: J. C. Graham & Co., 1884).

5. D. Michael Quinn, "The Mormon Hierarchy, 1832-1932: An American Elite," Ph.D. diss., Yale University, 1976.

6. "Sarah M. Kimball," in *Representative Women*, 26-27.

7. Minutes of the Female Relief Society of Nauvoo, 17 Mar. 1842, archives, historical department, Church of Jesus Christ of Latter-day Saints, Salt Lake City, Utah; hereafter LDS archives. This and other documents from LDS archives are used with permission. Of the twenty women listed, two names, Athalia Robinson and Nancy Rigdon, have been stricken through, and subsequent histories of the Relief Society based on a later typescript of the minutes have listed only eighteen women as having attended. A likely explanation for the striking out is in the notion that when Mormons left the church, as these two daughters of Sidney Rigdon did,

"their names were blotted out, that they were remembered no more among the people of God" (Al. 1:24).

8. Nauvoo Census, 1842, microfilm, LDS archives.

9. William Lawrence Foster, "Between Two Worlds: The Origins of Shaker Celibacy, Oneida Community Complex Marriage, and Mormon Polygamy," Ph.D. diss., University of Chicago, 1976, 224-28.

10. Nauvoo Relief Society Minutes, 30 Mar. 1842.

11. Names courtesy Andrew Ehat.

12. John Taylor, in Harrisville Ward General Minutes, 29 June 1881, LDS archives. For an account of these events from the viewpoint of Emma Smith, see Linda King Newell and Valleen Tippets Avery, *Mormon Enigma: Emma Hale Smith* (Garden City, NY: Doubleday, 1984).

13. West Jordan Ward Relief Society Minutes, 7 Sept. 1868, LDS archives.

14. Kenneth W. Godfrey, "Winter Quarters: Glimmering Glimpses into Mormon Religion and Social Life," unpublished ms. in possession of Leonard J. Arrington.

15. Eliza R. Snow, Diary, 1846-49, 1 Jan. 1847, microfilm, LDS archives.

16. Carroll Smith-Rosenberg, "The Female World of Love and Ritual: Relations Between Women in Nineteenth Century America," *Signs* 1 (Autumn 1975): 1-29.

17. Richard L. Jensen, "Clothing the Indians and Strengthening the Saints: Organized Activity of Mormon Women During the 'Lapse' of the Relief Society, 1844-1867," *Task Papers in LDS History,* No. 27 (Salt Lake City: Historical Department of The Church of Jesus Christ of Latter-day Saints, 1979), 2.

18. Wilford Woodruff Diary, 31 Dec. 1866; also year end summary for 1867, 1868, LDS archives.

19. Susa Young Gates, *History of the Young Ladies' Mutual Improvement Association . . .* (Salt Lake City: General Board of the YLMIA, 1911), 31.

20. Minutes of the Senior and Junior Cooperative Retrenchment Association, 1870-73, LDS archives.

21. *Woman's Exponent* 5 (1 Dec. 1876): 98.

22. Estelle Freedman, "Separatism as Strategy: Female Institution Building and American Feminism, 1870-1930," *Feminist Studies* 5 (Fall 1979): 514.

23. *Deseret News Weekly,* 11 Aug. 1869.

24. Leonard J. Arrington, "The Economic Role of Pioneer Mormon Women," *Western Humanities Review* 9 (Spring 1955): 164.

10.
Notes on Mormon Polygamy

Stanley S. Ivins

TIME WAS WHEN, IN THE POPULAR MIND, MORMONISM MEANT ONLY polygamy.[1] It was assumed that every Mormon man was a practical or theoretical polygamist. This was a misconception, for there were always many of these Latter-day Saints who refused to go along with the doctrine of "plurality of wives." It was accepted by only a few of the more than fifty churches or factions which grew out of the revelations of the prophet Joseph Smith. Principal advocate of the doctrine was the Utah church, which far outnumbered all other branches of Mormonism. And strongest opposition from within Mormondom came from the second largest group, the Reorganized Church of Jesus Christ of Latter Day Saints, with headquarters at Independence, Missouri.

This strange experiment in family relations extended over a period of approximately sixty-five years. It was professedly inaugurated on 5 April 1841 in a cornfield outside the city of Nauvoo, Illinois, with the sealing of Louisa Beaman to Joseph Smith. And it was brought to an official end by a resolution adopted at the 74th annual conference of the Utah church on 4 April 1904. Since that time those who have persisted in carrying on with it have been excommunicated. But the project was openly and energetically prosecuted during only about forty years. For the first ten years the new doctrine was kept pretty well under wraps, and it was not until the fall of 1852 that it was openly avowed and the Saints were told that only those who embraced it could hope for the highest exaltation in

169

the resurrection. And during the fifteen years prior to 1904, there were only a few privately solemnized plural marriages. So it might be said that the experiment was ten years in embryo, enjoyed a vigorous life of forty years, and took fifteen years to die.

The extent to which polygamy was practiced in Utah will probably never be known. Plural marriages were not publicly recorded, and there is little chance that any private records which might have been kept will ever be revealed.

Curious visitors to Utah in the days when polygamy was flourishing were usually told that about one-tenth of the people actually practiced it. Since the abandonment of the principle, this estimate has been revised downward. A recent official published statement by the Mormon church said: "The practice of plural marriage has never been general in the Church and at no time have more than three per cent of families in the Church been polygamous." This estimate was apparently based upon testimony given during the investigation into the right of Reed Smoot to retain his seat in the United States Senate. A high church official, testifying there, referred to the 1882 report of the Utah Commission, which said that application of the anti-polygamy laws had disfranchised approximately 12,000 persons in Utah. The witness declared that since at least two-thirds of these must have been women, there remained no more than 4,000 polygamists, which he believed constituted less than 2 percent of the church population. The error of setting heads of families against total church membership is obvious. Using the same report, Senator Dubois concluded that 23 percent of Utah Mormons over eighteen years of age were involved in polygamy. Later on in the Smoot hearing, the same church official testified that a careful census taken in 1890 revealed that there were 2,451 plural families in the United States. This suggests that at that time, 10 percent or more of the Utah Mormons might have been involved in polygamy.

Of more than 6,000 Mormon families, sketches of which are found in a huge volume published in 1913, between 15 and 20 percent appear to have been polygamous.[2] And a history of Sanpete and Emery counties contains biographical sketches of 722 men, of whom 12.6 percent married more than one woman.[3]

From information obtainable from all available sources, it appears that there may have been a time when 15 or possibly 20 percent of the Mormon families of Utah were polygamous. This leaves the great majority of the Saints delinquent in their obligation to the principle of plurality of wives.

While the small proportion of Mormons who went into polygamy may not necessarily be a true measure of its popularity, there is other evidence that they were not anxious to rush into it, although they were constantly reminded of its importance to their salvation.

A tabulation by years of about 2,500 polygamous marriages, covering the whole period of this experiment, reveals some interesting facts. It indicates that until the death of the prophet Joseph Smith in the summer of 1844, the privilege of taking extra wives was pretty well monopolized by him and a few of his trusted disciples. Following his death and the assumption of leadership by the twelve apostles under Brigham Young, there was a noticeable increase in plural marriages. This may be accounted for by the fact that during the winter of 1845-46, the Nauvoo temple was finished to a point where it could be used for the performance of sacred rites and ordinances. For a few weeks before their departure in search of a refuge in the Rocky Mountains, the Saints worked feverishly at their sealings and endowments. As part of this religious activity, the rate of polygamous marrying rose to a point it was not again to reach for ten years. It then fell off sharply and remained low until the stimulation given by the public announcement in the fall of 1852 that polygamy was an essential tenet of the church. This spurt was followed by a sharp decline over the next few years.

Beginning in the fall of 1856 and during a good part of the following year, the Utah Mormons were engaged in the greatest religious revival of their history. To the fiery and sometimes intemperate exhortations of their leaders, they responded with fanatical enthusiasm, which at times led to acts of violence against those who were slow to repent. There was a general confession of sins and renewal of covenants through baptism, people hastened to return articles "borrowed" from their neighbors, and men who had not before given a thought to the matter began looking for new wives. And as one of the fruits of "the Reformation," plural marriages skyrocketed to a height not before approached and never again to be reached. If our tabulation is a true index, there were 65 percent more of such marriages during 1856 and 1857 than in any other two years of this experiment.

With the waning of the spirit of reformation, the rate of polygamous marrying dropped in 1858 to less than a third and in 1859 to less than a fifth of what it was in 1857. This decline continued until 1862 when Congress, responding to the clamor of alarmists, enacted a law prohibiting bigamy in Utah and other territories. The answer of the Mormons to this rebuke was a revival of plural marrying to a point not previously reached except during the gala years of the Reformation.

The next noticeable acceleration in the marriage rate came in 1868 and 1869 and coincided with the inauguration of a boycott against the gentile merchants and the organization of an anti-Mormon political party. But this increased activity was short-lived and was followed by a slump lasting for a dozen years. By 1881 polygamous marrying had fallen to almost its lowest ebb since the public avowal of the doctrine of plurality.

With the passage of the Edmunds Act of 1882, which greatly strengthened the anti-polygamy laws, the government began its first serious effort to suppress the practice of polygamy. The Mormons responded with their last major revival of polygamous activity, which reached its height in 1884 and 1885. But with hundreds of polygamists imprisoned and most of the church leaders driven into exile to avoid arrest, resistance weakened and there was a sudden decline in marriages, which culminated in formal capitulation in the fall of 1890. This was the end except for a few under-cover marriages during the ensuing fifteen years while the experiment was in its death throes.

If there is any significance in this chronicle of polygamous marrying, it is in the lack of evidence that the steady growth of the Utah church was accompanied by a corresponding increase in the number of such marriages. The story is rather one of sporadic outbursts of enthusiasm followed by relapses, with the proportion of the Saints living in polygamy steadily falling. And it appears to be more than chance that each outbreak of fervor coincided with some revivalist activity within the church or with some menace from without. It is evidence that far from looking upon plural marriage as a privilege to be made the most of, the rank and file Mormons accepted it as one of the onerous obligations of church membership. Left alone they were prone to neglect it, and it always took some form of pressure to stir them to renewed zeal.

The number of wives married by the men who practiced polygamy offers further evidence of lack of enthusiasm for the principle. A common mistaken notion was that most polygamists maintained large harems, an idea which can be attributed to the publicity given the few men who went in for marrying on a grand scale. Joseph Smith was probably the most married of these men. The number of his wives can only be guessed at, but it might have gone as high as sixty or more. Brigham Young is usually credited with only twenty-seven wives, but he was sealed to more than twice that many living women and to at least 150 more who had died. Heber C. Kimball had forty-five living wives, a number of them elderly ladies who never lived with him. No one else came close to these three men in the point of marrying. John D. Lee gave the names of his nineteen wives but modestly explained that "as I was married to old Mrs. Woolsey for her soul's sake, and she was near sixty years old when I married her, I never considered her really a wife. . . . That is the reason that I claim only eighteen true wives." And by taking fourteen wives, Jens Hansen earned special mention in the *Latter-day Saint Biographical Encyclopedia,* which said: "Of all the Scandinavian brethren who figured prominently in the Church Bro. Hansen distinguished himself by marrying more wives than any other of his countrymen in modern times." Orson Pratt, who was chosen to deliver the first public discourse on the subject of plural marriage and became its most able defender, had only ten living wives, but on two days a week apart, he was sealed for eternity to more than two hundred dead women.

But these men with many wives were the few exceptions to the rule. Of 1,784 polygamists, 66.3 percent married only one extra wife. Another 21.2 percent were three-wife men, and 6.7 percent went as far as to take four wives. This left a small group of less than 6 percent who married five or more women. The typical polygamist, far from being the insatiable male of popular fable, was a dispassionate fellow, content to call a halt after marrying the one extra wife required to assure him of his chance at salvation.

Another false conception was that polygamists were bearded patriarchs who continued marrying young girls as long as they were able to hobble about. It is true that Brigham Young took a young wife when he was sixty-seven years old, and a few others followed his example, but such marriages were not much more common with the

Mormons than among other groups. Of 1,229 polygamists more than 10 percent married their last wives while still in their twenties, and more than one half of them before arriving at the still lusty age of forty years. Not one in five took a wife after reaching his fiftieth year. The average age at which the group ceased marrying was forty years.

There appears to be more basis in fact for the reports that polygamists were likely to choose their wives from among the young girls who might bear them many children. Of 1,348 women selected as plural wives, 38 percent were in their teens, 67 percent were under twenty-five, and only 30 percent over thirty years of age. A few had passed forty, and about one in a hundred had, like John D. Lee's old Mrs. Woolsey, seen her fiftieth birthday.

There were a few notable instances of high speed marrying among the polygamists. Whatever the number of Joseph Smith's wives, he must have married them all over a period of thirty-nine months. And Brigham Young took eight wives in a single month, four of them on the same day. But only a few enthusiasts indulged in such rapid marrying. As a rule it proceeded at a much less hurried pace. Not one plural marriage in ten followed a previous marriage by less than a year. The composite polygamist was first married at the age of twenty-three to a girl of twenty. Thirteen years later he took a plural wife, choosing a twenty-two-year-old girl. The chances were two to one that having demonstrated his acceptance of the principle of plurality, he was finished with marrying. If, however, he took a third wife, he waited four years and then selected another girl of twenty-two. The odds were now three to one against his taking a fourth wife, but if he did so, he waited another four years and once more chose a twenty-two-year-old girl, although he had now reached the ripe age of forty-four. In case he decided to add a fifth wife, he waited only two years, and this time the lady of his choice was twenty-one years old. This was the end of his marrying, unless he belonged to a 3 percent minority.

Available records offer no corroboration of the accusation that many polygamous marriages were incestuous. They do, however, suggest the source of such reports in the surprisingly common practice of marrying sisters. The custom was initiated by Joseph Smith, among whose wives were at least three pairs of sisters. His example was followed by Heber C. Kimball, whose forty-five wives included Clarissa and Emily Cutler, Amanda and Anna Gheen,

Harriet and Ellen Sanders, Hannah and Dorothy Moon, and Laura and Abigail Pitkin. Brigham Young honored the precedent by marrying the Decker sisters, Lucy and Clara, and the Bigelow girls, Mary and Lucy. And John D. Lee told how he married the three Woolsey sisters, Agatha Ann, Rachel, and Andora, and rounded out the family circle by having their mother sealed to him for her soul's sake. Among his other wives were the Young sisters, Polly and Lovina, sealed to him on the same evening. The popularity of this custom is indicated by the fact that of 1,642 polygamists, 10 percent married one or more pairs of sisters.

While marrying sisters could have been a simple matter of propinquity, there probably was some method in it. Many a man went into polygamy reluctantly, fully aware of its hazards. Knowing that his double family must live in one small home and realizing that the peace of his household would hinge upon the congeniality between its two mistresses, he might well hope that if they were sisters the chances for domestic tranquility would be more even. And a wife consenting to share her husband with another could not be blamed for asking that he choose her sister instead of bringing home a strange woman.

The fruits of this experiment in polygamy are not easy to appraise. In defense of their marriage system, the Mormons talked much about the benefits it would bring. By depriving husbands of an excuse for seeking extra-marital pleasures and by making it possible for every woman to marry, it was to solve the problem of the "social evil" by eliminating professional prostitution and other adulterous activities. It was to furnish healthy tabernacles for the countless spirits waiting anxiously to assume their earthly bodies. It was to build up a "righteous generation" of physically and intellectually superior individuals. It was to enhance the glory of the polygamist through a posterity so numerous that in the course of eternity he might become the god of a world peopled by his descendants. And there was another blessing in store for men who lived this principle. Heber C. Kimball, Brigham Young's chief lieutenant, explained it this way: "I would not be afraid to promise a man who is sixty years of age, if he will take the counsel of brother Brigham and his brethren, that he will renew his age. I have noticed that a man who has but one wife, and is inclined to that doctrine, soon begins to wither and dry up, while a man who goes into plurality looks fresh, young and sprightly. Why is this?

Because God loves that man, and because he honors His work and word. Some of you may not believe this; but I not only believe it—I also know it. For a man of God to be confined to one woman is small business; for it is as much as we can do now to keep up under the burdens we have to carry; and I do not know what we should do if we had only one wife apiece."[4]

It does appear that Mormon communities of the polygamous era were comparatively free from the evils of professional prostitution. But this can hardly be attributed to the fact that a few men, supposedly selected for their moral superiority, were permitted to marry more than one wife. It might better be credited to the common teaching that adultery was a sin so monstrous that there was no atonement for it short of the spilling of the blood of the offender. It would be strange indeed if such a fearful warning failed to exert a restraining influence upon the potential adulterer. . . .

When it came to fathering large families and supplying bodies for waiting spirits, the polygamists did fairly well but fell far short of some of their dreams. Heber C. Kimball once said of himself and Brigham Young: "In twenty-five or thirty years we will have a larger number in our two families than there now is in this whole Territory, which numbers more than seventy-five thousand. If twenty-five years will produce this amount of people, how much will be the increase in one hundred years?"[5] And the *Millennial Star* reckoned that a hypothetical Mr. Fruitful with forty wives might at the age of seventy-eight number among his seed 3,508,441 souls while his monogamous counterpart could boast of only 152.[6]

With such reminders of their potentialities before them, the most married of the polygamist must have been far from satisfied with the results they could show. There is no conclusive evidence that any of Joseph Smith's many plural wives bore children by him. Heber C. Kimball with his forty-five wives was the father of sixty-five children. John D. Lee with only eighteen "true wives" fell one short of Kimball's record, and Brigham Young fathered fifty-six children, approximately one for each wife.

Although the issue of the few men of many wives was disappointing in numbers, the rank and file of polygamists made a fair showing. Of 1,651 families more than four-fifths numbered ten or more children. Half of them had fifteen or more and one fourth, twenty or more. There were eighty-eight families of thirty or more, nineteen of forty or more, and seven of fifty or more. The average number of children per family was fifteen. And by the third or fourth generation some families had reached rather impressive proportions. When one six-wife elder had been dead fifty-five years, his descendants numbered 1,900.

While polygamy increased the number of children of the men, it did not do the same for the women involved. A count revealed that 3,335 wives of polygamists bore 19,806 children, for an average of 5.9 per woman. An equal number of wives of monogamists taken from the same general group bore 26,780 for an average of 8. This suggests the possibility that the overall production of children in Utah may have been less than it would have been without benefit of plurality of wives. The claim that plurality was needed because of a surplus of women is not borne out by statistics.

There is little doubt that the plural wife system went a good way toward making it possible for every woman to marry. According to Mormon teachings, a woman could "never obtain a fullness of glory, without being married to a righteous man for time and all eternity." If she never married or was the wife of a gentile, her chance of attaining a high degree of salvation was indeed slim. And one of the responsibilities of those in official church positions was to try to make sure that no woman went without a husband. When a widow or a maiden lady "gathered" to Utah, it was a community obligation to see to it that she had food and shelter and the privilege of being married to a good man. If she received no offer of marriage, it was not considered inconsistent with feminine modesty for her to "apply" to the man of her choice, but if she set her sights too high, she might be disappointed. My grandmother, who did sewing for the family of Brigham Young, was fond of telling how she watched through a partly open doorway while he forcibly ejected a woman who was too persistent in applying to be sealed to him. Her story would always end with the same words: "And I just couldn't help laughing to see brother Brigham get so out of patience with that woman." However, if the lady in search of a husband was not too ambitious, her chances of success were good. It was said of the bishop of one small settlement that he "was a good bishop. He married all the widows in town and took good care of them." And John D. Lee was following accepted precedent when he married old Mrs. Woolsey for her soul's sake.

As for Mr. Kimball's claims concerning the spiritual uplift to be derived from taking a fresh young wife, what man is going to quarrel with him about that?

The most common reasons given for opposition to the plural wife system were that it was not compatible with the American way of life, that it debased the women who lived under it, and that it caused disharmony and unhappiness in the family. To these charges the Mormon men replied that their women enjoyed a higher social position than those of the outside world and that there was less contention and unhappiness in their families than in those of the gentiles. There is no statistical information upon which to base a judgment as to who had the better of this argument.

In addition to these general complaints about polygamy, its critics told some fantastic stories about the evils which followed in its wake. It was said that through some mysterious workings of the laws of heredity, polygamous children were born with such peculiarities as feeble-mindedness, abnormal sexual desires, and weak and de-formed bodies.

At a meeting of the New Orleans Academy of Sciences in 1861, a remarkable paper was presented by Dr. Samuel A. Cartwright and Prof. C. G. Forshey. It consisted mainly of quotations from a report made by Assistant Surgeon Robert Barthelow of the United States Army on the "Effects and Tendencies of Mormon Polygamy in the Territory of Utah." Barthelow had observed that the Mormon system of marriage was already producing a people with distinct racial characteristics. He said: "The yellow, sunken, cadaverous visage; the greenish-colored eye; the thick, protuberant lips; the low forehead; the light, yellowish hair, and the lank, angular person, constitute an appearance so characteristic of the new race, the production of polygamy, as to distinguish them at a glance. The older men and women present all the physical peculiarities of the nationalities to which they belong; but these peculiarities are not propagated and continued in the new race; they are lost in the prevailing type." Dr. Cartwright observed that the Barthelow report went far "to prove that polygamy not only blights the physical organism, but the moral nature of the white or Adamic woman to so great a degree as to render her incapable of breeding any other than abortive specimens of humanity—a new race that would die out—utterly perish from the earth, if left to sustain itself."[7]

When one or two of the New Orleans scientists questioned

the soundness of parts of this paper, the hecklers were silenced by Dr. Cartwright's retort that the facts presented were not so strong as "those which might be brought in proof of the debasing influence of abolitionism on the moral principles and character of that portion of the Northern people who have enacted personal liberty bills to evade a compliance with their constitutional obligations to the Southern States, and have elevated the Poltroon Sumner into a hero, and made a Saint of the miscreant Brown."[8]

Needless to say there is no evidence that polygamy produced any such physical and mental effects upon the progeny of those who practiced it. A study of the infant mortality rate in a large number of Mormon families showed no difference between the polygamous and monogamous households.

It is difficult to arrive at general conclusions concerning this experiment in polygamy, but a few facts about it are evident. Mormondom was not a society in which all men married many wives, but one in which a few men married two or more wives. Although plurality of wives was taught as a tenet of the church, it was not one of the fundamental principles of the Mormon faith, and its abandonment was accomplished with less disturbance than that caused by its introduction. The Saints accepted plurality in theory, but most of them were loath to put it into practice, despite the continual urging of leaders in whose divine authority they had the utmost faith. Once the initial impetus given the venture had subsided it became increasingly unpopular. In 1857 there were nearly fourteen times as many plural marriages for each one thousand Utah Mormons as there were in 1880. Left to itself undisturbed by pressure from without, the church would inevitably have given up the practice of polygamy, perhaps even sooner than it did under pressure. The experiment was not a satisfactory test of plurality of wives as a social system. Its results were neither spectacular nor conclusive, and they gave little justification for either the high hopes of its promoters or the dire predictions of its critics.

NOTES

1. "Polygamy" is used here rather than the technically correct "polygyny" because it is the term generally employed to designate this Mormon experiment in marriage.

2. Frank Esshom, *Pioneers and Prominent Men of Utah* (Salt Lake City, 1913).

3. W. H. Lever, *History of Sanpete and Emery Counties, Utah* (Ogden, 1898).

4. *Journal of Discourses* (Liverpool, 1854-86), 5:22.

5. Ibid., 4:224.

6. *Latter-day Saints' Millennial Star* 19 (June/July 1857): 384, 432.

7. See *DeBow's Review* 30 (Feb. 1861): 206.

8. Ibid.

11.
Divorce among Mormon Polygamists: Extent and Explanations

*Eugene E. Campbell
and Bruce L. Campbell*

STUDIES OF MORMON POLYGAMY HAVE TENDED TO EMPHASIZE THE origin and motivation for the practice, courtship techniques, inter-family relationships, economic adjustments, housing arrangements, and legal difficulties, but very little has been written concerning divorce. Kimball Young has one short chapter in his *Isn't One Wife Enough?*, but he admitted that he had "no adequate information as to the number of church divorces, granted annually or in toto."[1] He believed that most divorces were granted by bishop's courts but said, "apparently some separations were managed by the President of the Church directly."[2] To further complicate matters, it may never be possible to secure an accurate divorce rate for polygamous marriages because it is not known how many marriages took place, since plural marriages were not recorded officially. Stanley Ivins contended that "there is little chance that any private records which might have been kept will ever be revealed."[3]

Nevertheless recent studies have revealed that 1,645 divorces were granted by Brigham Young during the period of his presidency and that many of these were obtained by prominent pioneer leaders involved in the practice of plural marriage. Unfortunately most of these records do not state the grounds for these divorces nor the number of children involved nor even if they were the result of

181

polygamous marriages. However, they do indicate that many Mormon marriages during this period were unstable and that official attitudes toward divorce were lenient.[4]

Despite the lack of documentary evidence that these divorces resulted from polygamous marriages, there are reasons to believe that most if not all of these certificates were issued to polygamists. First, many prominent men known to be polygamists are listed on these records of divorce. The names of many general authorities of the LDS church as well as stake and ward leaders are included. Second, several cases reveal that two or more wives were divorced from one man on the same day. The most unusual case is that of George D. Grant who was divorced from three wives on the same day and from a fourth wife within five weeks. More conclusive evidence is the fact that Brigham Young did not have authority to grant civil divorces terminating monogamous marriages, but as president of the church he alone had the right to sever polygamous relationships. Polygamous marriages were always extralegal, and in the Mormon system only the president had the right to authorize marriages and divorces. The incoming and outgoing correspondence of the pioneer leader is replete with requests for permission to take extra wives as well as to be divorced from them.

It should be noted that polygamous marriages continued to be solemnized by Brigham Young's successors, John Taylor and Wilford Woodruff, for thirteen years after President Young's demise, and it seems logical to believe that they also granted divorces. If they granted them in similar numbers, it is likely that there were well in excess of 2,000 divorces granted prior to the 1890 Wilford Woodruff Manifesto. Since officially there were only an estimated 2,400 men practicing polygamy in 1885,[5] 2,000 or more divorces might be higher than the national divorce rate in 1890 which was about one divorce per 1,000 existing marriages per year.

Evidence from D. Michael Quinn's prosopographical study of early LDS church leaders tends to bear out these assumptions. He discovered that of the seventy-two general authorities who entered plural marriage, thirty-nine were involved in broken marriages, including fifty-four divorces, twenty-six separations, and one annulment.[6]

George Levinger in his article on "Marital Cohesiveness" discusses three factors related to marital stability: positive attractions within the marriage, barriers to divorce, and alternative attractions outside the marriage.[7] Some notable positive attractions within marriage are the status it gives, attraction to the spouse, children, and financial success through the economic cooperation of family members. Alternative attractions outside the marriage include such considerations as a new partner or increased status. If the marriage relationship is poor, escaping the marriage may be seen as an alternative attraction. In most societies, however, there are barriers to divorce such as "the emotional, religious and moral commitments that a partner feels toward his marriage or toward his children; the external pressures of kin and community, of the law, the church and other associational membership."[8] In Mormon theology, marriage "for time and all eternity" was the key to exaltation and eternal glory. Such marriages sealed by the priesthood would endure forever and give men and women the possibility of eternal increase whereby they could achieve godhood, ruling over their progeny. Such concepts put successful marriage at the top of the Mormon value system and supplied many of the positive attractions of plural marriage.

Gradually plural marriage became such an important institution in the Mormon subculture that some leaders were teaching that it was essential for eternal exaltation. For example, in 1886 the Mutual Improvement Association of Hyrum, Utah, began producing weekly manuscript newspapers that were passed around the community from home to home. The first edition of the *Evening Star* contained a sermon by a local leader on the front page that began "no one may be saved in the celestial kingdom of God unless he enters into the practice of plural marriage." A later edition asserted that "Abraham, the friend of God, was a polygamist. We have no account of the Lord appearing to Abraham before he had taken his second wife."[9] Another example of Mormon beliefs in this regard was suggested by Apostle Orson Pratt in the first official announcement and defense of polygamy in 1852. Asserting that polygamy was a sacred order that had been the practice of such biblical figures as Abraham, Jacob, and others, he then suggested "that there were several holy women that greatly loved Jesus—such as Mary, and Martha her sister, and Mary Magdalene; and Jesus greatly loved them, and associated with them much, and when he arose from the dead, instead of first showing himself to his chosen witnesses, the Apostles, he appeared first to these women, or at least to one of them, namely Mary Magdalene.

Now, it would be very natural for a husband in the resurrection to appear first to his own dear wives, and afterwards show himself to his other friends."[10]

Although this was not official church doctrine, there was considerable pressure in Mormon communities to enter polygamy. During one of the October general conference meetings in 1875, Apostle Wilford Woodruff asserted: "We have many bishops and elders who have but one wife. They are abundantly qualified to enter the higher law and take more, but their wives will not let them. Any man who will permit a woman to lead him and bind him down is but little account in the Church and Kingdom of God. The law of Patriarchal marriage and plurality of wives is a revelation and commandment of God to us, and we should obey it."[11]

Despite such teachings, Stanley Ivins theorized that even without pressure from the federal government Mormons would still have given up polygamy, perhaps even sooner than they did. He stated that "far from looking upon plural marriage as a privilege to be made the most of, the rank and file Mormons accepted it as one of the onerous obligations of church membership. Left alone, they were prone to neglect it, and it always took some form of pressure to stir them to renewed zeal."[12]

Kimball Young believed that "a marriage and family system such as polygamy, superimposed as it was upon Christian monogamy with all its values, was, at times, bound to induce such stress as to require some official form of divorce."[13] Both Young and Ivins seem to support the proposition that in the particular circumstances of Mormon polygamy, the positive attractions to polygamous unions were so few that in spite of theological barriers against divorce, many would desire to be freed from plural marriages. Kimball Young also noted that in many cases couples separated without divorce. He maintained that "while the records are often rather uncertain, the inference may be drawn that there was a general public acceptance of the idea that if a man and woman could not get along, they were free to break up and seek new mates."[14] In some cases, the wife would leave for California or return to her home in the East or run off with another man.

Thus even if it is believed that the positive attractions to polygamy were limited, it should not be assumed that because Mormons strongly advocated polygamy and the eternal family concept, the barriers against divorce, at least in polygamous unions, were very strong. Church leaders recognized the difficulties involved in establishing a different marriage system, and their own limited experience convinced them that there would be failures. In addition to the normal problems that arise in marriage relationships, the Mormon concepts of millennialism, feelings of romantic love, and lack of proven standards of conduct and behavior all contributed to the relatively high ratio of divorce among Mormon polygamists.

Millennialism. There are numerous evidences that LDS church leaders and members alike expected to witness the second coming of Jesus Christ and planned to participate in his millennial kingdom. A case in point was the millennialist fervor expressed at the dedication of the cornerstones of the Salt Lake Temple in 1853 and Orson Pratt's warning in 1855 that "this event [Jesus Christ's second coming] is nearer than this people are aware of."[15] In 1862 Brigham Young's statement to a group of his colleagues at the site of the Salt Lake Temple was even more explicit: "I expect this temple will stand through the millennium . . . and this is the reason why I am having the foundation of the temple taken up. . . . If we do not hurry with this, I am afraid we shall not get it up until we have to go back to Jackson County, (Missouri) which I expect will be in seven years."[16]

Millennial expectations rose to a considerable height during the so-called Reformation in the years 1856 to 1858, and apparently many plural marriages were contracted as a result of this extreme religious pressure. Stanley Ivins's study summarized these developments as follows: "As one of the fruits of 'the Reformation,' plural marriages skyrocketed to a height not before approached and never again to be reached. If our tabulation is a true index, there were 65 percent more of such marriages during 1856 and 1857 than in any two years of this experiment."[17]

An interesting glimpse of this period is provided by a letter from Wilford Woodruff to George A. Smith in April 1857: "We have had a great reformation this winter; some of the fruits are: all have confessed their sins either great or small, restored their stolen property; all have been baptized from the presidency down; all are trying to pay their tithing and nearly all are trying to get wives, until there is hardly a girl 14 years old in Utah, but what is married, or just going to be. President Young has hardly time to eat, drink or sleep, in consequence of marrying the people and attending the endowments."[18]

In fact competition for wives was so intense that several men asked permission to marry girls under the age of fourteen. One man was given permission but was counseled by Brigham Young to "preserve her intact until she is fully developed into womanhood." To another who requested permission to marry two sisters, he wrote, "I do not wish children to be married to men before an age which the mothers generally can best determine." A third applicant was advised, "Go ahead, but leave the children to grow."[19] Circumstances that promoted such pressures may be seen in the following letter written to Brigham Young at the height of the Reformation by a resident of Fillmore, Utah: "My circumstances is this, my wife has been cut off from the Church and Bishop Brunson commanded me to have no more to do with her as wife that I was free from her, and go and get me a good wife, and a half a dozen of them if I wanted them, but did not tell me where to go, as it is evident that I must go somewhere else than Fillmore as there is 56 single men here besides all the married ones that are on the anxious seat to get more and only 4 single women. Now Sir would it not be [be a] good policy for me to go on a Mission to the States or England if you thought best I know of some good women in the States of my own Baptizing that might be got besides many more."[20]

The pressure to marry polygamously appears to have been intense, and little attention was paid to the future stability of such marriages because of the belief that the coming millennium would solve such earthly problems. This pressure to marry for religious reasons may not have taken into account the necessary compatibility of the marriage partners. Additionally many of the normal problems of marriage, such as earning a livelihood, personality adjustment, the sexual relationship, jealousies, and child rearing were all magnified in plural marriage. When the idealism of millennial expectations subsided, many couples discovered the incompatibility of their plural marriage, and divorce or separation seemed to be the solution to their dilemma.

Apparently the field of eligible women one had to choose from became very limited in some areas, and compatibility in such marriages became even more problematic. Thus the millennialist orientation of the early Mormons tended to induce them to contract plural marriages for religious reasons, and this led to strains and tensions in the everyday management of marriage.

The leaders of the church were well aware of the strains in polygamous marriages. Speaking on polygamy in September 1856 at the height of the Reformation, Brigham Young said: "[I]t is frequently happening that women say they are unhappy. Men will say 'My wife, though a most excellent woman, has not seen a happy day since I took my second wife;' . . . another has not seen a happy day for five years. It is said that women are tied down and abused: that they are misused and have not the liberty they ought to have; that many of them are wading through a perfect flood of tears, because of the conduct of some men together with their own folly. I wish my own women to understand," he continued, "that what I am going to say is for them as well as others, and I want those who are here to tell their sisters, yes, all the women of the community, and then write back to the States, and do as you please with it. I am going to give you from this time to the 6th day of october next, for reflection, that you may determine whether you wish to stay with your husbands or not, and then I am going to set every woman at liberty and say to them, Now go your way, my women with the rest, go your way. And my wives have got to do one of two things; either round up their shoulders to endure the afflictions of this world, and live their religion, or they may leave, for I will not have them about me. I will go into heaven alone, rather than have scratching and fighting around me."[21]

Two weeks later at general conference, Young announced that he would fulfill his promise by releasing women under "certain conditions and that is that you will appear forthwith at my office and give good and sufficient reasons, and then marry men that will not have but one wife."[22]

On 15 December 1858 George A. Smith called on the church president to make application for a divorce in behalf of Nicholas Groesbeck from his second wife. Young said that when a man married a wife, he took her for better or worse and had no right to ill use her; a man that would mistreat a woman in order to get her to leave him would find himself alone in the worlds to come. He said he knew of no law to give a man in polygamy a divorce. He had told the brethren that if they would break the law, they should pay for it; but he did not want them to come to him for a divorce as it was not right. He then appealed to George A. Smith for confirmation of his position. Smith said, "President Young it is with you as it was with Moses. There is no law authorizing divorce, but through the hardness of the people you are obligated to permit it."[23] Three days later Young said: "It is not right for the brethren to divorce their wives the way they do. I am determined that if men don't stop divorcing their wives, I shall stop sealing. Men shall not abuse the gifts of God and the privileges the way they are doing. Nobody can say that I have any interest in the matter, for I charge nothing for sealings, but I do charge for divorcing. I want the brethren to stop divorcing their wives for it is not right."[24]

Although Young was opposed to divorce and was seriously concerned about the number of men divorcing their wives, it appears that he was willing to grant divorces when the people requested it. In the case of women, he seemed especially generous in freeing them from an unhappy marriage. On one occasion in a meeting with George A. Smith and others, he complained that "many men who come to him to get sealed would say 'thank you Brother Brigham,' and when a woman wanted to leave they were too stingy to get [buy] a bill of divorce."[25] His advice to a woman who came to him for counsel, was to "stay with her husband as long as she could bear with him, but if life became too burdensome, then leave and get a divorce." Then he remarked that other than a little scripture on the subject, he was not aware that the Lord had given any special revelations on the subject of divorce.[26]

Young was in a difficult position. As head of the LDS church he could have made obtaining divorces more difficult, but such a move could have resulted in rather undesirable (from his perspective) outcomes. If pressure was needed to force people into polygamy and divorce became difficult to obtain, perhaps fewer people would be willing to enter into plural marriages. And if Kimball Young's observation that the subculture allowed for casual separation of incompatible couples is correct, any attempt to strengthen the barriers to divorce may have only increased the number of Saints who were marrying and divorcing and remarrying outside of any authority— church or state. Perhaps President Young sensed that if he were to have any reasonable control over polygamy he must permit some divorces.

Thus although statements about the family and the eternal nature of the marriage covenant might lead one to conclude that the barrier against divorce in Mormon polygamy was strong, there were other factors tending to reduce that barrier. In fact the belief in millennialism may have operated to increase marriage tensions, resulting in a rather ambivalent attitude toward divorce in the Mormon subculture.

William J. Goode in his article on love suggests that the theoretical importance of this universal psychological potential (romantic love) is "to be seen in the sociostructural patterns which are developed to keep it from disrupting existing social arrangements."[27] Romantic love posed a dilemma for Mormon polygamists because it had the potential to disrupt marriages contracted for religious reasons rather than for love or personal attraction. On the other hand many Mormons of marriageable age were influenced by the American norm of romantic love as the most acceptable basis for marriages.

This norm was rather new to America, but a study of the reactions of foreign visitors to American marriage customs between 1800 and 1850 noted that they universally reported the startling conclusion that romantic love was the basis for marriage in America during that era.[28] Romantic love is explosive enough in and of itself, but combined with a futuristic millennial spirit and the openness of the western frontier, it created a potentially volatile situation in the Mormon communities. Bessie Strong, the second wife of Aaron Strong, remarked, "In the beginning of the movement men took wives because it was a sacred duty, but in later years they were beginning to take them more because they fell in love with younger women. And when they did this, the older wife often suffered. Men abused the Principle."[29] The difficulties encountered in trying to manage love in Mormon polygamy were described by Richard Ballantyne, founder of the Mormon Sunday school system:

"How delicate is the position of man in plural marriage who loves his wives and who in turn is loved by them. Every move he makes, in his relation or intercourse with them, is an arrow that pierces deep into the heart of one or the other. Even his very looks and thoughts are read; true, often misinterpreted to mean partiality for one at the expense of another, be he ever so fair and good in his intention. How difficult his situation. What can he do to please them all? In trying to solve this question his difficulties only increase. A thousand thoughts and plans may come into his mind, but there is only one true solution. He must please God. In doing this, it may be hoped that bye and bye, he may also please them.

"Again, the situation is only aggravated when we discover the natural jealousy of the sex gradually unfolding itself. We speak of the attitude women should assume, and which, I have no doubt, they will hereafter be educated to assume, when the love of God and godliness predominates over low and sensual passions; but of this I do not now write, but of things that have existed in the past, and that, somewhat modified by experience for the better, exists today.

"Jealousy, then allied to its twin sister, Hatred, manifests its hideous form in various ways. In its extreme aspects it is said to be 'cruel as the grave,' which swallows up and consumes its victim. But even in a modified form its influence makes much trouble to the husband. Out of it comes selfishness which destroys that nice sense of justice which should exist in every household. Then discontent; murmurings; deceit, slander, misrepresentations."[30]

An interesting letter supporting the idea that love and polygamy were antithetical, written by a prominent Mormon educator whose father was a polygamist, contains the following excerpt:

"This is a subject I know a great deal about; my father was a polygamist—as good as the general run—probably no better, but he just was not able to keep harmony in the family. In all my research, when you are able to get all the way to the bottom, you will find heartaches. The women try to be brave, but no woman is able to share a husband *whom she loves* with one or more other women. And the second and third wives have even a harder time.

"Only a few of the women involved in polygamy asked for a divorce simply because it was not a popular thing to do. Convention would not allow it. But I can show you journal after journal when a wife is talking from her heart . . . that they felt . . . bitter . . ."[31]

On the difficulty of combining love and plural marriage Kimball Young concluded: "Perhaps Brigham Young and others were wise when they pooh-poohed romantic love as a factor in polygamous situations. Certainly there is some evidence in a few of our records that where the wives did not seem to be particularly fond of their husbands in the romantic sense, they were able to make a better adjustment than were those who were romantically involved with their spouses."[32]

It appears that in the Mormon system, romantic love and millennial ideas were not entirely consistent. Millennial zeal and pressures to obtain new wives were a threat to the stability of existing love marriages. On the other hand if the first marriage was not based on love, a new plural relationship based on romance was also a threat to existing relationships.

Anomie. Emile Durkheim, the French sociologist, theorized that society was needed to place some constraints on the behavior of men and women but that society could be disturbed by some painful crisis or by beneficent but abrupt transitions so that momentarily it could no longer regulate the affairs of humanity.[33] This is known as the state of anomie or normlessness. Durkheim describes this state as follows: "the scale is upset; but a new scale cannot be immediately improvised. Time is required for the public conscience to reclassify men and things. So long as the social forces thus freed have not regained equilibrium, their respective values are unknown and so all regulation is lacking for a time. The limits are unknown between the possible and the impossible, what is just and what is unjust, legitimate claims and hopes and those which are immoderate."[34] In a societal state of anomie, suicide rates increase, according to Durkheim, and divorces also increase—a sort of anomic suicide.[35] Divorce rates increase not because there are more bad husbands and wives, or even bad marriages, but because of a lack of regulations in the social structure including the marriage and family system.

It cannot be argued that polygamy per se is related to the state of normlessness. George Murdock, a noted anthropologist, has demon-strated that polygyny is the preferred marriage system in a majority of societies he studied. He points out, however, that polygyny poses some personal adjustment problems that may not arise in monogamy, such as sexual jealousy, but that societies that favor polygyny have elaborate social mechanisms to control the interaction of husband and wives in marriage. Speaking of the Mormon experience he wrote: "It is very probably their internal troubles in making the institution operate harmoniously, rather than external pressures, that induced the Mormons ultimately to abandon polygamy. That it can be made to work smoothly is perfectly clear from the evidence of ethnography."[36] It is here argued that Mormon polygamy developed within a context of normlessness or anomie, resulting from millennialist expectations that alienated Mormons from conventional society. As Thomas O'Dea suggests: "The very separateness of the Mormon group removed them still further from the inhibitions that discourage innovation in the general society. They were not really a part of conventional society. Moreover, hostility set them further apart, increased their separateness, and thereby further weakened the bonds of convention. As separateness encouraged innovation, innovation in return increased separateness by providing a creedal basis for evolving peculiarity."[37]

In addition to "evolving peculiarity," Mormons were moving en masse to establish a new society in the Great Basin, involving immigrants from Europe, Canada, and the United States, many of whom had left parents, spouses, even children, as well as jobs and secure positions in their communities in order to embrace the new faith and gather to the new Zion. Lives were in a state of flux, and pragmatic adjustments were the order of the day.

Robert Flanders believes that Joseph Smith and many of his prominent followers (such as Brigham Young and Heber C. Kimball) were alienated from the greater American culture and that they saw themselves living in a world they needed to prepare for the cataclysmic second coming of Jesus Christ. "Specifically, he [Joseph Smith] believed himself called to found the pre-millennial kingdom of God on earth. In this age of the Prophet Joseph, tens of thousands believed, even during his own brief lifetime."[38] Acting on this belief Mormons gathered to Zion at various times in New York, Iowa, Missouri, and Illinois only to be driven to the Rocky Mountains by their fellow Americans. For many Mormons the society of the United States was corrupt and antithetical to their religious goals so that society no longer regulated them. But the new society of Mormonism with its millennialist future orientation had not developed into anything resembling a mature social system with the many forms of checks and balances that are needed to regulate any society. A condition of anomie existed in which "the limits are unknown between the possible and the impossible, what is just and what is unjust, legitimate claims and hopes and those which are immoderate."

Rudger Clawson, defendant in the first polygamy case to come to trial under the Edmunds law, revealed the Mormon position regarding society's laws when he said: "I very much regret that the laws of my country should come in conflict with the laws of God; but whenever they do, I shall invariably choose the latter. If I did not so express myself, I would feel unworthy of the cause I represent. . . . The law of 1862 and the Edmunds law were expressly designed to operate against marriage as practiced and believed by the Latter-day

Saints. They are therefore unconstitutional and, of course, cannot command the respect that a Constitutional law would."[39]

Eleanor J. McLean married Parley P. Pratt in polygamy while still married to Hector McLean, although she was separated from him. When asked if she had divorced McLean before she married Pratt, she answered: "No, the sectarian priests have no power from God to marry; and a so called marriage ceremony performed by them is no marriage at all; no divorce was needed. . . . The priesthood, with its powers and privileges can be found nowhere upon the face of the earth but in Utah."[40] Such a dichotomy between the laws of God and the laws of humankind is strongly expressed in many early Mormon writings. The roots of anomic thought can be seen in such statements.

Another interesting case is that of Apostle Orson Hyde who eventually married nine wives and had three divorces. He was assigned to Carson Valley to serve as probate judge in 1854. When it became apparent that he should spend the winter of 1854-55 there, he wrote Brigham Young as follows: "But if I do stay, I want a wife with me. Either Marinder or Mary Ann or someone else, say Sister Paschall—I will leave it to you to determine. . . . If you think it not wisdom for anyone to come to me from the lake, may I get one here if I can find one to suit . . . ? The chances to get a wife here are not very many even if a man wanted to get one in this country. Women are scarce and good ones are scarcer still!"[41] His wife Mary Ann was sent to him, and after spending the winter with her, he proposed to leave her "here with her sister, having taken up a good ranch that will do for both, and not knowing what my future destiny may be."[42] Marriage for Hyde seems to have been a temporary convenience. Such an attitude would not have been honored in a well-established community that had developed strict standards of conjugal behavior.

Consider the case of George Stringham who married Polly Hendrickson in 1820 and raised a family of six children. In 1858 after all of the children were married, he married a much younger woman polygamously and moved from the home of his first wife, leaving her almost destitute. This embittered some of the children, and one daughter gave vent to her feelings in a letter written to her mother in 1860, portions of which follow:

"Mama, you was telling me of your trials. Oh how sorry it makes me feel for you to think you have to live alone, but I am glad you are as well satisfied with your lot, but I don't know how you can believe it is right for an old man to put away an old woman after they have raised a great family of children for them, and get a young one, and I tell you I don't believe there is any God in it. I would like to know what poor miserable woman was made for. If that is right they are no better off than the beasts, I tell you mama I can't believe that it is a just God to require such as that of women, for when he created them, he made the woman his helpmate. He didn't say for a while or till they was old and tired of them and then put them away for a younger one or another and leave the old one in sorrow and trouble. I tell you mama, the man that does it will have to answer for. How many times I heard you say that you believed that a man would have to answer for the trouble he made for woman. I don't know how you can believe it for the way I look at it its against the Bible and strongly against the Book of Mormon. I know I shall always believe it, you know it says that was the downfall of the Nephites, they getting wives and concubines. The God was angry with them and destroyed them off from the earth, because it was not right. If it had been right why didn't he make more than one for old Adam, I tell you mama it is not right nor never was nor never will be for God has not changed."[43]

This arrangement lasted fourteen years, and then in his old age he returned to his first wife. Apparently there were no powerful social mechanisms to regulate Stringham's behavior.

Another unusual case was that of Thomas Grover. A widower with six children, he married a woman with three children of her own before becoming involved in polygamy. Later he claimed that while praying for a testimony on plural marriage the Lord showed him in a vision the woman he should marry. He subsequently met her, married her, and she ultimately bore him twelve children. In later life when it became apparent that Grover was never going to make much of a mark in the world, his wife Hannah became restless and hard to live with. She began suggesting divorce and even wrote to Daniel H. Wells, a member of the First Presidency of the LDS church, proposing that Grover's entire family including wives and children be sealed to Wells. Wells advised her to stay with her husband, because "Thomas Grover is as good a man as I am" and cautioned her to keep the situation secret. However Hannah left her husband and went to live with her son Thomas in Nephi. On 14 November 1871 she was sealed to Daniel H. Wells in the Endowment House.[44] There is no record of her securing a divorce or having her sealing to Grover canceled, although that would have been the normal procedure. There appear to have been no checks on her behavior.

This case may be an example of a doctrine that appears to be rooted in anomie which was preached by Brigham Young in October 1861: "But there was a way in which a woman could leave a man lawfully—when a woman becomes alienated in her feelings and affections from her husband, it is his duty to give her a bill and set her free—it would be fornication for a man to cohabit with his wife after she had thus become alienated from him. . . . Also, there was another way in which a woman could leave a man—if the woman preferred a man *higher in authority* and he is willing to take her and her husband gives her up. There is no bill of divorce required, in [this] case it is right in the sight of God."[45]

All of these cases appear to share a common normless quality about them—the limits on action and the source of those limits are not at all clear. In this regard Kimball Young remarked: "It would by no means be assumed that conflict was the inevitable aspect of plural family life. The real problem was that the difficulties could not be easily settled because the culture did not provide any standardized way for handling these conflicts. For the most part, these people genuinely tried to live according to the Principle, but when they applied the rules of the game borrowed from monogamy, such as not controlling feelings of jealousy, they got into real trouble."[46]

Thus the regulations in American monogamy emphasizing romantic love and interpersonal attractions as social mechanisms were not easily adapted to Mormon polygamy. Murdock reports that in those societies preferring polygyny as a marriage system, the majority prefer sororal polygyny, the marriage of one man with two or more sisters. Kimball Young reports that about 19 percent of the Mormon families he studied practiced sororal polygyny and that this method worked quite well; but when other wives were added who were not sisters, difficulties multiplied.[47] This practice, far from universal, appears to have occurred because there were no limits rather than because it was a preferred mode of marriage. The example of John D. Lee marrying the mother of three of his wives "for her soul's sake" and others marrying a mother and daughter at the same time are examples of a lack of limits that would not have been tolerated in other more well-established societies.

For polygamous norms Mormons could and did turn to the

Old Testament. Even then they had problems adapting those teachings to their needs. For example, although the practice of sororal polygamy was frequently used in Mormon polygamy, the code of the Old Testament forbade this practice. Queen and Haberstein's description of Hebrew attitudes makes that clear: "The Hebrews, like all other peoples, had laws prohibiting marriage between persons with certain degrees of kinship and affinity. In earliest times stress was laid on the mother's line. Thus a man might marry his half-sister if they had different mothers, but not if they had the same mother. In those early days the prohibition included mother's sister, mother and daughter. Later regulations extended the ban to paternal half-sisters, stepmother, mother-in-law and daughter-in-law. The levitical code barred, in addition to the preceding, marriage of any man with any wife of his father, his father's sister, father's brother's wife, daughter's daughter, son's wife or daughter, brother's wife and wife's sister (during the lifetime of the wife)."[48]

The rules governing marriage in Jewish culture developed over thousands of years and reflected the move from a migratory life to a more sedentary one. Many of the regulations were not compatible with the Mormon circumstance. In the Mormon situation the extended family was not a particularly important structure. Intergenerational ties and living conditions were not prominent for a number of reasons. When a marriage broke up, the family also was broken. Queen and Haberstein say: "the Hebrew family for most purposes, was not the small conjugal group, but the household or ever larger kinship group. Marriage was not unimportant, but the wedded couple was absorbed in the consanguine family of the three generations and many collateral relatives."[49]

Although Mormons may have wished for regulation out of the Old Testament, it did not seem compatible with their circumstance; there is little indication that the Old Testament was ever used as a serious guide to their marriage regulation. There were rules, however. The first wife's permission was supposed to be obtained before another wife was taken. Each wife was to have a separate house or apartment of her own, and the husband was supposed to show evidence that he could support additional households. But these rules were not followed carefully. There were no rules governing courtship procedures nor the number of wives a man might marry.

Conclusions. Evidence has been represented in this essay

indicating that the Mormon system of polygamy was not one of consistent and strong regulation. In fact in many ways it appears to have been a system in which unusual practices developed as the limits were not clear to those involved. The divorce rate and number of separations were high not because polygamous marriage was difficult in this American context per se but because the context of Mormon polygamy was a state of anomie or normlessness caused by the Saints' millennialist belief system and the instability of their lives in colonizing the Great Basin. The explosive nature of this system can be seen in the troubles Mormons experienced with their American contemporaries in the West and Midwest.[50]

The only standards for conduct were the actions and advice of church leaders, and they could not be fully effective in regulating plural marriage for many reasons. They apparently claimed no special inspiration for regulating such a system, and their own limited experience with polygamy allowed them to propose only individualistic solutions to many problems.

Because of the sub rosa nature of the practice of polygamy, one could not always take statements about it from church leaders at face value. Some things were said for private information and others for public consumption. This often left the membership of the church without a clear guide for action. During the 1880s when federal agents were arresting Mormon polygamists and sending them to prison, lying and other forms of deception to protect polygamists, especially husbands, were expected and applauded by the Mormon community.

President Wilford Woodurff's Manifesto in 1890 publicly announced that the church leader "advised" members to abide by the law. However, Charles W. Penrose claimed authorship of the Manifesto and asserted that it was written to satisfy the federal government and was not taken seriously by the Mormon hierarchy.[51] It is certain that plural marriages were approved and performed by church leaders in Mexico and elsewhere until a second manifesto in 1904. Mormon fundamentalists, who have continued the practice of polygamy to the present, believe that LDS church leaders made secret ordinations in order to guarantee the continuance of the practice. In anomic circumstances, if the only voice of possible regulation is muted or ambivalent, a fluid marriage system may be expected. Given such circumstances perhaps the number of marriage failures and divorces among Mormon polygamists should not be surprising, but the fact that so many succeeded in developing happy marriage relationships and producing fine families should command both wonder and respect.

NOTES

1. Kimball Young, *Isn't One Wife Enough?* (New York: Henry Holt, 1954), 234. Technically Mormons practiced polygyny, the marriage of one man to two or more women. However, in the Mormon subculture polygamy is always taken to mean the marriage of one man to two or more wives. In this essay polygamy, polygyny, and plural marriage will all refer to the Mormon practice.

2. Ibid., 235.

3. Stanley Ivins, "Notes on Mormon Polygamy," *Western Humanities Review* 10 (1956): 230.

4. Box containing nine folders, plus several ledgers, archives, Historical Department, Church of Jesus Christ of Latter-day Saints, Salt Lake City, Utah; hereafter LDS archives.

5. See B. H. Roberts, *A Comprehensive History of the Church of Jesus Christ of Latter-day Saints, Century 1,* 6 vols. (Salt Lake City: Deseret News Press, 1930), 6:149, who "estimates that male members practicing polygamy represented only 2% of church population," which was about 120,000 in 1888.

6. D. Michael Quinn, "Organizational Development and Social Origins of the Mormon Hierarchy, 1832-1932: A Prosopographical Study," M.A. thesis, University of Utah, 1973, 248-91. Although there were eighty-one failures listed among church leaders, they were involved in more than 400 marriages.

7. George Levinger, "Marital Cohesiveness and Dissolution: An Interpretive Review," *Journal of Marriage and the Family* (1965): 248-91.

8. Ibid., 20.

9. Eugene E. Campbell, "Social, Cultural and Recreational Life," in *The History of a Valley: Cache Valley, Utah-Idaho,* eds. Joel E. Ricks and Everett L. Cooley (Salt Lake City: Deseret News Publishing Co., 1956), 418.

10. Young, 39-40.

11. Matthias F. Cowley, *Wilford Woodruff . . .* (Salt Lake City: Deseret News, 1909), 490.

12. Ivins, 232.

13. Young, 226.

14. Ibid., 452.

15. Louis G. Reinwand, "An Interpretative Study of Mormon Millennialism during the Nineteenth Century . . .," M.A. thesis, Brigham Young

University, 1971, 81, 86.

16. Journal History, 22 Aug. 1862, LDS archives. Mormons equate "going back to Jackson County" with the beginning of the Millennium.

17. Ivins, 231.

18. Journal History, 1 Apr. 1857.

19. Brigham Young, Outgoing Correspondence, 22-26, LDS archives.

20. Brigham Young, Incoming Correspondence, 5 Mar. 1857, LDS archives.

21. *Journal of Discourses,* 26 vols. (Liverpool, 1854-86), 4:55.

22. Wilford Woodruff Journal, 6 Oct. 1856, LDS archives.

23. Journal History, 18 Dec. 1858.

24. Ibid., 15 Dec. 1858.

25. Ibid., 15 Nov. 1858.

26. Brigham Young's Office Journal, 5 Oct. 1861, LDS archives.

27. William J. Goode, "The Theoretical Importance of Love," *American Sociological Review* 24 (1959): 47.

28. Frank Furstenberg, Jr., "Industrialization and the American Family: A Look Backward," *American Sociological Review* 31 (June 1966): 326-37.

29. Young, 385.

30. Richard Ballantyne Journal, 234, LDS archives.

31. George Shepherd Tanner to Max Tanner, copy in our possession.

32. Young, 209.

33. Emile Durkheim, *Suicide,* trans. John A. Spalding and George Simpson (New York: Free Press, 1951), 252.

34. Ibid., 253.

35. Ibid., 273.

36. George P. Murdock, *Social Structure* (New York: MacMillan Company, 1949), 31.

37. Thomas F. O'Dea, *The Mormons* (Chicago: University of Chicago Press, 1957), 54-55.

38. Robert Flanders, "To Transform History: Early Mormon Culture and the Concept of Time and Space," *Church History* 40 (1971): 110.

39. *Salt Lake Tribune,* 4 Nov. 1884.

40. Stephen Pratt, "The Last Days of Parley P. Pratt," *Brigham Young University Studies* (1975): 20.

41. Albert Page, "Orson Hyde and the Carson Valley Mission, 1855-57," M.A. thesis, Brigham Young University, 1970, 22.

42. Ibid.

43. Letter from Sabra Stringham to Polly Stringham, 10 June 1860,

copy in our possession.

44. Mark Grover, "The Effects of Polygamy upon Thomas Grover," seminar paper in our possession.

45. Conference Reports, 8 Oct. 1861, reported by George D. Watt, LDS archives; also found in the journal of James Beck, 8 Oct. 1861, LDS archives. A more careful study of the marriages of Zina Huntington Jacobs and Mary Elizabeth Rollins Lightner may be justified in light of this pronouncement.

46. Young, 209.

47. Ibid., 111.

48. Stuart A. Queen and Robert W. Haberstein, *The Family in Various Cultures* (New York: J. B. Lippincott Co., 1967), 167.

49. Ibid.

50. The Mountain Meadows Massacre is another indication of the relative normlessness that existed in the Mormon subculture at that time.

51. Minutes of the trial of Matthias F. Cowley for violation of the Manifesto, 27 Apr. 1911, Special Collections, Marriott Library, University of Utah. Penrose later became a member of the First Presidency.

12.
After the Manifesto: Mormon Polygamy, 1890-1906

Kenneth L. Cannon II

MANY MORMONS RESPONDED WITH SURPRISE WHEN THE RESIGNATIONS OF Elders John W. Taylor and Matthias F. Cowley from their quorum were announced during the church's April 1906 general conference. Some others were undoubtedly relieved. The dismissal of Taylor and Cowley represented the first action taken by church authorities against members who advocated the continuation of plural marriage contrary to federal law.[1] During the previous sixteen years, Mormondom had seen two Manifestos, a number of "official" statements (and numerous contradictory private ones by church leaders), and a secretive but persistent practice of "the principle" by church leaders and laymen.

This phenomenon of "new polygamy" is overwhelmingly affirmed by recent historical research.[2] Post-Manifesto polygamy was variously received by church leaders of the period (1890-1906), whose differing opinions caused a great deal of stress in the leading quorums.[3] Since in theory only the church president had authority to sanction the performance of new plural marriages, the sentiments of the three men who held that office during this transitional period—Wilford Woodruff, Lorenzo Snow, and Joseph F. Smith—are especially significant.[4]

While it may be impossible to know exactly what the attitudes of these three men were, several sources prove enlightening, including: their statements and actions and how these were perceived by others; the approximate number of plural marriages performed during the incumbency of each; the officers in whose call to the church hierarchy each president had a central role; and the attitudes (and changes in attitude) of other general authorities during this period. Conclusions derived from these investigations shed further light on the difficult process the Mormon church experienced in ultimately abandoning its practice of plural marriage.

President Wilford Woodruff's Manifesto of September 1890 signaled the official end of polygamy in the Mormon church. This ambiguous statement asserted that church leaders were not teaching or encouraging polygamy nor were they allowing members to enter into it. Woodruff denied that polygamous marriages had been carried out during the previous year, declared his intent to submit to the laws of the land, and vowed to use his influence to have church members "do likewise."[5] Apparently Woodruff and his two counselors, George Q. Cannon and Joseph F. Smith, did stop allowing couples to be married in polygamy for a short time after issuing the Manifesto, although a few couples who had been authorized to but had not entered polygamy before the Manifesto and one or two couples immediately after the Manifesto who agreed to move to Mexico were permitted to do so.[6] Privately, the president told the apostles that he expected polygamists to continue to support their wives, implying that this support included cohabitation.[7]

In October the following year, Woodruff and other church leaders publicly testified that plural marriage had ceased, that "the Manifesto was intended to apply to the Church of Jesus Christ of Latter-day Saints everywhere in every nation and country," and that "we are giving no liberty to enter into polygamous relations anywhere." Those who failed to obey the law would be subject to church discipline.[8] Woodruff later privately explained his remarks to fellow church leaders, stating that "he was placed in a position on the witness stand that he could not answer other than he did."[9]

As early as 1893, however, new plural marriages were performed in Mexico, an idea initially proposed by George Q. Cannon. Woodruff evidently agreed with his first counselor's idea, letting Cannon direct this new polygamy so that he would not participate directly as church president.[10] Cannon's responsibility included choosing and setting apart certain church leaders to perform the

marriages.[11] In that year at least two couples were married polygamously in Mexico, apparently with the approbation of Woodruff and
his two counselors.[12]

Throughout the mid-1890s the following scene was repeated
on numerous occasions. Church members who continued to believe
that polygamy was necessary to their exaltation would approach
Woodruff, asking if there was some way of accomplishing a plural
marriage. In some cases Woodruff probably told them that for the
present plural marriages were not permitted; others he referred to
George Q. Cannon, who interviewed them and told them of possibilities of plural marriage outside the United States. If the couple was
willing to relocate in order to enjoy the benefits of polygamy, Cannon
would send them to a church leader in Mexico or Canada, such as
Alexander F. MacDonald, George Teasdale, or Anthony W. Ivins,
who would perform the marriage.[13] Cannon undoubtedly also told
the couple to keep secret what he had told them so that unfriendly
non-Mormons or federal officials would not learn of the new
marriages.

Between 1893 and 1896 at least two marriages were performed every year. In 1897, the first full year after Utah attained
statehood, the number of plural marriages jumped nearly five-fold.
Political pressures created by attempts for statehood subsided after
Utah became a state, and church leaders realized they could allow
more polygamous marriages than before because federal interference would be minimized.[14] Potential charges of duplicity would not
be as damaging. While this in no way greatly liberalized the number
of Mormons who could marry in polygamy, it might have changed
attitudes enough to cause the increase in number of marriages
solemnized.[15]

These marriages and Wilford Woodruff's private clarifica-
tions of his public statements repudiating polygamy were not, however, matters of general knowledge, a situation which resulted in
confusion for many Mormons as they were left to their own interpretations of their leaders' public pronouncements.[16] Some who heard
rumors of Woodruff's true feelings concerning polygamous cohabitation probably did not believe them; others felt that the president
was only beating "the devil at his own game" by having members go
outside the United States to contract plural marriages. There seems
to have been little criticism of such marriages among those Latter-day

Saints who knew about them.

During Woodruff's presidency five men—Marriner W. Merrill, Anthon H. Lund, Abraham H. Cannon, Matthias F. Cowley, and Abraham Owen Woodruff—were appointed to the Quorum of the Twelve Apostles. All were firmly committed to "the principle."[17] Elders Merrill, Lund, and Cannon were involved in polygamous activities during Woodruff's administration. Although it is uncertain whether apostles Matthias Cowley or Owen Woodruff participated in such activities between their calls in 1897 and President Woodruff's death in 1898, it is certain that both were engaged in polygamy thereafter.

Among the twelve apostles and the First Presidency between 1890 and 1898, at least 58 percent of the members took an active part in post-Manifesto polygamy. If Matthias Cowley and Owen Woodruff are included, the proportion rises to 70 percent.[18] Historical records indicate that only two men seem to have had qualms about the continuation of polygamy during President Woodruff's lifetime: Francis M. Lyman and Lorenzo Snow.[19]

When Lorenzo Snow acceded to the presidency in late 1898, he charted a course different from his predecessor. Shortly after becoming president he announced that plural marriage would not be preached, for it was contrary to the laws of the land.[20] The national embarrassment of the church on the subject of polygamy which accompanied B. H. Roberts's election to and subsequent exclusion from the U.S. House of Representatives in the last two years of the nineteenth century may have strengthened Snow's conviction that the church's promises needed to be kept.[21] As president he felt he was in a position to bring the church's public position and private practices more into harmony.

In December 1899 and January 1900 Snow published statements in the *Deseret News* denying that any plural marriage had been performed with proper authority since 1890 and affirming that no such marriages had been or would be approved by him.[22] In a meeting with the apostles in January 1900, Snow expressed the fear that some new marriages were being solemnized without his knowledge or sanction. According to the Journal History account of the meeting, "[President Snow], without reference to anyone present, said that there were brethren who still seemed to have the idea that it was possible under his administration to obtain a plural wife and have her sealed to him. He authorized and requested the brethren present to correct this impression wherever they find it. He said emphatically that it could not be done. President Cannon moved that this be seconded as the mind and will of the Lord. Seconded by Brother Lyman and carried unanimously."[23] A year later Snow privately expressed the same sentiments to Apostle Brigham Young, Jr., stating he had never given his consent for plural marriage and adding, "God has removed this privilege from the people."[24]

Both church leaders and the general membership of the church seem to have perceived a change in church policy instituted by Snow's administration. In 1911, for example, Apostle Francis M. Lyman expressed his belief that Snow had changed the basic position of the church toward the continuation of plural marriage when he took office in 1898,[25] and Elder John Henry Smith told Alexander MacDonald in May 1901 that no more plural marriages were to be performed.[26]

Only statements made by Matthias Cowley in his 1911 trial for membership give any indication that Snow might have allowed some plural marriages to be performed. Cowley testified that when he once approached the president about solemnizing a plural marriage, Snow told him that he "would not interfere with Brother Woodruff's and Cannon's work."[27] It appears, therefore, that Snow indirectly consented to some plural marriages which had been authorized earlier by Woodruff and Cannon, especially before Snow made his strong statements in late December 1899 and January 1900. Almost all other evidence indicates Snow conscientiously tried to put a stop to new polygamy. He was largely unsuccessful.

While signals from Salt Lake City indicated the abandonment of polygamy, plural marriages continued to be solemnized in the Mexican colonies by John W. Taylor, Matthias Cowley, and others.[28] Mexican colonists probably assumed that Lorenzo Snow's statements were simply new attempts to ward off outside suspicion and interference. The only indication that Snow's strict position on new polygamy might have been to some extent followed in the Mexican colonies is that the number of marriages solemnized there by Anthony W. Ivins dropped drastically during Snow's presidency. It is possible that Ivins, who often claimed he never solemnized a marriage without proper authority, did not believe that Snow was permitting many marriages and therefore performed very few.

The statistics indicate that in 1899, the first full year of Lorenzo Snow's presidency, the number of plural marriages decreased by almost 200 percent, evidence of Snow's unwillingness to allow new marriages.[29] In 1900, however, the total number of marriages actually *rose* by more than 150 percent, a fact that seems especially ironic in light of Snow's public statements of late 1899 and 1900. In 1901 the total number of marriages remained high, but the number of these performed by Ivins remained a low 15 percent.[30]

These numbers are directly related to an increasing polarization in church leadership. Whereas most plural marriages during Wilford Woodruff's administration were performed outside the United States, a number of marriages after 1898 were performed in America, apparently initiated by members of the church leadership. Marriner W. Merrill, Matthias Cowley, John W. Taylor, Frank Y. Taylor, George M. Cannon, John M. Cannon, Hugh J. Cannon, Henry S. Tanner, and Owen Woodruff are some of the prominent leaders who married plural wives in the United States during Snow's presidency.[31] Yet Snow almost certainly had nothing to do with these marriages and may have had no knowledge of them.

Why did these leaders continue in a practice to which the church president was so openly opposed? One possibility is that Snow's two counselors, George Q. Cannon and Joseph F. Smith, sanctioned plural marriages without Snow's knowledge between 1898 and 1901.[32] For example, when Cannon set apart Matthias Cowley to perform polygamous marriages in 1898 or 1899, he told him to talk to no one about the marriages.[33] This indicates that Cannon and perhaps Smith believed so deeply in polygamy that they were willing to keep their actions from the church president. With the First Presidency thus divided, members of the Twelve would have received mixed signals from the highest governing body of the church.

Thus for the first time since the 1840s, there existed sharply polarized positions about plural marriage in the leading quorums of the church. The two men called to the Twelve during Lorenzo Snow's administration reflected the president's beliefs and increased that polarization. Rudger Clawson, a one-time polygamist, had only one wife when he was called as an apostle in 1898, but he also opposed Joseph F. Smith's "Second Manifesto" of 1904 because he felt it would cause much heartache.[34]

Reed Smoot, Snow's other appointee, was a monogamist and one of a rising group of Mormons who was ready to discard the nineteenth-century practices which had brought so much ill will on the church. By doing this these younger Mormons hoped to assimilate their church into the mainstream of American society. This is not to say Smoot was not committed to the church. Indeed, it was because of his commitment and his assessment of what Mormonism had to do to survive that he supported the abandonment of "unusual" Mormon practices.[35]

Other members of the quorum, such as Francis M. Lyman, began openly to oppose the continuation of polygamy. Some, such as John Henry Smith, apparently changed their attitudes after Lorenzo Snow became president. Still other apostles and even members of the First Presidency simply did not follow Snow's directions. This divergence of opinion among the hierarchy caused tensions and, as historian Thomas Alexander has suggested, was one of the things which threatened the collegiality of the leading quorums of the church at the turn of the century.[36]

The confusion and division persisted in the administration of Joseph F. Smith, Snow's successor. The extent of Smith's involvement in post-Manifesto polygamy is clouded by conflicting evidence. He apparently performed the plural marriage in 1896 of Apostle Abraham H. Cannon and Lillian Hamblin while he was second counselor in the First Presidency.[37] He knew about the new plural marriages being performed during Lorenzo Snow's administration and almost certainly approved of them. And there is evidence that Smith allowed new marriages to be performed during his presidency. Orson Pratt Brown, a bishop in the Mexican colonies, related that on a visit to Salt Lake City he presented Smith with the marriage records of Alexander F. MacDonald. The president reportedly surveyed the record, stated that "all of this work that Brother MacDonald performed was duly authorized by me," and told Brown to keep the record in Mexico so that a search in Salt Lake City could not unearth the records if federal marshals were to get permission to look for just such materials.[38] Additionally a child of a plural marriage performed in 1903 by Anthony W. Ivins stated that Joseph F. Smith sent a letter to Ivins authorizing that marriage.[39]

In a 1911 telegram to Reed Smoot, Smith implied his tacit approval of the marriages: "If the president [of the United States] inquires about new polygamy tell him the truth. Tell him that President Cannon was the first to conceive the idea that we could consistently countenance polygamy beyond the confines of the Republic where we have no chartered law against it, and consequently he authorized the solemnization of polygamy in Mexico and Canada after the Manifesto of 1890, and the men occupying presiding positions who became polygamists since the manifesto did it in good faith."[40]

Smith's choice of men to be appointed to high church office suggests that he may have facilitated the eventual demise of polygamy by choosing men who were willing to abandon the practice. Of the men appointed to the First Presidency or quorum of twelve between 1901 and 1906, three—John R. Winder, Charles W. Penrose, and Orson F. Whitney—were polygamists and four—Hyrum M. Smith, George Albert Smith, George F. Richards, and David O. McKay—were monogamists. There is no indication that any of the seven were involved in post-Manifesto polygamy.

Additionally there exist statements, both public and private, that seem to indicate Smith's opposition to the principle. In 1902 he told Brigham Young, Jr., that no plural marriages were "taking place to his knowledge in the Church either in the U.S. or any other country." He further stated, "It is thoroughly understood and has been for years that no one is authorized to perform any such marriages."[41] In a meeting of the apostles in November 1903, Smith told the leaders that "he had not given his consent to anyone to solemnize plural marriages" and "that he did not know of any such cases." He went on to insist that if members of the church were entering into polygamous marriages they were bringing trouble "upon the whole community."[42]

In 1904 Smith was called to testify before the Senate Committee on Privileges and Elections investigating Reed Smoot, who had recently been sent to the U.S. Senate by Utah's state legislature. His testimony included the following statement: "It has been the continuous and conscientious practice and rule of the church ever since the manifesto to observe that manifesto with regard to plural marriages; and from that time till to-day there has never been, to my knowledge, a plural marriage performed with the understanding, instruction, connivance, counsel, or permission of the presiding authorities of the church, in any shape or form; and I know whereof I speak, gentlemen, in relation to that matter."[43] Evidence collected during the Smoot investigation had created bad publicity for the church, and there was great pressure on Smith to reaffirm Mormonism's repudiation of polygamy.[44] Despite opposition from some members of the hierarchy, he therefore issued a statement in April 1904 reaffirming the 1890 Manifesto's prohibition of marriages "violative of the laws of the land." He denied that marriages had taken place and went on to announce the prospective policy of the church that anyone thereafter performing or entering into a plural marriage would be subject to excommunication.[45]

The case for abandonment of post-Manifesto polygamy was strengthened during this period by changes in the Quorum of the Twelve Apostles. Brigham Young, Jr., a proponent of polygamy and president of the quorum, died in 1903. He was succeeded by Francis M. Lyman, the apostle most opposed to the continuation of the practice. The vacancy in the quorum was filled by George Albert Smith, who also favored abandonment. Charles W. Penrose, who had similar feelings, replaced Owen Woodruff at his death in mid-1904.

However, other apostles—Marriner W. Merrill, John W. Taylor, Matthias Cowley, and George Teasdale—interpreted the 1904 Manifesto much as Wilford Woodruff's Manifesto had been interpreted by church leaders in the early 1890s. These men believed that plural marriages still could be performed outside the United States. Abiding by this interpretation, Cowley was married to a woman in Canada in 1905, and Taylor solemnized marriages outside the country.[46]

The senate's investigation of Reed Smoot continued in 1904 and 1905, and the Committee on Privileges and Elections was still interested in having apostles Taylor and Cowley appear before it. Smoot wrote in a letter to President Smith that all he heard in Washington was "Taylor and Cowley, Taylor and Cowley."[47] Pressure was mounting on the First Presidency and Twelve either to force these apostles to testify or to discipline them in some way.[48] In October 1905 Taylor and Cowley were asked to submit their resignations to Francis M. Lyman, president of the Twelve, to be announced if the need arose.[49]

Smoot, constantly called upon to defend the church and its reluctance to discipline Taylor and Cowley, had wanted the two men dropped from the quorum for some time but knew that the body would not do so unless absolutely necessary.[50] The apostle-senator must have been relieved when George F. Gibbs, secretary to the First Presidency, telegraphed him on 7 December 1905 that Smoot could use the resignations whenever the time seemed ripe. Yet Smoot replied in a long letter to the First Presidency that he did not want to be responsible for the "sacrifice" of Taylor and Cowley and that their resignations would do no good at the present. He did add, however, that the announcement should be made at some future time to placate anti-Mormon feelings in Washington, D.C.[51] But the same day that he wrote the letter, Reed Smoot received a telegram from Gibbs to the effect that the sentiments of the church fathers had changed and that the "brethren" were not in favor of "sacrificing" Taylor and Cowley for the time being.[52] However, by the next week Francis M. Lyman wrote Smoot telling him that he was "at perfect liberty to use the resignations" whenever he saw fit.[53]

On 9 March 1906 Charles W. Penrose wrote Smoot asking that he forestall a decision of the senate committee in his case until after the April conference of the church because of actions that would occur there which would have a bearing on the case.[54] Between December 1905 and April 1906, it had been decided that Taylor and Cowley should no longer serve as members of the quorum.

In April three new apostles were sustained to replace Marriner W. Merrill, a leading proponent of post-Manifesto polygamy who had died earlier that year, and Taylor and Cowley. The addition of these men firmly placed in the majority the faction favoring the abandonment of polygamy. When George Teasdale died in 1907, the entire group of men who favored continuing new marriages was gone from the quorum, either through death or dismissal.[55]

Taylor and Cowley believed that they would be reinstated after the whole affair blew over;[56] Smoot feared that would be the case. However, the prevailing sentiment among the Twelve was such that not only were the two not reinstated as apostles, they were further disciplined by their former quorum—five years later Cowley was disfellowshipped and Taylor excommunicated.[57]

Thus through the first several years of Joseph F. Smith's presidency, it appears that he allowed plural marriages to continue. He carefully denied connection with the practice on several occasions but qualified his statements by such phrases as "to my knowledge" and marriages "violative of the laws of the land."

Regardless of these denials, Smith's accession to the presidency signaled to many people a relaxation of church policy in relation to polygamy, both at home and in the Mexican colonies.[58] Several people close to Smoot, for example, doubted that Smith would issue any statement affirming the church's abandonment of plural marriage. Smoot's personal secretary, Carl A. Badger, expressed surprise when he learned of Smith's 1904 statement.[59] Couples married between 1901 and 1904 believed their marriages had been performed with proper authorization.[60] Cowley testified in 1911 that he believed Smith "was not opposed to these marriages if it could be done without trouble with the government."[61] Thus Cowley as well as others who continued to perform marriages believed that at the very least Joseph F. Smith did not oppose new marriages if they could be done unobtrusively.

The perception of this relaxed attitude is reinforced by the available numbers of marriages performed. According to the accumulated data (which are certainly not complete) five marriages were solemnized in 1901 after Joseph F. Smith was sustained as president. Twenty marriages were performed the next year, and there were thirty-three marriages in 1903, more than in any other year between 1890 and 1904. By the time the "second Manifesto" was issued in April 1904, ten marriages had already been performed. Apparently the last marriage sanctioned by the proper authorities before the Second Manifesto was solemnized on 29 March 1904; the couple had been told to move up their marriage date because a statement might be forthcoming in April conference.[62]

Anthony Ivins's marriage record book also reveals that he solemnized more marriages during the Smith administration than during the previous two administrations combined. Since Ivins insisted on authorization for the ceremonies he performed, it would suggest that Joseph F. Smith did sanction a number of marriages during those first years of his presidency.[63]

Thus Joseph F. Smith's attitudes toward the practice of polygamy seem ambivalent. He not only gave the public and the U.S. government inaccurate views of the practice, but he also kept his support of "new polygamy" from some of his fellow church leaders. His public statements and testimony before the senate committee could be explained by asserting "he had had to say what he did in Washington to protect the Church."[64] But how could he explain his statements to the quorum made at a time when he was consenting to plural marriages?

Smith probably did not feel he could outwardly go back on policies Lorenzo Snow had established because of possible disapproval from such powerful apostles as Francis M. Lyman. However, a larger proportion of the apostles was still favorably disposed to plural marriage when Smith became president; perhaps he privately told some of them he approved of their polygamous activities while placating others by making statements against the continuation of polygamy.[65] In any case, it is certain that such men as Francis M. Lyman and Reed Smoot believed for many years that Smith had had nothing to do with the new polygamy.[66]

During the three administrations and sixteen years following the 1890 Manifesto, there existed a notable ambiguity toward polygamy in the ruling councils of the church. Wilford Woodruff advocated the continued practice and apparently made this clear to his fellow church leaders, though he and they scrupulously kept it secret from the public and most of the church. Lorenzo Snow seems to have been straightforward in his opposition to the continued practice of polygamy and made his feelings known to the apostles. Joseph F. Smith supported the practice but evidently was careful in his selection of church leaders to whom he made his feelings known.

The common denominator in the administrations of Presidents Woodruff and Snow seems to have been George Q. Cannon. It was apparently Cannon who conceived of the idea that plural marriages could be performed outside the United States, and it was he who authorized men to perform plural marriages during Woodruff's presidency. Cannon also apparently secretly authorized plural marriages during Snow's administration despite Snow's opposition and Cannon's supposed acceptance of the president's views. Cannon died in April 1901, seven months before Snow's death.[67] After Cannon's death apostles such as Matthias Cowley, John W. Taylor, Marriner W. Merrill, George Teasdale, and Owen Woodruff carried on his work. After Snow's death these church leaders worked with the approval (whether tacit or explicit) of the new president, Joseph F. Smith.

The men ordained as apostles under Woodruff and Snow largely reflected each man's attitudes on polygamy. Woodruff's appointees supported the continuation of polygamy while the men called by Snow did not. Smith seemingly recognized that despite his own feelings, the church needed to show its good faith by eventually abandoning the practice completely and so called men who would facilitate such an abandonment.

During Woodruff's term as president, there was generally harmony in the ruling quorums of the church on the question of polygamy, for only a few apostles opposed its continuation in the first few years after the Manifesto. The harmony was disrupted, however, when Snow assumed office. Although a few leaders modified their views to be more in harmony with his, a majority did not. When Smith became president in 1901, he attempted to placate both factions by allowing polygamous marriages while denying he was doing so. His Manifesto of 1904 reaffirmed the church's official termination of plural marriage; but for almost two years thereafter, he did nothing to discipline those who refused to follow the dictates of this Second Manifesto. In late 1905 the Quorum of the Twelve Apostles was still vacillating on the question of what to do to its members who failed to abide by the 1904 ruling. Not until 1906 when three new apostles were appointed was there close to a consensus in the quorum favoring the abandonment of polygamy.

But the tensions and difficulties of polygamy did not end in 1906. It was not until three years later that a committee was formed to investigate members of the church who persisted in the active practice of polygamy.[68] In 1911 a policy was propounded to the effect that marriages performed before 1904 would be recognized as valid by the church.[69] Throughout the years that followed, Mormons who continued to take new wives were disciplined by the LDS church, and many of these people formed sects which are loosely identified as Mormon "fundamentalist" groups. These are the major surviving vestiges of a very difficult period of Mormon history.

NOTES

1. The official reason for the resignations was that Taylor and Cowley "found themselves out of harmony with the Presidency of the Church and the Quorum to which they belonged" (*Seventy-sixth Annual Conference of the Church of Jesus Christ of Latter-day Saints* [Salt Lake City: Deseret News Press, 1906], 93-94). Of interest is that Taylor and Cowley signed the resignations in October 1905 and that they were held for approximately six months before they were released. In fact, most of the apostles believed that the resignations were not to be made public (or, for that matter, effective)

other than if absolutely necessary because of events in the U.S. Senate's investigation of Reed Smoot. See D. Michael Quinn, "LDS Church Authority and New Plural Marriages, 1890-1904," *Dialogue: A Journal of Mormon Thought* 18 (Spring 1985): 102. Some believe the dismissals were politically motivated; see Victor W. Jorgensen and B. Carman Hardy, "The Taylor-Cowley Affair and the Watershed of Mormon History," *Utah Historical Quarterly* 48 (Winter 1980): 30-33. Other church authorities did not believe the dismissals were political, however, Francis M. Lyman explicitly stating such—that Taylor and Cowley were truly out of harmony with the quorum. See *The Trials for the Membership of John W. Taylor and Mathaias [sic] F. Cowley* (West Jordan, Utah: Mormon Underground Press, n.d.), 10; hereafter *Trials*. Apostle John Henry Smith believed Taylor and Cowley were forced to resign because they had performed plural marriages in the United States and had not limited such marriages to foreign countries (Joseph W. Musser Journal, 22 July 1909, archives, Historical Department, Church of Jesus Christ of Latter-day Saints, Salt Lake City, Utah; hereafter LDS archives).

In this essay "continuation" of polygamy refers solely to the solemnization, sanction, and contraction of new plural marriages and does not refer to the continued cohabitation of couples married in polygamy before the issuance of the 1890 Manifesto. The terms "polygamy" and "plural marriage" are used instead of the technically more correct "polygyny" because of their common usage in Mormon lore.

2. Michael Quinn's article is by far the most comprehensive treatment and analysis of polygamy from 1890 through 1905 as well as the best review of events immediately leading up to the issuance of the Manifesto in September 1890. Other treatments of this difficult subject and period are found in Richard S. Van Wagoner, *Mormon Polygamy: A History* (Salt Lake City: Signature Books, 1986); Thomas G. Alexander, *Mormonism in Transition: A History of the Latter-day Saints, 1890-1930* (Urbana: University of Illinois Press, 1986); and Jorgensen and Hardy.

3. An excellent analysis of the stresses the leading quorums of the church experienced in this difficult period is found in Thomas G. Alexander, "To Maintain Harmony: Adjusting to External and Internal Stress, 1890-1930," *Dialogue: A Journal of Mormon Thought* 15 (Winter 1982).

4. Michael Quinn has shown that there may have been post-Manifesto polygamous marriages that did not require the approval of the church president as in the case of the death of or divorce from a polygamist's first (and therefore legal) wife and the subsequent legal marriage of the polygamist to a woman to whom he had not previously been married. Quinn, 52-54.

5. *Deseret Weekly News,* 4 Oct. 1890. A more accessible copy of the Manifesto can be found in current LDS editions of the Doctrine and Covenants.

6. Abraham H. Cannon Journal, 2 Nov. 1890, Special Collections, Harold B. Lee Library, Brigham Young University, Provo, Utah; Quinn, 59-61.

7. Ibid., 1 Oct. 1890.

8. *Deseret Weekly News,* 24 Oct. 1891.

9. Abraham H. Cannon Journal, 12 Nov. 1891.

10. Joseph F. Smith to Reed Smoot, 1 Apr. 1911, as quoted in Jorgensen and Hardy, 36; Carl A. Badger Journal, 19 Mar. 1904, LDS archives; *Trials,* 14-18. See Quinn, 61-62. Church leaders believed that there were no laws against polygamy in Mexico and perhaps Canada. In fact polygamy was illegal in both countries. Quinn, 16-19; Jorgensen and Hardy, 17-18.

11. *Trials,* 14-16; Stanley S. Ivins to Juanita Brooks, 25 Feb. 1955, Utah State Historical Society; hereafter USHS.

12. Family Group Records of Willard Carroll and Joseph Cardon, Genealogical Department of the Church of Jesus Christ of Latter-day Saints, Salt Lake City (hereafter LDS Genealogical Department); *Salt Lake Tribune,* 1, 16 Aug., 1 Oct. 1910. Apostle George Teasdale, then leader of the Mexican colonies, apparently performed the Carroll marriage and might also have performed the Cardon sealing. Quinn found eleven polygamous marriages between July 1892 and early 1894 in Mexico and Canada, although only four were authorized by the First Presidency. Quinn, 61-62, 75-77.

13. Joseph T. Bentley Oral History, interviews by Gordon Irving, 1976, typescript, 1-2, James H. Moyle Oral History Program, LDS archives; Mildred Call Hurst Oral History, interview by Jessie Embry, 1976, typescript, 12, LDS Polygamy Oral History Project, Charles Redd Center for Western Studies, Brigham Young University, hereafter Redd interviews; Jorgensen and Hardy, 18-19; Stanley S. Ivins to Juanita Brooks, 25 Feb. 1955; George Q. Cannon to Anthony W. Ivins, 27 Dec. 1897, 1 Feb. 1898, USHS; H. Grant Ivins, "Polygamy in Mexico," 4 unpublished paper, USHS.

14. Joseph F. Smith, for example, viewed Utah's statehood as a turning point. He believed that after statehood was attained, sentiments softened, at least toward continued polygamous cohabitation. *Proceedings before the Committee on Privileges and Elections of the U. S. Senate in the Matter of the Protests Against the Right of Hon. Reed Smoot, A Senator from Utah, to hold His Seat,* 4 vols. (Washington, D.C.: Government Printing Office, 1904-1906), 1:130; hereafter *Proceedings.* Quinn raises the possibility that ninety-year-old Wilford Woodruff took a polygamous wife in 1897, forty-nine-year-old lecturer Lydia Mary von Finkelstein Mountford, who joined the church during a visit to Salt Lake City in February 1897. Quinn, 63-65.

15. Another possible explanation is that the Anthony W. Ivins marriage record (USHS), which begins in 1896, distorts the numbers I

worked from. It is possible that the number of marriages in the Ivins record raises the total number just enough to distort the record and provide misleading results. This possibility is unlikely, however, because almost all marriages performed by Ivins were listed in the same independent sources as other marriages during the period.

16. There was even confusion about the continuation of polygamous cohabitation. See, for example, Gary James Bergera, "'A Glimmer of the Same Light': The Personal Voice of One Woman's Reaction to Plural Marriage and the Issuance of the Woodruff Manifesto," unpublished paper, 1980, 8-14. A majority of church general authorities continued to cohabit with their plural wives after the Manifesto. See my "Beyond the Manifesto: Polygamous Cohabitation among LDS General Authorities after 1890," *Utah Historical Quarterly* 46 (Winter 1978): 30.

17. Marriner W. Merrill strongly favored the continuation of polygamy. He reputedly solemnized marriages after 1890, took a plural wife in 1900 or 1901, and remained strong in his advocacy of polygamy to his death (Anthon H. Lund Journal, 9 Jan. 1900, LDS archives; *Proceedings* 1:408-18; Jorgensen and Hardy, 14; *Trials,* 15). Anthon H. Lund, a lifetime monogamist, performed at least one and probably more polygamous marriages during Wilford Woodruff's presidency (Personal History of F. F. Hintze in possession of R. Sears Hintze; Jorgensen and Hardy, 13; Quinn, 62-63).

18. It is possible, of course, that the proportion was even higher.

19. Snow's feelings are documented below. Other evidence comes from statements made after Woodruff's death. Francis Lyman told Joseph W. Musser in 1914 that President Cannon and apostles Merrill, Teasdale, Cowley, Woodruff, and Taylor "had brot [sic] reproach upon the church and had done wrong" (Musser Journal, 16 Feb. 1914). One source indicates that Lyman was out of harmony with his quorum as late as 1903 on the question of polygamy (Joseph Eckersly Journal, 2-6 Sept. 1903, LDS archives).

20. Journal History, 15 Sept. 1898, LDS archives.

21. See Davis Bitton, "The B. H. Roberts Case of 1898-1900," *Utah Historical Quarterly* 25 (Winter 1975): 27-46.

22. *Deseret News,* 8 Dec. 1899, 8 Jan. 1900. Snow claimed that "no member or officer has any authority whatever to perform a plural marriage or enter into such a relation."

23. Journal History, 11 Jan. 1900. The statement was probably made in part in response to pro-polygamy sentiments expressed by Marriner W. Merrill and George Teasdale several days before in a meeting of the Twelve (Anthon H. Lund Journal, 9 Jan. 1900; John Henry Smith Diary, 10 Jan. 1900). All members of the First Presidency and Twelve were there except Brigham Young, Jr.

24. Brigham Young, Jr., Journal, 13 Mar. 1901, LDS archives.

25. *Trials,* 5, 14.

26. John Henry Smith Diary, 27 May 1901.

27. *Trials,* 15-16. Michael Quinn found that Anthony W. Ivins performed plural marriage ceremonies for Mexican colonists (who, according to Quinn, did not need First Presidency authorization) from October 1898 until July 1899, when Lorenzo Snow made it clear that this was not appropriate in his view. Quinn, 69-70.

28. Ibid., 14-18; Family Groups Records; *Salt Lake Tribune,* 1, 16 Aug., 1 Oct. 1910.

29. The numbers I use are drawn from a compilation of 150 marriages substantiated in each case by at least two and generally more sources. In addition, I have found evidence of at least seventy-five other marriages but have not yet sufficiently documented them for inclusion here. For more information, see the original printing of this essay in *Sunstone* 8 (Jan.-Apr. 1983): 35n71.

30. The number of plural marriages performed by Anthony W. Ivins in 1900 is also low, indicating that he at least took the church president's attitude seriously.

31. Ellen Steffensen Cannon to Katherine Cannon Thomas, 28 Dec. 1953, original in my possession; Family Group Records; *Trials,* 15-18; Taylor, *Rocky Mountain Empire,* 84; *Salt Lake Tribune,* 1 Oct. 1910.

32. Cannon and Smith had been in the First Presidency together since 1879 and for much of that time had taken care of the church's business together. Given their close relationship, it is possible that the two cooperated on the direction of the new polygamy.

33. *Trials,* 15-18. Cowley claimed that all the marriages he performed in 1900 and 1901 had been authorized by Cannon.

34. Anthon H. Lund Journal, 4, 6 Apr. 1904.

35. Later as a U.S. senator, Smoot was sensitive to the bad publicity the church received because of his position in Washington. Other younger Mormons who felt much as Smoot did included his personal secretary Carl A. Badger and probably J. Reuben Clark, Jr.

36. Alexander, "To Maintain Harmony," 50-52.

37. Cannon and O'Higgins, *Under the Prophet in Utah* (Boston: n.p., 1911), 176-79; *Proceedings,* 4:476. The tradition in the Cannon family is that Smith performed the Abraham H. Cannon-Lillian Hamlin marriage on a pleasure cruise from Los Angeles to Catalina Island. Lewis M. Cannon, a close friend and cousin of Abraham who later married Hamlin in another polygamous marriage, believed that Orson Smith, a local church leader in northern Utah, performed the ceremony (Carl A. Badger Journal, 9 Dec. 1905). Michael Quinn argues that "Orson Smith" was a code name for Joseph F. Smith and that Joseph F. Smith performed the wedding in the Salt Lake

temple. Quinn points out that the marriage was a proxy marriage in which Abraham stood in for his deceased brother David. Quinn, 83-84. Abraham Cannon died shortly after returning from his honeymoon in California with Lillian Hamlin. The daughter born to this union, Marba (Abram spelled backwards), is testament that the marriage was more than a proxy ordinance between Lillian and the departed David. Family Group Records of Abraham H. Cannon, LDS Genealogical Department. Smith denied involvement in the matter a number of times (see for example, Joseph F. Smith to Reed Smoot, 9 Apr. 1904, Reed Smoot Correspondence, Special Collections, Harold B. Lee Library, Brigham Young University), but always in the context of a marriage performed on board a ship. Quinn, 84-85n303. Smith and his wife Edna accompanied the newly-wed Cannons on their honeymoon to California, thus giving rise to the alleged (and traditional) setting of the marriage ceremony. Quinn, 83-84.

38. Orson Pratt Brown, Journal, 67-68, USHS.

39. *The Most Holy Principle*, 4 vols. (Murray, UT: Gems Publishing Co., 1970-75), 4:86. This is made more credible when the circumstances are considered. If Anthony Ivins refused to perform marriages unless they were authorized by the First Presidency, he would have had to receive some recommendation or notification to perform the marriage from that body. George Q. Cannon had used the medium of ambiguous letters; it is possible that Smith did the same thing after Cannon's death.

40. Joseph F. Smith to Reed Smoot, 1 Apr. 1911. In Smith's telegram, it was stated that marriages had been performed both in Canada and Mexico with church authority. In a letter from George Gibbs to Reed Smoot on 21 April 1911, Smoot was instructed that inclusion of Canada in the telegram was a mistake and that the only place where the late plural marriages took place was in Mexico (Reed Smoot Correspondence, LDS archives).

41. Brigham Young, Jr., Journal, 5 June 1902, New York Public Library.

42. Journal History, 19 Nov. 1903; John Henry Smith Diary, 19 Nov. 1903.

43. *Proceedings*, 1:129.

44. Reed Smoot's senate seat was important to the church, and it was threatened by the charges of new polygamy. Much of the non-Mormon public viewed the charges of new polygamy with distaste and the LDS church was placed in an unfavorable light at a time it was courting acceptance by American society at large.

45. *Seventy-fourth Annual Conference of the Church of Jesus Christ of Latter-day Saints* (Salt Lake City: Deseret News Press, 1904), 76. Of the apostles present at the conference, at least Owen Woodruff and Rudger

Clawson opposed issuing the statement (Anthon H. Lund Journal, 4, 6 Apr. 1904).

46. *Trials,* 15-17. Quinn suggests that Joseph F. Smith may have continued his contradictory approach to plural marriage for a time after April 1904. Quinn, 105.

47. Reed Smoot to Joseph F. Smith, 8 Dec. 1905, Reed Smoot Correspondence, LDS archives.

48. Smith told Smoot in April 1904 that Taylor and Cowley "have stated their own cases, and they will have to abide the results themselves," but he did nothing to discipline them at the time (Joseph F. Smith to Reed Smoot, 9 Apr. 1904, Reed Smoot Correspondence, LDS archives).

49. Copies of both resignations are included in the Reed Smoot Correspondence, LDS archives. The most salient parts of Taylor's resignation are set out in B. H. Roberts, *A Comprehensive History of the Church of Jesus Christ of Latter-day Saints,* 6 vols. (Salt Lake City: Deseret News Press, 1930), 6:400.

50. Reed Smoot to Joseph F. Smith, 7 Feb. 1905; Reed Smoot to the First Presidency, 8 Dec. 1905, Reed Smoot Correspondence, LDS archives.

51. George F. Gibbs to Reed Smoot, 7 Dec. 1905; Reed Smoot to First Presidency, 8 Dec. 1905, Reed Smoot Correspondence, LDS archives.

52. George F. Gibbs to Reed Smoot, 8 Dec. 1905, Reed Smoot Correspondence, LDS archives.

53. Francis M. Lyman to Reed Smoot, 15 Dec. 1905, Reed Smoot Correspondence, LDS archives.

54. Charles W. Penrose to Reed Smoot, 9 Mar. 1906, Reed Smoot Correspondence, LDS archives.

55. George F. Richards, Orson F. Whitney, and David O. McKay replaced Merrill, Taylor, and Cowdery in 1906. Anthony W. Ivins replaced George Teasdale.

56. Samuel W. Taylor, "Interviews with Nettie M. Taylor," 15 Jan. 1936, 4, and Raymond W. Taylor to Samuel W. Taylor, 3 May 1937, both as cited in Jorgensen and Hardy, 33.

57. *Trials,* 12, 18.

58. Ivins, "Polygamy in Mexico," 9; E. H. Callister to Reed Smoot, 27 Mar. 1904; James Clove to Reed Smoot, 29 Mar. 1904, Reed Smoot Correspondence, LDS archives.

59. Carl A. Badger to Ed Jenkins, 7 Apr. 1904, Badger Papers, Lee Library.

60. Emma Romney Eyring, "The Story of My Life," unpublished manuscript, 1953; Joseph T. Bentley Oral History, 1-2; Theodore C. Bennion Oral History, interview by Jessie Embry, 1976, typescript, 2, Redd interviews. President Smith indicated in 1911 that these marriages were approved of by

the church (Joseph F. Smith to Reed Smoot, 11 Apr. 1911) as did Heber J. Grant in the 1930s (Heber J. Grant to Katherine H. Allred, 15 Nov. 1935, First Presidency Letterpress Book, LDS archives).

61. *Trials,* 16. John W. Taylor almost went so far as to say that Smith had authorized him to perform the marriages he did (*Trials,* 7).

62. Hilda B. Farr Oral History, interview by Victor Jorgensen, 1972, typescript, 3, Oral History Department, California State University, Fullerton, as quoted in Jorgensen and Hardy, "The Taylor-Cowley Affair," 26.

63. Ivins Marriage Record. Ivins wrote his son Grant, "You can count on it[—]I have never performed a marriage seremony [sic] without proper authority" (Anthony Ivins to Grant Ivins, 7 Mar. 1911, USHS).

64. Stanley S. Ivins Journal, 19 Nov. 1944.

65. John W. Taylor strongly intimated that Joseph F. Smith had told him of his support of new polygamy (*Trials,* 7).

66. Reed Smoot to First Presidency, 8 Dec. 1905; Joseph W. Musser Journal, 22 July 1909.

67. One can only speculate as to what action Cannon would have taken in relation to the continuation of polygamy had he become church president.

68. George F. Richards Journal, 14 July 1909, LDS archives.

69. Anthony W. Ivins Journal, 19 Dec. 1910, USHS; H. Grant Ivins, "Polygamy in Mexico," 17; Heber J. Grant to Katherine H. Allred, 15 Nov. 1935. However, when John W. Taylor was reinstated into the church posthumously in 1965, the decision was made not to have the sealings restored between Taylor and his last three wives (two of whom he married in 1901). Delbert L. Stapley wrote Taylor's son, Raymond, "It is a rule followed by the Genealogical Society that if a marriage took place after the manifesto, that such marriages are not recognized nor will permission be given to seal such women to the man she or they were supposedly sealed to. Regardless of the sincere purpose of the women, they, as well as your father, were in violation of both the civil law and the law of the Church" (Delbert L. Stapley to Raymond W. Taylor, 4 June 1966, Marriott Library, University of Utah). Henry E. Christiansen then wrote Taylor on 2 February 1967 and affirmed what Stapley had written (Henry E. Christiansen to Raymond W. Taylor, 2 Feb. 1967, Marriott Library, University of Utah).

13.
The Metamorphosis of the Kingdom of God: Toward a Reinterpretation of Mormon History

Klaus J. Hansen[1]

POLYGAMY, CONTRARY TO POPULAR OPINION, SEDUCED FEW MEN INTO the seraglio that was Mormonism in the mind of Victorian America. Yet it lured several generations of historians—not to speak of journalists and popular novelists—into believing that its theory and practice provided the major key to understanding the "Mormon question." Not all historians succumbed to this point of view[2]; nevertheless further evidence requires another look at the problem suggesting that the idea of a political kingdom of God, promulgated by a secret "Council of Fifty," is an important key to understanding the Mormon past.[3] The polygamy conflict, it now appears, was merely that part of the iceberg visible above the troubled waters of Mormon history. Some church leaders, for example, once they had reconciled themselves to the inevitability of the attack on polygamy, in a number of instances subtly invited assaults on this "relic of barbarism" in order to shield an institution of infinitely greater significance for Mormon history, the political kingdom of God.

When in 1890 Mormon president Wilford Woodruff issued the Manifesto, ostensibly ending the practice of polygamy, he did so to save not only the church but also the kingdom of God. The semantic distinction between the two terms—the one denoting strictly an ecclesiastical body, the other a political organization intended to prepare the world for a literal, political government of Jesus Christ during the Millennium—originated with Joseph Smith, who taught those attending the secret sessions of the Council of Fifty in Nauvoo that "The Kingdom of God is a separate organization from the Church of God."[4] To those who understand this difference, it will be apparent that if the Manifesto marked a watershed in Mormon history because it heralded the beginning of the end for polygamy, the following twenty years, though lacking the dramatic impact of Woodruff's pronouncement, divided Mormon history even more conclusively and permanently because they witnessed the decline and virtual disappearance of the idea of the political kingdom of God so vigorously promoted by the Council of Fifty in the nineteenth century. This kingdom had existed for the most part *sub rosa*. Therefore its death, though accompanied by much agony, failed to attract as much attention as the death of plural marriage. Polygamy died with a bang, the political kingdom of God with a whimper. Hence those who understand the history of the political kingdom of God can better comprehend the magnitude of the political and intellectual transformation accompanying its death.

That history began formally in the spring of 1844, when Joseph Smith initiated some of his closest associates into the highly secret Council of Fifty to set up the "kingdom of Daniel by the word of the Lord."[5] Officially known among its members as "The Kingdom of God and His Laws with the Keys and Powers Thereof and Judgment in the Hands of His Servants," the council was described by John D. Lee as "the Municipal department of the Kingdom of God set up on the Earth, from which all law eminates, for the rule, government & controle of all Nations Kingdoms & toungs and People under the whole Heavens but not to controle the Priesthood but to council, deliberate & plan for the general good & upbuilding of the Kingdom of God on earth."[6] Joseph Smith even insisted that "there may be men acting as officers of the Kingdom of God who will not be members of the Church of Jesus Christ of Latter-day Saints."[7] Although it is doubtful that the Saints were able to persuade many non-Mormons to join the Council of Fifty, their projected inclusion in the "Government of God" was essential, for it allowed Mormons to insist that at least theoretically they observed the American doctrine of separation of church and state.[8] This theory played an important role in defending the Saints from the perennial accusations advanced by enemies that in Mormondom church and state were one.[9]

Yet even if non-Mormons had accepted this Mormon version of separation of church and state, there were other reasons why the suspected ideas and practices of the Council of Fifty became one of the major causes provoking the harrowing persecutions of the Saints. Non-Mormons clearly could not countenance the establishment of a separatist Mormon state, under whatever political theories. But the creation of a Mormon nation state to prepare the way for the government of God was precisely one of the major goals of the Council of Fifty.[10] For Joseph Smith and his successors believed that the Millennium could not be ushered in merely by spiritual preparation. If the law was to go forth from Zion, and the word of the Lord from Jerusalem, both the church *and* kingdom had to be organized prior to Jesus' reappearance in the clouds. This idea was in keeping with the strong Mormon belief that God required the active participation of men and women to fulfill his purposes. The Saints believed that the Lord's coming was imminent and that his return would be delayed only if—through wickedness or sloth—they failed to pave the way. Among present-day Mormons few even of the most fervent and literal-minded are able to equal the zeal and the degree of expectation which compelled most of their ancestors to anticipate the second coming at any moment.[11]

In the imagery of Daniel's prophecy the kingdom of God was likened to a stone which, loosened from the mountaintop without a hand, would crush all worldly governments and kingdoms in its path, finally filling the whole world.[12] Non-Mormons, who could be as literal-minded as the Saints, therefore believed that the Mormon kingdom like Mohammed's was to conquer the world by fire and sword. Nothing, however, could be further from the truth. Joseph Smith insisted emphatically that the kingdom was to be ushered in through peaceful means, although some of his followers did not always follow this injunction.[13] Still the Mormon prophet faced a problem—a problem that plagued the Saints not only in Missouri and Illinois but that followed them relentlessly even into the recesses of the "everlasting mountains"—how to organize such a kingdom peacefully within the boundaries of the United States. Viewed from the vantage point of historical hindsight, it is therefore clear that with the formation of a nucleus government for the kingdom of God primarily consisting of members of the Council of Fifty, the prophet had crossed the Rubicon. That the Saints would cross the Mississippi had thus become almost inevitable.

To Joseph Smith in 1844, this was of course not so obvious. True, he seems to have realized that a temporal kingdom of God in an area surrounded by non-Mormons faced at best a precarious future. But what if through a bold stroke he could capture the United States for the kingdom? The Council of Fifty thought there might be a chance and nominated the Mormon prophet for the presidency of the United States. Council of Fifty member George Miller wrote hopefully, "If we succeeded in making a majority of the voters converts to our faith, and elected Joseph president, in such an event the dominion of the kingdom would be forever established in the United States."[14] As a result the Council of Fifty decided to send all available elders on missions to campaign for the prophet and to preach Mormonism at the same time. "If God goes with them," remarked Apostle Willard Richards, "who can withstand their influence?"[15]

To anyone who believed with the faith of a Willard Richards, Smith's candidacy clearly was not as irrational as it may appear from hindsight. Still, the Mormon prophet was realistic enough not to stake the entire future of the kingdom of God on this plan. He therefore commissioned three members of the Council of Fifty to negotiate with Sam Houston for the acquisition of a large tract of land between the Nueces and Rio Grande rivers for the possible establishment of a Mormon state that would serve as a buffer between Mexico and Texas. The Mormon emissaries styled themselves plenipotentiaries, perhaps in a somewhat over-eager anticipation of their hoped-for future status.[16] That these hopes were within the bounds of official teachings regarding the kingdom of God is confirmed by as realistic a Mormon leader as George Q. Cannon, who as late as 1862 told a group of elders about to depart for a church mission that the kingdom of God was "to become a political power, known and recognized by the powers of the earth; and you, my brethren, may have to be sent forth to represent that power as its accredited agents . . . at the courts of foreign nations."[17]

As an alternate possibility to the Texas venture, Smith commissioned scouting expeditions of the Council of Fifty to search out a possible location for the kingdom in the trans-Mississippi west.[18] At the same time Orson Hyde, emissary of the council in Washington, had instructions to negotiate with the federal government for that very purpose. Hyde significantly reported that the Saints could expect little federal support for their plan and advised the prophet and his associates that "if the Saints [are to] possess the kingdom, I think they will have to take it; and the sooner it is done the more easily it is accomplished."[19] As it soon turned out this was the only alternative left to the Mormons. For with the death of their prophet, which followed within weeks, the Saints had to bury any hopes of capturing the kingdom through gaining the presidency of the United States. The establishment of the kingdom in Texas meanwhile had also become unfeasible. Under the forceful leadership of Brigham Young therefore the Council of Fifty attempted to set up the kingdom in the Rocky Mountains.

Although the Council of Fifty never fully realized its goal of establishing the kingdom of God as a separate nation in the Great Basin, it ceaselessly worked in that direction for as long as possible. When Brigham Young and the Council of Fifty organized the exodus, they knew that the territory which they planned to colonize belonged to Mexico. In an epistle circulated in the autumn of 1845, Young admonished the Saints that removal beyond the boundaries of the United States was a test of orthodoxy: "If the authorities of this church cannot abide in peace within the pale of this nation, neither can those who implicitly hearken to their wholesome counsel. A word to the wise is sufficient."[20] When the leaders of the church finally learned of the ratification of the treaty of Guadalupe Hidalgo, however, there was nothing they could do, as Frederick Logan Paxson pointed out long ago, "but make the best of these facts and to seek from the United States the same sort of autonomy they had received from Illinois."[21]

As a matter of fact the Council of Fifty tried to do better than that. Although Brigham Young apparently realized in 1847 that it was impossible to cut the political threads with the United States in the near future, he did his best to render those threads as thin and weak as possible. As a result the Council of Fifty launched the state of Deseret at a time when it was in absolute political control of the Great Basin, so as to present the federal government with the accomplished fact of a kingdom of God before non-Mormons could hamper its development. And even before the establishment of Deseret, the Council of Fifty observed at least a theoretical separation of church and state. As James Clark was the first to point out, the origins of Great Basin government can hardly be attributed to "well established precedents of frontier impatience and restlessness."[22] The fact is that the Mormons had migrated to the Rockies precisely for the purpose of setting up their own government, a government that was only incidentally an adaptation to frontier conditions. A commonly held opinion is that the state of Deseret was created because the United States had not yet provided a government for the region and because the presence of gold seekers and other gentiles required a civil magistrate.[23] This interpretation is incorrect. Had a government already existed in the area, the Mormons most likely would not have migrated there. On the other hand even if gold seekers and others had not come to the Great Basin, the Council of Fifty would still have set up a formal government, along precedents worked out by Joseph Smith in 1844.[24]

It was obvious, of course, that sooner or later the Saints had to supplement the state of Deseret with a governmental organization approved by Washington, if only to keep relations with the "states" as amicable as possible. Moreover, statehood need not necessarily have diminished the power of the Council of Fifty appreciably. The doctrine of states' rights, which had worked to the detriment of the Saints in Missouri and Illinois, could be used to great advantage in maintaining a considerable degree of independence for the political kingdom of God at a time when the Civil War amendments to the Constitution and their interpretation were still in the future. Had Deseret achieved statehood, the political control of the Council of Fifty probably would have continued with little outside interference. Utah senator Frank Cannon's later assertion that the Mormons attempted to gain admission into the union in order to escape its authority thus contains a kernel of truth.[25] That Deseret in 1850 failed to be admitted as a state, however, was not a consequence of anti-Mormon sentiment in Congress, so evident in all later attempts. The sectional controversy worked just as effectively to frustrate Mormon hopes when the southern bloc in Congress combined with northern advocates of popular sovereignty to relegate the Mormon kingdom to territorial status under the compromise of 1850.[26]

But even as a territory the kingdom of God enjoyed a

considerable degree of autonomy. Territorial secretary Benjamin Ferris observed that from 1851 on "the laws of the United States have been *nominally* in operation," although in reality the Mormons governed themselves.[27] The territorial government ruled *de jure*, while the state of Deseret continued to be the real authority accepted by the Saints. When in 1855 Brigham Young could boldly announce that "The Kingdom of God is actually organized and the inhabitants of the earth do not know it,"[28] the context of the speech made it clear that he was not referring to the church. Only too soon, however, it became apparent that non-Mormons knew more about the kingdom of God than Mormons suspected. As a result relations with the federal government deteriorated, culminating in the Utah War, 1857-58. When President James Buchanan sent an ill-starred military expedition to Utah in 1857, it was as much to suppress an alleged Mormon rebellion as to suppress polygamy, although as Richard Poll has pointed out, the Democrats were in dire need of stealing some of the thunder from the Republican "twin relics" platform of 1856 to prove to a reform-minded north that they too were against at least one relic of barbarism (the other being slavery).[29]

To Brigham Young the expedition meant something else. He announced publicly that perhaps the Lord was about to cut the thread between the kingdom of God and the United States.[30] Privately he wrote to Thomas L. Kane "that the time is not far distant when Utah shall be able to assume her rights and place among the family of nations."[31] This renewed enthusiasm for the kingdom of God also affected the subalterns of the prophet. Thomas Tanner of the Nauvoo Legion signed a letter to his commanding officer Col. Ellerbeck as "Captain of the Royal Artillery, Deseret."[32] Although the Lord by allowing for a peaceful settlement of the conflict indicated that he apparently did not want the thread cut at this time, Mormon leaders continued to prepare their Rocky Mountain empire for the day when they could permanently hoist the flag of the kingdom.

Three years later these hopes seemed to be on the verge of realization, with the bombardment of Fort Sumter portending the fulfillment of Joseph Smith's prophecy that war beginning in South Carolina would envelop the earth and lead to the "full end of all nations."[33] Young taught that north and south would destroy each other, leaving the kingdom of God to take over the reins of government of the United States.[34] As a result the Council of Fifty vigilantly kept its organization intact for the time when the political kingdom of God could send its accredited ambassadors abroad. In a special message to the legislature of the extra-legal state of Deseret in 1862, Brigham Young reminded its members, "This body of men will give laws to the nations of the earth . . . when the time comes, we shall be called the Kingdom of God . . . Joseph Smith organized this government before, in Nauvoo, and he said if we did our duty, we should prevail over all our enemies. We should get all things ready, and when the time comes, we should let the water on the wheel and start the machine in motion."[35] But the time never came. In vain the Saints kept waiting for the finger of the Lord to lift the yoke of oppression from their shoulders and raise his chosen people to nationhood. Disappointment and frustration thus played an important part in the metamorphosis of the kingdom of God.

Nevertheless a Mormon nationalism of such profound intensity would not die overnight, especially in view of its strong theological and philosophical roots. This is a point that cannot be emphasized enough. For it may be possible to argue that the Mormons developed an incipient nationality primarily as the result of enforced unity and physical isolation on the frontier—an inevitable consequence of certain environmental and sociological phenomena. That this influence existed cannot be denied. Park and Burgess, those eminent American sociologists, called attention to it over forty years ago: "Once the sect has achieved territorial isolation and territorial solidarity, so that it is the dominant power within the region that it occupies, it is able to control the civil organization, establish schools and a press, and so put the impress of a peculiar culture upon all the civil and political institutions it controls. In this case it tends to assume the form of a state, and become a nationality. Something approaching this was achieved by the Mormons in Utah."[36]

This influence, however, was only secondary. The primary source of Mormon nationalism in the Great Basin was intellectual and must be traced to the theology and political philosophy of Joseph Smith as it had originated in the Burned-over District and matured in Ohio, Missouri, and Illinois.[37] That the Rocky Mountain frontier placed its own indelible environmental stamp on this form of nationalism seems self-evident. Thus, although the concept of Mormon nationalism was not the product of the Great Basin environment, that environment encouraged the practice of such theories. It was, of course, precisely for this reason that Brigham Young and the Council of Fifty sought out their Rocky Mountain refuge. But regardless of any environmental influences, Mormon leaders had internal—i.e., theological—motivations for establishing the kingdom of God, motivations that would have appeared in some form no matter where they had settled.

The same internal motivation resulted in Mormon political unity and highly centralized control of all political activities. It is frequently claimed that this political cohesion and lack of pluralism were primarily a response to persecution. In the absence of conflict, so the argument runs, Mormon institutions would have been as democratic as those of the United States itself. The disappearance of the Mormon People's Party after the Manifesto, the subsequent dissolution of the anti-Mormon Liberal Party in 1893, and the alignment of Utah along national party lines are sometimes cited as proof of the validity of this point of view.[38] This explanation, however, is too simple, involving the old *post hoc propter hoc* fallacy. An examination of the political theory of the kingdom of God reveals that persecution or not, the Saints were committed to political unity.[39]

The practical results of such a philosophy, to non-Mormons at any rate, seemed singularly un-American. When William H. Hooper, a member of the Council of Fifty, "campaigned" for the seat of territorial delegate to congress in 1856, Apostle George A. Smith, who accompanied the aspirant on his election campaign, informed the Saints of Mount Pleasant, Utah, "What we do we should do as one man. Our system should be Theo-Democracy,—the voice of the people consenting to the voice of God."[40] Needless to say Hooper was "elected." As long as the Council of Fifty controlled politics, Mormon elections were hardly anything more than a "sustaining" of the official candidates. If, however, on rare occasions the people might actually nominate a candidate not approved by the hierarchy, "counsel" by the leaders usually sufficed to bring about the desired results. Hosea Stout, for example, recorded in his diary that on 2 August 1855 he went to Davis County in order to persuade the people to withdraw the name of a popular bishop, Anson Call, for nomination for the impending election to the legislature and place John D. Parker in his stead. The change was apparently made without much protest. But what Stout did not record and what the people of Davis County apparently did not know was that Parker belonged to the

Council of Fifty, having been called by none other than Joseph Smith.[41]

In light of these ideas and practices it appears that the transformation of the idea of the kingdom of God from a political to a purely ecclesiastical concept and the cessation of centralized control over Mormon politics by the hierarchy involved a penetrating and painful intellectual transformation of assumptions that were basic to the very fiber of the social and political systems of the kingdom of God. What were the causes for this metamorphosis? They may be classified, perhaps somewhat arbitrarily, into four categories: (1) persecution, (2) the decline of millennialism, (3) the inherent American patriotism of the Saints, (4) and the fact that the kingdom of God had fulfilled important functions and outlived its usefulness.

The promotion of the political kingdom of God by Mormon leaders was one of the major reasons why the Saints were driven so relentlessly for over half a century. Although this point must have been obvious to Wilford Woodruff, it is evident he believed that cessation of polygamy would end or at least diminish the reforming zeal of those crusading for monogamy, thus depriving the political enemies of Mormonism of indispensable support for their crusade against the kingdom of God. The Manifesto clearly was primarily a tactical maneuver to save not only the church but if possible the political kingdom as well. The preservation of the church alone as a religious institution would have made the restitution of polygamy impossible—as demonstrated by the history of Mormonism since 1890. But if the kingdom of God could have been preserved, it might have been possible to continue polygamy once the non-Mormon onslaught had spent itself.

With the advantage of hindsight, this argument may appear as a mere begging of the question. But to Woodruff continuation of the political kingdom of God seems to have been a real alternative. True in 1889 the First Presidency of the church publicly declared "that this Church does not claim to be an independent, temporal kingdom of God, or to be an *imperium in imperio* aiming to overthrow the United States of any other civil government" and once again affirmed its traditional public position that "Church government and civil government are distinct and separate in our theory and practice, . . ."[42] To those who understood the political theory of the kingdom of God, however, this declaration was in complete harmony with the one issued four years later at the completion of the Salt Lake Temple in 1893 by a convocation of 115 select church leaders, who unanimously affirmed that "the Presidency of the Church are set to govern and control the affairs of the Church and Kingdom of God . . . that upon their shoulders rests the responsibility of teaching, governing, controlling and counselling the Church and Kingdom of God in *all* things on the earth."[43]

Perhaps Woodruff was merely clutching at straws in an attempt to evade the inevitable. But he was not the only one who attempted to keep alive the belief that the kingdom of God and with it the church would be delivered from the enemy in the near future. In 1900 Woodruff's successor Lorenzo Snow affirmed at a special priesthood meeting in the Salt Lake Temple that "there are many here now under the sound of my voice, probably a majority, who will live to go back to Jackson County [site of the New Jerusalem] and assist in building that temple."[44]

By making polygamy the major issue the church leaders could always maintain that the persecution of the Saints was of a *religious* nature, involving a violation of their constitutional rights. The enemies of Mormonism, of course, also knew their Constitution. Thus John Hyde insisted that "as a religion, Mormonism cannot be meddled with; as a civil policy it may."[45] Frederick T. Dubois of Idaho, prominent leader in the anti-Mormon crusade, showed that the major motivations behind the attack on polygamy were political: "Those of us who understood the situation were not nearly as much opposed to polygamy as we were to the political domination of the Church. We realized, however, that we could not make those who did not come actually in contact with it, understand what this political domination meant. We made use of polygamy in consequence as our great weapon of offense and to gain recruits to our standard. There was a universal detestation of polygamy, and inasmuch as the Mormons openly defended it we were given a very effective weapon with which to attack."[46]

To the frustration of the gentiles, the Saints always denied the allegations pertaining to the political kingdom. And they could do this most effectively without being technically untruthful, for, according to the Mormon principle of separation of church and state, the political kingdom of God was not a church organization. Thus Mormon leaders could keep their enemies quite effectively in the dark. Gentiles, of course, sensed this without being able to support their charges with sufficient evidence. When the full story of the role of the kingdom of God in the anti-polygamy crusade is revealed, the verdict of future historians might well be that in 1890 the Saints merely lost a battle, being as yet undefeated in the war. Enemies of Mormonism apparently realized this; the continued altercations with the Saints for at least another twenty years at any rate seem to indicate that the gentiles were less than satisfied with their "victory" in 1890. Mormon leaders all the while continued their tactics of deflecting the renewed onslaught on the kingdom. In the Smoot hearings, for example, Mormons were charged with attempting to cloud the real issues (i.e., relationship of church and state in Mormon dominated areas) by "trying to force the protestants to issues which they themselves have never raised" (i.e., polygamy).[47] Thus these tactics ironically backfired, providing the Saints with subtle means for defending the kingdom. If these Mormon defense measures were partially successful, internal reasons may have been as important as external ones for the metamorphosis of the kingdom.

Millennialism is perhaps the most obvious example. The Mormon church can of course honestly assert that no transformation in doctrine has occurred. But the perpetuation of doctrinal theories does not preclude a fundamental intellectual transformation. To this day orthodox Latter-day Saints believe that Jesus Christ will return and that in time all earthly governments but that of the kingdom of God will disappear. Nevertheless not many Mormons at the present time have organized their lives in such a manner that at practically any moment they can prepare themselves for and welcome this event as a literal occurrence. Not that nineteenth-century Saints could always say that of themselves. But they experienced definite and sustained periods of profound expectation. As the years wore on, however, without deliverance in sight, a certain spirit of resignation spread among the faithful. True, some Mormons believed that the Edmunds Act was a harbinger of the Millennium, and in 1890 there was a widespread belief among church members that Joseph Smith's prediction of 1835—that fifty-six years would "wind up the scene"—would be fulfilled.[48] But such enthusiasm was short-lived. In 1903 Benjamin F. Johnson, an original member of the Council of Fifty, could not conceal his disappointment when he remarked that "we were over seventy years ago taught by our leaders to believe that the coming of Christ and the millennial reign was much nearer than we believe it to be now."[49] Johnson's belief seems to have been shared by the majority of the Mormons. By projecting the certain and inevitable return of Jesus Christ to an undetermined future date, the Saints had removed a major motivation for building the political kingdom. Not even the optimistic pronouncements of a church president at the turn of the twentieth century could prevent this decline of millennial expectations.

Possibly of even greater significance for the transformation of the kingdom was the basic American patriotism of the majority of the Saints. This statement may appear to contradict implications of Mormon disloyalty to the U.S. government inherent in the separatist nationalism of the kingdom of God. To the gentiles, of course, the disloyalty of the Saints was merely axiomatic. And they could marshal enough evidence to prove to their own satisfaction that the Mormon protestations to the contrary were either untruthful or absurd. The Saints, on the other hand, pointed out that loyalty to the constitution of the United States was a basic element of their faith.[50]

But how could such allegiance be reconciled with kingdom building? A circular letter which church leaders addressed to the world in 1846 reveals one attempted solution: "Our patriotism has not been overcome by fire, by sword, by daylight or midnight assassinations which we have endured; neither have they alienated us from the *institutions* of our country."[51] Brigham Young in cruder fashion elaborated on this concept by drawing a distinction between the Constitution and the "damned rascals who administer the government."[52]

The intellectual position of the leaders of the kingdom of God was nevertheless fraught with difficulties. The gentiles clearly would not accept it. Judge Thomas J. Anderson, for example, had this to say: "Will men become attached to the principles of the Constitution of the United States when they hear the government constantly denounced as tyrannical and oppressive? It would be as unreasonable to expect to gather grapes from thorns, or figs from thistles."[53] What Anderson of course failed to understand was that men do not always think and do what appears reasonable to others. One of the major problems was that Mormons and gentiles were using the same words in totally different context and with conflicting connotation. Moreover, equally authentic democratic and patriotic motives inspiring

Mormons existed side by side with the separatist tendencies that found expression in the political kingdom of God.

As Thomas O'Dea pointed out, these conflicting concepts could coexist because "the Mormons never worked out consistently the political implications of their religious philosophy."[54] But sooner or later there came a point in the lives of most Saints when they had to decide which loyalty took precedence. John D. Lee presents a moving illustration of this conflict in a journal entry made in 1851, while on his way to southern Utah as a member of the Iron County Mission. Among the colonists was a large group of converts from the British Isles who accused Lee of "causing national feelings by speaking of great battles that had been fought by the Americans." Vowed Lee, "I hope never again to excite that kind of National Feelings. All governments on earth but one are corrupt & that is the government of God that is my National Interest."[55] As a member of the Council of Fifty, Lee of course knew more about this "national Interest" than those who were traveling with him.

As Mormon isolation decreased after the Civil War, however, a younger generation, which had not experienced the persecutions in Missouri and Illinois or the hardships of the exodus, had little use for this national interest and exerted pressure upon the kingdom to identify with the mainstream of American life.[56] The first important manifestation of internal discontent with separatism was the Godbeite movement. Although the chief demand of the insurgents was the cessation of economic isolation, these men also wanted a closer identification of Mormonism with the United States both politically and culturally. Several years after his excommunication, Edward W. Tullidge, for instance, insisted that the idea of a separatist political kingdom of God was in fact a distortion of what he conceived to be the true meaning and purpose of Mormonism. Rather, he affirmed it was the divine mission of the church "to give a more glorious destiny to the American nation itself."[57] Young had the heretics excommunicated primarily on grounds that they refused to acknowledge the prophet's right to dictate to them "in all things temporal and spiritual."[58]

It is an ironic commentary on social and intellectual change that the liberalism of the Godbeites has become the conservatism of twentieth-century Mormonism, a change vividly illustrated by the testimony of the church leaders in the Smoot hearings. When in 1903 a powerful group of senators protested against seating Reed Smoot, senator from Utah, on the grounds that he was a member of a hierarchy controlling political affairs in Utah in violation of agreements presumably made in 1890 and that his election ignored the principles of separation of church and state, most Mormon leaders, church president Joseph F. Smith among them, were subpoenaed by the committee. In a particularly significant statement that would have startled Brigham Young considerably, Smith testified, "Our people are given the largest possible latitude for their convictions, and if a man rejects a message that I may give him but is still moral and believes in the main principles of the gospel and desires to continue his membership in the church, he is permitted to remain and he is not unchurched."[59] This statement, of course, was an affirmation of future intention rather than past practice.

The political kingdom of God understandably received considerable attention at these hearings, with the writings of Orson Pratt coming under particularly close scrutiny. These no self-respecting critic of Mormonism could ignore, particularly not the famous assertion that "The Kingdom of God . . . is the only legal government that can exist in any part of the universe. All other governments are illegal and unauthorized. God, having made all beings and worlds, has the supreme right to govern them by His own laws, and by officers of His own appointment. Any people attempting to govern themselves by laws of their own making, and by officers of their own appointment, are in direct rebellion against the Kingdom of God."[60] Perhaps no other statement by a Mormon leader gained as much notoriety in anti-Mormon literature. The task of refuting Pratt before the committee fell to Apostle James E. Talmage, whom the church had appointed to digest the massive testimony of its witnesses and iron out any contradictions. Talmage attempted to demolish Pratt's statement by drawing support from a remark by Brigham Young, who had once dismissed Pratt's "vain philosophy" as being "no guide for Latter-day Saints."[61] What Talmage did not reveal to the committee was that Young had levelled the charge in a totally different context and that the Mormon leader shared Pratt's views regarding the kingdom of God.[62]

Talmage's approach, however, was the only realistic one, especially since church leaders in the past had defended the kingdom against the gentiles only by pointing out that church and state were separate in Mormondom and that the charge of church control of politics was a distortion because in a Mormon community the political leaders inevitably belonged to the church.[63] Mormon leaders obviously could not publicly reverse their stand on a doctrine as fundamental as that of the political kingdom of God, especially since they had always denied its existence to the gentiles. Hence church leaders could only continue to affirm that a political kingdom of God was in no way part of the Mormon dream. The hierarchy could exorcise the separatist tendencies of Mormonism only by insisting that they had never existed. The intellectual transformation of Mormonism could best be accomplished under the pretense that it was not going on.

Because gentile accusations frequently distorted Mormon aims and because the enemies of Mormonism were unaware of the distinction between church and kingdom, church leaders could quite effectively bury the political kingdom of God by taking refuge behind semantics without being technically guilty of untruthfulness. Even before Talmage took the stand, the First Presidency had published an article in the 1903 Christmas edition of the *Deseret News* reiterating its public stand on the kingdom of God. The Mormon organization, the article affirmed, "does not attempt to exercise the powers of a secular government, but its influence and effects are to strengthen and promote fidelity to the law and loyalty to the nation where its followers reside. The phrase 'church and kingdom' . . . [denotes] solely an ecclesiastical organization. It is separate and distinct from the state."[64]

The presidency could not have chosen its words more carefully. The word *kingdom* as used in this context had always been synonymous with *church* in Mormon usage. Any mention of the *political* kingdom of God was of course scrupulously avoided, although ironically the avowed purpose of the church "to strengthen and promote fidelity to the law and loyalty to the nation where its followers reside" was applicable to the political kingdom of God as well. Mormon leaders must have known that this statement—introduced by Talmage as evidence for the defense in the Smoot hearings and reminiscent of the one issued shortly after the Manifesto, as well as foreshadowing the official declaration of the church regarding relations of church and state published in 1907—could be interpreted by gentiles as a Mormon concession. Yet to those who understood the true purposes of the political kingdom, it was nothing of the kind. In fact the statement could be viewed as a subtle statement of defense in behalf of the kingdom. It was of course a supreme paradox that the Mormon leaders could apply a theoretical separation of church and state to the very purpose of preventing such a division.

Nevertheless although the Saints regarded Smoot's vindication as a victory for their side, church leaders would not have been able to survive many such victories. For with each new controversy the survival of the political kingdom depended increasingly on a private interpretation of words. As time went on it became more and more apparent that the kingdom could not live by semantics alone, especially when it was being deserted by its own citizens.

Led by a vocal minority of intellectuals in the Godbeite tradition, a new generation of Mormons began to identify with the mainstream of American culture. Frank Cannon, later to become a notorious enemy of his own people, illustrated through a description of his patriotic feelings sentiments that were most likely shared by many young Mormons. During a stay in Washington some time before the Manifesto, he remarked, "I wonder whether another American ever saw that city with such eyes of envy, of aspiration, of wistful pride, of daunted admiration. Here were all the consecrations of a nation's memories, and they thrilled me, even while they pierced me with the sense that I was not and might well despair of ever being, a citizen of their glory."[65]

On a more intellectual level, Nels L. Nelson, professor of English at Brigham Young University, attempted to show in his *Scientific Aspects of Mormonism*[66] how much Joseph Smith had anticipated the thought of Charles Darwin, John Fiske, T. H. Huxley, and Herbert Spencer. Nelson was looking for evidence to demonstrate that Mormonism was in the mainstream of Western thought and culture and in the forefront of those forces that were pushing America ever onward and upward in a cosmic process of scientific and moral evolution; he was satisfied that he had found this evidence in abundance.

Even more important in this enterprise was the work of the historian. Liberal students of Mormon history, for example, insisted that the separatist tendencies of Mormonism had existed only as a figment of the imagination of the enemies of the church. To these writers the Turner thesis provided a ready-made vehicle for the

Americanization of Mormon history. In fact these scholars probably would have invented Frederick Jackson Turner had he not existed, so readily did they apply the frontier hypothesis to the Mormon past. By portraying the Saints as typical frontiersmen, they created the impression that Great Basin social and political institutions from their inception reflected the values of American democracy. Whatever departures had occurred from the main currents of American thought and behavior were mere back eddies, explainable as temporary but necessary responses to a hostile environment. Once the Mormon pioneers had conquered this environment, the true American character of the pioneers, both socially and politically, would reveal itself. These historians had thus employed one of the most time-honored uses of history—that of reading the present into the past in order to reshape the future along ways parting from the old—to the reconstruction of the Mormon past.[67]

Yet all these efforts might have failed had it not been for the fact that Mormon nationalism had outlived its usefulness. The idealistic conception of a temporal kingdom of God that would dominate the world could comprise a powerful motivating force for a society of farmers and artisans to carve an inland empire out of a hostile environment and thus provide a physical basis of survival for Mormonism. In fact the positive leadership of the Council of Fifty may well have been one of the primary reasons why Mormonism, unlike most sects originating in the early half of the nineteenth century, not only survived but continued to thrive. Yet having successfully accomplished its important mission of establishing a home for the Saints, the Council of Fifty may have found it difficult to employ the millennialistic vision of a world empire as the justification for the more mundane direction of everyday Mormon endeavors, especially in view of the onslaught of a hostile world that attempted to crush this empire, partly in response to the ideas and activities of the very organization that created it.[68]

Several years ago the founder and leader of the Theocratic Party, Homer A. Tomlinson, appeared on the campus of Princeton University to campaign for his election to the presidency of the United States in preparation for the establishment of the kingdom of God in America with himself as king and president. Tomlinson proclaimed his doctrines to a cheering crowd of 1,500 undergraduates. After the speech they mockingly paraded him around the campus. His picture in jest appeared on the front page of the *Daily Princetonian* the following day.[69]

The Mormon kingdom of God was spared such a fate—a fate far worse than persecution—because at one of the most crucial periods of its history it had responded to the values of twentieth-century American culture, at the same time preserving much of its identity. And yet paradoxically without the existence and the activities of the Council of Fifty, which contributed much to building the Great Basin Kingdom, Mormonism might well have failed to enjoy its present stature and prestige within the framework of accepted American religious values and persuasions.

NOTES

1. Nearly thirty-five years have passed since Alfred Bush and I first presented our thinking on the Council of Fifty and the Kingdom of God in 1957, and more than twenty-five years since the publication of "The Metamorphosis of the Kingdom of God." It is only to be expected, then, that with the flowering of Mormon history in the intervening years, the topic under discussion may require some revision. I hope to report on the evolution of my own thinking in some detail elsewhere. Yet I do think it appropriate to place "The Metamorphosis," if briefly, within the context of evolving Mormon scholarship.

The facts and arguments advanced in "The Metamorphosis" were discussed more fully in my book *Quest for Empire: The Political Kingdom of God and the Council of Fifty in Mormon History* (East Lansing: Michigan State University Press, 1967). They are part of what may be called a "first-generation kingdom school" that focused largely on the Council of Fifty and its significance in the kingdom—initiated, among others, by G. Homer Durham, "A Political Interpretation of Mormon History," *Pacific Historical Review* 13 (June 1944): 136-50; Alfred L. Bush and Klaus J. Hansen, "Notes Towards a Definition of the Council of Fifty," 1957, unpublished ms.; Hyrum L. Andrus, *Joseph Smith and World Government* (Salt Lake City: Deseret Book, 1958); and James R. Clark, "The Kingdom of God, the Council of Fifty, and the State of Deseret," *Utah Historical Quarterly* 26 (Apr. 1958): 130-48. Michael Quinn reported on the discovery of additional sources in 1980, refining and adding to but not significantly altering the earlier factual basis ("The Council of Fifty and Its Members, 1844 to 1945," *Brigham Young University Studies* 20 [Winter 1980]: 163-93).

If there is general agreement on the facts, the same cannot be said for interpretation. While the above scholars (with the exception of Quinn) stressed the importance of the Council of Fifty, Andrus insisted that the political kingdom was to be a world government fully implemented only after the second coming of Jesus Christ. A more recent study by Andrew F. Ehat, "'It Seems Like Heaven Began on Earth': Joseph Smith and the Constitution of the Kingdom of God," *Brigham Young University Studies* 20 (Spring 1980): 253-79, also stressed the religious and transcendent nature of the kingdom. Most other scholars have argued that the kingdom was very much in the world, in preparation for the Millennium. Millennialism has been the subject of numerous scholarly studies in the past thirty-five years and promises to be a continuing source of controversy, with discussion being further advanced by the forthcoming research of Grant Underwood.

A first dissenter from the kingdom school was Gordon Thomasson, who questioned the existence of the kingdom and argued that "it is not necessary to have recourse to an hypothetical political kingdom of God to understand Church involvement in politics"—an opinion that found a sympathetic hearing among those who preferred a more traditional interpretation of Mormon history ("Foolsmate," *Dialogue: A Journal of Mormon Thought* 6 [1971], 3/4:148). Others, particularly Quinn, while accepting the importance of the political kingdom, contended that the significance of the Council of Fifty has been exaggerated (see his "The Council of Fifty and Its Members"). After weighing evidence on both sides, Marvin Hill has recently taken a kind of middle ground, suggesting that "whether the Council of Fifty was central, mere symbol, or a revolutionary government, it came as the culmination of a long period of church political involvement in which the Saints sought to have the political balance of power" (*Quest for Refuge: The Mormon Flight from American Pluralism* [Salt Lake City: Signature Books, 1989], xvi). Hill, however, also asserted that by focusing too exclusively on the Council of Fifty, I slighted "the complex origin and nature of Mormon ideals" (ibid.). In *Quest for Refuge* (the title appears to be in direct response to the title of my *Quest for Empire*), Hill argued "that the Mormon quest for political power came not from a rising estimation of man's capabilities to usher in his own millennium, as Hansen supposed, but rather from a terrible fear that the people could not govern themselves without divine direction" (ibid.)—thus the subtitle of his work: *The Mormon Flight from American Pluralism*. Hill's work clearly represented the informed thinking of a scholar who has a thorough command both of Mormon sources and the larger context of American cultural history. In future work, I hope to show that while I have benefited from Hill's insight I also believe that our disagreements are outweighed by a fundamental consensus on the significance of the kingdom of God in Mormon history. In that sense, I am also in agreement with Jan Shipps's *Mormonism: The Story of a New Religious Tradition* (Urbana: University of Illinois Press, 1985), who likewise sees the political kingdom as an essential element in the Mormon tradition. Perhaps it may not seem unreasonable to see Hill and Shipps as leading representatives of a second generation of the kingdom school, focusing less on the Council of Fifty and more on the larger implications of the kingdom.

Another controversy was generated by my perhaps overly pointed juxtaposition of polygamy versus the political kingdom in the opening paragraph to "The Metamorphosis." No doubt, if I were to write this essay today, I would be inclined to open with less dramatic flourish. Certainly, recent scholarship has focused on the political consequences of polygamy. Edward Leo Lyman, in *Political Deliverance: The Mormon Quest for Utah Statehood* (Urbana: University of Illinois Press, 1986), makes short shrift of the political kingdom, though note should be taken of Vernon H. Jensen's dissenting opinion, "The Lyman Thesis," in *Dialogue: A Journal of Mormon Thought* 21 (Summer 1988): 9-11. In his forthcoming *Solemn Covenant: The Mormon Polygamous Passage* (from University of Illinois Press), Carmon Hardy, while not as dismissive of the political kingdom as Lyman, also makes a strong case for the primacy of polygamy in the political struggle. Nevertheless, I am not ready to yield the field completely, holding fast to a major point only implied in the following article and articulated more directly in *Quest for Empire* that "plural marriage was part of the social order of the political kingdom, . . . [and] could only be practiced in ethical and moral terms within the kingdom (54). Instead of an either/or proposition—polygamy or the political kingdom—future interpretations should pay closer attention to the interrelationship between the two.

These remarks briefly indicate what I hope to demonstrate more fully in future work: that (with apologies to Mark Twain) reports of the death of the kingdom school of Mormon history have been exaggerated.

2. See, for example, Leonard J. Arrington, *Great Basin Kingdom: An Economic History of the Latter-day Saints, 1830-1900* (Cambridge, 1958); David Brion Davis, "The New England Origins of Mormonism," *The New England Quarterly* 26 (June 1953): 147-68; Durham, "A Political Interpretation of Mormon History"; Robert J. Dwyer, *The Gentile Comes to Utah: A Study in Religious and Social Conflict, 1862-1890* (Washington: Catholic University of America, 1941); Howard R. Lamar, "Political Patterns in New Mexico and Utah Territories," *Utah Historical Quarterly* 28 (Oct. 1960): 377-87; William Mulder, *The Mormons in American History* (Salt Lake City: University of Utah Press, 1957); Richard D. Poll, "The Mormon Question Enters National Politics, 1850-1856," *Utah Historical Quarterly* 25 (Apr. 1957): 117-31; Richard D. Poll, "The Political Reconstruction of Utah Territory, 1866-1890," *Pacific Historical Review* 27 (May 1958): 111-26; Jan Shipps, "The Mormons in Politics: The First Hundred Years," Ph.D. diss., University of Colorado, 1965.

3. Andrus, *Joseph Smith and World Government*; Arrington, *Great*

Basin Kingdom, 31-32, 39-40, 50-62; Fawn M. Brodie, *No Man Knows My History, The Life of Joseph Smith the Mormon Prophet* (New York: A. A. Knopf, 1945), 356-57; Juanita Brooks, *John Doyle Lee* (Glendale, CA: A. A. Clark, 1962); Alfred L. Bush and Klaus J. Hansen, "Notes Towards a Definition of the Council of Fifty," MS, 1957, Harold B. Lee Library, Brigham Young University; James R. Clark, "Church and State Relationships in Education in Utah," Ph.D. diss., Utah State University, 1958; Clark, "The Kingdom of God, the Council of Fifty and the State of Deseret"; Robert Bruce Flanders, *Nauvoo: Kingdom on the Mississippi* (Urbana: University of Illinois Press, 1965), 278-305; Klaus J. Hansen, "The Political Kingdom of God as a Cause for Mormon-Gentile Conflict," *Brigham Young University Studies* 2 (Spring/Summer 1960): 241-60; Klaus J. Hansen, "The Kingdom of God in Mormon Thought and Practice, 1830-1896," Ph.D. diss., Wayne State University, 1963; J. Keith Melville, "Theory and Practice of Church and State During the Brigham Young Era," *Brigham Young University Studies* 3 (Autumn 1960): 33-55; Thomas F. O'Dea, *The Mormons* (Chicago: University of Chicago Press, 1957), 165-68.

4. Brigham H. Roberts, ed., *History of the Church of Jesus Christ of Latter-day Saints*, 2d ed., 7 vols. (Salt Lake City: Deseret Book Co., 1946-50), 7:382; hereafter cited as HC.

5. HC 6:365.

6. Minutes of the Council of Fifty, 10 Apr. 1880, Harold B. Lee Library; Robert Glass Cleland and Juanita Brooks, eds., *A Mormon Chronicle: The Diaries of John D. Lee, 1848-1876*, 2 vols. (San Marino, CA: Huntington Library, 1955), 1:80; HC 6:260-67, 286, 331, 341, 343, 351, 356; 7:379-80.

7. HC 7:382. See also Brigham Young, 8 July 1855, *Journal of Discourses*, 26 vols. (Liverpool: Latter-day Saints' Book Depot, 1855), 2:310; hereafter JD.

8. John D. Lee, in *Mormonism Unvailed* (St. Louis, 1877), 173, insists that a non-Mormon identified only as Jackson became a member of the Council of Fifty. Thomas L. Kane possibly may have been a member. At any rate Brigham Young discussed matters with the "Colonel" of such a confidential nature as he was accustomed to discuss only in the privacy of the council. See Brigham Young to Thomas L. Kane, 1 Sept. 1858, in Edward Eberstadt and Sons, *Western America in Documents* (New York, 1963), 111.

9. Thus George Q. Cannon was quoted in *Truth* 2 (1 Aug. 1936): 43. It should be emphasized, however, that the Saints were hardly consistent. Parley P. Pratt for one could see no distinction between church and state (JD 1:173-74).

10. Cleland and Brooks, *Mormon Chronicle*, 1:80; John Taylor, JD 6:23-24; Young to Kane, in Eberstadt, *Western America*, 111.

11. See particularly the early issues of the *Latter-day Saints' Millen-*

nial Star, esp. 6 (15 Oct. 1845): 140-42, as well as numerous revelations in D&C, esp. 34:7, 35:27; 43:17-35; 49:7; 52:43; 112:24, 34.

12. Dan. 2:44-45.

13. HC 6:365: "It will not be by the sword or gun that this kingdom will roll on."

14. *Correspondence of Bishop George Miller with the Northern Islander from His First Acquaintance with Mormonism up to Near the Close of His Life. Written by Himself in the Year 1855* (n.p., n.d.), 20-23; HC 6:356.

15. HC 6:232.

16. *Correspondence of Bishop George Miller,* 20.

17. *Millennial Star* 24 (15 Feb. 1862): 103.

18. HC 6:222; James Emmett was instructed to establish a settlement at the Missouri River. Dale Morgan, ed., "The Reminiscences of James Holt: A Narrative of the Emmett Company," *Utah Historical Quarterly* 23 (Jan. 1955): 7.

19. HC 6:275-77, 372.

20. Ibid., 7:478-79.

21. Frederick Logan Paxson, *History of the American Frontier,* 1763-1893 (New York: Houghton Mifflin Co., 1924), 349.

22. Clark, "The Kingdom of God," 133. The quotation is from Leland H. Creer, *The Founding of an Empire: The Exploration and Colonization of Utah* (Salt Lake City: Bookcraft, 1947), 313.

23. Leland H. Creer, *Utah and the Nation* (Seattle: University of Washington Press, 1929), vii, and *The Founding of Empire,* 312; Andrew L. Neff, *History of Utah, 1847-1869* (Salt Lake City: Deseret News Press, 1940), 108.

24. Brigham Young was always emphatic that he was merely carrying out the plans of Joseph Smith in this respect. See JD 17:156; Journal History, 19 Jan. 1863, archives, historical department, Church of Jesus Christ of Latter-day Saints, Salt Lake City, Utah.

25. Frank J. Cannon and George L. Knapp, *Brigham Young and His Mormon Empire* (New York: Fleming H. Revell Co., 1913), 117.

26. Poll, "The Mormon Question," 117.

27. Benjamin G. Ferris, *Utah and the Mormons* (New York: Harper and Bros., 1856), 167.

28. JD 2:310.

29. Poll, "The Mormon Question," 131.

30. Journal History, 2 Aug. 1857.

31. 1 Sept. 1858, in Eberstadt, *Western America,* 111.

32. Ibid., 106.

33. D&C 87.

34. Diary of Charles Walker, 28 Apr. 1861, Utah State Historical

Society, Salt Lake City.

35. Journal History, 19 Jan. 1863. The best account of the Mormons in the Civil War is Gustive O. Larson, "Utah and the Civil War," *Utah Historical Quarterly* 33 (Winter 1965): 55-77.

36. Robert E. Park and Ernest W. Burgess, *Introduction to the Science of Sociology* (Chicago, 1921), 872-73, as quoted in Thomas F. O'Dea, "Mormonism and the Avoidance of Sectarian Stagnation: A Study of Church, Sect, and Incipient Nationality," *American Journal of Sociology* 60 (Nov. 1954): 293. O'Dea's article is one of the most stimulating on this complex problem.

37. Whitney R. Cross, *The Burned-over District: The Social and Intellectual History of Enthusiastic Religion in Western New York, 1800-1850* (Ithaca: Cornell University Press, 1950), 138-50.

38. See, for example, Therald N. Jensen, "Mormon Theory of Church and State," Ph.D. diss., University of Chicago, 1938, 82-95.

39. For representative selections of the political thought of Mormon leaders on this question, see Heber C. Kimball, JD, 6:129; *Millennial Star* 5 (Mar. 1845): 150; Parley P. Pratt, *Key to the Science of Theology* (Liverpool: F. D. Richards, 1855), 70; HC 5:61; John Taylor, JD 7:326.

40. Journal History, 12 July 1865.

41. Juanita Brooks, ed., *On the Mormon Frontier, The Diary of Hosea Stout,* 2 vols. (Salt Lake City: University of Utah Press, 1964), 2:559 Parker was initiated into the Council of Fifty on 19 March 1844; see HC 6:267.

42. *Official Declaration* (Salt Lake City, 12 Dec. 1889).

43. Diary of L. John Nuttall, 19 Apr. 1893, Special Collections, Harold B. Lee Library. Frank Cannon, moreover, insisted that he had heard Woodruff remark "that it was the right of the priesthood of God to rule in all things on earth, and that they had in no wise relinquished any of their authority." Frank J. Cannon and Harvey J. O'Higgins, *Under the Prophet in Utah* (Boston: C. M. Clark, 1911), 153.

44. John Mills Whitaker Journal, 16 Oct. 1887, Marriott Library, University of Utah.

45. John Hyde, *Mormonism: Its Leaders and Designs* (New York: W. P. Fetridge, 1857), 307-308.

46. Autobiography of Frederick T. Dubois, MS, 29, Idaho Historical Society, as quoted in Grenville H. Gibbs, "Mormonism in Idaho Politics, 1880-1890," *Utah Historical Quarterly* 21 (1953), 291.

47. U.S. Congress, Senate, *Proceedings Before the Committee on Privileges and Elections of the United States Senate in the matter of the Protests Against the Right Hon. Reed Smoot, a Senator from the State of Utah, to Hold His Seat,* 4 vols. (Washington, 1904-1907), 1:126; see also Cannon and O'Higgins, 34-36, 115. Homer Durham's observation that "any purposeful internal direction of the political power inhering in the church may be said to have ceased with

the dissolution of the People's Party, June 10, 1890," thus bears revision; "A Political Interpretation of Mormon History," 148. Frank Jonas, who shared with a whole generation of Mormon historians the belief that the political struggle ended in 1890, has recently revised his former opinion, pointing out that "actually the transition from the turbulence of the territorial period to the relative quiet of later years was not easy"; "Utah: Crossroads of the West," in *Western Politics* (Salt Lake City: University of Utah Press, 1961), 274.

48. HC 2:182; *Millennial Star* 52 (Oct. 1890): 675-76.

49. Benjamin F. Johnson to George S. Gibbs, Apr.-Oct. 1903, MS, 18, Harold B. Lee Library.

50. D&C 101:76-80; HC 3:304.

51. Quoted in Dale Morgan, *The Great Salt Lake* (Indianapolis: Bobbs-Merrill Co., 1947), 223.

52. Journal History, 8 Sept. 1851, 4. For a brief discussion of this problem, see Franklin D. Daines, "Separatism in Utah, 1847-1870," *Annual Report of the American Historical Association for the Year 1917* (Washington, 1920).

53. Quoted in M. W. Montgomery, *The Mormon Delusion* (Minneapolis, 1890), 310.

54. O'Dea, *The Mormons*, 171.

55. John D. Lee, "Journal of the Iron County Mission," ed. Gustive O. Larson, *Utah Historical Quarterly* 20 (July 1952): 260.

56. Persecution thus served as an effective propaganda foil enabling Mormon leaders to keep the Saints unified. See O'Dea, "Mormonism and the Avoidance of Sectarian Stagnation."

57. *Tullidge's Histories* (Salt Lake City: Juvenile Instructor, 1889), 154.

58. Edward W. Tullidge, "The Godbeite Movement," *Tullidge's Quarterly Magazine* 1 (Oct. 1880): 32.

59. *Smoot Proceedings*, 1:97-98; an excellent introduction to Smoot in a broader context is Milton R. Merrill, *Reed Smoot: Utah Politician* (Logan, UT: Utah State University Press 1953).

60. Orson Pratt, *The Kingdom of God* (Liverpool: R. James, 1851), 1.

61 *Deseret News*, 23 Aug. 1854.

62. Especially revealing is a note by Brigham H. Roberts in the James E. Talmage Papers, Harold B. Lee Library, which is a request for information that would minimize the temporal and political aspects of the kingdom of God: "The above references are wanted to aid Brother Talmage in forming testimony to be given before the Senate Investigating Committee." See also *Smoot Proceedings*, 3:25.

63. For Talmage's testimony, see *Smoot Proceedings* 3:35-38.

64. 19 Dec. 1903.

65. Cannon and O'Higgins, *Under the Prophet in Utah*, 66.

66. (New York, 1904).

67. Some representative Mormon works in this tradition are Creer, *Utah and the Nation* and *The Founding of an Empire*; Milton R. Hunter, *Utah in Her Western Setting* (Salt Lake City: Deseret News Press, 1943); Neff, *History of Utah*; and Levi Edgar Young, *The Founding of Utah* (New York: C. Scribner's Sons, 1923). Of considerable interest is a letter of Neff to George H. Brimhall, president of Brigham Young University, 1 Apr. 1906, Brimhall Papers, Harold B. Lee Library: "To my mind the greatest fact in American history is the spread of settlement from the Atlantic seaboard to the Pacific ocean. And I hope to ascertain the relative part of the Mormons in blazing the trail and opening up the continent to settlement." Others following this same interpretation are Ray Allen Billington, *Westward Expansion, A History of the American Frontier* (New York: MacMillan, 1949), 532 ff.; Dean D. McBrien, "The Influence of the Frontier on Joseph Smith," Ph.D. diss., George Washington University, 1929; and Thomas Weldon, "The Turner Thesis and the Mormon Frontier," M.A. thesis, Stetson University, 1964. Two carefully reasoned studies refuting the concept of Mormonism as a frontier religion are Whitney R. Cross, *The Burned-over District*, 138-50; and S. George Ellsworth, "A History of Mormon Missions in the United States and Canada, 1830-1860," Ph.D. diss., University of California, 1950, 327-42.

68. Several colleagues suggest that I overemphasize the role and importance of the Council of Fifty, since it is difficult to decide in a particular instance whether Brigham Young and other Mormon leaders acted in their ecclesiastical capacities or as members of the council. And even if the two functions can be separated, such knowledge may not always prove very enlightening. Frank Jonas, for example, reports in "Utah: Crossroads of the West," 273, that "Former United States Senator Elbert D. Thomas (Utah 1933-51) used to relate that Brigham Young, with the traditional American concept of separation of church and state strongly in mind, sat on one side of his desk in the morning, when he did state business, and then moved his chair to the other side, when he did church work in the afternoon." And yet in the light of this very theory of separation of church and state, there can be no question that Mormon leaders, when performing political functions, acted in their authority as members of the Council of Fifty.

69. 2 Dec. 1960.

14.
"To Maintain Harmony": Adjusting to External and Internal Stress, 1890-1930

Thomas G. Alexander

IN HIS LANDMARK ORGANIZATIONAL STUDY, GERMAN SOCIOLOGIST Max Weber outlined three forms of authority: traditional, charismatic, and legal. Originally charismatic under Joseph Smith and to some extent under Brigham Young, by the late nineteenth century leadership in the Church of Jesus Christ of Latter-day Saints (LDS) had become traditional. Leaders no longer functioned outside acknowledged lines of authority but operated with clearly established relationships to one another and to Mormon church membership. The presidency of the church automatically passed to the president of the Council of the Twelve. Being called to the First Presidency or to the Twelve immediately vested church leaders with authority both in the priesthood sense and in the sense of personal prestige, more the original meaning of the Latin *auctoritas*.[1]

Just as the leadership of the church was not charismatic by the late nineteenth and early twentieth centuries, neither was it legal. It was not governed by the "rule of law and not of men." Church leaders had not yet separated church money and equipment from their private property. In fact as late as Lorenzo Snow's death in October 1901, the question arose whether his property and church property were one and the same, and the separation was not completely solidified until 1922 and 1923 during Heber J. Grant's administration. Furthermore well into the twentieth century and to a lesser extent today, most general authorities did not depend completely on their positions for a living. Since a bureaucracy requires a money economy, a true bureaucracy within the church could not be organized before 1908 when the church sifted to a money system by abolishing payments in scrip and kind.[2]

Administratively the system of government dominant in the church today was largely set in the late nineteenth and early twentieth century, when leadership was traditional and its structure was shifting from charismatic to more bureaucratic forms of leadership. Under Joseph Smith, administration centered in the prophet, who generally made final decisions and exercised personal authority. Although the current prophet still has the power of making final decisions on all questions, a church bureaucracy operating under fixed rules handles most administrative matters. The Church Office Building housing the bureaucracy at 50 East North Temple rather than the Church Administration Building housing most general authorities at 47 East South Temple operates the church's day-to-day affairs. Bureaucrats know the files and rules and provide continuity of administration. In the administrations of Joseph F. Smith (1901-18) and Heber J. Grant (1918-45), reading committees drawn from the First Presidency and Twelve approved texts for church use, and the First Presidency considered and appropriated the exact sum of the church's share for the construction of a new chapel. Today the bureaucracy handles both matters, though ultimate approval still rests with the First Presidency and Twelve as it would with administrative officers in any bureaucratic system.[3]

If the church organization in the late nineteenth century was post-charismatic and pre-bureaucratic, it was also unlike classical pre-bureaucratic forms of organization which typically are avocational and directed by persons of independent means. An example would be a medieval fiefdom ruled by a vassal of a king. The situation of the general authorities was much different. In virtually every case, a large part of their outside incomes was linked to church-controlled businesses like ZCMI, Consolidated Wagon and Machine, or Hotel Utah, or they were beholden to the church for outstanding loans. In some cases, as with James E. Talmage and John A. Widtsoe, church stipends provided their entire or principal income.[4] Thus financially the church's hierarchy had some characteristics of a bureaucracy though church funds were not the only source of income for its organizational leaders.

Yet the form of organization was collegial, essentially a pre-bureaucratic form. Many commentators on church government have missed this point. Frank Cannon's *Under the Prophet in Utah* pictures the church as an autocracy run by Joseph F. Smith; Samuel W. Taylor's recent study offers a similar emphasis.[5]

Doctrinally and historically the church leadership thus exhibited both hierarchical and collegial elements. Both are built into the scriptural injunctions about church government. Doctrine and Covenants 107 declares that "the Presidency of the High Priesthood . . . has a right to officiate in all offices in the church" (v. 9), indicating a hierarchical superiority to other quorums in the church. At the same time the Twelve, "special witnesses of the name of Christ," are said to "form a quorum, equal in authority and power to the three presidents previously mentioned" (vs. 23-24)—a collegial element. In addition, the seventy "form a quorum equal in authority to that of the Twelve special witnesses or Apostles" (vs. 25-26).

In light of these dual characteristics, crises—often those associated with succession in the First Presidency—made the conflict between hierarchy and collegiality more conspicuous than did operational problems. There are, of course, exceptions to this generalization.[6] In most cases, however, Timothy Ware's generalization made about conciliarism in the Greek Orthodox Church holds for the LDS church as well: "In the Church, there is neither dictatorship nor individualism, but harmony and unanimity; men remain free but not isolated, for they are united in love, in faith, and in sacramental communion. In a council this idea of harmony and free unanimity can be seen worked out in practice. In a true council no single member arbitrarily imposes his will upon the rest, but each consults with the others, and in this way all freely achieve a 'common end.'"[7]

When schismatic tendencies and disharmony have developed in the LDS church, in a number of cases the Twelve resolved them by collegial action. An instructive parallel is the operation of the cardinals during medieval schisms in the Roman Catholic Church.[8] Like the succession dispute between Urban VI and Clement VII, the crisis at the death of Joseph Smith not only posed the question of succession but also of a unified church's continued existence.

At the death of Joseph Smith, the Twelve acted on behalf of

God and of the general church as a council to preserve the body of the Saints from dissolution and the church from destruction. In practice, of course, schism did develop, but in general the largest portion of the church membership recognized the collegial authority of the Twelve and followed them to the west.

Crises also developed as Mormonism made the transition from the nineteenth to the twentieth century. In these cases the sources of strain came in the attempt to define the political, social, economic, and doctrinal position of the church and its leadership as the church moved from a highly unitary, internally rigid body to a more pluralistic organization. Under those conditions, the standard of conduct of church members and the limits of conformity for members and leaders alike changed rapidly, straining the internal harmony of the general authorities and leading to the removal of some.

Although church leadership is partly hierarchical and partly collegial, the model for deliberations of the First Presidency and Council of the Twelve is collegial. As each general authority is inducted into the Council of the Twelve, he is so instructed. Perhaps the best example of this is found in the journal of James E. Talmage. Francis M. Lyman, then president of the Twelve, told Talmage after having him set apart that during the deliberations of the Twelve and First Presidency, he must feel free to present his views as vigorously as he chose. After the body made a decision, however, he must leave the meeting supporting the decisions, duty-bound not to discuss the deliberations or any disagreements which might have developed in the council. Because of a curious interpretation of that charge, Talmage's journal changed radically. Before his apostleship, he wrote fully and freely about the operation of the church. Afterward it was virtually silent on matters of church organization and policy. Yet apostles Anthon H. Lund, Reed Smoot, George F. Richards, and Heber J. Grant understood the charge differently.[9]

The collegial principle under which the First Presidency and Twelve operated was, as they called it, "harmony." In general it worked very well for day-to-day operations and in developing internal programs such as the priesthood reform movement, temple cere-mony revisions, and alterations of temple garment styles.[10]

Perhaps the best example of this ability to reach harmony on matters not involving larger issues is found in the codification of doctrine undertaken during the 1890s and culminating in the publication in 1899 of James E. Talmage's *A Study of the Articles of Faith*. In 1894 the First Presidency asked Talmage, then a lay member, to give a series of lectures on the doctrines of the church. Four years later he was asked to rewrite the lectures and present them to a committee for consideration as an exposition of church doctrine.[11]

In the process Talmage reconsidered and clarified some doctrines which had been poorly defined before. For example, during the 1894 lectures, George Q. Cannon, first counselor in the First Presidency, "expressed his opinion that the Holy Ghost was in reality, in the image of the other members of the God-head—a man in form and figure; and that what we often speak of as the Holy Ghost is in reality but the power or influence of the spirit." The First Presidency, however, "deemed it wise to say as little as possible on this as on other disputed subjects," perhaps since the nature of the Holy Ghost was somewhat equivocal in the writings of Joseph Smith.[12]

After the 1894 discussion Talmage published an article in the *Juvenile Instructor* incorporating Cannon's views and also reproduced the position in the *Articles of Faith* manuscript. He was somewhat surprised when the First Presidency approved that section practically without revision. The controversial opinion of 1894 had by 1899 become the published doctrine of the church.[13]

Harmony floundered, however, on the shoals of larger traditional interests—changes which seemed alterations in basic principles (plural marriage or organic evolution) or which involved larger political interests (dietary rules, member involvement in politics) or a combination (the League of Nations controversy).

It is, I believe, at these stress points which challenged collegiality and traditional authority that we best see the operation of harmony. This is partly true because "the Brethren" often did not comment on discussions when harmony easily prevailed. Essentially, the Council of the Twelve and First Presidency faced from the 1890s through the early 1930s the difficulties of any traditional society under the stress of acculturation, attempting the task of, in Peter Berger's phrase, "world maintenance" while trying to define a new twentieth-century Mormonism within an increasingly pluralistic society. Under these conditions it is not surprising that traditional leadership was strained by both measures which broke with previous tradition and those that continued it.[14]

Perhaps the most difficult problem church leadership faced was determining the role of the general authorities in national politics. In the nineteenth century, the church had been politically unitary rather than pluralistic. Local and general authorities decided political questions in the church's interest, as they perceived it. In territorial Utah the church-operated People's Party held virtually all political offices until conditions in 1889 and 1890 contributed to several anti-Mormon Liberal Party victories. In 1891 church leadership formally disbanded the People's Party and urged members to divide into the two major parties. Since the Republican Party had been most vigorous in its anti-Mormon activities, leaders feared that most members would become Democrats, essentially remaining unitary. Their solution was to have Republican general authorities actively solicit membership while Democratic general authorities remained relatively silent.[15]

Some Democratic general authorities, such as Moses Thatcher of the Twelve and B. H. Roberts of the First Council of the Seventy, objected. Thatcher, who had been in and out of difficulty for opposing his colleagues on expenditures for economic development, for supporting a strong millennialist position, and for differences with fellow apostle Marriner W. Merrill, declined to obey and was threatened with exclusion from the dedication of the Salt Lake Temple in 1893 until he recanted.[16]

In late 1893 the anti-Mormon Liberal Party similarly disbanded, and its members joined the two major parties. Most became Republicans, tipping the scale enough to elect Frank J. Cannon, son of George Q. Cannon of the First Presidency, as territorial delegate and a GOP majority to the Utah constitutional convention of 1895. In 1895 Utahns elected a Republican majority to the legislature and state offices.[17]

Thatcher and Roberts together with Presiding Bishop William B. Preston and Apostle John Henry Smith served in the state constitutional convention, and Thatcher and Roberts intended to run as Democratic candidates for the U.S. senate and congress in 1895. Thatcher and Roberts thought that since church members were now politically divided and the church had given up its political dictation, the American tradition of liberty required no prior restraint and hence no permission to run for office.[18]

On the eve of the election in the priesthood meeting of the

October 1895 general conference, Joseph F. Smith, second counselor in the First Presidency, attacked Roberts and Thatcher, charging they were out of harmony since they had not sought permission to run. Smith seems to have had three motives. He was concerned about balance between the two political parties; he was an extremely partisan Republican of long standing; and he was concerned about the need of the general authorities to act in harmony. He insisted that all church officials secure permission from their quorum to run for office to determine whether they would be spared from their ecclesiastical duties.[19]

Discussed by the First Presidency and Twelve, largely in Thatcher's absence since he was ill during much of the next six months, Smith's views were codified in the so-called Political Manifesto and approved by both bodies shortly before the April 1896 general conference. Thatcher refused to sign. Late in the year, after various efforts by his colleagues had failed, he was dropped from the quorum and ordered not to exercise his priesthood. He forestalled excommunication the next year only by recanting.[20]

The Thatcher case posed the classic conflict of traditional leadership—personal liberty and collegial authority. The goals of the First Presidency and Twelve included balancing church membership between the two parties and safeguarding the internal harmony necessary to lead the church. In this case the council faced a combination of external and internal stress. The external stress came both from demands that the church cease political dictation and from Republican Party officials. If the church had indeed given up political dictation, however, could the quorum in good conscience demand control over its members' political activities?

The council resolved the issue by insisting that the church had no desire to control politics but that it had a right to control the actions of quorum members. In the interest of harmony, each member had to receive approval to participate in outside political activities that might compete with his ecclesiastical duties. Thatcher, believing that this solution infringed upon his personal liberty refused to subordinate his own interests to the council's need for harmony and was expelled.

The incident reveals another feature of the council's operation—a relatively greater emphasis on hierarchy than on collegium. Though permission to run for political office had been necessary before 1891, it was apparently not necessary again until Joseph F. Smith opened his attack on Roberts and Thatcher in October 1895. Smith was fourth in line for the presidency and a counselor in the First Presidency. As such, his public statements carried considerable weight. Even today a preemptive public statement or leak of a public position by a senior general authority may dictate the public position of the council on a particular question.[21]

An even more complex case is that of dietary code found in the Word of Wisdom. The current interpretation of abstention from alcohol, tea, coffee, and tobacco had been enunciated by Joseph Smith, Hyrum Smith, and Brigham Young but was not codified until 1898-1905. As the general authorities reached consensus, the First Presidency sent circular letters to stake presidents and bishops outlining the policy, and members of the council began catechizing local officials about adherence to the rules.[22]

After 1905 council disagreement left the meaning of the Word of Wisdom to focus on public policy. Some apostles such as Heber J. Grant, then a senior member of the Twelve, believed that adherence to the Word of Wisdom required members to promote Prohibition. Grant, an active Democrat, could insist on that position since the Democratic Party was largely Mormon. Republicans Reed Smoot and Joseph F. Smith saw the situation more from the perspective of Republican gentile businessmen, many of whom opposed Prohibition. The situation was further complicated by evangelical Protestants who initiated the Prohibition movement in Utah and chided church leaders for moral sloth.[23]

Even for Mormon Republicans the situation was not simple. President Smith and Elder Smoot feared dividing the Republican Party and strengthening the anti-Mormon American Party, which controlled Salt Lake City government from 1905 through 1911. After 1911 they were apprehensive about the possibility of reviving an anti-Mormon coalition against ecclesiastical influence in the Prohibition question. On the other hand, a number of prominent Mormon Republicans, led at first by a reluctant Nephi L. Morris, president of the Salt Lake Stake, favored Prohibition and fought Smoot and his political machine on this and other issues. This breach widened into a full rupture after the Republican Party refused to support statewide Prohibition in 1912 and a group of so-called "Prohibition Republicans" reconstituted themselves as the Progressive Party, supporting

Theodore Roosevelt for the U.S. presidency and Morris for Utah governor.[24]

Breaches of harmony were virtually unavoidable under these circumstances. Joseph F. Smith and Reed Smoot preached abstinence and at times even Prohibition from the pulpit. In private they counseled political moderation, though at times favored local option. This visible contradiction between official and unofficial signals confused the general church membership. The penultimate conflict took place in 1915 when William Spry, Utah governor, in part with President Smith's support, pocket-vetoed a bipartisan Prohibition bill, divided the Republican Party, and thus committed political suicide. Republican Nephi L. Morris lost a bid for governor in 1916, while the Democratic Party behind German-Jewish businessman Simon Bamberger carried the governorship and the legislature.[25]

Heber J. Grant's pro-Prohibition stand also challenged harmony. A member of the national board of the Anti-Saloon League, Grant championed Prohibition from the pulpit and platform. Joseph F. Smith resignedly said that he had "frequently tried to modify his zeal," but Grant did "as he wishes." The legislature had passed a 1909 local option bill which Spry had, to a furor among Prohibition supporters, pocket-vetoed. Grant, who believed the liquor interests had bought the governor and Smoot's political machine with Republican support, planned a strong Prohibition speech for the April 1909 conference. Francis M. Lyman, president of the Council of the Twelve, however, apparently sensing a breach of harmony, asked his colleague to speak on the "peaceable things of the Kingdom." Annoyed, Grant nevertheless decided obedience was better than sacrifice and followed Lyman's counsel.[26]

In this case the strain on harmony was external. Harmony was achieved first on local option as a compromise and later on statewide prohibition. Breaches in that harmony came because of extracollegial stress caused when members worked publicly for positions generally opposed by the council's consensus. Late in 1915 when the overwhelming majority in Utah clearly favored statewide Prohibition, Smoot and Smith came out publicly and privately in favor of Prohibition, thus reuniting the council and reestablishing harmony. By the time, however, irreparable damage had been inflicted on the political machine Smoot had so carefully organized and President Smith had so fully supported. In this case stress had little

inside effect but resulted in tremendous external repercussions as
members of the church, looking for signals to reinforce the harmony
they expected, were understandably confused by the conflicting
rumors.

A third breach of harmony was created by the problem of
new plural marriages. Between the Manifesto of October 1890 ostensibly ending new plural marriages and the Second Manifesto of April
1904 when Joseph F. Smith strongly interdicted the practice, members of the Twelve and First Presidency sanctioned and performed
various marriages both in the United States and abroad.[27]

When the election of Reed Smoot as senator from Utah and
the resultant investigations brought some of these marriages to light,
general authorities reexamined their policy of approving new plural
marriages. Obviously it was a costly one. Church leaders had agreed
to end plural marriage in exchange for statehood; now their good
faith was suspect. The extent to which members of the First Presidency and Twelve participated in these decisions is not yet determined, nevertheless, the revelation of new marriages caused serious
external and internal stress.

The First Presidency and Twelve did not arrive at a consensus
on a course of action until after 1904, and their new policy was as
difficult to implement as it had been to reach. Plural marriage had
been so thoroughly ingrained in the Latter-day Saint community that
neither a public pronouncement nor a hierarchical decision could
easily eliminate it. Apostle Marriner W. Merrill, for instance, insisted
in one discussion that no year would go by without some children
being born to plural marriages and that the Manifesto of 1890 was
not a revelation from God.[28]

Some of the most politically minded, including Reed Smoot,
Francis M. Lyman, and Joseph F. Smith, feared adverse public opin-
ion and pressed vigorously to stop the new marriages. In 1906 the
Twelve dropped Matthias F. Cowley and John W. Taylor from their
ranks for openly advocating continued plural marriage and Marriner
W. Merrill, another advocate, died. George F. Richards, Orson F.
Whitney, and David O. McKay, none of whom was a polygamist or
attached to the principle of plural marriage, replaced them.[29]

Even then not until 1911 could the First Presidency and
Twelve reach a consensus sufficient to try Taylor and Cowley for their
membership in spite of the two apostles' continued efforts to influ-

ence others to enter new plural marriages. It was privately whispered that Smoot and Lyman were out of harmony for pressing so hard to end new plural marriages while public pronouncements stressed that church leadership had resolved the question and that offenders would be tried. As in the case of Prohibition, contradictory public and private signals left many members unable to perceive a consensus within the highest quorums of the church.

The hardening resolution, however, became apparent in 1909, two years before the Cowley and Taylor trials, when a special committee of apostles was formed under Francis M. Lyman to prosecute new polygamists despite resistance to the prosecutions both from the membership and from local leaders.[30]

In an apparent attempt to reeducate the general membership and public, the leaders reinterpreted "celestial marriage" and "new and everlasting covenant"—previously understood to mean plural marriage. In various places, including testimony before the senate committee investigating Reed Smoot, James E. Talmage emphasized that the terms actually referred to sealing for time and eternity in the temple. Results of the trials were publicized through church periodicals. Gradually members became convinced of the new consensus, and those who refused to change were disciplined or forced underground.[31]

In this case the sources of strain on harmony were extremely complex. Like the cases of political involvement and the Word of Wisdom, continued plural marriages created outside political pressure, but of a different sort, since there was no incentive outside the church to maintain the plural marriage system. Internally, however, the stress was enormous since a high percentage of general and local church leaders either were or had been polygamists. In addition, opposition from within the Twelve stemmed from members like Abraham O. Woodruff, George Teasdale, Marriner W. Merrill, and Matthias F. Cowley, normally the most loyal of members. It was only as they died or were expelled that a new consensus formed. By the time the Lyman committee was appointed in 1909, only seven of the fifteen members of the First Presidency and Twelve had been in the leadership when Reed Smoot was elected to the senate in 1903.

Conflicting interests also appeared in the League of Nations controversy following World War I. Here a majority of the Twelve and all of the First Presidency publicly supported the league and

adopted a resolution that council members would not oppose the
league. Because of his opposition to the league covenant as drafted,
Reed Smoot ran into considerable difficulty, though his support of
Henry Cabot Lodge's reservations rather than William Borah and the
irreconcilables left him a loophole.[32]

However, Smoot opposed the league and attacked those who
supported it by working through James Casey, editor of the *Herald-
Republican,* a Mormon church-sponsored Republican Party newspaper. Its attacks on B. H. Roberts, Richard W. Young, president of the
Ensign Stake and close friend of President Heber J. Grant, and
Anthony W. Ivins, a member of the Twelve and Grant's cousin,
angered members of the Twelve and led eventually to the
newspaper's sale.[33]

As in the case of new plural marriages, leaks from the council
meetings left the public impression that the council had changed its
position to support Smoot. This led in turn to a confrontation
between Smoot and several other council members. He promised to
make the matter clear in a public speech but feared losing the 1920
senatorial election, a fear which Heber J. Grant, a Democrat, shared.
Recognizing the important role a member of the Twelve could play
in Congress, Grant allowed Smoot to turn his denial into an equivocal
statement. The dispute was never resolved but died with potential
United States membership in the League in 1921. Its principal results
were contributing to the demise of the *Herald-Republican,* strengthening the position of Democratic apostles such as Anthony W. Ivins,[34]
and polarizing millennarian sentiment within the church. Some
members believed as Smoot that neither the League nor any other
earthly power could prevent war and pestilence on earth until Jesus
Christ's second advent. Others such as George F. Richards saw the
League as an agency for promoting world peace which would allow
the gospel to spread in preparation for the Second Coming.[35]

A fourth major breach in harmony came from the conflict
between a literal interpretation of the Bible on the one hand and the
theory of evolution through natural selection and higher criticism of
biblical texts on the other.

Since the late nineteenth century, speeches and articles in
the *Improvement Era* and other church magazines generally allowed
rather wide latitude, all the way from Joseph Fielding Smith's biblical
literalism to John A. Widtsoe's belief that evolution may take place

within "orders." On the authenticity of the Bible, the *Improvement Era* had published the views of University of Utah professor Frederick J. Pack and others indicating that the earth was millions of years old and that events like Noah's flood could not possibly have taken place literally since there was not enough water, time, or heat to accomplish the indicated flooding and evaporation. In 1921 Anthony W. Ivins and Charles W. Penrose of the First Presidency observed that some biblical stories like Jonah and Job might not be literally true.[36]

The crisis, however, centered on the question of humankind's age on the earth. Joseph Fielding Smith rejected any scientific evidence which did not agree with his "Adam was the first man" interpretation of the scriptures. B. H. Roberts's unpublished manuscript "The Truth, The Way, The Life," dealt with biblical literalism and organic evolution by including pre-Adamic humans. After a long discussion the Twelve refused to approve either Roberts's or Smith's views. Smith disobeyed, however, preaching and publishing on the topic. This publication and the ensuing controversy which surrounded it disturbed President Grant, not because he agreed with one position but because he feared disharmony. James E. Talmage attempted to smooth over the disharmony in a speech denying organic evolution while allowing a scientific view of the earth's age.[37]

The Political Manifesto, the Word of Wisdom, new plural marriages, and the League of Nations had each been tied to a political or social concern. In the case of evolution and the Bible, the problem was doctrinal: what was the nature of creation, the development of beings, the nature of biblical texts, and the relationship of humanity to God? Though evolution and related questions required a reexamination of basic doctrinal positions, they were perhaps least disruptive, partly because they did not involve practical concerns and partly because the church had a long tradition of discussion on the nature of humankind and creation. Brigham Young, for instance, had speculated that Adam had been brought to the earth rather than having been created or born here.

From these five issues during a period of rapid change and adjustment, the historian can make some generalizations about stress within the Mormon ecclesiastical polity. In each case the First Presidency and Twelve related basic problems to the need for maintaining harmony in the face of disruptive internal and external influences.

In virtually ever case, if they could not achieve actual consensus, they thought it important to maintain the appearance of harmony in order to maintain morale and promote brotherhood. The common contemporary tactic of lay members opposing one another by citing a favorite general authority or scripture to support their position can be extremely disruptive. Such controversy is even more divisive in a collegial situation.

Thus disruptions of collegial harmony could in extreme cases lead to discipline and severance from the quorum, as with Moses Thatcher and Matthias F. Cowley, or excommunication, as with John W. Taylor. In other instances official displeasure rested upon Reed Smoot, Joseph Fielding Smith, and B. H. Roberts. Issues of basic doctrines, as with new plural marriages, or of doctrine combined with public policy, as with the Word of Wisdom, caused the most difficulty over the longest period of time.

Since church leadership had already shifted from charismatic to traditional authority, the stress resulting from these challenges reveals much about how a traditional organization maintains consensus while simultaneously legitimizing change. In some cases leaked reports of quorum debates allowed church members the comfort of recognizing that they were not alone—either in clinging to tradition or in favoring change. Dissension could be allowed over conflicting goals, as in the apparent either-or choice between supporting the League of Nations and reelecting Reed Smoot, or in the conflict between supporting Prohibition and keeping the Republican Party unified. On some issues dissent could not be tolerated. Moses Thatcher, Matthias F. Cowley, and John W. Taylor were unwilling to maintain harmony at the cost of personal convictions and found ultimately that their collegium could not allow this deviance.

The main tasks of charismatic leadership are rallying converts and true believers; traditional leadership must concern itself with both internal harmony and outside pressures. Between 1890 and 1930 the church accepted for the first time the necessity of finding a way for God's kingdom to coexist with Caesar's. At least four of the five issues discussed were directly related to external pressures imposed by the need for accommodation. The Political Manifesto required division into political parties because of outside pressure. Prohibition was in part the result of pressure from evangelical Protestant denominations who thought that professed Mormon beliefs in abstinence should require Mormon opposition to all alcoholic use in the community. Various groups with Victorian moral standards feared and hated plural marriage. The League of Nations controversy pressured the church leadership to take an interest in national politics. Only in the evolution controversy was there little compelling outside pressure, and perhaps for that reason it was the easiest to resolve or ignore.

In retrospect the church leadership's efforts to maintain legitimacy during a rapid transition from being a religious monopoly to being a competing religious movement strained its internal structure. As long as the Latter-day Saints monopolized secular and religious interests in Utah territory, they could "utilize the entire society" as their "plausibility structure" in world maintenance. After the monopoly was broken, they used "social engineering" to maintain the structure, and an important feature of that engineering was the principle of "harmony."[38]

The disruption of collegial harmony is probably not out of proportion to the stress. If the removal of three members from the quorum is used as a measure of stress, the only period which exceeds this one came in the wake of the Missouri persecutions when seven were dropped, though two of them returned to the quorum. Even after the murder of Joseph Smith, the succession crisis, and the exodus from Illinois, only three were dropped from the Twelve, indicating that perhaps the stress associated with the problems in Illinois were not greater than those associated with accommodating the norms of Victorian America.

NOTES

1. Max Weber, *From Max Weber: Essays in Sociology,* trans. and eds. H. H. Gerth and C. Wright Mills (New York: Oxford University Press, 1946), 196-252; Peter M. Blau, *On the Nature of Organizations* (New York: Wiley, 1974), 42-43; on the history of the LDS church, see James B. Allen and Glen M. Leonard, *The Story of the Latter-day Saints* (Salt Lake City: Deseret Book Co., 1976); and Leonard J. Arrington and Davis Bitton, *The Mormon Experience* (New York: Alfred A. Knopf, 1978).

2. Weber, *From Max Weber,* 197; Anthon H. Lund Journal, 5, 6, 21, and 24 Nov. 1901 and 6 Mar. 1902, archives, historical department, Church of Jesus Christ of Latter-day Saints, Salt Lake City, hereafter LDS archives; Marriner W. Merrill Journal, 27 Feb. 1902, LDS archives; Journal History, 26

Nov. 1923, LDS archives; Leonard J. Arrington, *Great Basin Kingdom: An Economic History of the Latter-day Saints, 1830-1900* (Cambridge, MA: Harvard University Press, 1958), 409. All documents from LDS archives are used by permission.

3. Weber, *From Max Weber,* 214. Fifty East North Temple, the Church Office Building, houses mostly middle- and lower-echelon officers, while the Church Administration Building at 47 East South Temple is the office building in which the First Presidency and Twelve are located.

4. Weber, *From Max Weber,* 107, 214. On business interests, salaries, and other connections among the church's hierarchy, see D. Michael Quinn, "The Mormon Hierarchy, 1832-1932: An American Elite," Ph.D. diss., Yale University, 1976, 127-30; John A. Widtsoe, *In A Sunlit Land: The Autobiography of John A. Widtsoe* (Salt Lake City: Deseret News Press, 1952), 161; George F. Richards Journal, 30 Jan. 1925, LDS archives; Heber J. Grant Diary, 12 June 1928, LDS archives.

5. Frank J. Cannon and Harvey J. O'Higgins, *Under the Prophet in Utah: The National Menace of a Political Priestcraft* (Boston: C. M. Clark Publishing Co., 1911); Samuel W. Taylor, *Rocky Mountain Empire: The Latter-day Saints Today* (New York: MacMillan, 1978); Jan Shipps, "Writing about Modern Mormonism," *Sunstone* 4 (Mar.-Apr. 1979): 43-48; James E. Talmage Journal, 10 Nov. 1901, Special Collections, Harold B. Lee Library, Brigham Young University, Provo, UT. On 23 November 1918 as the Council of the Twelve considered the reorganization of the First Presidency upon the death of Joseph F. Smith, Anthon H. Lund wrote in his diary: "As a people we have learned the meaning of Section 107 in Doctrine and Covenants which tells us that the Twelve form a quorum equal in authority with the First Presidency, and they have also learned that Seniority in quorums means authority. (This may be called an unwritten law of the Church, but we have seen how it tends to harmony.)"

6. See D. Michael Quinn, "Joseph Smith III's 1844 Blessing and the Mormons of Utah," *Journal of the John Whitmer Historical Association* 1 (1981): 12-27, and *Dialogue: A Journal of Mormon Thought* 15 (Summer 1982); Gary James Bergera, "The Orson Pratt-Brigham Young Controversies; Conflict Within the Quorums, 1853-1868," *Dialogue: A Journal of Mormon Thought* 13 (Summer 1980): 7-49; and Reed C. Durham, Jr., and Steve H. Heath, *Succession in the Church* (Salt Lake City: Bookcraft, 1970).

7. Timothy Ware, *The Orthodox Church* (Baltimore, MD: Penguin Books, 1963), 23.

8. See Brian Tierney, *Foundations of the Conciliar Theory: The Contribution of the Medieval Canonists from Gratian to the Great Schism* (Cambridge: Cambridge University Press, 1955), 2-23.

9. James E. Talmage Journal, 8 Dec. 1911. For similar comments,

see Grant Diary, 5 Apr. 1900; John Henry Smith Journal, 4 Oct. 1903, Western Americana, University of Utah; and George Albert Smith Journal, 6 Oct. 1903, University of Utah.

10. William G. Hartley, "The Priesthood Reform Movement, 1903-1922," *Brigham Young University Studies* 13 (Winter 1973): 137-56; George F. Richards, Journal, 15 Nov., 10, 27, 28 Dec. 1921, 3 June, 7, 13 July, 31 Aug. 1922, 9 Dec. 1926, and 25 Jan. 1927.

11. U. S. Senate, *Committee on Privileges and Elections of the United States Senate in the Matter of the Protests Against the Right of Hon. Reed Smoot, a Senator from the State of Utah to Hold His Seat,* 4 vols. (Washington, D.C., 1904-1906), 3:4 (hereafter cited as *Proceedings*); Lund Journal, 5 Jan. 1899; Talmage Journal, 27 Dec. 1898; see also Thomas G. Alexander, "The Reconstruction of Mormon Doctrine: From Joseph Smith to Progressive Theology," *Sunstone* 5 (July-Aug. 1980): 28.

12. Talmage Journal, 5 Jan. 1899; D&C (1883 ed.), 54-55.

13. Talmage Journal, 9, 16 Jan. 1899; Lund Journal, 13 Jan. 1899.

14. In a sense the LDS church was confronting a challenge to legitimacy not unlike the model with which Peter L. Berger deals in *The Sacred Canopy: Elements of a Sociological Theory of Religion* (Garden City, NY: Doubleday, 1967). This was a period in which the LDS leadership faced an almost classical problem of "world maintenance." As Berger pointed out, "when a challenge appears . . . [the old verities] can no longer be taken for granted. The validity of the social order must then be explicated both for the sake of the challengers and of those meeting the challenge. The children must be convinced, but so must their teachers" (31); see also Robert H. Wiebe, *The Search for Order, 1877-1920* (New York: Hill and Wang, 1967), 44-75.

15. Gustive O. Larson, *The Americanization of Utah for Statehood* (San Marino, CA: Huntington Library, 1971), 284-90; Kenneth W. Godfrey, "Was There More to the Moses Thatcher Case than Politics?" paper presented to a joint Mormon History Association/Utah Endowment for the Humanities session, 1, 3 Nov. 1979, 21-22. For a thorough treatment, see Edward Leo Lyman, "The Mormon Quest for Utah Statehood," Ph.D. diss., University of California, Riverside, 1981.

16. Godfrey, "Moses Thatcher," 8, 9, 11, 12, 16, 17, 19, 20, 26, 29, 31.

17. Ibid, 25-26. Larson, *Americanization of Utah,* 296-97.

18. B. H. Roberts, *A Comprehensive History of the Church of Jesus Christ of Latter-day Saints,* 6 vols. (Salt Lake City: Deseret News Press, 1930), 6:330-31; Marriner W. Merrill, *Utah Pioneer and Apostle: Marriner Wood Merrill and His Family,* ed. Melvin Clarence Merrill (n.p., 1937), 192.

19. Roberts, *Comprehensive History,* 6:330-31.

20. Merrill, *Utah Pioneer and Apostle,* 198-99, 205, 207, 209; *Proceed-*

ings, 1:170, 563; Milton R. Merrill, "Reed Smoot, Apostle in Politics," Ph.D. diss., Columbia University, 1950, 4; Roberts, *Comprehensive History*, 6:335-36.

21. A recent example of this same phenomenon was the controversy over the volume by Allen and Leonard cited above. Although initially released in an unusually large edition that sold out rapidly, it was not republished for nearly fifteen years. Reportedly a senior general authority disliked the book. Allen and Leonard were told by other members of the Twelve, however, that they liked the volume and considered it an important contribution to Mormon history.

22. For a general discussion of the development of the Word of Wisdom, see Paul H. Peterson, "An Historical Analysis of the Word of Wisdom," M.A. thesis, Brigham Young University, 1972; *Journal of Discourses*, 26 vols. (Liverpool: F. D. & S. W. Richards, 1855-85), 12:27-32; Grant Diary, 5 May, 30 June 1898; Lund Journal, 31 Aug., 2 Sept., 9 Jan. 1900, 26 June 1902; Emmeline B. Wells Journal, 8 Sept. 1900, Special Collections, Harold B. Lee Library; John Henry Smith Journal, 5 July 1906; First Presidency to C. R. Hakes, 1 Aug. 1902, to John W. Hess, 31 Oct. 1902, and to H. S. Allen, 1 Nov. 1902, First Presidency, letters sent, LDS archives; George Albert Smith Journal, 5 Aug., 2 Sept. 1905, 27 May, 2 June, 16 June 1906.

23. For a general discussion of these interests, see Bruce T. Dyer, "A Study of the Forces Leading to the Adoption of Prohibition in Utah in 1917," M.S. thesis, Brigham Young University, 1958; Grant Diary, 15 Mar., 12, 16 Nov. 1908; Lund Journal, 2 Oct. 1908; Journal History, 4, 6 Oct. 1908. For a discussion of the national prohibition movement, see Joseph Gusfield, *Symbolic Crusade: Status Politics and the American Temperance Movement* (Urbana: University of Illinois Press, 1963). Gusfield's thesis that the middle class tried to regain its status by imposing Prohibition on the lower classes seems not to apply to Utah since the main support for Prohibition came from a group already holding high status and opposition came from a similar group in the Republican party. The only exception might be found in the Prohibition Republicans. See also James H. Timberlake, *Prohibition and the Progressive Movement, 1900-1920* (Cambridge, MA: Harvard University Press, 1963), who sees the Prohibition crusade as part of the movement for progressive reform; and Norman H. Clark, *Deliver Us from Evil: An Interpretation of American Prohibition* (New York: Norton, 1976), both of whom see Prohibition as part of the American reform movement.

24. Lund Journal, 23, 26, 27 Jan., 3 Feb., 15, 17 Mar., 17 Nov. 1909; John Henry Smith Journal, 26 Jan. 1909, 4 Oct. 1911; Dyer, "Prohibition in Utah," 29-31, 43-44, 55; Grant Diary, 23 Mar. 1909; Reed Smoot Diary, 9 Oct., 11, 17 Nov. 1909, 4 Oct. 1911, Special Collections, Harold B. Lee Library; Reuben Joseph Snow, "The American Party in Utah: A Study of Political Party Struggle During the Early Years of Statehood," M.A. thesis,

University of Utah, 1964.

25. Joseph F. Smith, "Editor's Table: Temperance and Prohibition," *Improvement Era* 12 (Aug. 1909): 830-33; Lund Journal, 5 Mar. 1915; Jan Shipps, "Utah Comes of Age Politically: A Study of the State's Politics in the Early Years of the Twentieth Century," *Utah Historical Quarterly* 35 (Spring 1967): 109-11.

26. Lund Journal, 2 Oct. 1908, 15, 17 Mar. 1909; Journal History, 14 Oct. 1908, 20 Mar. 1909; Grant Diary, 12, 16 Nov. 1908, 23 Mar., 6 Apr. 1909; Joseph F. Smith to Reed Smoot, 15 Feb. 1909 in Joseph F. Smith Letterbooks, LDS archives; Dyer, "Prohibition in Utah," 43-44.

27. Lund Journal, 2 Oct. 1900, 28 Sept. 1906; John Henry Smith Journal, 9, 10 Jan. 1900; *Proceedings*, 1:110-11, 389-90, 406, 422, 487-88, 2:68, 141-43, 295-96; Joseph F. Smith to Reed Smoot, 9 Apr. 1904, Joseph F. Smith Letterbooks; Cannon and O'Higgins, *Under the Prophet*, 177; Grant Diary, 9 Oct. 1898; George Q. Cannon to Anthony W. Ivins, 27 Dec. 1897, Ivins Family Papers, Utah State Historical Society, Salt Lake City; Anthony W. Ivins, excerpts from the A. W. Ivins Recordbook of Marriages, Utah State Historical Society; B. Carmon Hardy and Victor W. Jorgensen, "The Taylor-Cowley Affair and the Watershed of Mormon History," *Utah Historical Quarterly* 48 (Winter 1980): 4-36.

28. Matthias F. Cowley, *Cowley's Talks on Doctrine* (Chattanooga, TN: Ben E. Rich, 1902), 180-82; Joseph Eckersley Journal, 26 Dec. 1904, LDS archives; Lund Journal, 9 Jan. 1900, 18 Nov. 1903; Journal History, 19 Nov. 1903; John Henry Smith Journal, 9, 10 Jan. 1900, 19 Nov. 1903; Joseph F. Smith to Samuel L. Adams, 24 Dec. 1903, Joseph F. Smith Letterbooks; Talmage Journal, 14 Oct. 1904; Merrill, *Utah Pioneer and Apostle*, 147; *Proceedings*, 1:408-10.

29. Lund Journal, 5 Apr. 1906; First Presidency to Heber J. Grant, 12 Apr. 1906, First Presidency, letters sent.

30. George F. Richards Journal, 14 July 1909 and passim. Richards's journal provides excellent documentation for the various trials.

31. James E. Talmage, "The Story of Mormonism," *Improvement Era* 4 (Oct. 1901): 909; Smoot Hearings, 3:42-45.

32. James B. Allen, "Personal Faith and Public Policy: Some Timely Observations on the League of Nations Controversy in Utah," *Brigham Young University Studies* 14 (Autumn 1973): 77-98; Smoot Diary, 22 Sept., 12 Oct. 1919, 29, 30 July, 5 Aug. 1920; Lund Journal, 5 Aug. 1920.

33. Lund Journal, 30 Jan., 3 Feb. 1919; Grant Diary, 30 Jan., 31 July 1919, 17 July 1920; Smoot Diary, 20 Aug., 12 Oct. 1919.

34. James H. Moyle to Heber J. Grant, 29 Apr. 1920; Grant to Moyle, 13 May 1920, cited in James Henry Moyle, *Mormon Democrat: The Religious and Political Memoirs of James Henry Moyle*, ed. Gene A. Sessions (Salt Lake

City: Historical Department of the Church of Jesus Christ of Latter-day Saints, 1975), 258-65; Grant Diary, 23 Oct. 1920; Smoot Diary, 23, 24 Oct. 1920; Lund Journal, 21 Oct. 1920.

35. Lund Journal, 28 July 1920; George F. Richards Journal, 3 Oct., 4 Nov. 1919. On the nature of Mormon millennialism, see Grant Underwood, "Seminal Versus Sesquicentennial Saints: A Look at Millennialism," *Dialogue: A Journal of Mormon Thought* 14 (Spring 1981): 32-44.

36. John A. Widtsoe, *Joseph Smith as Scientist: A Contribution to Mormon Philosophy* (Salt Lake City: General Board, Young Men's Mutual Improvement Associations, 1908), 109-13; Joseph Fielding Smith, *Man, His Origin and Destiny* (Salt Lake City: Deseret Book Co., 1954); Charles W. Penrose and Anthony W. Ivins to Joseph W. McMurrin, 31 Oct. 1921, First Presidency, letters sent; Frederic W. Pack, *Science and Belief in God* (Salt Lake City: Deseret News, 1924).

37. Grant Diary, 8 Apr. 1927, 22 May 1930; 16, 25 Jan. 1931; Truman G. Madsen, "The Meaning of Christ—The Truth, The Way, The Life: An Analysis of B. H. Roberts's Unpublished Masterwork," *Brigham Young University Studies* 15 (Spring 1975): 260 and passim; Duane E. Jeffrey, "Seers, Savants, and Evolution: The Uncomfortable Interface," *Dialogue: A Journal of Mormon Thought* 8 (Autumn-Winter 1973): 63-65. On 25 January 1931, Heber J. Grant wrote in his diary, "After reading the articles by Brothers [B. H.] Roberts and [Joseph Fielding] Smith, I feel that sermons such as Brother Joseph preached and criticisms such as Brother Roberts makes of the sermon are the finest kind of things to be let alone entirely, I think no good can be accomplished by dealing in mysteries, and that is what I feel in my heart of hearts these brethren are both doing." See also James E. Talmage, "The Earth and Man" (1931; reprt., Provo, UT: Brigham Young University, 1976). On Brigham Young University's vault copy of the published version of this speech is a notation "False doctrine" in Joseph Fielding Smith's hand.

38. See Berger, *Sacred Canopy*, 49-50.

15.
Sheaves, Bucklers, and the State: Mormon Leaders Respond to the Dilemmas of War

Ronald W. Walker

THE QUESTION OF HOW THE LATTER-DAY SAINT CHURCH SHOULD respond to armed conflict has long troubled Mormons. Can they refuse to bear arms because of their religion? Could there be grounds for a military crusade? In addition to juxtaposing pacifism and military participation, warfare also poses the question of allegiance. Do Saints owe their primary loyalty to conscience, church, or nation? These issues are difficult, for Mormon scripture and heritage speak ambiguously of both pacifism and war—of "sheaves" as well as "buck-lers." Mormon leaders have answered the dilemmas of war differently at different times, weighing in the process, shifting LDS attitudes toward millennialism and Americanism.[1]

The earliest testing grounds for the Saints' attitudes toward violence and war were their conflicts with non-Mormon neighbors. Mormonism had scarcely commenced when in January 1831 Joseph Smith warned his almost 200 New York followers of the threat of persecution. But rather than urging resistance, his revelation counseled them to "escape the power of the enemy" by moving west.[2]

Northern Ohio and western Missouri became the twin centers of the Mormon gathering. The former was such a scene of conflict that at times members "had to lic every night for a long time

267

upon our arms to keep off mobs."[3] At first the Saints responded to
the Missouri turmoil pacifically. "So tenacious were they for the
precepts of the gospel," a participant later wrote, that "the Mormons
had not so much as lifted a finger, even in their own defence."[4]
Indeed during these dark moments, six leading elders "offered
themselves a ransom for the church, willing to be scourged or die, if
that would appease . . . [the Missourians'] anger."[5] Such abnegation
reflected not only inferior numbers but a theology admonishing
church members to forgive their tormentors at least three times
before resisting. Even then should a Saint "spare" his oppressor, he
would be rewarded for his righteousness.[6]

But as Missouri hostilities continued, Mormon reaction har-
dened. When faced with almost certain expulsion from Jackson
County, the Saints "found that they would be justified by the law of
both God [and] man, in defending themselves, their families and
houses."[7] Their ineffectual defense and consequent eviction occasioned yet a more militant response. In the belief that Missouri
governor Daniel Dunklin would reinstate the expatriates on their
lands but would not provide a standing defense, Joseph Smith, who
had remained in Ohio, organized the paramilitary "Zion's Camp."
The heavily armed company eventually swelled to more than 200 men
as it marched from Ohio to Missouri, personally led by the Mormon
prophet.[8]

The marching of a private army across the American wilderness aroused both fear and misunderstanding. Missourians viewed
the group as an instrument of retribution, while some church leaders
complained of "the transformation of God's kingdom into a warrior
band."[9] Lending weight to these feelings, Mormon rhetoric was often
bellicose. The authorizing revelation for Zion's Camp spoke of the
need to redeem Jackson County by "power" and suggested the
possibility of sacrificing life for the cause. Moreover, the Saints' loose
and excited speech gave the impression that Zion would be forcibly
delivered.[10]

From the beginning of the crisis, the Mormon prophet
believed that the persecutions of his followers resulted partly from
their own misconduct and consequently a revelation urged them to
reform their behavior, forego retribution, and pursue lawful redress.
Before proposing Zion's Camp, Smith sought to defuse the controversy by interposing either state or federal troops between Mormons

and their rivals.[11] As the party marched to Missouri, the "Camp" lifted a white banner with "PEACE" inscribed in red lettering and the group displayed an unusual frontier reverence for animal life. Smith cautiously confirmed to the Missouri governor their defensive purposes.[12] When Dunklin reversed his position and refused to place the Mormons on their lands, Smith, who was out-manned and without government sanction, disbanded his group. An accompanying revelation decried the immediate use of force and urged the Saints to "sue for peace" even "to the people that have smitten you."[13]

By 1838 Mormons could hardly suppress their outrage. Continuing violence weighed heavily on LDS leaders living in Missouri. Sidney Rigdon, Smith's assistant and spokesman, vowed the Saints would never be aggressors, but his promise was overwhelmed by his other unrestrained words: "We take God and all the holy angels to witness this day, that we warn all men in the name of Jesus Christ, to come on us no more forever. [F]or from this hour, we will bear it no more, our rights shall no more be trampled upon with impunity. The man or set of men who attempts it, does it at the expense of their lives. And that mob who comes on us to disturb us; it shall be between us and them a war of extermination, for we will follow them, till the last drop of their blood is spilled, or else they will have to exterminate us: for we will carry the seat of war to their own houses, and their own families, and one party or the other shall be utterly destroyed."[14] Like a roaring fireball, Rigdon's printed and widely circulated oration ignited a final wave of fury. By mid-October the embattled Smith sanctioned an aggressive defense, while some of his followers organized themselves into secret bands that replied to Missouri mobocracy in kind.[15] Later the Mormon leader denied any personal role in the conflict.[16] Before the final confrontation he was captured, and the Saints in his absence agreed to leave the state rather than fight.

The Missouri turmoil toughened Mormon attitudes. The pacifism of earlier days lost its appeal. Instead Mormons resolved in the future to deal with their enemies from a position of strength and consequently at Nauvoo, Illinois (and later in Utah), formed the "Nauvoo Legion." This army of several thousand well-trained soldiers was seen as a necessary "mantle of protection" while living in the "western wilds" so far removed from stable government. And in the martial atmosphere of the times, military titles became fashionable for both church and civic leaders, while military auxiliaries organized and drilled the city's youth.[17] Smith, who had rejoined his followers, noted another purpose for the conscripts: the legion "will enable us to show our attachment to the state and nation . . . whenever the public service requires our aid, thus proving ourselves obedient to the paramount laws of the land, and ready at all times to sustain and execute them."[18] Despite their persecutions, Mormons awaited their nation's call to arms.

The Nauvoo Legion, with its curious blend of religion, patriotism, and military display, was poorly conceived to allay the confusion surrounding the new faith. No more reassuring was the legion's manpower, numbering more than a quarter of the entire United States Army in 1845. Excessive and seemingly threatening, it made Smith appear to be a Mohammed bent on religious crusade.[19] The result was predictable. As in Missouri, Mormon force summoned counterforce. Smith was assassinated, and mobs again sought to expel the Saints from their homes.

The Saints remained self-controlled. "We would fight our way clear," an LDS editorial noted the legion's military superiority. But "we will suffer wrong rather than do wrong. . . . The gospel whispers peace."[20] Only after most church members had begun their westward hegira did a small remnant of Mormons and their allies unsuccessfully defend their community. The Nauvoo Legion failed to be the Damoclean sword which its detractors thought.

The Mormon or Utah War of 1857-58 embroiled the Saints in yet another civil conflict. Responding to rumors of Mormon defiance to national authority, U.S. president James Buchanan dispatched an American army to Utah. The Saints had left Illinois with their loyalties badly fractured, upset not so much with America as with Americans. Consequently though they aggressively pursued statehood for Utah, their sense of grievance led them to tangle repeatedly with federal territorial appointees, who in the LDS view violated their right of self-government. Like their seventeenth-century New England ancestors, Mormons presented the paradox of a patriotic but restless citizenry.[21]

For the persecution-conscious Mormons, the national army seemed the crowning proof of American perfidy. Instead of investigating the territorial officers' colored reports of LDS disloyalty, Buchanan dispatched several thousand soldiers without announcement or explanation. Furthermore church leaders heard talk that

General Harney, the expedition's initial leader, hoped for a sanguinary adventure. According to his biographer, Harney "had fully determined, on arriving at Salt Lake City, to capture Brigham Young and the twelve apostles, and execute them in a summary fashion."[22] Young, who had succeeded Smith, did not conceal his outrage. "I swore in Nauvoo, when my enemies were looking me in the face, that I would send them to hell across lots, if they meddled with me," he stormed, "and I ask no more odds of all hell today."[23]

Even before receiving firm news of the army's approach, Young began defensive preparations, including, by virtue of his authority as territorial governor, the reactivation of the Nauvoo Legion. Later Mormons fortified their eastern passes, marshaled public opinion for war, and sought alliance with the Great Basin Indians.[24] Yet as government troops approached, Young appeared ambivalent and less than resolute. "Are you going to contend against the United States?" he asked his congregation. "No. But when they come here to take our lives solely for our religion, be ye also ready."[25]

In truth Mormon speech and actions were sometimes inconsistent. On the one hand, church leaders initially used force to harass the invaders. Small companies of the legion were ordered to impede the advancing American army with all means short of bloodshed. "Annoy them in every possible way," read the legion's orders. "Use every exertion to sta[m]pede their animals and set fire to their trains. Burn the whole country before them, and on their flanks."[26] During these tense months in late 1857, Mormons probably would have defended their communities had the Utah expedition attempted to test their defenses. This wartime atmosphere in turn helped produce the tragedy at Mountain Meadows. Feeling threatened and giving way to a mass hysteria not uncommon during war, members of the southern Utah militia and Indian allies killed almost 100 emigrants passing through the territory.[27]

On the other hand, as Mormon and American troops approached open battle in the spring of 1858, Young consciously weighed policies and principles and resolved a peaceful course. Doubtless the settlers from their mountain bastions could inflict heavy losses upon eastern soldiers. Yet the cost of such a campaign would be great and even then an ultimate American victory was likely. To such practicality Young added pacifism. "It is better to lose property," he asserted, "than the lives of men, women, and children."[28]

Thereupon church members abandoned their homes and recommenced their hegira, this time to an undetermined location to the south. But the situation ended less dramatically. Satisfied that reports of Mormon disloyalty were largely fictitious, Buchanan's newly arrived territorial governor promised to isolate the army from LDS communities if the Mormons would return to their homes. They agreed, and the so-called war ended without battle casualties.[29]

Although the Utah War was the last armed confrontation between Saints and their fellow American citizens, Mormons would encounter difficulties with Great Basin Indians for at least another decade. These tribes offered only spasmodic resistance to well-organized churchmen. Despite some initial attacks, Mormon leaders generally tried to pacify their Indian neighbors. "Never retaliate a wrong," Young counseled. "Independent of the question of exercising humanity towards so degraded and ignorant a race of people," he declared, it was "manifestly more economical, and less expensive, to feed and clothe them, than to fight them."[30] To be sure Mormons erected defensive fortifications and occasionally launched punitive expeditions against marauding tribes. Worse, some rank-and-file members treated Indians with cold, frontier brutality. Yet as non-Mormon military observers conceded, Young and his closest associates generally urged conciliation and used force as a last resort.[31]

The Mexican War of 1846-48 provided the first test of Mormon attitudes and conduct during a national war. Its timing could not have been more unfortunate. The expatriates had just begun their western exodus, and their distress-filled camps were dispersed across the length of Iowa. Not surprisingly when American army officers solicited 500 Mormon volunteers to march on Mexican California, most were unenthusiastic. As one diarist wrote, the call for a battalion "needed considerable explaining for every one was about as much prejudiced [against it] as I was at first."[32]

However, Brigham Young reacted differently. Earlier he had sought federal aid for emigration, and while he had hoped to receive a government contract for the construction of a series of forts enroute to Oregon, a Mormon-American army appeared equally to serve his purposes. The proposal would transport 500 Mormons at government expense to the proximity of their new homeland, while the troops' pay could help to finance the migration of the remainder of the destitute church. By providing volunteers the Mormons could allay prejudice with a demonstration of their patriotism, possibly become the dominant American settlement in California, and secure federal approval—so vitally required—of their temporary settlement on midwestern Indian lands.[33]

"This is the first time the government has stretched forth its arm to our assistance," enthused Young, "and we received their proffers with joy and thankfulness." When some of his followers hesitated to enroll, he reminded them of their Americanism. "Suppose we were admitted into the Union as a State and the government did not call on us, we would feel ourselves neglected." Besides, Young reminded, it was the state governments of Missouri and Illinois and not the national government that had inflicted their past distress. After Young's endorsement, the U.S. Army officer who managed the induction found the Mormons to be "entirely patriotic."[34]

If church members were somewhat divided in their attitudes toward the battalion, the church press reflected a similar ambivalence about the war in general. At times the press boasted that American arms and institutions were ordained to a high and glorious role. The English *Millennial Star,* reflecting the American sentiments of its editorial writers, declared, "The long reign of intolerance that has darkened the dominions of Mexico must receive a fatal blow from American arms, and the more tolerant genius of American institutions."[35]

But more often patriotism and Americanism had a detached and tepid quality. Certainly war was not license for unbridled conduct. As the battalion began its 2,000-mile march that secured California without battle, Apostle Parley Pratt counseled LDS conscripts neither to "Misuse their enemies" nor "spoil their property." The Mexicans, in fact, were "fellow human beings to whom the gospel is yet to be preached."[36]

More than Christian brotherhood and missionary zeal shaped Mormon attitudes. Their persecutions had alienated the Saints from fellow Americans and as a result made their support of the war half-hearted. The *Millennial Star* often sounded like a Whiggish anti-war newspaper. "In their blindness and lust of dominion" and "under the 'banner—*might makes right*'," one editorial declared, Americans "grasp at the wide extended dominions of Mexico."[37]

Mormon scorn of American conduct also reflected their millenarianism. They viewed the Mexican War as divine judgment and as the beginning of the promised terror announcing the millennial era. "God will use the American arms to break down papal domination" in Mexico, Orson Hyde, another church leader, warned, "then [he will] do as seemeth him good."[38] What Hyde hinted at, other editorials made clear. The Saints "are conscious that they are leaving cities and nations which are destined to be shaken by the insupportable blasts of adversity," declared the *Star*. "The wicked shall slay the wicked, and the spirit of God shall be taken from all rebellious flesh."[39]

To be sure the Mormon position during the Mexican War was confusing. The church leaders' pursuit of self-interest and their dedication to civil authority and Americanism were not always reconcilable with their dark, millennial forecasts. The result was the idealization of abstract American principles and institutions. At the same time Mormons took a jaundiced view of Americans. The latter would be required by Providence to pay a heavy price for their rejection of the prophets and the persecution of God's people.

While Mormon conduct during the Mexican conflict established a precedent of military service, the Civil War proved a partial exception. At best the Saints provided only token support to the Union cause. Outwardly Utahns conformed to legal requirements. Although their territorial status exempted them from wartime conscription, Mormons complied with the national government's request in 1862 to guard briefly communication lines between forts Bridger and Laramie. Moreover, they paid Washington's war tax of $26,982 and repeatedly rejected southern entreaties which reportedly promised confederate statehood on the Saints' terms.[40] Yet Mormon behavior was more circumspect than enthusiastic, embracing the letter rather than the spirit of the union cause.

The respect of church leaders for American government by no means had vanished. "We are tried and firm supporters of the Constitution and every Constitutional right," Young declared in April 1862. He regarded secessionists as "fanatics" who "were determined to ruin if they could not rule."[41] To attest to their loyalty, Utahns in 1861-62 made a third plea for statehood, which if successful presumably would have committed them to an active military role in the war. "We show our loyalty by trying to get in [the Union] while others are trying to get out," Utah's territorial delegate to congress asserted, "notwithstanding our grievances, which are far greater than those of any of the Seceding States."[42]

But Mormon support for the war was never strong. Young viewed abolitionists as "black-hearted Republicans," who had "set the whole national fabric on fire."[43] Subsequent federal policy in Utah deepened his outrage. Although wanting to conciliate Mormons at least for the duration of the conflict, President Abraham Lincoln successively appointed two inept and irritating governors.[44] And no situation during the Civil War rankled the Saints more than the presence of California Volunteers in Utah. Ostensibly charged with preventing the disruption of territorial communications by Indian raiders, the troops stationed themselves on the western slopes of the Wasatch Range. There with their artillery easily commanding Salt Lake City, they built a permanent camp.

While these specific events alienated Mormons, the larger explanation for their Civil War discontent lay in their resurgent millennialism. The first events of the conflict seemed to confirm their long-held scenario of the end. During the South Carolina nullification controversy thirty years before, Joseph Smith had forecast that the millennial wars would start with a rebellion in South Carolina and would in turn involve the northern and southern states. The latter, he predicted, would call on Great Britain as well as other nations for support and thus would begin a chain of events leading to universal war. Fort Sumter and its aftermath seemed to fulfill these projections almost to the letter.[45]

Smith's prophecies firmly cast millennialism on the Mormon consciousness, influencing churchmen in at least three major ways. First, with the "last days" close at hand, Mormons disengaged themselves from institutions and events—including the struggle between the states. The United States government was seen as twenty-five years past its zenith and rapidly declining in its corruption to a sure demise.[46] Why spend blood and treasure in a lost cause?

Second, the Saints began to plan for a post-millennial era. "We shall make preparations for future events," Heber C. Kimball, Young's counselor, declared. "The South will secede from the North, and the North will secede from us, and God will make this people free as fast as we are able to bear it."[47] Church leaders could now discern the divine purpose in their forced migrations. While the world trembled on the edge of Armageddon, the Saints dwelled peacefully in their mountain valleys.[48] Preserving their strength by avoiding any wartime engagements, they could at the proper time step forth, as their prophetic tradition held, to preserve American political institutions for a new world order. Perhaps, as Kimball predicted, Young might yet occupy the U.S. presidential chair.[49]

Third, as a reaction to these impulses there emerged in Mormon thinking a decidedly pacifist strain. During the Civil War years, Young often spoke of the desirability of peace. "A large share of the ingenuity of the world is taxed to invent weapons of war," he declaimed. "What a set of fools!"[50] Personally the church president was attracted neither to fighting nor to military display. "If we could have our choice, it would be to continually walk in the path of peace," he said during the height of the hostilities, "and had we the power, we would direct the feet of all men to walk in the same path." Nor did Young condemn the behavior of those who fled west to escape the war. "I think they are probably as good a class of men as has ever passed through this country," he commented. "I have no fault to find with them."[51]

As the war progressed Mormon millennialism and alienation varied in inverse degree to the strength of the union's arms. Accordingly, as Appomattox approached, the tone of the church-owned *Deseret News* became more pro-northern. Yet when Lee surrendered the newspaper treated the event with silence. Young had predicted that the Civil War would bring "years and years" of turmoil, though there would be "seasons that the fire will appear to be extinguished."[52] Apparently Mormon leaders believed Appomattox to be one of these insignificant delays in the holocaust. Or perhaps they began to sense the imprecision of their millennial calculations.

If the Civil War marked the high tide of Mormon alienation, reaction to the Spanish-American conflict expressed the Saints' growing conciliation with American society. During the early 1890s the church discarded plural marriage, political solidarity, and centralized economics, which previously had inhibited its entrance into the American mainstream. In return Congress rewarded Utah with statehood in 1896. Finally free from irritating disputes with the American government, the Mormon community for the first time could express its patriotism freely, and during the Spanish War it did so enthusiastically, compensating for past insinuations of disloyalty.[53]

Like their fellow Americans, Mormons were filled with the excitement of the hour. The *Deseret News* painted Cuban conditions as barbarous and medieval, a reflection of the "stolid, sullen, animal nature" of the Spanish race. By the first week of April 1898, the church newspaper had reduced the issues down to whether Spain would lose Cuba with or without compensation. Should the latter happen, it promised that Mormons would not be inactive. "If our glorious Union shall become involved in war," an editorial declared, "she will never number, in all her armies a truer, a braver, or better soldier than the Mormon recruit."[54]

Most Saints were unaware of their own nation's aggressiveness in the dispute, which presumably could have been amicably resolved. Mormons with the majority of their fellow citizens including most clergy believed that peace lay in Spanish and not American conciliation. When President William McKinley finally led the United States into war, it was because most Americans, including a majority of Latter-day Saints, preferred hostilities to any delay or compromise in solving the Cuban imbroglio.[55]

During the early months of 1898, even though public opinion in Utah and elsewhere outraced national policy, the church consistently supported McKinley's slower pace. The *Deseret News* described itself as aloof from "the sensation-monger influence," though its rhetoric often belayed the claim, and hoped that "peaceable means" might yet be brought to bear.[56] Furthermore some of the sermons of the church's general conference in April 1893 urged peace. The influential George Q. Cannon, first counselor to President Wilford Woodruff, cited Joseph Smith's pacifistic revelation: "We must proclaim peace; do all in our power to appease the wrath of our enemies; make any sacrifice that honorable people can to avert war."[57]

The church leader who most withstood the popular clamor was Brigham Young, Jr. In a tabernacle discourse only days after Congress accepted the war resolution, the apostle urged a response patterned after his father's Civil War policy. The American government should be sustained, Young held, and if national defense required, he himself would bear arms. But such a case seemed unnecessary. Rather he urged Mormons to remain home and donate their wages to the war effort. Behind his public phrases lay his private opposition to the war. "Let the wicked slay the wicked," he wrote confidentially in his diary. The war is an "unrighteous cause."[58] Young was restating the Saints' lingering tradition of a peaceful Zion sequestered from the world and its corollary, a limited loyalty to civil authority. But Americanism had become the watchword. The Mormon first presidency voiced its strong displeasure to Young and moved quickly to disassociate itself from his position.[59]

Soon any hesitation about the war disappeared from church rhetoric. "It is gratifying to know that in the issues involved our country is wholly right," declared the *Improvement Era,* while the *Young Woman's Journal* obliquely found the Spanish to be "wicked, reckless men." In turn the First Presidency issued a statement which affirmed the absolute loyalty of the Mormon people.[60] To prove its words the church leadership telegraphed local leaders to encourage troop enlistment, while the directors of the church-related ZCMI department store apparently offered half pay to volunteering employees for the duration of the war.[61] With the names of prominent LDS families among its enlistments, Utah became one of the first states to fill its initial quota of 500 volunteers. Troops left Utah amid enthusiastic cheers and, in at least some cases, after receiving protective blessings administered in the Salt Lake Temple.[62]

The sweeping success of American arms converted the *Deseret News* into a powerful exponent of expansionism. The idea of an American empire, at once spiritual, economic, and territorial, secularized one of the most cherished LDS images. The little stone in Daniel's vision no longer was seen to represent Mormonism's mission. Instead it came to symbolize the new American empire which had "struck the image of the Old World imperialism on its feet of iron and clay and shattered it to the four winds."[63] The obligations of the nation's expanded sovereignty seemed awesome: "Then for reclamation, reformation, purification and the infusing of new and healthier blood into the shrunken arteries of the captive colonies! What a mighty, burdensome, long-enduring and withal upright, philanthropic, Christian-like labor this will be! It is the bringing of order out of chaos; the dragging from the dark recesses of ignorance and superstition millions of human beings and placing them within the benevolent power of human progress."[64] In addition the newspaper explicitly proclaimed prevailing Anglo-Saxon racism and envisioned a grand British-American civilizing influence. Clearly Mormons were ready to shoulder the white man's burden.[65]

LDS flirtation with imperialism quickly passed. Yet the fact that Mormons even expressed such ideas was nonetheless important. Like the larger reaction of the church to the Spanish-American War, it indicated Mormonism's cultural direction. The Saints during the war had blended religious and national symbols, displayed their patriotism for public effect, and vigorously reflected the American mood. They had become a part of pluralistic America.

The outbreak of World War I did not surprise Mormons. While their newspapers and magazines sometimes reflected the belief of many western intellectuals that warfare was obsolete, far more often Mormons adhered to their millennial heritage that the Civil War had muted but by no means subdued. Each of Brigham Young's four successors reaffirmed the approaching apocalypse, with President Wilford Woodruff warning in 1894 of calamities which within two decades would bring "mighty changes among the nations of the earth."[66] Twenty years and four days later, Archduke Francis Ferdinand of Austria-Hungary was assassinated at Sarajevo.

At the war's beginning the Saints' millennial assessment found an expression in President Woodrow Wilson's strict neutrality. LDS president Joseph F. Smith believed that the conflagration at last fulfilled the Mormon prophecy of an entire world at war except for Zion—for he defined Zion as not just the western valleys of the Saints but the entire western hemisphere.[67] "As a nation we certainly have just cause to be thankful for [the] peace that prevails in our midst, and it is to be hoped that nothing will occur to disrupt it," he wrote in November 1914. Believing the war to be "without adequate cause" and "the supreme crime of all history," he was content that events should run their course while Zion-America remained at peace.[68]

Smith remained resolute in his views even as Wilson began to move the nation toward intervention. The Mormon president was, as a friend described him, "a man of peace," but his reluctance for war was also reinforced by his strong Republican partisanship.[69] "Consistency is a Jewel," he wrote derisively of the Democrats' 1916 presidential campaign slogan, "Wilson Has Kept Us Out Of War."[70] Reflecting Smith's views, church periodicals continued to call for peace at the same time Wilson was formally requesting a congressional war declaration. And when America joined the western allies, Smith rendered at best proper and unemotional support: "Worldly ambition, pride, and the love of power, determination on the part of rulers to prevail over their competitors in the national games of life, wickedness at heart, desire for power, for worldly greatness, have led the nations of the earth to quarrel with each other and have brought them to war and self-destruction. I presume there is not a nation in the world today that is not tainted with this evil more or less. It may be possible perhaps, to trace the cause of the evil, or the greatest part of it, to some particular nation of the earth; but I do not know." Smith urged Mormons to bear American arms and hoped that somehow the allied armies might increase worldwide liberty and righteousness. But he had no illusions of the allies' purity. God "is working with men who never prayed, men who never have known God, nor Jesus Christ. . . . God is dealing with nations of infidels."[71]

Most Mormons, however, were far less restrained, and as the war continued Smith himself became an earnest advocate of the American cause. "Whether the United States is rightfully at war does not for the present concern any American," declared the *Deseret News* several days after the congressional declaration of war. "His country is at war, and unless he is ready to give it every ounce of efficient support he can command, his place is not among Americans."[72] Charles W. Penrose, Smith's counselor, conceded that while non-resistance "under certain circumstances" was justified, the present crisis was not one of them. "Jesus was no milksop," he declared.[73] While generally phrasing their support in terms of citizenship and the flag, church leaders did not doubt the justice of the cause. For instance Smith came to believe the contest pitted freedom against despotism and toward the end of the war joined other leading American churchmen in petitioning for the unconditional surrender of the "autocratic and military leaders" of the central powers.[74] What was at first a dubious exercise had become a crusade.

Mormons fervently joined the cause. Perhaps due to Smith's original hesitation, the church did not participate in the first Liberty Bond drive. Thereafter its fund raising was strenuous. "Those who have money and do not support the Government will find that there will be other ways to make them do their duty," pointedly wrote Heber J. Grant, president of the twelve apostles and chief fund-raiser for the Mormon community. With church tithes and organization committed to the activity, Utah repeatedly oversubscribed the government's financial requests.[75] By September 1918 the state had over 18,000 men under arms, almost half of them volunteers. Rural districts responded with enlistments more promptly than urban areas—a non-Mormon official explaining the difference by the high incidence of church members outside of Utah's cities.[76] President

Smith offered $3,500 in wartime agricultural prizes, while LDS mag-
azines preached economy and patriotism.[77] "For the prompt and
effective part our own people have played [in the war]," the First
Presidency proudly wrote upon the war's conclusion, "they . . .
deserve the highest commendation."[78]

Mormon enthusiasm was a microcosm of the nation. World
War I united Americans, including the Saints, like no other national
war. Moreover Mormon millennial perceptions made them, like
other religious fundamentalists, particularly susceptible to Wilsonian
rhetoric. For leaders such as B. H. Roberts, the conflict promised to
be "the war to end all wars" after which "there shall come world peace,
and the earth shall rest."[79] Likewise Wilson's views on democracy
deeply touched Mormons. Below the surface of President Smith's
wartime remarks flowed the current of *vox populi, vox Dei*: worldwide
democracy would manifest God's will by bringing peace, improving
the world's social order, enhancing LDS proselyting and perhaps
ushering in the millennial era.[80] If Mormons deviated from wartime
sentiment, they "out-Wilsoned" Wilson by making religious overtones of his speech explicit.

Certainly their language and emotions seemed inflamed for
even wartime passions. "As yet we have no knowledge of human flesh
being fed to [German] prisoners," the *Relief Society Magazine* declared,
"but we know that disease germs have been injected into their blood,
and it has been said that women have been nailed to doors within
churches, after the brutes into whose hands they have fallen have
accomplished their wicked purposes." Even Apostle James E. Talmage in the spirit of the times could not resist commenting on the
ironic fate of former LDS missionaries to Germany. In the past they
had gone with only their testimonies and scriptures as defense; now
they go "with Browning guns as their instruments of persuasion."[81]

Such expressions violated President Smith's call for dispas-
sion during the war, but they also understandably offended German-
American Mormons. The war for the first time pitted Mormon
against Mormon, and the Saints in Germany obediently responded
to church counsel by sustaining their government and defending
their fatherland.[82] But the psychological situation of Utah's German-
Americans was more taxing. With nativism surging around them and
torn by conflicting national and cultural traditions, they reacted
erratically. Some gathered in secret meetings and hardly concealed

their alienation from both Mormonism and Americanism. Their suspicious, wartime behavior led to a few of them being arrested and detained, as Utah followed a pattern occurring elsewhere in the United States. "It is a very critical time for our nationals as well as [for the] German saints," a contemporary diarist aptly recorded, "and great wisdom and understanding is necessary to successfully meet the present needs."[83]

Mormon German-Americans were not the only members dissatisfied with church policy. Discontent was sufficiently widespread that the First Presidency took note. "Some of our people, some that are very pacific[,] become critical as to our war policy," acknowledged Charles W. Penrose, Smith's counselor. While conceding that war was generally wrong, Penrose insisted that "when the Lord commands or inspires his servants to counsel the sons and daughters of Israel to lend their aid in the work of righteous warfare, that is different."[84] While the church press had treated pacifism and conscientious objection respectfully prior to the American war declaration, it later strongly warned Mormons against the slightest deviation in allegiance. "There is small patience today with one whose loyalty comes under the least question," admitted the *Deseret News*, advising anyone with reservations to keep "his acts above suspicion and his mouth shut."[85]

The Mormons' surging emotions and high expectations did not diminish overnight. To many general authorities, including the newly sustained church president, Heber J. Grant, Wilson's proposed League of Nations promised that the wartime crusade might bear a lasting and universal peace.[86] Likewise the movements of the 1920s to outlaw war and encourage disarmament rekindled a few similar hopes.[87] But the rise of the fascist powers mocked the Saints' peaceful hopes. As a result the crusade of 1917-18 would become for many a source of deep disillusionment.

As World War II approached, Mormons displayed a pacifist tendency unequaled in their tradition since the Civil War. Yet they were more likely to denounce the evils of war than recommend an unequivocal pacifism. And Mormons in the 1930s still felt a sense of estrangement—not because of their lack of integration into the American community, as formerly, but rather the opposite. They now shared with most other Americans, especially conservative religionists, the sense of betrayal occasioned by the undelivered hopes of

World War I.[88] The interwar years had transformed President Heber J. Grant from an energetic wartime fund-raiser into a thorough-going skeptic over the purposes of war. His counselors, David O. McKay and especially J. Reuben Clark, whose Quaker ancestry and personal orientation strongly compelled him toward pacifism, voiced similar views.[89] Thus Mormonism during the 1930s joined that generation's crusade—the crusade for isolationism.

The First World War seemed replete with "lessons," and LDS authorities actively proclaimed them: American and European vital interests were incompatible; war was a perversion of patriotism; economic profiteering lay at the root of warfare; true neutrality was non-judgmental; another conflagration would end civilization or occasion a cataclysmic economic depression.[90] "Never again for the United States," resolved the *Deseret News*.[91] The prevailing disillusionment led British Mission president Hugh B. Brown to embrace warmly the Munich appeasement. "While some may accuse us of truckling to tricksters and forsaking the weak," he wrote, "still we thank God that we had stout-hearted men at the helm who knew what value the world was getting for the price they had to pay."[92]

When war finally commenced in 1939, Mormon churchmen remained aloof. "Each side [of the conflict] claims to believe it is in the right," the First Presidency wrote with clear skepticism. Privately it considered the hostilities to be "merely a breaking out again of the old spirit of hatred and envy that has afflicted Europe for a period of a thousand years at least." Indeed a year after the fall of France, church leaders not only believed that the United States was militarily secure but, if first counselor Clark's statements were representative, that the European democracies conspired to have America finance the war for empire.[93] There was even a hint that in case of an American war declaration Mormons might exercise the right of conscientious objection. Rather than fighting, leaders believed that America could best proclaim its mission by peaceful, moral example.[94]

Church policy was more than an outcropping of submerged pacifism or an expression of World War I disillusionment. President Franklin D. Roosevelt and the New Deal deeply alienated the Mormon presidency. "Our nation cannot be preserved if the present governmental policies shall continue," the presidency wrote.[95] President Grant privately believed that Roosevelt was neither an "honest man" nor wise in his policies. "It is one of the regrets of my life that

I cannot take the stu[m]p against the . . . new deal," he wrote only eight days before Pearl Harbor. Grant in fact feared that Roosevelt was seeking war to assume dictatorial power.[96] Following the Japanese attack Grant privately accused the American president of "destroying the nation to the best of his ability by trying to get us in [to the] war when there was no need for it." Throughout the remainder of the conflict, Grant continued to suspect Roosevelt's motives and to believe as late as January 1945 that proper policy could have avoided the American declaration of war.[97] Only the fear of politically dividing the church restrained his public expression.

The church's wartime pronouncements reflected Grant's private misgivings. "Both sides [of the conflict] cannot be wholly right; perhaps neither is without wrong," began Mormonism's most far-reaching statement on war, issued on April 1942: "The Church is and must be against war. The Church itself can not wage war, unless and until the Lord shall issue new commands. It cannot regard war as a righteous means of settling international disputes; these should and could be settled—the nations agreeing—by peaceful negotiations and adjustment." While remonstrating against war, the statement did not endorse pacifism. When "constitutional law . . . calls the manhood of the Church into the armed service of any country to which they owe allegiance," the presidency continued, "their highest civic duty requires that they heed that call." Thus leaders renewed their allegiance to military service while objecting to war. Grant, who believed the message to be "wonderful," tried to honor Clark, the actual author of the text, by allowing him to affix his signature to the document. However, Clark declined to do so.[98]

By April 1942 already 6 percent of the total church population served in the American forces or in defense-related industries, and by the conflict's end 5,714 LDS men had been killed, wounded, or were missing in action. The church itself purchased over $17,000,000 in government bonds, while President Grant personally donated to war charities and urged his grandchildren to bear arms.[99] As the war progressed second counselor David O. McKay and other general authorities characterized it as a moral struggle to preserve liberty. The Axis leaders were seen as "cruel, ambitious warlords" and Hitler, though unnamed, as "the world's chief gangster." But the response of Grant and Clark was more guarded. Neither publicly defended the war's issues, while the First Presidency itself gave at best muted support. Its warmest expression called for an allied victory, though "noble men" and "more Christ-like nations" were required for a permanent peace.[100]

While dispassionately removed from the excessive moralizing of World War I, the official Mormon response raised serious questions. By refusing any moral pronouncements, the First Presidency opened itself to the charge of subjugating principle to obedience, especially in view of the war's fascist and anti-Semitic challenges. In the United States the effect was eased by the statements of other general authorities who exceeded the narrow and cautious official declarations of the presidency. However, in Germany where Mormonism in 1939 had over 15,000 adherents, church policy passively confirmed the Third Reich. Although isolated cases of Mormon resistance to Nazism did occur, including one teenager, Helmuth Huebner, who was beheaded for distributing anti-government propaganda, most members loyally if at times fearfully supported the regime. Perhaps 600 German Saints gave their lives for it.[101]

The Mormon presidency answered the question of the war's responsibility by fixing moral guilt on government rulers—presumably in this case both axis and allied. Their "lust for unrighteous power and dominion over their fellow men" might instigate war, the presidency held, but in the process political leaders "put into motion eternal forces [of justice which] they do not comprehend and cannot control." God himself would overrule and determine justice, the presidency seemed to be saying, relieving citizens of the need to disobey an unjust sovereign. The roots of such teaching extended to the First World War when Mormons had differentiated between the acts of the German regime and its citizenry.[102] This explanation satisfied the majority of German and American Saints, but a few Mormon-Americans refused to fight and gained conscientious objector status.[103]

Following Japanese surrender, the Mormon presidency immediately reasserted its anti-militarism. Its letter to Utah's congressional delegation denounced peacetime conscription as carrying the "gravest dangers to our Republic." Such a program, the churchmen declared, foreshadowed a further decline in American moral values and posed a threat to democracy and to peace.[104] Nor had the First Presidency's perspective concerning the Second World War changed. "The recent spread of barbarism and violence over Europe and the

Orient is still shocking the sensibilities of humanity," it proclaimed a
year after the war's end. Clark in turn denounced the American use
of the atom bomb as "the crowning savagery of the war" and as
"fiendish butchery."[105] In the eyes of LDS leaders, the war had ended
as it had begun—pursuing folly and barbarism.

The "official" Mormon response to the war had parallels
elsewhere. Its theoretical pacifism, cooling internationalism, and
limited verbal support for the issues of the conflict closely corre-
sponded with the wartime patterns of other American religious
groups. And like them these ideas were particularly apparent at
Mormonism's highest hierarchical levels.[106] But if the Mormon
leadership's response typified religious America, paradoxically it also
served the growing international interests of the church. By renounc-
ing war and rendering to each competing Caesar his military due, the
religious movement departed from the narrow nationalism of its
birth.

The dispassionate but supportive pronouncements of World
War II became canon for subsequent responses. During the early
stages of the Cold War, Mormons responded to their country's call
with a unanimity which precluded debate. The Korean War transpired in virtual ecclesiastical silence, although Clark did offer an
obiter dictum on its technical illegality.[107] Even during the Vietnam
struggle when some church members again questioned their military
obligation, the Mormon pulpit only occasionally and obliquely discussed the war. "Though all the issues of the conflict are anything but
clear," characteristically declared one apostle, Boyd K. Packer, "the
matter of citizenship responsibility is perfectly clear." As with other
scripturally-oriented but non-activist clergy, Mormon leaders urged
compliance to "the highest civic duty" of armed service.[108]

While consistent with past precedents, the church's reaction
to the Cold War masked an altered perspective. The Mormon war
position of 1942 had been born during a period when many were
alienated from government, but it meshed with the leadership's
growing trust in the American administration's war policies. By 1970
this distrust of Washington had all but disappeared. "It is not possible
for an individual citizen to have the information that is available to
the President and the Congress," wrote the First Presidency's office,
"and without all of the facts he is not in a position to judge [the
correctness of the war]." Indeed the First Presidency expressed its

"complete confidence" in the national government and in its ability to pursue the Vietnam conflict to an honorable conclusion.[109] Clearly the affirmative climate of the Eisenhower years, the specter of communism, the social unrest of the 1960s, as well as the long-standing Americanism of the Saints had turned the Mormon leaders to the state.

Only a minority of members disagreed with the official policy. "I cannot allow myself to take refuge by shifting moral responsibility to the laws of my country or the orders of my leaders," declared one young war protester. "I must have higher loyalties than man's laws and governments—to principles, to conscience, to God."[110] In response to such dissent, the First Presidency acknowledged that a member might become a conscientious objector—but by virtue of personal conscience and not because of church doctrine or membership.[111] Thus as in previous moments of wartime tension, the conflict between Mormon pacifism and Mormon civil obedience again surfaced.

Mormon reaction to war has drawn on an uneven heritage. Like other Christians, Latter-day Saints mix pastoral and martial images. God's church is a little flock, the earth a white field ready for harvest, and converts "sheaves" which have responded to the "waters of life." Yet shields and bucklers, rods and swords, conquerors and armies also characterize LDS canon.[112] The example of Mormonism's founding prophet seems as ambivalent. "Renounce war and proclaim peace," Joseph Smith recorded in a formal revelation. Moreover Smith advised against the unnecessary taking of animal life, even the life of predators.[113] Yet he bore the title of lieutenant-general, commanded over 2,500 troops, took sword exercises, possessed an "armor-bearer," exuded the expansionist spirit of Manifest Destiny and dedicated the Nauvoo Temple while dressed in full military regalia.[114]

Mormon scriptures somewhat clarify the LDS position. While detailing approvingly the pacifism of 1,000 converts who chose death rather than armed resistance, the Book of Mormon obviously sanctions as one of its central themes the defense of family and self, rights and property, and nation and religion—but only upon divine permission.[115] There is another stipulation: defenders should use forbearance; a first strike defense policy is equated with defeat.[116]

In addition to their idea of a restrained and religiously

sanctioned defense, Mormons have another belief that has affected
their reaction to war. They strongly support "the powers that be"—in
war as well as in peace. "Let no man break the laws of the land," one
revelation counseled. "He that keepeth the laws of God hath no need
to break the laws of the land."[117] The need to sustain civil authority
by arms has been heightened by the reverence Mormonism gives to
the land of its birth. More than a homeland, America is a promised
land, possessed of a holy history and sacred future. God ordained the
Constitution. Thus by deifying its past and future and declaring its
government divinely instituted, Mormons view the defense of the
United States as a holy venture.[118]

Mixing peaceful and militant symbols and calling for both
civil obedience and peaceful restraint to war, the ambiguous Mormon
heritage has left room for considerable variation. However, there
have emerged several discernible patterns. A strain of "qualified"
pacifism has continued throughout the church's experience, best
seen in the Saints' own turmoils but by no means absent during
national war. Tentative and conditional, more often vocal than
substantial, it has surfaced most strongly when members experience
a sense of alienation as during the Civil War and post-World War I
eras. In peacetime church periodicals have reflected such sentiment
by praising conciliation, arms limitation, disarmament proposals, and
for non-Mormons, conscientious objection and pacifism. These expressions have largely disappeared during actual wartime conditions—either discarded or privately kept. But below "official" church
levels, anti-war sentiment has often been present even during wartime conditions. Such small, disparate, and estranged groups as
"other-world" millennialists, Utah's German-Americans of the First
World War, or the social activists of the 1960s have given Mormon
"pacifism" a continuing voice.

However, a categorical pacifism has never been a dominant
Mormon response. With the exceptions of early Missouri settlers and
subsequent but infrequent dissenters to the church's rule, few Saints
have totally opposed warfare—even those who have objected to
specific national wars. Indeed as the religious movement has matured, church leaders have increasingly seen military service as a
religious obligation and state support as a virtue. The Nauvoo Legion
in Illinois and the Mormon Battalion in the Mexican War, whatever
their other justifying motives, were also expressions of the church's

civil loyalty. While the Saints' qualified allegiance during the Civil War proved an aberration, the Spanish-American War began the formal routinization of Mormon military service. By World War II the First Presidency's stated allegiance had become so dominant that it denied wartime accountability for rank and file and ceded to national states both immediate and ultimate responsibility for war-making. Thereafter as during the southeast Asia conflict, Mormon confidence in the purposes and integrity of government has grown.

This trend toward state support has modified the church's theocratic outlook. As the secular state became dominant, the prospect of the Mormon theocracy receded and with that dimming, Mormon civil loyalties became more firmly attached to the American government. The process paralleled New England's transfer of civil allegiance following the gradual decline of the Congregational establishment during the mid-nineteenth century.[119] Moreover the Second World War terminated the theocratic ideal that Mormon leaders should declare by revelatory counsel the justness and appropriateness of armed resistance. Nationalism and the growing internationalization of the church required not only international military compliance during the war but demanded that such compliance be automatic and dispassionately neutral.

Wars also altered the hopeful anticipations of Mormon millennialism. The emotion, which powerfully impelled early Mormonism, peaked during the Civil War and doubtless contributed to the Saints' limited war activity. The prospect of the American Republic's imminent fall weakened normal responsibilities. In turn the First World War produced a less potent and secularized millenarianism. But while both conflicts fanned millennial fires, neither ushered in the kingdom. Consequently Mormons increasingly sensed that warfare was a statement of its time—a demonstration of evil—rather than an immediate herald for the promised day. Ironically while wars originally strongly stirred millennial spirits, by the mid-twentieth century, their unfulfilled hopes cooled the impulse.

The Saints' altered theocratic and millennial viewpoints indicate a changed perspective toward the American mainstream. Early Mormonism appeared both to contemporaries and to later historians to be "outside" and perhaps hostile to the dominant tendencies of Jacksonian America.[120] The movement's reaction to warfare, however, paralleled its gradual conciliation with prevailing Americanism.

The wartime opinions of Mormon leaders increasingly matched those of other conservative churchmen, while church membership at large expressed sentiments indistinguishable from the nation of their citizenship—whether American, German, or English.[121] Mormonism retained its deep antipathy for the humanistic and secular trends of the modern era. But by sustaining government and by placing aside such notions as theocracy and polygamy, the church by the latter half of the twentieth century has emerged as a conservative voice very much from within the conventional fold of society.

While for many the Mormon affinity for the state carries deep moral implications, church leaders appear untroubled. Only rarely have they raised the issue of conscience; nor have they generally justified wartime policy by citing their strongest moral argument—the danger that civil disobedience might lead to anarchy. Obviously their vision has centered on the practical questions of protecting and expanding the church's mission. More than expediency their policy is premised in the Christian assurance of divine power and rewards. An omnipotent and eternal deity, transforming the events of war to conform with his will, eventually will judge both wicked and righteous—if in yet another sphere. Our duty is to obey our government, whatever its virtue. Clearly emphasizing personal purity instead of social responsibility and affixing culpability for war upon government leaders, the formula focuses on a combatant's purposes of heart and resulting conduct rather than the wartime issues of the moment.

The Mormon moral position is symptomatic of the church's larger reaction to war. Competing patterns of Christian pacifism and military service, church and state allegiance, Americanism and internationalism, as well as the millennial tension between an ideal and an actual world have produced a variety of responses. Yet LDS leaders themselves have followed a generally consistent path. Scripturally conservative and "other-worldly" in stressing personal salvation, they have usually pursued restraint in their own conflicts while supporting the bearing of arms in national wars. Their policy parallels the historic approach toward war of pietistic Christianity. Not only has the religious movement subordinated social consequence to individual purity, but perhaps as a partial result, it has also become susceptible to and even supportive of contemporary nationalism. The dilemmas of war have brought Mormon leaders to yield to the unrelenting demands of modern society while reposing ultimate faith in an eternal reckoning.

NOTES

1. During the last decades scholars have begun to examine Mormon attitudes concerning war. See D. Michael Quinn, "The Mormon Church and the Spanish-American War: An End to Selective Pacifism," *Pacific Historical Review* 43 (Aug. 1974): 342-66; Robert Jeffrey St, "Mormonism and War: An Interpretative Analysis of Selected Mormon Thought Regarding Seven American Wars," M.A. thesis, Brigham Young University, 1974; and for a miscellaneous collection of articles and documents, Gordon C. Thomasson, ed., *War, Conscription, Conscience and Mormonism,* 2d ed. (Santa Barbara, CA: Mormon Heritage, 1972).

2. Doctrine and Covenants of The Church of Jesus Christ of Latter-day Saints (Salt Lake City: Church of Jesus Christ of Latter-day Saints, 1921), 38:28-32; hereafter D&C.

3. Joseph Smith to Edward Partridge, 30 Mar. 1834, in Max H. Parkin, "Kirtland: A Stronghold for the Kingdom," in *The Restoration Movement: Essays in Mormon History,* eds. F. Mark McKiernan, Alma R. Blair, and Paul M. Edwards (Lawrence, KS: Coronado Press, 1973), 82.

4. John Corrill, *Brief History of the Church of Christ of Latter-day Saints* . . . (St. Louis: Printed for the Author, 1839), 19; "Interview with Alexander W. Doniphan," *Kansas City Journal,* 24 June 1881, in *Saints' Herald,* 1 Aug. 1881; Warren A. Jennings, "Zion is Fled: The Expulsion of the Mormons from Jackson County, Missouri," Ph.D. diss., University of Florida, 1962.

5. "To His Excellency, Daniel Dunklin, Governor of the State of Missouri," *The Evening and Morning Star* (Kirtland, OH), 2 (Dec. 1833): 114; Corrill, *Brief History,* 19.

6. D&C 98:23-31.

7. *Times and Seasons* 1 (Dec. 1839): 19.

8. Sidney Rigdon and Oliver Cowdery, "Dear Brethren," Kirtland, Ohio, 10 May 1834, broadside, archives, Historical Department, Church of Jesus Christ of Latter-day Saints, Salt Lake City, Utah (hereafter LDS archives); and "Letter of the First Presidency to the Scattered Saints," 9 Jan. 1834, Journal History, LDS archives. Peter Crawley and Richard L. Anderson, "The Political and Social Realities of Zion's Camp," *Brigham Young University Studies* 14 (Summer 1974): 406-20, places the Missouri expedition in its historical context.

9. Martin Harris, "Unpublished Statement of January 23, 1847," New York Public Library, copied in the Stanley Ivins Collection 11:44, Utah State Historical Society, Salt Lake City.

10. D&C 103, esp. vv. 15, 27-28. For the high emotionalism of the time, see "J. M. Henderson to the Independence, Missouri, Postmaster," Chagrin, Ohio, 29 Apr. 1834, first published in *Missouri Intelligencer,* 7 June 1834, and subsequently quoted in H. C. Smith, *Journal of History* 7 (Oct. 1915): 486-87.

11. D&C 101, esp. vv. 1-9 and 76-80; and "Letter of the First Presidency to the Scattered Saints," 9 Jan. 1834, Journal History.

12. Joseph Smith, *History of the Church of Jesus Christ of Latter-day Saints, with Introduction and Notes by B. H. Roberts,* 2d ed. rev., 7 vols. (Salt Lake City: Deseret News Press, 1948), 2:71-72; hereafter cited as HC. James H. Hunt, *Mormonism: Embracing the Origin, Rise and Progress of the Sect* (St. Louis: Ustick and Davies, 1844), 146-47; and "Saints to Dunklin," 24 Apr. 1834, in Journal History.

13. D&C 105:14, 29-31, 38-41. The revelation, however, did not preclude the future use of force.

14. "Oration Delivered by Mr. S. Rigdon, on the 4th of July, 1838 . . .," reprinted in *Brigham Young University Studies* 14 (Summer 1974): 527.

15. HC 3:162. For an account of the climatic events in Missouri, including the Mormon secret bands and Smith's possible knowledge of their activities, see Leland H. Gentry, *A History of the Latter-day Saints in Northern Missouri from 1836 to 1839* (Provo, UT: Department of Seminaries and Institutes of Religion, 1965), 213-44.

16. HC 5:489-90; Corrill, *Brief History,* 40-41.

17. "Remarks on Chartered Rights," *Times and Seasons* 4 (15 Dec. 1842): 42; "Minutes of the Nauvoo Legion," undated, LDS archives; Robert Bruce Flanders, *Nauvoo: Kingdom on the Mississippi* (Urbana: University of Illinois Press, 1965), 112, 326; Joseph Smith III, *Journal of History* 3 (Apr. 1910): 132; and *Hawkeye and Iowa Patriot,* 18 Mar. 1841, in Kenneth W. Godfrey, "Causes of Mormon non-Mormon Conflict in Hancock County, Illinois, 1839-1846," Ph.D. diss., Brigham Young University, 1967, 142. The latter states the Nauvoo City Charter passed legislation conscripting all men between the ages of eighteen and twenty-five into the legion. Apparently the enactment was enforced by public opinion and not legal penalties.

18. HC 4:269. According to Smith another reason for the legion was to provide the means of fulfilling the Mormon militia responsibility without having to serve with those unsympathetic to their faith, ibid., 5:489-90 and *Times and Seasons* 2 (15 May 1841): 416.

19. The legion did not originate the image of Mormonism as Islamic militarism but certainly revived it. Kenneth W. Godfrey, "Mormon Non-Mormon Conflict," 138-44, reviews the adverse public reaction to the Mormon army.

20. John Taylor, *The Nauvoo Neighbor,* 29 Oct. 1845.

21. By residing outside a state boundary but within American territory, Mormons were without the constitutional assurance of self-government. As perhaps the single exception to the rule, Utah repeatedly was denied the promise of speedy statehood as proposed by the Northwest Ordinance of 1784. Not only did this delay cause tension, but so did the men appointed to fill territorial offices. As in colonial America these "foreign" appointed officials were at times unsympathetic to local needs.

22. Quoted in Norman F. Furniss, *The Mormon Conflict, 1850-1859* (New Haven: Yale University Press, 1966), 121.

23. Brigham Young, *Journal of Discourses*, 26 vols. (London: Latter-day Saints' Book Depot, 1854-86), 5;78; hereafter cited as JD.

24. Juanita Brooks, *The Mountain Meadows Massacre*, 2d ed. (Norman: University of Oklahoma Press, 1970), 15-35.

25. Brigham Young, JD 5:127.

26. Quoted in Edward W. Tullidge, *The History of Salt Lake City and Its Founders* (Salt Lake City: By the Author, 1886), 172. Young later claimed that the legions' scorched-earth policy was instituted without his consent; see "Brigham Young MS," 4 Oct. 1859, LDS archives. The reverse side of the legion's orders frequently bore the phrase, "Shed no blood," *Deseret News,* 23 May 1877.

27. Brooks, *Mountain Meadows Massacre.*

28. Brigham Young, JD 7:46. Young's declaration was similar to Smith's "Fishing River Revelation," cited earlier. On both eventual force was not ruled out, conditioned on the sanctification of the Saints.

29. The Mormon Fabian tactics, however, had destroyed seventy-four wagons containing perhaps 300,000 pounds of foodstuffs as well as capturing 1,400 head of cattle. Furniss, *The Mormon Conflict,* 116, 144; B. H. Roberts, *A Comprehensive History of the Church of Jesus Christ of Latter-day Saints* (Salt Lake City: Deseret News Press, 1930), 4:283-85.

30. *Millennial Star* 17 (28 Apr. 1855): 261; 19 (18 Apr. 1857): 248.

31. Howard A. Christy, "Open Hand and Mailed Fist: Mormon-Indian Relations in Utah, 1847-52," and "The Walker War: Defense and Conciliation as Strategy," *Utah Historical Quarterly* 46 (Summer 1978): 216-35, and 47 (Fall 1979): 395-420; Howard Stansbury, *Expedition to the Valley of the Great Salt Lake of Utah . . .* (Philadelphia: Lippincott, Grambo, & Co., 1852), 148-49; and J. W. Gunnison, *The Mormons, or Latter-day Saints . . .* (Philadelphia: Lippincott, Grambo, & Co., 1852), 146.

32. Hosea Stout, *On the Mormon Frontier: The Diary of Hosea Stout, 1844-1861,* ed. Juanita Brooks (Salt Lake City: University of Utah Press, 1964), 1:177.

33. *Times and Seasons* 6 (20 Jan. 1845): 1,096; Brigham Young, *Manuscript History of Brigham Young,* comp. Elden Jay Watson (Salt Lake City:

By the author, 1971), 221-24; and Journal History, 14 Aug. 1846, 3.

34. Young, *Manuscript History*, 205, 226, 264-65. Also see *Millennial Star* 9 (1 May 1847): 137.

35. *Millennial Star* 9 (15 June 1847): 187.

36. Quoted in Stout, *On the Mormon Frontier*, 1:179.

37. The unsigned editorial probably was written by Orson Spencer, a New Englander by birth and education, *Millennial Star* 9 (1 Mar. 1847): 73. Indeed Mormon representatives in Washington artfully displayed the church's ambivalence toward the American government, threatening to seek British or Mexican succor if American aid was not forthcoming; see W. Ray Luce, "The Mormon Battalion: A Historical Accident?" *Utah Historical Quarterly* 42 (Winter 1942): 32, 38n.

38. *Millennial Star* 9 (1 Mar., 15 June 1847): 69, 178.

39. Ibid., 9 (1, 15 Nov. 1847): 330-31, 346-47.

40. E. B. Long, *The Saints and the Union: Utah Territory During the Civil War* (Urbana: University of Illinois Press, 1981); Gustive O. Larson, "Utah and the Civil War," *Utah Historical Quarterly* 33 (Winter 1965): 59-61; Orson F. Whitney, *History of Utah* (Salt Lake City: George Q. Cannon Sons, 1893), 2:93; and "Interview with Brigham Young, Jr.," *Philadelphia Morning Post*, 1 Nov. 1869, in Stanley P. Hirshon, *The Lion of the Lord: A Biography of Brigham Young* (New York: Alfred A. Knopf, 1969), 257-58.

41. Whitney, *History of Utah*, 2:93; *Deseret News*, 16 Apr. 1862. Young's assertions are paraphrased by Whitney.

42. William H. Hooper to George Q. Cannon, 16 Dec. 1860, *Millennial Star* 23 (12 Jan. 1861): 30. There was an element of game playing to these statehood petitions based, as we shall see, upon Mormon millennial calculations. Prior to Utah's third bid for entry into the union, Young confidentially wrote: "We are very thankful that Congress has not admitted us into the Union as a State. However, we shall continue to tease them on that point so long as they pretend to legislate for the past Union. . . ." Young to Hooper, 7 Feb. 1861, Brigham Young Papers, Coe Collection, Yale University, in Klaus J. Hansen, *Quest for Empire: The Political Kingdom of God and the Council of Fifty in Mormon History* (East Lansing: Michigan State University Press, 1967), 166.

43. JD 10:110.

44. Gustive O. Larson, *Outline History of Territorial Utah* (Provo, UT: Brigham Young University, 1972), 206-16, and Larson, "Utah and the Civil War," 61, 72-73. Lincoln regarded the Morrill Act as impolitic and made no attempt to enforce it.

45. This important revelation, found in D&C 87, did much to shape LDS perceptions of war. Widely circulated in the early preaching of church leaders, at first it was withheld from publication; see Brigham Young, JD 8:58.

Later it was printed in England in 1851 in the Pearl of Great Price, compiled by Franklin D. Richards (Liverpool: F. D. Richards, 1851), 25, and in the United States in *The Seer* (Washington, D.C.), Apr. 1854, 241. Smith received a confirming revelation, 12 July 1843, which while not printed during his lifetime is now found in D&C 130:12-13. For additional early references to it, see Jedediah M. Grant's statement, Journal History, 2 Apr. 1854, 2; Andrew Jenson, *Historical Record,* 25 June 1846; *New York Times,* 31 July 1858.

46. *Deseret News,* 2 Jan., 6 Mar. 1861, 26 Mar. 1862. See also Brigham Young, JD 9:5.

47. JD 9:7. See also Long, *Saints and the Union,* 20.

48. For instance, Brigham Young, JD 9:5 and Wilford Woodruff, ibid., 10:215-16.

49. T. B. H. Stenhouse, *The Rocky Mountain Saints* (New York: D. Appleton and Company, 1873), 376.

50. Brigham Young, JD 8:324. For a useful compilation of Young's pacifist statements, see Hugh Nibley, "Brigham Young and the Enemy," *The Young Democrat* (n.d., n.p.), copy in LDS archives.

51. Brigham Young, JD 10:248. For Young's self-confessed lack of militarism, see Edward W. Tullidge, *Life of Brigham Young; or Utah and Her Founders* (New York: Tullidge and Crandall, 1876), 30.

52. JD 9:143. Reportedly on the Sunday preceding the Appomattox surrender, Young predicted four more years of war, Stenhouse, *Rocky Mountains Saints,* 610.

53. Quinn, "The Mormon Church and the Spanish-American War," 342-66.

54. *Deseret News,* 5, 23 Apr., 2 May 1898.

55. Walter LaFeber, *The New Empire: An Interpretation of American Expansion, 1860-1898* (Ithaca, NY: Cornell University Press, Cornell Paperbacks, 1966), 379-406. The sentiment and role of the American clergy in the crisis has been warmly debated, although recent opinion has downplayed its aggressiveness, Winthrop Hudson, "Protestant Clergy Debate the Nation's Vocation, 1898-1899," *Church History* 43 (Mar. 1973): 110-18.

56. *Deseret News,* 2 Apr. 1898.

57. *Conference Reports of the Church of Jesus Christ of Latter-day Saints, April 1898* (Salt Lake City: Church of Jesus Christ of Latter-day Saints), 86; hereafter cited as CR. The discourses of Brigham Young, Jr., B. H. Roberts, Wilford Woodruff, John Henry Smith, and Francis M. Lyman also discussed the issue; ibid., 26-28, 32, 56, 58-61. Elsewhere Cannon declared, "There is probably as little provocation for our nation to engage in war at the present time as can usually be found when difficulties arise between nations" (*Juvenile Instructor* 33 [15 Apr. 1898]): 315).

58. Journal History, 24 Apr. 1898, 2; Brigham Young, Jr., Diary, 22,

24, 28 Apr. 1898, LDS archives.

59. To counter the influence of Young's sermon, a strongly stated editorial was prepared at President Woodruff's request and placed in the 25 April 1898 edition of the *Deseret News*. For activity behind the scenes, Journal History, 25, 26 Apr. 1898, 2-3. Several local church authorities were favorable to Young's speech, including President Angus Cannon of the Salt Lake Stake. Cannon believed the discourse to be "dictated by the Holy Ghost" but "unwise"; Brigham Young, Jr., Diary, 29 Apr. 1898. See also Young's entries, 24-26 Apr. 1898.

60. *Improvement Era* 1 (May 1898): 521; *Young Woman's Journal* 9 (June 1898): 284; *Deseret News*, 25, 28 Apr. 1898.

61. Journal History, 30 Apr. 1898, 2.

62. Noble Warrum, *Utah Since Statehood*, 4 vols. (Salt Lake City: S. J. Clarke Publishing Company, 1919), 1:434-35. Brigham Young had at least eight descendants serve, including two who had graduated from West Point; Kenneth C. Kerr, "The Young as Soldiers," *Young Woman's Journal* 13 (July 1902): 313-14. For Woodruff's priesthood blessings, see Journal History, 3 May 1898, 2, and 28 May 1898, quoting the *Brigham City Bugler*.

63. *Deseret News*, 30 June 1898. The church newspaper phrased its support for expansionism in terms of civilization, humanitarianism, and even American economic betterment—denying its position favored "conquest, landgrabbing and military glory." The difference apparently lay in intent; see *Deseret News*, 9, 10, 28 June, 7, 14 July, 6, 30 Aug. 1898.

64. *Deseret News*, 6 Aug. 1898.

65. *Deseret News*, 1, 4 Aug. 1898. Even the anti-imperialists reflected the ethnocentrism of the time; Christopher Lasch, "The Anti-Imperialists, the Philippines, and the Inequality of Man," *Journal of Southern History* 24 (Aug. 1958): 319-31.

66. Journal History, Oct. 1914, 1, 2, 12-13. For a sampling of the attitudes of other church presidents: John Taylor, JD 19:305; *Juvenile Instructor* 76 (Apr. 1941): 168-69; *Instructor* 99 (Feb. 1914): 92-94. The Mormon periodicals' repeated doom-saying prior to World War I is found in *Millennial Star* 32 (16 Aug. 1870): 520-22; 47 (6 Apr. 1885): 218-19; 58 (25 June 1896): 408-09; 76 (26 Mar. 1914): 200; *Deseret News*, 9 June 1894 and 26 July 1900; and *Improvement Era* 14 (Feb. 1911): 350-52.

67. Joseph Smith to Isaac Russell, 11 Jan. 1916, First Presidency Letterbooks, LDS archives. Joseph Smith, Jr., had given a similar definition, *Teachings of the Prophet Joseph Smith*, ed. Joseph Fielding Smith (Salt Lake City: Deseret Book Company, 1970), 362.

68. Joseph F. Smith to Hyrum M. Smith, 7 Nov. 1914; Joseph F. Smith to J. M. Studebaker, 11 May 1915; and Joseph F. Smith to Arthur J. Brown, 22 Aug. 1914, First Presidency Letterbooks. The last quotations are

taken from an editorial of the Salt Lake *Herald,* 11 Aug. 1914, in which Smith expressed strong approval.

69. HC 6:467.

70. Joseph F. Smith to E. Wesley Smith, 7 Nov. 1916, First Presidency Letterbooks.

71. *Messages of the First Presidency of The Church of Jesus Christ of Latter-day Saints,* ed. James R. Clark (Salt Lake City: Bookcraft, 1971), 5:71. For church opposition to the American entry into the war as late as April 1917, see *Instructor* 52 (Apr. 1917): 190.

72. *Deseret News,* 9 Apr. 1917. Those who held contrary sentiment were invited to "surrender or migrate." Three days earlier the newspaper strongly repudiated its editorial policy of twenty years—and indeed the long-standing belief of President Smith—by belatedly embracing military preparedness; ibid., 6 Apr. 1917.

73. CR, Apr. 1917, 19-20.

74. Joseph F. Smith, *Instructor* 52 (Aug. 1917): 404, and 53 (Nov. 1918): 579.

75. Heber J. Grant to Loyal Americans of Utah, 15 Feb. 1918, George Albert Smith Papers, Special Collections, Marriott Library, University of Utah. Roberts, *Comprehensive History of the Church* 4:467-68, lists the financial contributions of the church and its members.

76. *Instructor* 52 (June, Aug. 1917): 296, 409; *Improvement Era* 21 (Sept. 1918): 1,024.

77. *Instructor* 52 (May 1917): 240. *The Relief Society Magazine* 5 (1918): 90-92, 161-63, 216-17, 280-82, 592-96, instructed church ladies in wartime economy and even included a lesson on "War and the Art of War Among Book of Mormon Peoples." As a further indication of Mormon support, general authority B. H. Roberts, despite his sixty years, volunteered as a military chaplain.

78. "The First Presidency to All Stake, Ward and Other Church Workers," 26 Nov. 1918, Heber J. Grant Letterbooks, Heber J. Grant Papers, LDS archives.

79. CR, Oct. 1916, 143; *Deseret News,* 12 Sept. 1914. Smith's two counselors wrote: "It surely appears that important events are rapidly moving on towards 'the great consummation'"; Lund and Penrose to Smith, 21 Oct. 1917, LDS archives. For other examples of millennial sentiment, see James E. Talmage, "The Federation of the World, A Thousand Years of Peace," *Improvement Era* 20 (Oct. 1917): 1,097; Fred L. W. Bennett, "The Ethics of War," ibid. (Mar. 1917): 425; Charlotte Stewart, "The Everyday Ways of Peace," *Young Woman's Journal* 26 (May 1915): 324; *Relief Society Magazine* 4 (July 1917): 408.

80. *Improvement Era* 17 (Sept. 1914): 1,076-77; CR, Oct. 1914, 7.

81. "War and the Art of War Among Book of Mormon Peoples," *Relief Society Magazine* 5 (Oct. 1918): 595; James E. Talmage, "'Mormonism' and the War," *Improvement Era* 21 (Oct. 1918): 1,030.

82. Gilbert W. Scharffs, *Mormonism in Germany: A History of the Church of Jesus Christ of Latter-day Saints in Germany Between 1840 and 1970* (Salt Lake City: Deseret Book, 1970), 58-60. During the war perhaps seventy-five German LDS soldiers lost their lives. If growth statistics are indicative, German Saints felt little tension between their nationalism and church allegiance, even after the entry of the United States into the war. LDS membership in Germany during the war years rose from 7,500 to 8,000 and rapidly increased in the immediate years thereafter.

83. John M. Whitaker, "Journal," 3:729, 733, Special Collections, Marriott Library, University of Utah. The journal entries are during Oct. and apparently early Nov. 1917.

84. CR, Oct. 1917, 20-21. As an example of such dissent, Bishop Heber Bennion, who formerly presided over the Taylorsville Ward, refused to concede that church membership obliged war support. The non-Mormon world was corrupt, he argued, and the Saints should leave it to its fate. Another bishop wrote that many Mormons "believe this war is an unrighteous war from both sides, and that the United States going into it, is only a furtherance of an unrighteous cause." Heber Bennion to George A. Smith, 14 Mar. 1918, George Albert Smith Papers, University of Utah; James Martin to Heber J. Grant, 28 May 1917, Heber J. Grant Papers.

85. *Deseret News,* 11 Dec. 1917. For similar comments, see *Instructor* 52 (Oct. 1917): 521, 530. Even following the American entry into the war, Mormon editorials occasionally treated conscientious objectors kindly—but with no mention of *Mormon* conscientious objectors, ibid., 10 Feb. 1916; *Millennial Star* 78 (23 Mar. 1916): 184-87; *Deseret News,* 16 June, 11 Dec. 1917; *Relief Society Magazine* 4 (Oct. 1917): 553-65.

86. Publicly Grant phrased his support cautiously: "The position of the Church of Jesus Christ of Latter-day Saints is that the standard works of the Church are not opposed to the league of nations"; *Improvement Era* 23 (Dec. 1919): 109. Church leaders were not united in supporting the league, see James B. Allen, "J. Reuben Clark, Jr., On American Sovereignty and International Organization," *Brigham Young University Studies* 13 (Spring 1973): 347-48.

87. B. H. Roberts, *Deseret News,* 14 Jan. 1928.

88. Norman Furniss, *The Fundamentalist Controversy, 1918-1931* (New Haven: Yale University Press, 1954), treats the bitter harvest of World War I on America's conservative religious establishment. For examples of Mormon sentiment, see *Deseret News,* 28 Jan. 1938, and *Millennial Star* 98 (5 Nov., 17 Dec. 1936): 712-13, 808-809.

89. Clark once proclaimed, "My ancestry is Quaker, and I am coming to believe that there is heredity, in ideas, and concepts, as well as in our physical being. So I loathe war, and all that goes with," *Improvement Era* 55 (Aug. 1952): 568.

90. *Deseret News,* 21 Nov. 1935, 8 Sept., 28 Oct. 1936, 15 Oct. 1938, 25 Apr. 1939. Also CR, Apr. 1937, 24; Apr. 1941, 69; Oct. 1941, 15.

91. *Deseret News,* 14 Sept. 1937.

92. *Millennial Star* 100 (6 Oct. 1938): 633. During the interwar period, Brown strongly condemned war as "sheer madness" and "stupidity"; ibid. 99 (4 Nov., 16 Dec. 1937): 710-11, 716, 802-804. Brown, a former professional soldier and future general authority, strongly championed the allied cause after the actual outbreak of hostilities.

93. CR, Oct. 1940, 7; First Presidency to William C. FitzGibbon, 11 Oct. 1941, LDS archives. The unpublished, eighteen-page FitzGibbon letter remains one of the more important Mormon statements on war. For Clark's repeated predictions of the European conspiracy, *Deseret News,* 7 June 1934, 24 June 1937; CR, Apr. 1937, 23, and Apr. 1941, 20.

94. General authority Richard L. Evans made the suggestion of possible LDS conscientious objection, though he also cited the Mormon tradition of upholding civil authority and military service; CR, Apr. 1941, 52. Also see First Presidency to William C. FitzGibbon, 11 Oct. 1941.

95. CR, Apr. 1941, 14.

96. Grant's growing mistrust of Roosevelt became explicit in December 1942. "Perhaps I do the President an injustice and I would not want to be quoted, but I sometimes think he [Roosevelt] is laying his plans in getting into the war to become a dictator"; Heber J. Grant to Silas S. Smith, 12 Dec. 1942, Heber J. Grant Letterbooks. Also see Heber J. Grant to George N. Peek, 29 Nov. 1941; Heber J. Grant to John W. O'Leary, 4 Nov. 1941; Heber J. Grant to Florence Pearson, 20 Jan. 1942; and Heber J. Grant to Eric Ryberg, 31 Jan. 1944; all in Heber J. Grant Letterbooks.

97. Heber J. Grant to Richard L. Evans, 8 Dec. 1941; Heber J. Grant to Edith [Young], 2 May 1942; Heber J. Grant to Katherine Ivins, 22 May 1942; Heber J. Grant to Silas S. Smith, 12 Dec. 1942; all in Heber J. Grant Letterbooks.

98. CR, Apr. 1942, 88-97. The text was subsequently reprinted in pamphlet form and distributed widely throughout the church. For Clark's authorship of the message, Heber J. Grant to his granddaughter Joy, 4 Oct. 1942, Heber J. Grant Letterbooks.

99. *Improvement Era* 45 (May 1974): 274; Harold B. Lee and Mark E. Peterson to the First Presidency, 30 Sept. 1947, George Albert Smith Papers; Heber J. Grant to J. Parley White, 14 Apr. 1942; Heber J. Grant to Tom [Judd], 7 Oct. 1942; and Heber J. Grant to Hugo B. Anderson, 18 Nov.

1942, Heber J. Grant Letterbooks.

100. *Millennial Star* 104 (23 Apr., 16 July 1942): 264-66, 450-52; 105 (21 Jan. 1943): 38-39; 107 (Jan. 1945): 5-8; CR, Oct. 1944, 79; *Improvement Era* 46 (Aug., Nov. 1943): 480, 656.

101. Scharffs, *Mormonism in Germany*, 91-116; Joseph M. Dixon, "Mormons in the Third Reich: 1933-1945," *Dialogue: A Journal of Mormon Thought* 7 (Spring 1972): 70-78. The executed Helmuth Huebner had three accomplices who were imprisoned.

102. CR, Apr. 1942, 95. Under President Grant's direction, Clark was apparently the first to crystallize the doctrine. For the World War I teaching, Joseph F. Smith, *Era* 20 (May 1917): 656.

103. The number of LDS conscientious objectors is uncertain but apparently exceeded ten, Thomasson, *War, Conscription, Conscience and Mormonism*, 26.

104. *Improvement Era* 49 (Feb. 1946): 76-77. The letter was dated 14 Dec. 1945 and was issued by President George Albert Smith. Grant had died the previous year.

105. *Millennial Star* 109 (Jan. 1947): 2-3; J. Reuben Clark, CR, Oct. 1946, 88, and Oct. 1948, 175.

106. F. R. Flournoy, "Protestant Churches and the War," *South Atlantic Quarterly* 42 (Apr. 1943): 113-45; Roland H. Bainton, *Christian Attitudes Toward War and Peace: A Historical Survey and Critical Re-evaluation* (New York: Abingdon Press, 1960), 14.

107. J. Reuben Clark, Jr., *Stand Fast By Our Constitution* (Salt Lake City: Deseret Book Company, 1962), 129. The church's general conferences were virtually devoid of any comment concerning the Korean War, though the *Deseret News* strongly denounced international communism and other church periodicals discussed the broad issue of Christianity and the war. See William E. Berrett, "Spirituality and Armed Conflict," *Improvement Era* 55 (Apr. 1952) 242, 271-73.

108. Boyd K. Packer, *Improvement Era* 71 (June 1968): 58-61. For other general authority comments, see ibid., 69 (Dec. 1966): 1,121-23; 71 (June 1968): 48-50, 79-81. The attitudes of other churches during the war is detailed by H. C. Quinley, "Protestant Clergy and the War in Vietnam," *Public Opinion Quarterly* 34 (Spring 1970): 43-52.

109. Letter of Joseph Fielding Smith, 20 Mar. 1970 [written and signed by Joseph Anderson, secretary to the First Presidency], published in Thomasson, *War, Conscription, Conscience and Mormonism*.

110. Eugene England, "The Tragedy of Vietnam and the Responsibility of Mormons," *Dialogue: A Journal of Mormon Thought* 2 (Winter 1967): 74. Also Knud S. Larsen, "A Voice Against the War," ibid. (Autumn 1967): 163-66, and essays in Thomasson, *War, Conscription, Conscience and*

Mormonism.

111. Letters of the First Presidency, ibid., xii, 4, and 5.

112. D&C 5:14; 10:66; 11:2; 27:15-18; 33:9; and 35:14. Such examples could be greatly multiplied.

113. Ibid., 98:16; HC 2:71-72.

114. HC 6:208, 275-77; *Times and Seasons* 6 (1 Feb. 1845): 789; Journal of Norton Jacob, typescript, LDS archives.

115. Al. 43:46-47 and 48:14-16. Illustrating the necessity of divine sanction, several Book of Mormon incidents found the righteous migrating to a new land rather than resisting aggression.

116. Morm. 4:1-4; Mos. 21:6-12; 3 Ne. 3:20-21. See also D&C 98:23-48.

117. D&C 134, esp. vv. 1-5. This statement apparently was written by Smith's associate, Oliver Cowdery, and at first was appended to the Doctrine and Covenants. Twentieth-century editions, however, have included it without distinction in Smith's revelations. Also see ibid., 58:21 and 98:4.

118. D&C 101:77, 80; 109:54, and 1 Ne. 13:19.

119. For an examination of the Congregational transfer of loyalty, James Fulton Maclear, "The True American Union of Church and State: The Reconstruction of the Theocratic Tradition," *Church History* 28 (Mar. 1959): 41-62.

120. Robert Flanders restates this familiar refrain in Mormon historiography within an important new context, "To Transform History: Early Mormon Culture and the Concept of Time and Space," ibid., 40 (Mar. 1971): 108-17.

121. Church members clearly were not immune to the pervasive patriotism common during war. Like the church's press in America, both the German *Der Stern* and the British *Millennial Star* united religion and nationalism during their country's wars. For example, during the Crimean War, 1854-56, the *Star* found Britain and France to be "on the side of right" and confidently predicted victory—partially because of national virtue and religiosity.

Epilogue:
"Justice Will Follow Truth"

B. H. Roberts

FRANKLY, THIS *HISTORY* [*A COMPREHENSIVE HISTORY OF THE CHURCH OF Jesus Christ of Latter-day Saints, Century I*] is pro-Church of the Latter-day Saints. Not, however, in the sense that the *Ecclesiastical History of Eusebius* is pro-Christian. In that work the author deliberately announces his intention to ignore those things disadvantageous to the Christian cause, and dwell upon those only which glorify it. This results in special pleading, not history.

Nor is this *History* pro-Church of the Latter-day Saints in the sense that Joseph Milner's *History of the Church of Christ* (4 Vols.) is pro-Christian; for he announces in his Introduction that as there have been persons from the time of our Savior whose disposition and lives have been formed by the rules of the *New Testament*, it is the lives of these men that he proposes to write as the history of the church; not their rites, ceremonies, or their religious controversies. "Nothing but what appears to me to belong to Christ's kingdom," he says, "shall be admitted: genuine piety is the only thing which I intend to celebrate." Such writing, of course, however excellent it may be for some purposes, is *not* "church history," but merely a history of piety within the church. Not in this sense, then, is this work pro-Church of the Latter-day Saints. The position is not assumed that the men of the New Dispensation—its prophets, apostles, presidencies, and other leaders—are without faults or infallible, rather they are treated as men of like passions with their fellow men. Bearing indeed a heavenly treasure, no less a thing than delegated authority from God to teach the gospel and administer its ordinances of salvation to the children of men; to gather modern Israel from among the nations of the earth,

303

and establish Zion; to perfect the lives of those who receive the truth the church proclaims, and prepare the world for its coming Lord, the rightful King of all the earth, Jesus the resurrected and glorified Christ. But while the officers and members of the church possess this spiritual "treasure," they carried it in earthen vessels; and that earthliness, with their human limitations, was plainly manifested on many occasions and in various ways, both in personal conduct and in collective deportment. But back of all that, and it should never be lost sight of, is the supreme fact—and it was a controlling element in all their proceedings—that they occupied such relations with God that they were, on occasion, moved upon to speak and act as God would speak and act. And *when* they spoke and acted as prompted by the inspiration of God, *then* what they said and what they did was the word and will of God, and the power of God unto salvation. This the writer has sought to bear in mind; as well as on the other hand to keep aware of the human limitations of these men in considering their work. No essential events in the history of the church in the New Dispensation of the gospel have been omitted because they might be considered detrimental to the reputation of either the leaders of the church or of its membership. Where conflicting evidence to a fact or state of facts was found to exist, and the evidence favorable to the church has been adopted in the text, the *per contra* evidence has been given either in modification of the text, or given in full in the footnotes; and where clearly reprehensible measures and policies have been adopted, these have been considered with the freedom that true historical writing must ever exercise.

It need not be said that this course has laid a heavy burden upon the writer of this *History*. It is always a difficult task to hold the scales of justice at even balance when weighing the deeds of men. It becomes doubly more so when dealing with men engaged in a movement that one believes had its origin with God, and that its leaders on occasion act under the inspiration of God. Under such conditions to so state events as to be historically exact, and yet, on the other hand, so treat the course of events as not to destroy faith in these men, nor in their work, becomes a task of supreme delicacy; and one that tries the soul and the skill of the historian. The only way such a task can be accomplished, in the judgment of the writer, is to frankly state events as they occurred, in full consideration of all related circumstances, allowing the line of condemnation or of justification to fall where it may; being confident that in the sum of things justice will follow truth; and God will be glorified in his work, no matter what may befall individuals, or groups of individuals. This the writer freely confesses has been the purpose of his work—not the vindication of men before the bar of history, but the justification of the ways of God to man; and to prove that God is true, though all men have to be condemned as weakling or even liars.

Let not this remark, however, be regarded as implying too great a censure upon the leading men of the New Dispensation. While many of them fell into grievous sins, and all of them at times plainly manifested errors of judgment and limitations of their conceptions of the greatness and grandeur of the work in which they were engaged, yet doubtless they were the best men to be had for the work, since they were chosen either directly of God, or else by a divinely appointed authority, and in either case called of God, and ordained to bring forth the work. And sure it is that good men and faithful have been found in sufficient number, and of such capacity, when helped of God, to proceed with the work of the Lord in the earth, and God has given it increase. . . .

CONTRIBUTORS

THOMAS G. ALEXANDER is professor of history at Brigham Young University in Provo, Utah. He is director of the Charles Redd Center for Western Studies, past president of the Mormon History Association, author of *Mormonism in Transition: A History of the Latter-day Saints, 1890-1930,* and co-author of *Mormons & Gentiles: A History of Salt Lake City.* "'To Maintain Harmony': Adjusting to External and Internal Stress, 1890-1930" was first published in *Dialogue: A Journal of Mormon Thought* 15 (Winter 1982): 44-58.

JAMES B. ALLEN, former Assistant Church Historian of the Church of Jesus Christ of Latter-day Saints, is Lemuel Redd Professor of Western History at Brigham Young University. He is past president of the Mormon History Association, author of *Trials of Discipleship: The Story of William Clayton, a Mormon,* and co-author of *The Story of the Latter-day Saints.* "The Significance of Joseph Smith's 'First Vision' in Mormon Thought" first appeared in *Dialogue: A Journal of Mormon Thought* 1 (Autumn 1966): 29-45.

LEONARD J. ARRINGTON was Church Historian of the Church of Jesus Christ of Latter-day Saints for ten years beginning in 1972. He is past director of the Joseph Fielding Smith Institute for Church History at Brigham Young University and was the first president of the Mormon History Association, which he helped to found. He is author of *Great Basin Kingdom: An Economic History of the Latter-day Saints, 1830-1900* and *Brigham Young: American Moses.* "The Search for Truth and Meaning in Mormon History" was first published in *Dialogue: A Journal of Mormon Thought* 3 (Summer 1968): 56-66, and subsequently anthologized in *Personal Voices: A Celebration of Dialogue,* ed. Mary L. Bradford (Salt Lake City: Signature Books, 1987), 63-77.

MAUREEN URSENBACH BEECHER is professor of English and senior research historian for the Joseph Fielding Smith Institute for Church History. She was founding president of the Association for Mormon Letters and is past president of the Mormon History Association. "The 'Leading Sisters': A Female Hierarchy in Nineteenth-century Mormon Society" first appeared in *Journal of Mormon History* 9 (1982): 25-39.

EUGENE E. CAMPBELL was professor of history at Brigham Young University and is past president of the Mormon History Association. The author of *Establishing Zion: The Mormon Church in the American West, 1847-69,* he died in 1986. Bruce L. Campbell, his son, is associate professor of family studies and consumer sciences at California State University at Los Angeles. "Divorce among Mormon Polygamists: Extent and Explanations" was first published in the *Utah Historical Quarterly* 46 (Winter 1978): 4-23.

KENNETH L. CANNON II is a lawyer practicing in Salt Lake City, Utah. He serves on the Advisory Board of Editors of the *Utah Historical Quarterly* and on the board of trustees of the Utah Heritage Foundation. He received the Mormon History Association's Francis M. Chipman Award to Outstanding Young Scholar in 1983. "After the Manifesto: Mormon Polygamy, 1890-1906" is a revision of an essay first appearing in *Sunstone* 8 (Jan.-Apr. 1983): 27-35.

MARIO S. DE PILLIS is professor of history at the University of Massachusetts at Amherst. He has been trustee and historical consultant for the restoration of the Shaker community of Hancock, Massachusetts. "The Quest for Religious Authority and the Rise of Mormonism" first appeared in *Dialogue: A Journal of Mormon Thought* 1 (Autumn 1966): 68-88.

ROBERT B. FLANDERS, professor of history at Southwest Missouri State University in Springfield, is author of *Nauvoo: Kingdom on the Mississippi.* "Dream and Nightmare: Nauvoo Revisited" was first published in *The Restoration Movement: Essays in Mormon History,* eds. F. Mark McKiernan, Alma R. Blair, and Paul M. Edwards (Lawrence, KS: Coronado Press, 1973), 141-66.

KLAUS J. HANSEN is professor of history at Queen's University in Kingston, Ontario. He is author of *Quest for Empire: The Political Kingdom of God and the Council of Fifty in Mormon History* and *Mormonism and the American Experience.* "The Metamorphosis of the Kingdom of God: Toward a Reinterpretation of Mormon History" first appeared in *Dialogue: A Journal of Mormon Thought* 1 (Autumn 1966): 63-83.

WILLIAM G. HARTLEY is associate professor of history and research historian for the Joseph Fielding Smith Institute for Church History at Brigham Young University. "Mormons, Crickets, and Gulls: A New Look at an Old Story" first appeared in *Utah Historical Quarterly* 38 (Summer 1970): 224-39.

STANLEY S. IVINS taught animal husbandry at the University of Nebraska. He died in 1967. "Notes on Mormon Polygamy" was first published in *Western Humanities Review* 10 (Summer 1956), 3:229-39, then in *Utah Historical Quarterly* 35 (Fall 1967): 309-21, and later anthologized in *Mormonism and American Culture,* eds. Marvin S. Hill and James B. Allen (New York: Harper & Row, 1972), 101-11.

DEAN L. MAY, former editor of *Journal of Mormon History,* is associate professor of history at the University of Utah in Salt Lake City. "A Demographic Portrait of the Mormons, 1830-1980" was first published in *After 150 Years: The Latter-day Saints in Sesquicentennial Perspective,* eds. Thomas G. Alexander and Jessie L. Embry (Provo, UT: Charles Redd Center for Western Studies, 1983), 37-69.

LINDA KING NEWELL, former co-editor of *Dialogue: A Journal of Mormon Thought,* is co-author of *Mormon Enigma: Emma Hale Smith.* "A Gift Given, A Gift Taken: Washing, Anointing, and Blessing the Sick among Mormon Women" first appeared in *Sunstone* 6 (Sept.-Oct. 1981): 16-25, and was subsequently anthologized as "Gifts of the Spirit: Women's Share" in *Sisters in Spirit: Mormon Women in Historical and Cultural Perspective,* eds. Maureen Ursenbach Beecher and Lavina Fielding Anderson (Urbana: University of Illinois Press, 1987), 111-50.

B. H. ROBERTS was a General Authority of the Church of Jesus Christ of Latter-day Saints from 1888 until his death in 1933. He was author of *New Witness for God* and other works. He served as Assistant Church Historian from 1902 to 1933. "Justice Will Follow Truth" is excerpted from *A Comprehensive History of The Church of Jesus Christ of Latter-day Saints, Century I,* 6 vols. (Salt Lake City: Church of Jesus Christ of Latter-day Saints, 1930), 1:vii-ix.

JAN SHIPPS is professor of history and religious studies at Indiana University-Purdue University at Indianapolis. She is past president of the Mormon History Association, author of *Mormonism: The Story of a New Religious Tradition,* and currently co-editor of *Religion and American Culture: A Journal of Interpretation.* "The Prophet Puzzle: Suggestions Leading Toward a More Comprehensive Interpretation of Joseph Smith" was first published in *Journal of Mormon History* 1 (1974): 3-20.

RONALD W. WALKER is professor of history and senior research historian for the Joseph Fielding Smith Institute for Church History at Brigham Young University. "Sheaves, Bucklers, and the State: Mormon Leaders Respond to the Dilemmas of War" first appeared in *Sunstone* 7 (July-Aug. 1982): 43-56.